EXCELSIO
ALSACE
DOMAINES
SCHLUMBERGER
GEWURZTRAMINER
KAVALIEROS
FAMILLE PERRIN
Château de Beau
CHATEAUNEUF-DU-PAPE
APPELLATION D'ORIGINE CONTROLÉE
Sancerre
CW00829407
HINON
de la Dioterie
MONOPOLE
2015
CAPELLAN
RIOJA
Encruzad
Quinta dos Roques . 2015
DÃO
Joh. Jos. Prüm
2016
Wehlener Sonnenuhr
CHATEAU
SMITH HAUT LA
2014
PAZO SEÑORA
ALBARIÑO
TEAR OF THE PIN
DRY WHITE WINE
RETSINA
appellation by tradition
R18
THE
MC
2018
G
CHÂTEAU GUIRAU
BORDEAUX BLANC SEC
2016
Côte
OT NOIR
DOMA DE LA CÔTE
CHATEAU
L'EGLISE-CLINET
1995
POMEROL
APPELLATION POMEROL CONTROLÉE
TERTRE ROTEBOEU
2004
ANSELMI
2015
CAPITEL CROCE
JEREZ
LO CORTADO
TRADICION
Product of Spain
VORS 30 YEARS
246/2150
Livio Felluga
Terre Alte
2017
Riesling Schloss
2009
ALSACE GRAND CR
Domaine Weinba
LE SOL
GIMBLETT GRAVELS
2013
BRUNO ROCCA
Rabajà 1999
PRODUCT
DOMAINE DE LA
RANGE DES P
2016
Morgon
Appellation Morgon Contrôlée
« Côte du Py »
Jean Foillard, 69910 Villié-Morgon
Produit de France
2014
NALLE
SONOMA COUNT
DRY CREEK VAL
88% ZINFANDEL
7% PETITE SIRAH + 5% CARIGNANE
SELVAPIANA
VIGNETO
BUCERCHIA
2015
GRAND VIN
DE
CHATEAU LATOU
PREMIER GRAND CRU CLASSÉ
2006
PAUILLAC
NAPA VALLEY
BERNET SAUVIGN
HATEAU RAYA
TEAUNEUF-DU-PAPE
2004
2013
NECKE
MARKT
ALTE REBEN
13,5% vol
BAROLO 2012
LA TURQU
CÔTE BRUNE
Côte-Rôtie
APPELLATION CÔTE-RÔTIE CONTRÔLÉE
Les Chétill
2002
Pierre Péte
CHAMPAGNE
Cuvée Spéciale
S MICHEL &
Chablis Grand Cru
GRENOUILLES
HAPEL DOWN
VINTAGE 2016
CESANI
VERNACCIA
naia
2018
Domaine
BERTHET-BONDET
2011
2011
CHATEAU - CHALON
Appellation d'origine contrôlée
Dom Pérignon
Vintage 2008
M.
GRAHAM
1977
VINTAGE
PORT
BOTTLED 1979
OPORTO
MUSCAT
OF AUSTRALIA
Royal Tokaji
5 Puttonyos Aszú
2013
Sauternes
2001
RAISED
-BY-
WOLVES
SEMILLON
2016
Feudo 2012
Etna Rosso
GIROLAMO RUSSO

67
PALL MALL

PHOTOGRAPHY BY JOAKIM BLOCKSTRÖM

67

PALL MALL

WINE & FOOD

RONAN SAYBURN MS & MARCUS VERBERNE

Publisher Jacqui Small
Editor Lucy Bannell
Art direction and design Lawrence Morton
Photography Joakim Blockström
Prop styling Cynthia Inions
Production director Marina Asenjo, BookLabs
Indexer Vanessa Bird

Printed and bound in China by C&C Offset Printing Co Ltd

67 Pall Mall, London SW1Y 5ES

67 Pall Mall, The Penthouse, Shaw Centre, 1 Scotts Road, Singapore 228208

67pallmall.com

First published in Great Britain in 2020 by 67 Pall Mall Ltd.

A CIP catalogue record for this title is available from the British Library.

ISBN 978 1 5272 5190 8

The first half of this book is all about wine. Ronan leads us through the mysteries of terroir, teaches us how to perform 'culinary CSI' by looking for visual and flavour clues, and gives a guide to how to store our precious bottles. He discusses the concepts behind pairing wine and food, plans a wine-led dinner, then gets into a detailed examination of white and red wine varieties.

Recipes come second, and Marcus has divided his 100 delicious dishes into chapters entitled Sea & river, Land, Garden and Sweet.

Throughout the book, the wines are cross-referred to the dishes and vice versa, with alternative wines suggested for each dish, and other foods chosen to match a style of wine. So we will never be short of ideas for a dish to go with that perfect bottle... or of a different bottle to go with a mouth-watering recipe.

Ronan has offered a plethora of other possible wine matches with each recipe, to give us even more choice. Please note that he lists them in price order, with the cheapest first.

A CHANCE TO LIFT THE VEIL ON THE DARK ART OF SOMMELIERS

'FOUNDED BY WINE lovers, for wine lovers' is the statement of intent that is at the centre of everything we do at 67 Pall Mall. The question that I ask myself every time a situation or opportunity presents itself is: 'what would I want as a wine lover?', because that goes to the heart of why I founded the Club with a group of my wine-loving friends; to try and solve some of the issues that face the wine lover in the early 21st century.

The main challenge we all face is cost and availability. In an expensive city such as London, restaurants have to charge a high margin on wine. This leaves the wine lover with a quandary: restaurant wine lists are getting more expensive, while the wines on them are becoming younger and more esoteric. Yet many of us who have been collecting wine for a while have cellars full of exactly what we would like to order in a restaurant... if only it were available and offered at a price that we remember from a few years ago. This is how the idea for the Club came about: a place that offers a huge wine list from over 40 countries, including 800+ wines by-the-glass, as well as unlimited corkage.

When Ronan and Marcus came to me with an idea for a book they wanted to write on matching wine with food, it fitted perfectly into the ethos of the Club. Its starting premise was to concentrate on the wines you want to drink, then construct a menu around your choices (not what most of us do, which is to look at it the other way around). This book puts wines centre-stage and seeks recipes to pair beautifully with them. Additionally, this is a chance to lift the veil on the dark art of sommeliers, who seem to effortlessly construct pairings that I would never consider... an opportunity not to be missed.

This is a book to be used. We have bound it so it will sit flat on your kitchen counter and hope that, in years to come, much-thumbed and sauce-splattered versions will adorn kitchens all over the world. While it would look equally beautiful on your coffee table, that would be missing its point. Go out and create!

Grant Ashton
FOUNDER & CEO

CLARE SMYTH

Food and wine matching is one of life's great pleasures. There are wines that go well with food, and then there are the moments when you just sit back and say: 'wow!' Those are the special moments, when you savour just how wine and food can elevate each other. Moments like these have stayed with me for years: a special wine with that phenomenal dish, shared with friends.

I first met Ronan many years ago at Restaurant Gordon Ramsay. Ronan was the respected head sommelier, I was at the beginning of my journey as a chef. It was a pressurised environment, yet Ronan always took time to show us when he sold an exceptional wine, and often let me taste it, too. Though I knew nothing about it, I was inspired by that first sip of fine wine.

I admired how Ronan could break

down such a vast subject into plain English, making it approachable and enjoyable to learn about, with a real common sense attitude. When he was giving wine tastings, it would seem so easy. Fast forward many years and Ronan is one of the world's great sommeliers, yet his easy-to-follow approach still comes through, as he shows with this book, a comprehensive guide on how to approach and enjoy wine.

Marcus has provided fantastic recipes, using quality ingredients, that can easily be prepared at home for any occasion. Like Ronan, he has a no-nonsense approach to food that results in great dishes that will be a delight on any table.

Even with good knowledge about wine, it is such a vast subject that it is always good to have an expert on hand, and this book is that expert. In these pages you will discover lots of inspiration, be given tons of ideas about how to nail those pairings and create those great 'wow' moments which will stay with you forever.

OZ CLARKE

One of the most reassuring sights any wine lover can see in a restaurant is the smiling, friendly face of Ronan Sayburn and his calm manner as he glides about the room. Some sommeliers think of themselves as superstars and act accordingly. Ronan is an omniscient superstar, but conducts himself in such a way that he makes everybody – from the most avid wine geek to the guest who knows little but wants some generous, sympathetic advice – feel at ease, confident that they're making the right choices.

Feeling confident, relaxed, optimistic... this is desperately important if you want to enjoy wine and food to the utmost, and it is something 67 Pall Mall puts at the heart of its operations, and has done from day one.

You'll never get the best out of wine and food if you only stick to what you know. Here, the skill of a great sommelier is to know just how far you want to be led into the wonderful world of something new.

Ronan writes as attractively as he talks, introducing concepts such as terroir, grape variety differences and wine and food compatibility with ease. And he has the best possible partner in this endeavour. Marcus is a passionate believer in terroir and originality in food, as well as being wickedly keen to challenge Ronan's wine skills to find perfectly matching wines.

Sometimes a wine and food match is blindingly obvious. If you're at 67 Pall Mall and you want simple but perfectly prepared Welsh lamb with a carefully decanted Pauillac, Marcus and Ronan will delight in giving you this. But the modern world of wine and food is about so much more than just the classic pairings. There are thousands of wines that didn't exist a generation ago. There are dozens of cuisines that chefs had barely heard of a generation ago. And it is this world that Ronan and Marcus attack with such joy and enthusiasm.

Food changes the flavour of wine. It may enhance. It may hinder. But it will change the wine. That's the challenge Ronan and Marcus so enjoy.

In this book, Ronan has collected 100 fascinating wines, to which Marcus has responded with really imaginative and mouth-watering recipes. And all irresistibly photographed. Right now I'm gazing at a chilled glass of Tio Pepe en Rama to go with baked salt cod, chorizo, tomato and chickpeas. Heaven.

terroir

MIGRATION OF THE VINE

The cradle of civilisation is said to have been Mesopotamia, the area between the Mediterranean Sea and the Caspian Sea that forms modern-day Iran and Iraq. It was one of the first societies, along with Georgia and China, to produce wine on a large scale, as long ago as 6,000 BC. A community that can combine the agricultural skills of grape growing with the chemistry of fermentation must, genuinely, be civilised.

Grapes moved with the Phoenicians into present-day Lebanon, then to Anatolia, before the Greeks took the vine across the Mediterranean to their homeland. The Greeks also planted vines in Italy, a place they called *Oenotria*, or 'the land of the vine'. The Romans spread the vine across Europe in their typically well-organised style. They also invented many aspects of viticulture and vinification that are still used today, such as training methods – planting vines in rows and positioning their shoots across horizontal wires – the use of sulphur as both an antiseptic and an antioxidant, the creation of storage vessels from amphorae to barrels and even cork closures. The mighty Roman Army took the vine on its travels, and there is a rich Roman history in many winemaking regions of France, such as Champagne, the Rhône Valley and St-Emilion.

Eventually, in the 16th century, Spanish and Portuguese conquistadors brought European vines and winemaking skills to the Americas. Much later, in the southern hemisphere, Scotsman James Busby, the Resident (the consular representative) to New Zealand in the early 19th century, took grapes to Australia and New Zealand, and perhaps even to South Africa as well.

Now, vines are grown all across the globe. But, while some Old World winemaking areas in Europe and the Mediterranean can boast hundreds of indigenous grape varieties, the New World is home to only a few dozen. And 'New World' itself is only a relative term; some areas have, in fact, been growing grapes for 150 years (and even since the 1650s, in the case of South Africa), though it is only in the last 50–60 years that they have started to produce wines of note.

Ironically, the indigenous vines of North America saved European vines after the spread of the *phylloxera vastatrix* mite during the late 19th century...

HOW A MITE SPREAD FRENCH WINEMAKING AROUND THE WORLD

Phylloxera vastatrix is a mite from the Americas that feeds on the roots of vines. Grapes from the genus *Vitis vinifera* are used for making the classic European wines (Chardonnay, Sauvignon and so on), while a lot of other *Vitis* genuses come from the Americas. During the Victorian period, there was a fashion for enormous botanical gardens full of rare varieties of plants. A lot of plant matter was moved around the world because of this craze, including some American *Vitis* genuses that were brought to Europe. Unfortunately, they were infested with *phylloxera*, which then migrated to the European varieties of vine. But, while *phylloxera* did not usually kill the American vines, it proved fatal to *Vitis vinifera*, which had no resistance; the mite cut off the food supply by gnawing through root nodules, and the vines died. In the two decades between the 1850s and 1870s, 40 per cent of all vines in France were destroyed. Winemakers desperately looked for a solution: they tried to flood *phylloxera* out, because you can drown the mite; they tried to burn it out, which unsurprisingly the vines couldn't withstand. Neither worked. It was thought that the wine business in France was finished. Eventually, a solution was found: grafting European vines on to American root stock. Bordeaux shifted to growing mostly Cabernet Sauvignon and Merlot, as these vines took the graft well.

However, the *phylloxera* infestation shaped the development of winemaking worldwide, as French wine growers scattered (often by invitation) to the New World of California, Chile and Argentina to make their living, taking Carmenere and Malbec vines with them (see pages 118 and 119). Other Bordeaux winemakers stayed in Europe, but trekked over the Pyrenees and started making Rioja in Spain (see page 119).

Parts of the world, including South Australia (Barossa and McLaren Vale), Colares in Portugal, Santorini, with its sandy, inorganic soils, and certain vineyards including Bollinger's 'Vielles Vignes Français' and Quinta do Noval's 'Naçional' have remained *phylloxera* free.

Most of South America has remained *phylloxera* free, Chile because of its four natural barriers – the Pacific, the Andes, the Atacama desert and southern glaciers – and Argentina due to meltwater flood irrigation and sandy soils that both mean *phylloxera* has never prospered there. The old Bordeaux varieties of Carmenere and Malbec therefore flourish here, as they don't take well to the grafting process.

PREVIOUS PAGE Overlooking Pinot Noir vines in the Rippon vineyard by Lake Wanaka in Central Otago, New Zealand

WHAT IS TERROIR?

A natural curiosity about how things work is essential if you want to be a good sommelier. It's not enough that grapes taste full and fruity; you should want to know *why* that is. In fact, when asking 'why?' in regard to how a wine tastes, you need to try to understand the question on a global scale.

'Terroir' is a French term that relates to all the natural factors that occur to create great wine: climate, geology and geography. Where the winds blow because of the presence or absence of a mountain range. How close to oceans, lakes or rivers the vineyards are. Where the cool sea breezes or ocean currents run. The angle and direction of the slopes on which grapes are planted, specifically whether they face into the sun in cooler areas, or out of the sun in hotter areas. What is the bedrock and what is its mineral content? What is the soil's composition and is it fertile or infertile? Winemaking talent and grape varieties can be changed, but these environmental factors cannot.

As the world spins eastwards, winds from the equator blow in huge circles, spiralling clockwise in the Northern Hemisphere and anticlockwise in the Southern Hemisphere (the Coriolis Effect). This affects every climate in the world and, of course, every winemaker.

There are three global soil types: igneous, metamorphic and sedimentary, all of which are formed from degraded rock from the Earth's plates. They keep recycling: igneous rock bubbles up from volcanoes and eventually is weathered down into fine material, then dragged back under the crust of the Earth by subducting plates (plates that are being forced underground), to be heated to magma once more. A winemaker must choose their vine to suit their soil.

The plates won't stop moving. Even now, as the Pacific Ocean floor spreads apart due to thermal magma plumes under the Earth's crust, the edges of the Pacific Ocean are being subducted under the surrounding continental land masses, causing a circle of volcanoes and seismic activity known as 'the Ring of Fire'. The ocean floor is covered with carbon, from dead sea life. As that gets dragged down, it starts to melt and release carbon dioxide. The gas pushes its way out to the surface and brings magma with it, creating volcanoes and mountain ranges (there are about 160 active volcanoes in the Andes alone).

Why is this significant? Because some great wine regions are found in valleys created by this process: the Napa Valley (leading to the Sierra Nevadas), Chile's Central Valley (positioned by the Andes), and Marlborough and Central Otago in New Zealand (the Southern Alps). They are also found in coastal ranges: Sonoma County and Santa Barbara in California, for example, and Casablanca and San Antonio in Chile. Others are in the elevated regions caused by uplifted mountains, such as the Mendoza and Salta areas of Argentina, the Bekaa Valley of Lebanon, or Yunnan province in the Himalayas. There are also the numerous volcanic areas of the Mediterranean: Santorini in the Aegean Islands, Vesuvius close to Naples in Campania, Etna on Sicily, the Canary Islands and the island of Madeira.

Rift valleys – caused by the relaxing of tectonic plate pressure and the resulting faulting and land collapse – formed famous wine landscapes such as Alsace and the Northern Rhône.

The best winemaking regions in the world are located between the latitudes of 28° to 50° in the Northern and Southern Hemispheres. In the north, this covers California, the classic European wine regions and parts of India, China and Japan (the latter three coming relatively late to the winemaking game). In the south, it covers southern South America, South Africa, Southern Australia and New Zealand.

A warm environment closer to the equator will produce grapes high in sugar but lacking acidity, while anything north of 50° (and therefore with cooler weather) will provide plenty of acidity but not enough sugar to make a balanced wine. There are always exceptions to this: Salta, in northern Argentina, sits at 24°, but is chilled by its altitude of 3,000m; Chateau Hornsby is in central Australia, close to Alice Springs. Presumably, winemakers at both vineyards struggle with the extremes of their environment.

THE THREE TYPES OF CLIMATE

MARITIME A land mass close to a large body of water. In summer, moving water helps cool the area (important in the Douro Valley); in winter, it helps move frosty air, keeping the land warm (vital in the Mosel Valley). Bordeaux and New Zealand are good examples of this climate. Crucially, a Maritime climate allows a long, cool growing season that – in a place such as Bordeaux – helps to create elegant tannins in the grape skins.

CONTINENTAL A land mass that gets very hot in summer and very cold in winter. The potential hazards here include occasional frosts in springtime, which crucially affect flowering of the vines, plus the early onset of cold weather in autumn, when grapes will struggle to ripen. Champagne and Burgundy are both examples of this kind of climate.

MEDITERRANEAN Generally hot during summer and with mild winters, due to either being close to an enclosed sea (as is the case in the Mediterranean) rather than a very large ocean with its Polar water currents, or to being a large hot land mass with internal thermal winds, such as the south coast of Australia, or South Africa.

Some of the best terroirs in the world

FRANCE: BORDEAUX

Bordeaux boasts some of the most hallowed hills on Earth, in viticultural terms. The *croupes*, or mounds of gravel that spread out like ripples on a pond in the Haut-Medóc (see below right), have for centuries provided wine lovers with many a muse into which to pour their love and admiration. But until the 17th century, most of this area was swampy marshland, it was only when Dutch engineers drained the waters that there was revealed a rocky gravel soil rich in minerals: perfect for growing grapes.

Ever since then, the best wines from Bordeaux have been considered the greatest and most expensive in the world. The first growths (*premiers crus*) – the highest classification – command such respect that the wines are sold long before they are bottled. Further to the south, fine white wines are produced, along with reds, in the arid, sandy and gravelly soil of Graves.

Bordeaux is famous for all three major styles of wine: white, red and sweet. Sauternes and Barsac produce some of the most unctuous, rich, decadent and sublime dessert wines on the planet.

The Médoc, also known as the Left Bank, is home to some of Bordeaux's most illustrious châteaux and expensive wines – the likes of Châteaux Latour, Margaux, Lafite-Rothschild and Mouton-Rothschild – making it the benchmark global standard for high-quality Cabernet Sauvignon blends. The Haut-Medóc produces 2.3 million cases of wine each year, a staggering number for an area known for such high quality.

During the last ice age in France, as glaciers melted and retracted, they carved out the huge Garonne estuary, grinding down rocks to create deep beds of gravel along the far eastern edge of the Médoc. The estuary is more than 10km wide at its broadest part and, with the Atlantic on its other side, creates a Maritime climate. Bordeaux is a relatively flat area; you could think of it as a beach, with rising and falling sea levels over many millennia depositing sand, silt and pebbles. (The highest point is Poujeaux in the Moulis region, only 45m above sea level.)

The Médoc peninsula is divided in two: the Médoc and the Haut-Médoc, the latter of which is the more southerly of the two and contains the famous communal appellations of Saint-Estèphe, Pauillac, Saint-Julien and Margaux. The commune boundaries are defined by where the gravel sits.

The most widely planted red grape in Bordeaux is Merlot, but in the Médoc, Cabernet Sauvignon dominates, with up to 85 per cent used by some producers in their blends. Cabernet ripens two weeks after Merlot, and the warm, free-draining gravel soils, the Maritime climate and – especially – warm, dry Septembers allow the tannins in the skins to develop finesse and elegance.

FRANCE: LIMESTONE OF CHAMPAGNE, THE LOIRE & BURGUNDY

The complex geology of Europe has been shaped by the movement north of the African plate pushing into the Eurasian plate, causing mountain ranges such as the Alps, Pyrenees and Massif Central to be formed.

In simplistic terms, during the Mesozoic period (260 million years ago), most of northern Europe was a shallow, warm sea where many shelled creatures (oysters, mussels, clam and corals) lived. When they died and sank to the seabed, the pressure of layering deposits caused their shells to compact and lithify into limestone. Deposits from the same period are found from the English South Downs down through France as a chalky marl, rich in seashell fossils.

Heavy deposits built up in the Paris area, causing a collapse of rock strata and creating the Paris basin. Erosion from (principally) the Seine, Aube, Yonne and Loire rivers caused the edges of this basin to become exposed. Many of France's famous wine regions can be found on these limestone edges, often known as the 'Kimmeridgian Chain'.

The main vineyard sites are the Aube region of Champagne, Chablis, Tonnerre and the Auxerrois wine areas of northern Burgundy, and Sancerre, Pouilly-Fumé and Menetou-Salon in the Loire Valley. The composition and water-retaining qualities of the soil make it perfect for *Vitis vinifera* vines.

A harder Oxfordian limestone and marl (a limestone-rich clay) can be found further south in the Côte d'Or. Limestone is present all over northern France and southern England, covering the vineyards of Kent, Dover and the Isle of Wight.

ABOVE Château Latour sits in a prime position next to the Gironde estuary, which helps to moderate the temperature. Positioned on a thick bed of gravel and sand, the soils are poor and free draining, forcing vine roots deep to source water and minerals. They are also warm, keeping heat at night and reflecting light in the day: ideal for Cabernet Sauvignon

FAR LEFT The soils on the Left Bank or Médoc are günzian gravels, created by glaciers during the last ice age. *Croupes* or mounds of this gravel define the appellations

LEFT The limestone escarpment of St-Emilion is one of only a few noticeable rises. The soils here have more sand, clay and limestone and only patches of gravel

FRANCE: CHÂTEAUNEUF-DU-PAPE, SOUTHERN RHÔNE VALLEY

This region became famous for wine production when Bertrand de Goth was 'promoted' from Archbishop of Bordeaux to Pope Clement V (his Bordeaux home later becoming Château Pape-Clement), and moved the papacy to Avignon. He established a castle in this region that was known as the 'new castle of the Pope'. The wines first gained their fame because of this. So highly sought-after were they that they were the first recorded to be faked, when barrels of dubiously sourced red had the bogus Châteauneuf-du-Pape branding seared on to them. This fakery in turn led to the very first *Appellation d'Origine Contrôlée* (AOC) laws being created in 1936 for these wines. AOC laws control which grape varieties, vineyards and winemaking practices are allowed to use a wine's name.

The Southern Rhône Valley sits in a Mediterranean climate, enjoying blisteringly hot, dry summers and mild, damp winters. The Mediterranean Sea has a cooling effect on this area, but the effect is not as marked as is that of the cold Atlantic on Bordeaux or Portugal, which both sit in a Maritime climate.

Fast-moving Alpine melt waters during the last Ice Age carried huge stones or *galets* the size of cantaloupe melons into the Southern Rhône river to create some extraordinary scenery. The stones get very hot during the day and continue transferring heat into the vineyard throughout the night. Not much can grow in this soil except gnarly old vines that are trained into bush shapes. Grenache is the dominant variety here and, grown in these soils and this heat, can make unpleasant wines lacking in structure: burningly alcoholic with jammy red fruit, soft tannins, low acidity and white pepper spice. This is why Syrah and Mourvèdre are often blended in, to bring acidity and tannins, reduce the raging alcohol and add dark berry fruit to the red jammy fruit, and black pepper spice to the white pepper. Mourvèdre also brings a wild animal gaminess. The three varieties complement each other to create complex and interesting wines.

But there is always an exception that proves the rule: the most highly regarded Châteauneuf-du-Pape is Château Rayas, made from 100 per cent Grenache. As it is grown in cool, sandy soils without the stony *galets*, it never get heavy or jammy.

BELOW *Galets roules*, or pudding stones, are found in the northern part of the Châteauneuf-du-Pape appellation and make for an impressive sight, though it is impossible for much other than vines to grow. These mini thermal storage heaters keep the vineyards warm well after the sun goes down

FRANCE: ALSACE

Alsace in north-eastern France has the mighty Rhine river and Germany's Black Forest mountains to the east, and is somewhat geographically segregated from the rest of France by the Vosges mountains to the west. It sits in a rift valley caused by a relaxing of tectonic plate pressure, which in turn causes a series of fault lines to develop and the land to collapse, leaving a valley between two mountain ranges.

The vineyards of Alsace lie in the foothills of the Vosges mountains, which shelter them from wind and rain. The rainfall in Colmar is only 500mm, making it, along with Marseilles, one of the driest cities in France. This lack of moisture – and, therefore, rot – makes it a great region for biodynamic wines, as growers don't need to spray against the mould that can develop in wetter regions.

Alsace contains some of the most diverse soil types in France, running the whole gamut from sandstone, clay and alluvial, through limestone, to volcanic and metamorphic. Riesling is widely grown here, a variety that intensely expresses the soil from which it comes, and so the Rieslings of Alsace are as diverse in their nuances of flavour as the region's soils.

The hot weather here also allows the production of slightly off-dry Pinot Gris and Gewurztraminer, as the grapes can accumulate plenty of sugar, and these wines are the perfect foil for the richly delicious Alsace cuisine.

ABOVE The foothills of the Vosges mountain provide east-facing slopes that are perfect for growing grapes. Overlooking the town of Guebwiller is Domaine Schlumberger's Grand Cru vineyard: Kitterlé

ITALY: TUSCANY

There is a lot of variability in Tuscany. The heart of the region – and the original 1716 designation of Chianti – falls entirely within the modern Chianti Classico zone, covering the four principal villages of Radda, Gaiole, Castellina and Greve.

There are many soil types in Tuscany, but the two most-lauded are *alberese* – a compact clay and limestone – and *galestro*, a granite and schistous clay soil often said to be found in the best vineyards. The proximity of a vineyard to the Tyrrhenian Sea on Italy's west coast produces different expressions of the Sangiovese grape. If it is down by the sea, close to Maremma or Bolgheri, the wines are deep coloured with dark fruit that can carry the weight of new oak. If it is in Chianti Rúfina, as the vineyards climb the spine of the Apennines and there is a drop in temperature, the wines are paler with increased acidity; Pinot Noir-like.

Basic Chianti can be quite grim, while Chianti Classico Gran Selezione and Brunello di Montalcino can be awe-inspiringly great. This may be in part due to the many clones of Sangiovese. A post-war boom in the wines, especially in America, saw high-yielding poor-quality clones, such as Sangiovese di Romagna, planted; these wines can be thin and very tart with sour cherry flavours and abrupt tannins. However, the Brunello clone in Montalcino and the Prugnollo Gentile of Montepulciano can both produce elegant, silky, complex wine.

So, if the wines can be so varied, why is Tuscany included here? Please extend plenty of poetic licence... it's the sunsets. The Tuscan landscape – with its rolling hillsides, terracotta-roofed villas and long cypress-lined driveways – is stunning as the landscape turns orange. This, along with the quality of simple Tuscan food, inevitably makes wine taste great. The psychology surrounding where, how and with whom wines are drunk is very important. Not very scientific, but true.

GERMANY: MOSEL

Germany is just about as far north as vines can be grown. There are two vital factors to be considered when choosing a great vineyard site in a colder climate: the slope and aspect of your vineyard, in other words, how steep it is and in which direction it faces. In German wine, sugar is king, and wine growers need to be clever about siting vineyards, taking advantage of the slopes to maximise precious hours of heat and sunshine. The Mosel, Saar and Ruwer rivers cut impossible doglegs and 'S'-shaped bends throughout their courses, and the vineyards cling to their valley sides. One thing they have in common is that they always face south or south-east, where they receive the early morning sun and warm up quickly, giving the vines a full day's sugar production. As the river twists, no vineyards are found on slopes facing north or west, as they don't receive enough sunlight. Crazy slopes can be found here: the vineyards of Urziger Würtzgarten or Bremmer Calmont rise at 60°; workers need mountaineering gear!

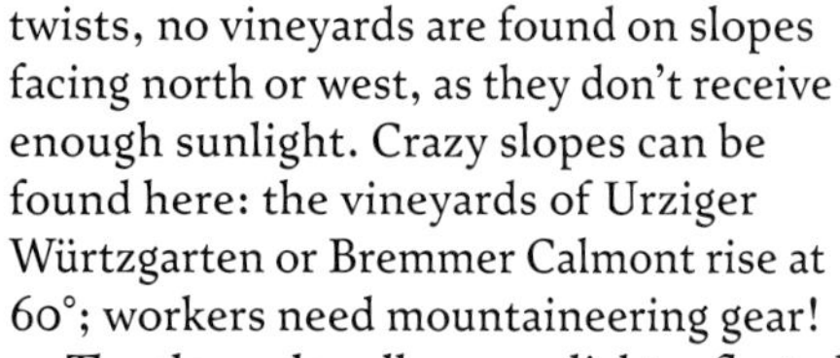

The slope also allows sunlight reflected from the river to penetrate the vineyards; while any cold, frosty air just slips down out of the vineyard and is drawn away by the moving river.

Riesling needs to ripen slowly and gracefully and this environment provides the correct conditions. Deep slate soils, both blue and red, heat up quickly in the day and provide warmth in the evenings.

A smoky, sulphurous note in the Rieslings from Mosel can be attributed to this slate and is occasionally very apparent (for example, in the wines of Weingut JJ Prüm, see page 52). Could it be because these slate soils lack sufficient nitrogen? Yeast needs nitrogen during fermentation and, if it is lacking, can become stressed and produce small amounts of sulphur. It's a complicated subject, but these flavours in Riesling from Mosel are found nowhere else.

These wines show taut, muscular, acidic strength, grace and delicacy from the fruit, a hint of residual sugar and a gentle 8.5 per cent alcohol. They walk the tightrope between acidity and sugar. To appreciate this tension and balance is the sign of a true wine lover.

LEFT Dramatic S-shaped bends create huge amphitheatres of vineyards, angled into the sun. The slopes cause frosty air to roll down and be carried away by the moving water. Also, sunlight reflects off the water, increasing the potential to ripen grapes

USA: NAPA VALLEY 'BENCHES'

As tectonic plates skate around on the Earth's surface, driven by hot magma plumes from the planet's core, they either collide, are pulled apart, or slide against each another. In California, the Pacific Oceanic plate is moving north and colliding with the North American plate and the two grind against one another along the San Andreas faultline (in ten million years' time, Los Angeles will be further north than San Francisco... you probably shouldn't worry too much about this). The collision of plates along a coast line causes a concertina-like effect on the topography and creates series of valleys, as well as some serious volcanic activity.

Napa Valley runs northwards from San Pablo Bay above San Francisco to the town of Calistoga. Either side of the Valley are the Mayacamas and Vacas mountain ranges. As the rain falls on these mountains, it washes alluvial pebbles, sand and loam down into the Valley floor, which fan out of the hillsides and create raised 'benches'. These stony, free-draining benches are perfect for Cabernet Sauvignon. They also give rise to the legendary 'Rutherford dust' of the area. André Tchelistcheff – the father of modern California winemaking – claimed that great Cabernet from here had allspice and cocoa flavours along with dusty powdery tannins, due to the deep soils and the long hanging times for the grapes, which allow polyphenols and anthocyanins to develop fully. The wines of the famous Martha's Vineyard, Opus One, Staiglin, Inglenook and Quintessa vineyards all display this characteristic.

USA: SONOMA COAST & RUSSIAN RIVER

Cold Alaskan water is pulled south along the western side of the USA by the Humboldt Current, chilling the coasts of Washington, Oregon and California.

Inland from California's coastal mountain ranges lies the broad Central Valley, then the Sierra Nevadas, eventually followed by the deserts of Death Valley. As the air here is hot, it rises, creating a vacuum effect to the west. This causes that cold Pacific air to get sucked through the gaps in the coastal range. When cold air meets warm air, precipitation happens, in the form of rain or fog. (Think of those iconic images of the Golden Gate Bridge shrouded in fog at the entrance to San Pablo Bay.)

Sonoma County enjoys a lot of this fog effect, especially when air is channelled through the Petaluma Gap and then south to Carneros and north into the Russian River Valley. The cool morning fog has burned off when the midday sun reaches its peak, but the effect is a large diurnal shift between daytime and night-time temperature. The cool night temperatures promote acid production in grapes, while the warm days allow for sugar production. A good wine must balance these elements.

This climate makes the region perfect for growing elegant Pinot Noir and classy Chardonnay. Compared to the Cabernet Sauvignon-dominant Napa Valley – the Bordeaux of California – Sonoma can happily be labelled the state's Burgundy.

BELOW This photo, taken above the fog line in Sonoma County, shows just how much dense fog floods into the valleys here. Drawn through gaps in the coastal mountains, it keeps that Pinot Noir and Chardonnay acidity bright and fresh, while warm, sunny afternoons pack sugar and flavour into the grapes

AUSTRALIA: COONAWARRA

Coonawarra is the Aboriginal word for 'honeysuckle'. The first vines were planted here as early as 1890 by pioneer John Riddoch and, by the 1950s, the potential for quality was established and companies such as Penfolds began producing dry red wines rather than the fortified Port styles that had historically been drunk in Australia.

This wine region is located in the limestone coast area of South Australia, on the border with Victoria. Located just 60km from the sea and chilled by cool sea breezes, it has a climate similar to that of Bordeaux. Australian soils are some of the oldest in the world – the Porongurup mountains in Western Australia are about 1.2 billion years old – and it's the soils of Coonawarra that mark this area out as unique. It sits on a 12 x 1 km rectangle of 'terra rossa', a deep red-coloured layer of iron oxide-based top soil, about 50cm thick, laid over limestone. It was one of the first New World regions to be delimited solely by its soil type.

The Cabernet Sauvignon grape works particularly well here, and you could swear that a slight sanguine ferrous tang can be tasted on the palate, as well as the trademark aromas of Australian mint and eucalyptus on the nose.

ABOVE 'Terra rossa' soils are a type of red clay, produced by limestone weathering over thousands of years and coloured by iron oxide. The water-retaining nature of this limestone, a proximity to cool ocean winds, and the chosen grape variety of Cabernet Sauvignon all add to the region's success

ARGENTINA: MENDOZA

The skyline of western South America is dominated by the longest mountain chain on earth: the Andes. It's only 50 million years old, so quite young in geological terms, and was created by the Pacific Nazca tectonic plate subducting (being forced under) the South American plate. During this process, carbon from dead plankton on the ocean floor returns to the surface, about 160km from the coastline, in the form of carbon dioxide, and with it comes magma and the creation of volcanoes. Similar to the Californian coastline (see page 16), Chile has a coastal range of mountains, a wide Central Valley, then another range of mountains (in Chile, this is the Andes). On the far side of the Andes is Mendoza, sitting very high on an elevated plateau 1,000–1,500m above sea level.

Astonishingly, the Andes have more than 160 active volcanoes that provide a rich wealth of minerals and metals that explain the region's long history of wine growing. In the early Victorian era, new engineering technology allowed the Chileans to mine deeper into the Andes, bringing certain families great wealth (Chile is still the world's largest producer of copper). These families travelled to Europe, and, on their travels, enjoyed the great wines of Champagne, Bordeaux and Burgundy. When *phylloxera* struck and destroyed 40 per cent of France's vineyards (see page 10), some Bordeaux winemakers moved to South America, bringing with them their most widely planted varieties: Carmenere, vital to Chile's wine industry, and Malbec, a huge success story in Argentina.

The high altitude of Mendoza brings cold temperatures (on average every 100m of altitude will cause a 1°C drop), while the combination of a high-altitude vineyard next to a mountain range with easterly winds creates a big rain shadow. This results in little rainfall and also little cloud cover, bringing plenty of blue skies and UV light that helps to thicken grape skins. It also provides little thermal insulation at night, as there is no cloud. So this region has a wide diurnal shift of day to night temperatures, from 5°C at night, which causes the grapes to build acid, to 35°C during the day, allowing for sugar production in the fruit. Due to the low rainfall, the vineyards are usually provided with controlled irrigation, which permits the development of an ideally balanced leaf canopy. Combined with organically poor sand and gravel soils, this results in perfectly ripe fruit.

Around two thirds of Argentinian wine production is in Mendoza and around 70 per cent of that is Malbec. The deep colours, vibrant black and blueberry fruit and aromas of violet and liquorice, along with almost sweet tannins, make these wines deservedly popular.

ABOVE The Andes are a magnificent backdrop for the vineyard workers in Mendoza, and act as a rain shadow; annual rainfall is around 200mm (London's is 621mm and Tuscany's is 777mm). Low rainfall means no cloud cover, therefore high UV rays and no thermal retention at night

APPEARANCE

When it comes to wine, you need to differentiate between drinking it purely for enjoyment, and tasting it professionally to assess its quality, or to reveal its origins. For those who like wine, hopefully the experience will fall somewhere in between; you can enjoy drinking it for the flavour alone, but also understand the intrinsic quality markers to look for and the typical characteristics of grape variety or country of origin that make us like it.

Clarity

Just by attention to the look of a wine, you can tell a lot about it. Firstly it should be clear, with nothing floating in it or any hazy appearance. (Some winemakers perform minimal filtration or fining, others ferment for extended periods on the grape skins. These wines may appear cloudy, and are for more specialist drinkers. They are like the wheat beer equivalent of the wine world, and not to everyone's taste.) In the vast majority of cases, you expect to see a clear, bright liquid that reflects light from its surface and has a brilliant lustre.

Colour

White wine ranges from a clear – almost water white – colour, through to a pale green tinge, to straw, lemon yellow, golden and eventually to copper or tawny. Many factors will affect the colour: the grape variety, whether a wine has been aged in oak barrels, or how much it has oxidised. A very young wine will often have a green tinge, while oaked wines tend to take on a golden colour. Older wine naturally oxidises, so deep golden tones in a glass of white may well reveal a 10- or 15-year-old wine that has gently been allowed to oxidise, to add complexity to its flavours. Generally speaking, white wine starts off pale and takes on colour with age.

Conversely, red wine starts off dark, almost black in colour and gets paler with age, turning from deep purple, through ruby and garnet, until finally arriving at tawny. The intensity of colour in red wines comes from components in the grape skins such as anthocyanins, that contain polyphenols and tannins. The colour of a specific wine will vary depending on factors such as the thickness of the grape skins or the amount of anthocyanins they contain, how long a winemaker leaves the juice in contact with the skins during fermentation, or the age of the wine.

In simplistic terms, polyphenols are deep purple, while tannins are brick red. A young wine is deeply coloured and tannic, as it contains plenty of both these substances. As red wine ages, polyphenol molecules begin to polymerise, joining together to form long chains. When these chains reach a certain size, they can no longer be held in suspension and start to drop out of a wine as sediment, making the wine lose its deep purple colour.

An ageing wine will, therefore, grow paler and begin to take on mahogany, brick-red tones from the tannins that still remain. A mature wine can be identified when the glass is tilted at a 45° angle and the meniscus of the wine is observed against a white background. The meniscus should show a brick red-orange hue, in general, that will reveal that the wine is seven to ten years old, or older (see below).

Thin-skinned grapes such as Pinot Noir, Gamay or Nebbiolo will make a pale coloured wine, as they are low in anthocyanins, the deep purple colour found in grape skins

A youthful wine from a variety such as Cabernet Sauvignon or Syrah, whose colour is deep. The rich hue extends right to the meniscus, indicating youth

Mature wine whose purple anthocyanins have polymerised, falling out of suspension. A red-brick orange meniscus is visible, which indicates it still has tannins

Oak ageing

Using oak barrels is a very ancient method of transporting wine. Before that, winemakers used clay amphorae, which were very heavy and not especially robust. Conversely, you can throw oak barrels about, or store them in the hold of a boat and use them as ballast while keeping the crew 'happy' at the same time. Once they had been drunk, the barrels could be filled with sea water and used as ballast once again.

To make an oak barrel, you need to cut a tree into staves. Depending where in the forest you get your oak from, or the species of oak you are using, you will get an open or a closed grain (a closed grain will have come from a tree in the centre of a forest, whereas an open grain indicates a tree on the outskirts). Famous oak forests in France include Limousin, Tronçais, Allier, Nevers and Vosges. The oak variety *Quercus sessilis* is tight-grained; *Querscus robur* is wide-grained.

A winemaker will want different types of barrel depending whether they want oxygen; for instance, they'd choose an open grain to let the air in and allow controlled oxidation of wine as it ages.

Barrel staves used to be left out in the open air for a couple of years. They got rained on, then dried, in the process gradually removing the resinous material and fresh wood characteristic of the oak.

To create a barrel shape, the staves are heated to make them flexible by toasting the oak, rolling the wood around a flame. All the wood sugars, such as vanillin, start to caramelise on the inside of the barrel, giving up their vanilla flavour. You can order barrels lightly toasted, or medium, or heavy, depending on the style of wine you are making. Big, heavy Australian Shiraz is usually aged in quite a heavily toasted barrel. A lighter toast gives more of a hazelnut, vanilla and popcorn characteristic. As a toast gets heavier, it gives dark chocolate or coffee flavours, due to the over-caramelised wood sugars. The French call these roasted flavours *torréfaction*.

At the time of going to press, a brand-new French oak barrel costs about €900. A 225-litre *barrique* – the Bordeaux standard (300 bottles) – will put €3 on the price of every bottle. To make a bottle of wine, you need 1–1.2kg of grapes, and, in 2018, 1kg of grapes in Champagne cost €5–8. So the grapes are only a little bit more expensive than the oak. To put oak into barrels of wine is very expensive and reserved for the top-quality bottles. If you go to any supermarket and buy a £5 Chardonnay that says 'oak' on the label, it will have been made with oak chips, such as those you buy to use on a barbecue. Winemakers can order those in different toasts, too, and they come in sacks, like a supersized teabag that you throw into a fermenting tank to give a kind of a breakfast cereal flavour. Good oak, in contrast, should complement a wine, not overpower it.

When looking at a wine, a golden colour will suggest ageing in oak. A white wine that is green in tone has probably not been aged in oak barrels.

Many grape varieties marry well with the flavour of oak, others – notably Riesling – do not (see page 50). There are various levels of oak flavour that a winemaker may desire, but oak should be used as a seasoning to wine, in the same way that a chef seasons food, and should not dominate.

American oak (*Quercus alba*) barrels are used in the USA, parts of Australia and in Rioja, and it imparts a sweeter, coconut flavour to wine.

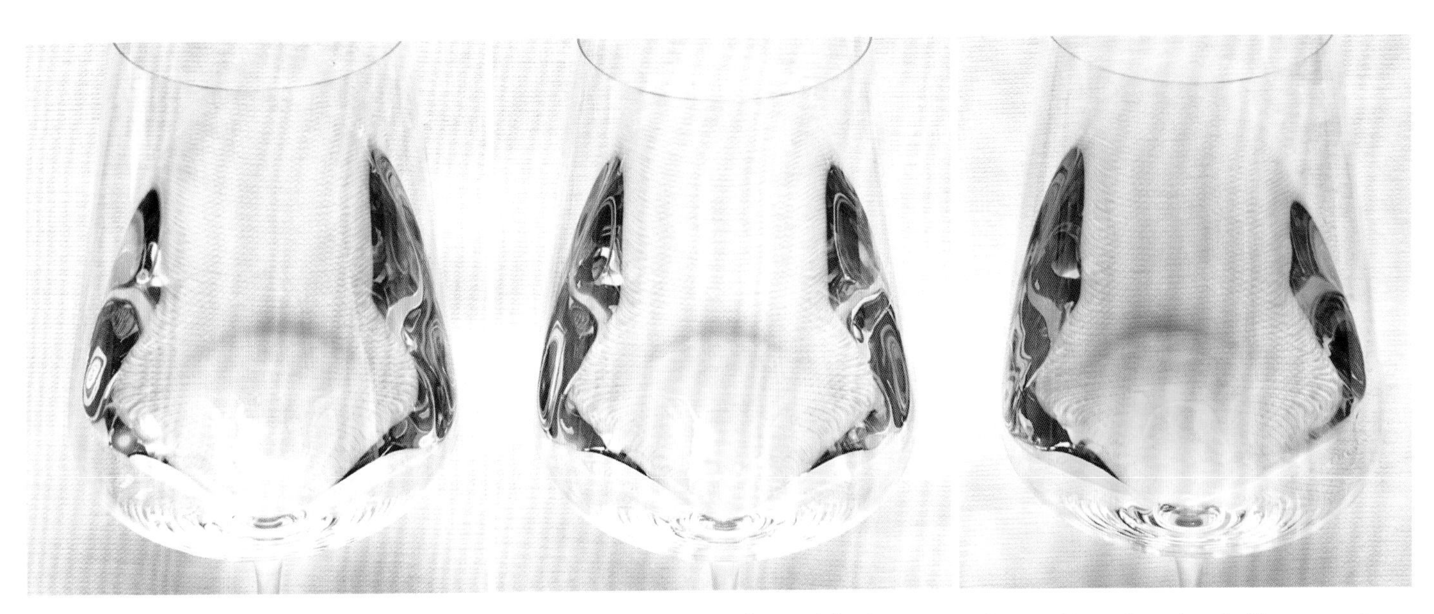

A bright, pale wine, with a touch of green, suggesting youth. Or it could have been aged in stainless steel, as oak adds gold tones. It may be Sauvignon Blanc or Riesling

This is a wine with more colour and depth, possibly indicating more age, or the oak-barrel ageing that gives golden tones, so it could be a Chardonnay

Deep gold in colour, almost with a copper hue, showing it's quite mature with lots of oak ageing; this could even be a dessert wine in which the grapes were affected by botrytis

'Legs'

If you swirl a wine around inside a well-polished glass and then hold it up to eye level, after ten seconds or so you should see a line appear a couple of centimetres above the wine's surface, on the inside of the glass. After another five to ten seconds, balls of liquid will begin to form along this line and drop down into the wine like tears or legs.

This is an indication of the amount of alcohol it contains; the phenomenon is caused by the interplay between adhesion, evaporation and surface tension of both water and alcohol. As a wine is swirled in the glass, the alcohol that reaches the highest part evaporates, leaving a lower surface tension to the wine beneath it. Therefore the wine is drawn up the inside of the glass to form a ball, which eventually gets too heavy and falls back down as a tear. The higher the wine is in alcohol – and therefore body in general – the larger and more pronounced these tears will be. (This is called the Gibbs-Marangoni Effect.)

Very rich, sweet wines will also show heavy viscosity, as the glycerol in the sugar will coat the inside of the glass and make the tears even more pronounced. For example, a Port or sweet Sherry will immediately have fast-forming, well-defined legs, due to its high sugar content and high alcohol level.

Crystals

You may sometimes see tiny crystals in the bottom of a bottle, or clinging to the underside of a cork. These are crystals of potassium bi-tartrate (known in cooking as cream of tartar), a natural acid found in fruits. Usually, this acid is held in the wine in solution, but if the wine is stored for prolonged periods of time at very cold temperatures, crystals will start to form.

Winemakers often perform a 'cold stabilisation' before bottling, in which the wine is chilled and filtered to remove most of the tartrates. The presence of these crystals, therefore, indicates minimum intervention or filtering by the winemaker, which is often a good thing.

Aroma

The aroma of wine is often its most intriguing and enjoyable aspect. Wine we call 'complex' is precisely that; it does not have a one-note fragrance (only – say – fruity); instead, it has scents that, each time we raise the glass, bring something different. For example, great white Burgundy may have aromas of pineapple, mango, citrus zest, hazelnut or macadamia nut, toasted brioche, vanilla and caramel.

These aromas are created when esters and aldehydes formed in wine during fermentation mirror the same molecular formula as the fruits or vegetables they suggest to us on the nose.

When smelling or 'nosing' wine, we can do it in two different states. Firstly when the wine has been poured and allowed to settle in the glass for a few minutes. Gently sniffing the wine like this will reveal the most volatile aromas of the grape variety and the fruit-like fragrances that it contains. These may be strong indicators of the variety, or the origin of the wine. For example, sharp green apple, cut grass, green asparagus or pea shoot aromas may be an indication of Sauvignon Blanc and – if the intensity is low and mineral – would indicate an Old World, cooler climate origin such as a Sancerre or Pouilly-Fumé from the Loire Valley in France. If the aromas are more intense – for instance containing papaya or passion fruit – that may indicate a New World origin, such as Marlborough in New Zealand or Casablanca in Chile.

A gentle swirling of the glass causes its inside to become coated with wine and helps the alcohol to evaporate, taking with it some of the lesser volatile aromas, the more subtle fragrances that may come from age, or from winemaking processes such as oak-barrel ageing. For example, mature red Burgundy, when still, will have red-fruit characteristics such as strawberry, cranberry and raspberry. After agitating in the glass, secondary leather, bacon and mushroom aromas often reveal themselves.

Palate

When tasting a wine, you must consider its structure, those things that initially hit our tastebuds. We are able to perceive five tastes: sweet, sour, salt, bitter and umami. (Vying for a place as the sixth basic taste are calcium, *kokumi*, piquancy, coolness, metallicity, fat and carbon dioxide… but these go beyond the remit of this book.)

You aren't likely to encounter saltiness in wine, even though you often may *think* you detect salinity in high-acid wines and draw the conclusion that it must be from a coastal origin. Dry Sherry – especially Manzanilla – often has this characteristic, but it's a flavour association, rather than actual salt in the wine. In other words, surprisingly, it's just your imagination. A chemical analysis would show that the wine did not contain salt.

Bitterness is undesirable and indicates a fault, or poor winemaking, maybe coming from harsh unripe tannins or cork taint (see page 34).

Umami is a savoury, mushroomy, gamey flavour. Although perceptions of a meaty or gamey character can be found in wines such as Northern Rhône Syrah (see page 92), it's doubtful that it's from the same source as that in meat.

Ultimately, it is the counterbalance between acidity (sourness) and sugar (sweetness) on which we assess wine. The growing environment for the vine, or the climate, is the determining factor for both (see page 11).

Conclusions

A well-practised tasting method, an understanding of classic grape aromas and tastes, mixed with a good knowledge of wine-producing regions, are the tools that we need to perform the vinous CSI involved in blind tasting. It's a process of connecting the dots until a logical conclusion presents itself.

For example, if presented with a 10-year-old red Rioja:

the appearance would be on the red-garnet side (not purple) and it would have a mahogany rim to the meniscus, indicating the wine has some age (see page 22). The aromas would be ripe and maybe slightly jammy, indicating that the grapes were grown in a hot climate, and dominated by red fruits such as strawberry. There would most likely be a strong aroma of oak, but not the vanilla of French oak, rather the toasted coconut of American oak. (Rioja winemakers traditionally use American oak as it was cheaper than French; because of the way American coopers sawed the wood, they got more staves out of each tree.)

Once you've identified the mahogany rim and jammy, strawberry, coconut oak flavours, the logical conclusion is that the wine is a mature Rioja.

RIGHT 'Legs', or tears, after swirling wine in a glass, can tell you about a wine's body, levels of alcohol and sugar

Zalto
DENK'ART

THE SERVICE OF WINE

GLASSWARE

Serving wine in decent glasses is crucial. By this, I don't mean expensive, as you can buy decent glassware for not much money. A good wine glass should be clear (so no coloured glass, or cut glass), so you can easily see the colour of the wine, its clarity, hues and viscosity (see pages 22–23). It should have a long stem, as you should hold a wine glass by the stem rather than the bowl, which both puts finger marks on the glass and warms the wine from the heat of your hand. A wine glass should have a high volume capacity: you should be able to get four to six large glasses from a bottle, and each of these should fill a glass only one-third full. This allows plenty of room to swirl the wine and help release all its aromas, without running the risk of accidentally throwing it all over your dinner companions.

Recommended producers: Riedel, Schott-Zwiesel, Spiegelau, Zalto.

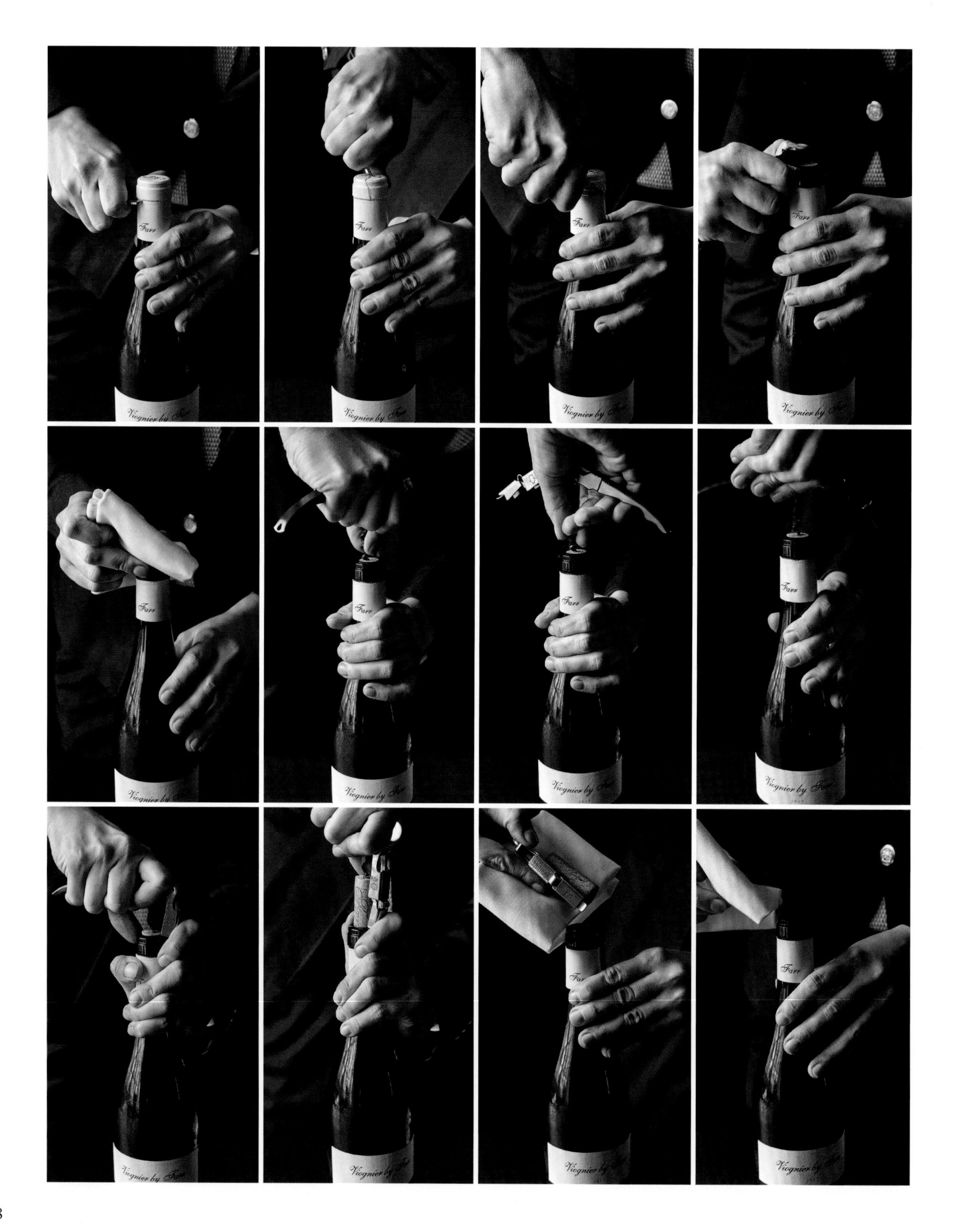
Farr
Viognier by

CORKSCREWS & OTHER CORK EXTRACTORS

The essential tool of the sommelier. A good corkscrew should have a long helix or 'worm', preferably Teflon-coated, and a pivoted arm to brace against the neck of the bottle. Avoid corkscrews that have a worm that looks like a large screw, as these tear the centre out of older corks.

A twin-pronged cork puller – a butler's thief or 'Ah-So' – is useful for extracting old or crumbly corks, so it's worth having one of these if you open older bottles regularly. At the Club we use a Durand corkscrew for delicate corks; combining twin prongs and a helix-style corkscrew.

With old wine, it is helpful to have a funnel and squares of muslin ready, in case some pieces of cork crumble into the wine. Sharply tap the neck of the bottle against a napkin: if done correctly, a few drops of wine will be expelled and – with them – the pieces of floating cork.

Broken corks that fall into the bottle can be extracted with a shoelace or string with a large knot tied in it. The trick is to pull the cork into the bottle neck with the knot beneath it; when you pull the shoelace out, the cork will come with it.

The ultimate bottle-opening device, used on very old bottles, is a pair of Port tongs. These are heated in a fire until red-hot, then clamped around the neck of a bottle. A cloth or feather dipped in ice water is stroked across the red-hot glass, causing the neck to break perfectly.

LEFT Cut the foil from the bottle neck (never try to insert a corkscrew through a foil). Wipe the glass under the foil, in case mould has got in there during storage. Use a good robust corkscrew with a Teflon-coated helix worm; the bottle should not rotate, only your wrist should move. Wipe the neck of the bottle again after the cork has been removed

ABOVE When tasting wine, look at its colour against a white surface, or a napkin (see page 22–23 for what it can tell you); then swirl the glass and look at the 'legs' (see page 24) to assess the wine's body, alcohol and sugar levels. Nose the wine before swirling, to gauge its primary aromas, and again after swirling, when secondary fragrances may be revealed

SERVING TEMPERATURES

A domestic fridge is set at around 5°C, which is too cold for almost all wines. Remember, the term 'room temperature' was coined during Victorian times, when it did not mean the centrally-heated 20°C that it can suggest today. At home, if you have had a wine out in your dining room for a few hours, return it to the fridge for 30 minutes or so to bring the temperature down; conversely, if a bottle has been in a temperature-controlled cool cellar or wine-fridge environment, bring it out 30 minutes before you intend to drink it.

The range of temperatures at which a wine 'should' be served can differ enormously, depending on what style of wine it is.

When you chill sparkling wine, it damps down the bubbles – which then release a lot more slowly – and accentuates the acidity. Young Champagnes and sparkling wines are often served as palate cleansers, so you want that good energy and the acidic freshness that makes you salivate. However, if an old Champagne is served too cold, all those flavours will be numbed, so treat it as you would a good white Burgundy and serve it at 12–14°C.

As the temperature at which white wine is served rises, the less acidity will have a say in its flavours. A German Riesling will taste flabby when it is served too warm; acid drives this style of wine, so it should generally be served cool, but not ice-cold, at 8–10°C.

Serving richer white wines too cold – such as a good Puligny-Montrachet that earns its price through subtle, nuanced flavours – masks acidity, fruit characteristics and delicately balanced flavours. Serve these wines at 12°C: cool but not chilled. If you are drinking a good white Burgundy and the glass is covered in heavy condensation, it is over-chilled.

Lighter styles of red wine, such as Pinot Noir and Gamay, showcase a bit more acidity, so they should be served at 14–15°C, still on the cooler side. Heavier styles of red wine, such as Syrah, should be served a little warmer, at 17–18°C. This is because these more powerful styles usually contain more alcohol and, if served too warm, the acidity will not balance and the alcohol sticks out, the fruit characteristics will be bland and the wine will seem very flabby.

Dessert wine should be served quite cold, in order to achieve the optimum balance of acidity and sweetness; 6–8°C is the recommended temperature range here. Too warm, and the wine will just taste sweet, its subtleties lost. A good rule of thumb is price: don't serve a £3,000 Château d'Yquem freezing cold!

DECANTING

There are three main reasons for decanting. The first is to aerate young wines. Wines are bottled in a low- or no-oxygen atmosphere to stop any premature ageing through oxidation. However, they have been shoved into a bottle and starved of the oxygen and air that help bring out the flavours and wake the wine up. Young wines can be decanted fairly rapidly, splashing and bubbling into the bottom of a decanter; it is not a delicate process, you are just trying to aerate the wine. Decanting is reserved for more expensive and complex young wines: if you buy £6 supermarket Sauvignon, you don't need to do it, but a £60 Meursault from a merchant would probably benefit.

The second reason for decanting is for old wines. They develop sediment, a kind of sand or grit that you can see in the bottom of the bottle. This fine silt is composed of anthocyanins (polymerised polyphenols, see page 22). You need to take the wine off its sediment, as it can taste bitter and make the wine appear hazy, and you need to do so gently. There are two ways of doing it: you could stand the bottle upright for 24 hours, so the sediment falls to the bottom. Or, if you haven't remembered to do that, carefully transport it in the same position in which it has been lying (this is why we use wine cradles, see right). Very gently and slowly decant it from the same angle in which it has been lying. In either case, light a candle under the bottle – or use the light from your phone – and look through the shoulder of the bottle at the light as you pour, so you can see sediment coming up like a wisp of smoke, and stop pouring before any of it reaches the decanter.

The third reason for decanting is temperature control. If you have kept good wines in a temperature-controlled storage fridge, they should not be served at that temperature (see above for more on serving temperatures). Decanting will bring the temperature of the stored wine up to the level you desire.

You can decant both red and white wine, and even consider gently decanting aged Champagne to open up the more subtle tertiary flavours that develop over time in the bottle (see overleaf for more on opening Champagne). Old Champagnes don't have many bubbles, so you must decant them gently.

CLEANING DECANTERS Be careful when cleaning decanters, as you don't want to leave anything inside that might affect the flavour of the next wine to be poured in. The old-school way is to break up eggshells and put them in the decanter with white wine vinegar. Swirl, and the sharp edges will clean the insides. Then wash thoroughly, to remove any vinegar taint. Some people use denture tablets, or tiny ball bearings. But always try to use vinegar rather than detergent as the cleaning agent, both because it usually works better and because it's not a good idea to use chemicals in decanters.

OPENING OLD WINES When you open an expensive bottle of old wine, always wipe under the foil once it is removed, in case mould has grown there under damp cellar conditions. Wipe again after removing the cork, for the same reason.

ABOVE If a wine has been stored on its side and you have not turned it upright for at least 24 hours before opening the bottle, then serve it in a cradle in a similar position in which it was stored, so any bitter-tasting sediment remains undisturbed at the bottom

RIGHT Lighting a candle and placing it under the shoulder of a bottle as you pour means you can stop when you see any sediment rising, before it reaches a glass or decanter

OPENING CHAMPAGNE

The first rule of opening Champagne is to make sure that the bottle is cold, which subdues the bubbles, as it's very messy otherwise! Ideally, keep the bottle in the fridge overnight, then move it to the freezer for the last 20 minutes before serving, if you find that your fridge isn't quite cold enough.

Young Champagne should be served cold, at 6–10°C. If it's an older wine, serve it warmer, to fully appreciate its tertiary flavours (see page 30).

An elegant way to prepare and serve Champagne is from an ice bucket, filled two-thirds with ice and one-third with water. The bottle should be placed in there for 15–20 minutes before opening.

Champagne and sparkling wines come with a pull tab on their foils. Often, when you use it, it can tear and doesn't look very elegant, so, if you have an expensive bottle of Champagne, you may prefer to use a knife to cut off the foil neatly.

You must always open Champagne safely, as the bottles contain the pressure of a double-decker bus tyre, and each is topped off with a cork armed with a metal cap. It is a lethal weapon. Along with squash balls, flying Champagne corks can cause some appalling eye accidents, if care is not taken.

As soon as you start to loosen the wire cage, make sure you have a firm grip on the neck of the bottle and that your thumb is firmly placed on top of the cork. Pull down the metal wire and push it away from the bottle neck. Move your hand up to the cork and put your other hand on the base of the bottle. Keeping a tight grip on the cork, twist the bottle by the base; don't twist the cork, as that may cause it to split in half. You will start to feel it come out slowly and gently. (Don't be tempted to open your hand to see how far it has come out.) It will release from the bottle with a soft sigh.

As corks get older, they become compressed by the glass bottle neck, so have less resistance in the neck of the bottle and will come out with comparative ease.

RIGHT There's no mystery to opening a good bottle of Champagne. First, make sure it's chilled, to avoid spraying your guests. Cut off the foil neatly (avoid using the pull tab, which can look messy), then ease back the wire cage from the cork, immediately covering the top of the cork with your thumb and keeping it there. With your other hand on the base of the bottle, rotate the bottle, not the cork, until the cork is eased out

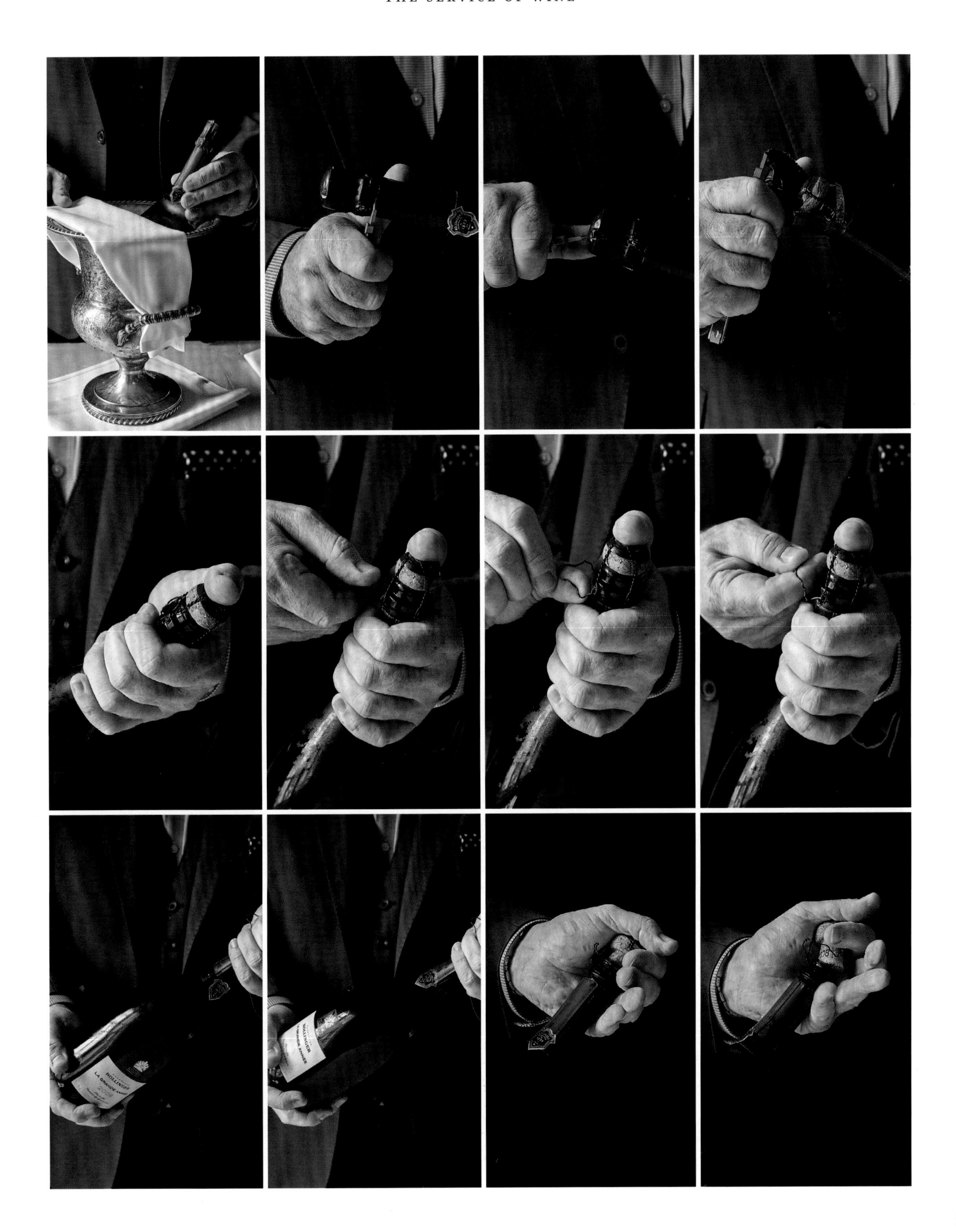
BOLLINGER
LA GRANDE ANNEE

WINE FAULTS & STORAGE

Cork taint

Caused by TCA (2, 4, 6-trichloroanisole), a type of chlorine that is a naturally occurring element. It used to be quite prevalent in corks, due to their old manufacturing process. When you pull the cork out of a corked wine, you are greeted by a horrible musty smell, strong and acrid, reminiscent of the inside of a rotten walnut. Naturally, this is very easy to spot in its more extreme cases.

It becomes more problematic to pinpoint when wine is only slightly corked; for TCA to be noticeable, there only have to be 10–12 nanograms present in each litre. That's when even wine experts and sommeliers start doubting themselves, as the odour could easily be mixed up with the tertiary flavours and aromas of some very good and non-corked wines (as it ages, some wines naturally take on a damp forest floor, mushroomy quality).

A lot of cork comes from Portugal; it is the bark of oak trees, evolved over time to stop the trees being killed by forest fires, as it acts like a fire jacket. Every eight years, you can harvest the cork from the tree trunks.

The cork farmers used to leave their harvest on the forest floor for several months, to start its process of drying out. During that time, moisture and mould would get into the bark. Then they took the cork to a factory and dipped it in bleach to clean it, which of course introduced chlorine. This combination of mould and chlorine is responsible for the development of TCA in cork.

Striations in cork are where TCA can hide and cause cork taint. There are about 800 million hexagonally shaped cells making up the structure of a cork, which is why they are so light (they contain so much air), but each can also provide a hiding place for TCA.

Cork taint was a particularly chronic problem in Portugal during the 1970s, following the Carnation Revolution, a social movement, when a lot of land was taken from wealthy landowners and redistributed to peasants. In the rush to make much-needed money from the newly acquired land, the novice bark farmers picked the cork from the forests too early, which only served to exacerbate the issue.

These days, the occurrence of corked wine is probably less than one per cent of all bottles opened, because Portugal has done a lot to clean up its act, while cork farmers are also using better technology to prevent cork taint.

Screwcaps

There isn't really much anti-screwcap snobbery any more, and the rise of the screwcap has forced the cork industry to address its issues with TCA. In the 1950s, experiments with screwcaps proved massively unpopular with the wine-buying public, so were abandoned. In the early 2000s, thanks to Jeffrey Grosset in the Clare Valley in Australia (see page 55), screwcaps were revived and started a worldwide trend, with Australia and New Zealand leading the charge.

Oxidation

While you would be unlucky to open a corked wine these days, oxidation is a far more common fault. It's the phenomenon you witness when you slice an apple and leave it to turn brown. Oxidation causes a darkening in colour: white wines turn golden or amber, while reds become a brownish colour. (It occurs less in red wines, because of the antioxidant effect of anthocyanins.) In oxidised wines, the fruit flavours tend to become quite heavy on the palate. Oxidation has become a common problem in European wines that have been shipped to the Far East, if they are not in refrigerated containers.

The oxidation process can also produce acetaldehydes, which act to give a Sherry kind of flavour to the wine. This chemical is formed of acetic acid, that shows a vinegar character, and ethyl-acetate, which has a nail polish aroma. As some of these fragrances are present in perfectly good wines anyway, it can be hard to tell where it is a fault and where it is a flaw!

To avoid oxidation, store wine – especially white wine – in relatively cool and dark conditions. So if you have been walking past your local off-licence for months, looking at that bottle of Dom Pérignon in the window… and suddenly it's half-price, then keep walking. It has light strike. In France, they say it has *le goût de lumière* ('the taste of light').

Heat damage

If you are planning to keep wine for a long time, it should be stored at 13°C or below. Any temperature higher than this can speed up the ageing process, which isn't a disaster but may mean that a 10-year-old wine ends up tasting like a 15-year-old wine.

Any school child knows that, when a liquid warms up, it increases in volume, and this puts pressure on a wine bottle's cork, which will get pushed out a tiny bit, maybe by as little as 0.5mm. When the temperature falls again, the wine will decrease in volume and the cork will be pulled in a little bit. This is known as thermal pistoning. If it happens over a period of time, it will break the oxygen seal of the cork and the wine will oxidise. To check for heat damage, look at the level of the wine in the bottle and for any sign of seepage around the foil.

Reduction

This is the presence in a wine of volatile sulphur compounds – the most common of which is hydrogen sulphide – and is, in theory, the opposite to oxidation as it can occur in an oxygen-free environment. Winemakers can protect their wines from oxidation by putting carbon dioxide 'blankets' in the barrels; these lie on the top of the liquid, as carbon dioxide is heavier than air, but a total absence of oxygen may cause a slight rotten egg or sulphurous smell to develop. You can prevent reduction by exposing wine to controlled amounts of oxygen during the winemaking process, and by using diammonium phosphate to add nitrogen.

Hydrogen sulphide compounds can also form due to a lack of nitrogen in fermenting grape must, which may cause yeast to become stressed (see Mosel soils, page 16). Natural forms of nitrogen can be introduced to must by planting cover crops, such as clover or rapeseed brassicas, between vineyard rows (this also helps with soil erosion if a vineyard is on a slope).

An old sommelier's trick is to add a pre-1992 British copper coin (made from 97 per cent copper) to a glass or decanter of the wine, which may help to remove some of the sulphurous aromas.

... and the exceptions that prove the rules

Normally, you don't want a second fermentation of wine in the bottle. But if you are making Champagne, you need it, as that is what creates the bubbles.

Aerobic yeast growth in a barrel (*flor*) is how you make Fino Sherry.

Oxidation is how you make Tawny Port, while very heavy oxidation makes Madeira. A slow, gradual oxidation in good-quality white Burgundy will add complexity to the wine.

You don't want mould growth on your grapes unless it is *botrytis cinerea* (see page 123), aka 'noble rot'.

The legendary wines from Château Musar in Lebanon's Bekaa Valley are very high in both volatile acidity (VA) and *Brettanomyces* (Brett) yeasts, yet they are considered delicious. And the wonderful 1947 Cheval Blanc has levels of VA so high that it is officially unfit for human consumption. (We served it by the glass at the Club after opening, and nobody died.)

MATCHING WINE AND FOOD

WHEN YOU WANT to create a perfect match between a wine and a particular dish, it is essential to consider the ingredients, the cooking techniques and the sauce served with a recipe. When you have the chance to pair a meal with a bottle of wine, it can be great fun and create a memorable experience. When entertaining at home, you have an advantage over us sommeliers. The truth is that sommeliers often have to compromise on wine recommendations: at a table where four people are having four different starters and four different main courses but want to share just one bottle of wine, it makes it impossible to perfectly pair everything. Much better, in that case, to go for a wine that everyone will enjoy. However, at home, where you as host will serve the same menu to all your guests, the following pages will give you some points to bear in mind.

The texture of the main ingredient and how it has been cooked will both help determine a good wine and food pairing; for instance, roast venison has a very different flavour and structure to steamed Dover sole. Stewing, grilling, poaching and barbecuing all have different effects on texture and taste.

RIGHT A perfect marriage of Super-Tuscan Sassicaia Cabernet Sauvignon with Oxtail & celery ravioli, root vegetables (see page 282)

SASSICA
2004
SASSICAIA

The Maillard reaction

This is the caramelisation of sugars and amino acids that occurs in a protein after applying direct heat. It's what creates the crust on a flame-grilled steak, or on seared scallops. Foods that have undergone extreme cooking techniques such as flame grilling or barbecuing generally pair well with the most intense wines from warm, sunnier climates, in which flavours and tannins are wrapped up in ripe, jammy fruits.

Many wines from the New World (Australia, Argentina or California), as well as warm-climate European styles from Spain and southern Italy fall into this category.

They pair well with foods such as beef, venison or boar that has been charred or roasted, especially recipes with dark sauces flavoured with dark berries, chocolate, juniper or liquorice.

The ripeness of the fruit, the texture of the tannins and the level of alcohol of a particular wine are all very important considerations. All foods that have undergone the Maillard reaction while cooking have a very deep, dark, meaty flavour, and a wine has to be bold and heavy to work with them. It has also got to have a lot of fruit and alcohol and high tannins: everything needs to be very upfront and punchy.

Sauces

While the main event on any plate is the protein, it can take a back seat at times, depending on the intensity of the sauce used with it. Echoing the flavours of a sauce with the wine you match to it can be a triumph: a sauce with a reduction of red wine or Port and flavoured with blackberries, bacon and black pepper to be paired with Syrah, for instance; or blackcurrant and mushroom with Cabernet; or cherry and cranberry with Tempranillo or Sangiovese. Australian Shiraz can be lifted with the addition of mint relish or rosemary to a sauce (see page 246). Chilean Carmenere served with grilled beef and herbaceous chimichurri is delicious (see page 280). Light cream or cheese sauces are best served with oakey, full white wines such as Burgundy or New World Chardonnay (see page 144). Green herb sauces such as salsa verde are best paired with high-acid, herbaceous whites such as Sauvignon Blanc or Verdicchio (see page 180).

Complement or contrast?

Pairing wine and food may mean serving light dishes with light wines and heavy dishes with heavy wines. These like-to-like flavour matches can be tremendously successful, such as green pepper or asparagus with a Marlborough Sauvignon Blanc; or creamy, cheesy and rich lobster thermidor with a full-bodied Sonoma Chardonnay; or even the classic combination of rich foie gras with an unctuous glass of Sauternes.

Contrasting food pairings can be more exciting both to invent and to taste, but run a higher risk of spectacular failure, too. Acidic wine will match with high-acid foods such as tomatoes, capers and vinaigrette, but counterbalance and contrast with rich, fatty or oily foods such as smoked salmon, charcuterie or pâtés. Tannic red wines will counteract the fat in well-marbled steaks. Sweet and salty combinations are probably the most obvious example of fortunate wine and food contrasts, such as the classic pairing of a glass of Port with Stilton cheese (for more on matching sweet wine with salty food, see right, and for pairing wine with cheese, see page 41).

Rich and fatty foods may be partnered with light wines, if they have an intense flavour. By intense, I mean those with very full fruit flavours and/or a sharp acidity that helps to cut through the fat. A slight sweetness in a wine, for instance, such as that found in a beautiful German Spätlese (late-harvested grapes that produce slightly sweet wines, see page 52), is excellent with a sumptuous, fat goose or duck; in the same way, rich and heavy Christmas pudding polarises itself against a light, frothy sweet Moscato d'Asti (see page 123), with its mouth-cleansing wash of acid and bubbles.

'It goes with where it grows'

The idea of pairing wines with dishes that come from the same country or region is very sensible, as the styles of cuisine and of wine will have grown in harmony together for many years. The phrase 'it goes with where it grows' is apt for this type of food and wine matching.

For example, the salt-marsh lambs that graze on the banks of the Gironde estuary are perfect matches to local wines from the Médoc; while Piedmontese Nebbiolo from Barolo or Barbaresco is an ideal choice with a hunter's catch of small game birds, wild boar stew or white Alba truffle. Sun-dried Italian tomatoes flavoured with thyme and oregano and served with polenta and meatballs are sublime with Chianti's Sangiovese grape (see page 262).

Acidity

This is found in food in the form of citrus and other fruit juices, wine sauces or vinegar. Wines must match the sharpness of a dish with similar levels of acidity, or they will taste dull and flat next to it.

Acidity in white wine can enhance the flavours of certain dishes, in the same way as a squeeze of lemon juice can improve food, or help bring out the brininess of shellfish. For example, try the juice of an Amalfi lemon drizzled over a platter of *fritto misto* in Capri, while sipping a glass of the region's crisp, dry Verdicchio, for a gastronomic epiphany, or try a similar seafood and acid pairing at home (see page 138).

Acidity clashes with tannins in red wines, causing the tannins to dominate. If this happens, a diner may accuse a perfect wine of having unbalanced or immature tannins; however, often, it is acidic ingredients on the plate that are the culprit. Although a food's acidity may not cause the wine to taste so bad that it is undrinkable, it may mean that the wine is best saved for an occasion that will flatter it more. If you are choosing red wines to drink with high-acid dishes, ensure that they are intense in acid and fruit, but low in tannins (see right).

White wines with high acidity include anything based on Sauvignon Blanc, such as New Zealand Sauvignon, Loire Valley Sauvignon (Sancerre or Pouilly Fumé); white Bordeaux blended with Semillon (Bergerac, Entre-Deux-Mers, Graves); or Fumé Blanc (oaked Californian Sauvignon). Some Chardonnays also fall into this category, often those from a cool climate without – or with little – oak influence (such as Chablis or northern Italian Chardonnay). Many white Italian grapes are high in acid, such as Malvasia, Verdicchio and Trebbiano, and so is Riesling (in Germany, those at Kabinett level), Vinho Verde, Muscadet and Chenin Blanc, the list goes on...

Red wines with low tannins and high fruit include Beaujolais, New World Grenache, some Pinot Noir, some Loire Valley reds, Italian Barbera and Bardolino and some young Spanish Tempranillo.

Salt and pepper

Classic combinations of salty food and sweet wines have been popular for centuries: Sauternes and Roquefort; Port and Stilton; sweet Oloroso Sherry with salted Marcona almonds...

Salt works as a flavour enhancer and will amplify the tannins in red wine. Interestingly, this means that people who habitually take a lot of salt with their food will usually favour lighter Beaujolais-style red wines, as they find all other red wines to be too tannic, tasting both bitter and immature. Wines with a naturally high fruit character also match well to salty foods to some extent, because of the sweet fruit's affinity to salt.

Acidity counters salt well, too, so Champagne and dry white wines are often served as aperitifs with salted nuts, olives or snacks. Another good match for these are Fino and Manzanilla Sherries, which have a slightly salty character anyway (for more on the saline taste apparent in some wines, see page 24).

When pairing wines with food, always search carefully for any salty flavours that might be hidden in dishes, such as Parma ham, bacon, anchovies, olives and so on.

Also be careful of pepper. While an exuberantly peppery dish can enhance simple, average-quality red wines by perking them up slightly, it can destroy the complex and subtle flavours that are so prized in fine old wines.

Sweetness

Sweetness in a dish must be matched or outweighed by the sweetness of the wine paired with it, or the wine will not even taste sweet and, instead, will appear thin and tart in contrast.

Some desserts are not very sweet but have a high acidity content, for instance fruit-based dishes such as thin apple tarts from Alsace. In such cases, a relatively light wine with high acidity is required alongside, such as Alsace *vendange tardive* (VT), German Spätlese or Auslese, Loire Côteaux du Layon, or Australian or New World late-harvest Rieslings, Semillons or Muscats.

More substantial dishes need heavier wines with more residual sugar, such as Sauternes, Alsace *sélection de grains noble* (SGN), German Beerenauslese or Trockenbeerenauslese, some Vouvrays, French *vin doux naturels* and Hungarian sweet Tokajis.

Only the heaviest wines work with very rich dishes with lots of sugar and syrupy textures, or with chocolate. These wines may be fortified and include Port, Madeira and Australian liqueur muscat, or can be very sweet due to *botrytis cinerea* (a penicillium mould that shrinks the grape, leaving a concentrated sugary juice, see page 123), such as is the case in the best sweet German wines or Sauternes (see pages 123–124).

Dry white wines will taste nasty and metallic with sweet dishes; the fruit flavours in the wine are stripped away by the sweet food and only the acid remains. Oaky or buttery flavours do not match well either.

For red wines, try those with very light tannins, high fruit, or black Muscats, Ports or Banyuls.

And remember all these rules when thinking of savoury dishes, too, in which sweet sauces, jellies and relishes have been used as part of the cooking process, or are to be served alongside the food as accompaniments.

Heat

Fiercely hot chilli or curry dishes are probably best with something creamy and fatty and non-alcoholic to drink served alongside, such as coconut milk, or yogurt-based drinks such as lassi. The fat in these traditional drinks helps to suppress capsaicin, the compound in chilli that is responsible for the pepper's heat. Cold and fizzy drinks, such as beer, actually increase the capsaicin's effect. Working for a year in Thailand as a scuba diving instructor taught me that lesson; after about six months eating hot dishes, I learned that a glass of milk would cool me down pretty effectively, rather than the five beers I had been trying before. I'm pretty sure, though, that the bar owner preferred it when I was ignorant of this fact...

Small amounts of green chilli in a dish can work alongside high-acid wines such as Sauvignon Blanc or dry Riesling (see page 130). Dried red chilli, often found in South American cuisines, can work with Malbec from Argentina or Carmenere from Chile (see page 280). As spice-heat levels increase in a dish, look for wines with some residual sugar, such as Alsace Pinot Gris, or Gewurztraminer, or German Rieslings, as the sweetness will help to counterbalance the heat (see pages 150, 163, 179 and 252).

... and matching food with high-tannin wines

Tannin can be very difficult to match with food; it causes metallic tastes with fish, and bitterness with salty and acidic flavours. Tannin is an essential part of the structure of red wine and generally accounts for it having a longer lifespan than white wine; it preserves the wine, but does fade with age.

Over time, polyphenols from the grape skins (made up of anthocyanin and tannin compounds) polymerise into long chains until they are too large to be held in suspension and fall to the bottom of the bottle as sediment (see page 22).

In young wines, the chains of tannin molecules may be long, but not large enough to fall, and can give the wine a coarse texture or feeling. This is increased as saliva causes the tannins to coagulate together, giving a gritty, mouth-furring effect on the palate. Take a tannic red wine, swirl it around your mouth and spit into a white basin: you will observe the small black flecks of tannin. The action of chewing helps to break this down. So full-bodied tannic wines need to be paired with rich protein dishes that require a bit of chewing.

The quantity of tannin can vary in a young wine, but it is the quality that makes the most difference in texture; small chains will probably lead to a wine with a smooth texture, whereas large chains can make a wine feel coarse.

The best food to eat with high-tannin red wines is therefore full-flavoured 'chewy' meat dishes, as a lot of chewing will moderate your perception of the tannin. Many good red wines may appear dry and austere on their own, but improve when paired with suitable food. More mature reds will have less tannin, and so can be matched with dishes that do not have such intense textures and flavours, such as simple roast leg of lamb with a sauce made from the cooking juices, or even hard cheeses.

TRICKY INGREDIENTS

EGGS Egg yolk coats the mouth in a very glutinous manner, and crumbly hard-boiled eggs have a sulphurous quality. As eggs usually are not eaten alone, except at breakfast, wines should be matched against the main flavour ingredient in an egg dish. This could be onion, bacon, salmon, or even red wine, as in Oeufs en Meurette (see page 196). To match with hollandaise sauce, Chardonnay is often best, with its creamy, buttery overtones and some oak (see page 144); if the hollandaise is more lemony, then choose assertive, crisp, high acid wines. Airy, light soufflés do not have a problem with the coating texture of the egg, so when matching food with soufflés, concentrate on the main flavouring. If it's cheese, you want a lactic flavour in the accompanying wine, so choose something that has been through malolactic fermentation. Try oak-aged, creamy-textured wine with soft acidity, such as a barrel-aged Chardonnay. A smoked salmon soufflé, on the other hand, works well with young, assertive Sauvignon Blanc. Mayonnaise can have similar issues to runny egg yolks, so you need a wine match with the acidity to cut through that oiliness. Therefore, with a Waldorf salad, an English Bacchus would work well, with its very strong celery and grapey character and high acidity (see page 307). Quail's and gull's eggs are more delicate in taste and match well with young Champagne, especially when hard-boiled and dipped in celery salt.

CERTAIN VEGETABLES Especially tricky to match with wine are artichokes, asparagus, fennel and spinach. Artichokes may make wines taste metallic or sweet, due to a chemical known as cynarin. Serving the vegetables with lemon juice, light vinaigrettes or lemony hollandaise (all difficult to match with wine in their own right) can help remedy this, as long as you choose young, punchy, crisp wines. Sauvignon Blanc works well, as does Chenin Blanc, Riesling or Pinot Grigio. Braising the vegetables, adding cream, Parmesan cheese or lemon juice is the best way to soften their edges, making it easier to match them to a wine. As the vegetable is often a side dish, it does not cause too many problems at a dinner.

TRUFFLES There is an affinity between truffles and the Nebbiolo grape of northern Italy. Truffles, with their deep, rich and earthy flavours, may overpower some wines, but should not cause issues when used sparingly as a garnish. Old Champagne works very well with white truffle (see page 314), although Richard Geoffroy – who has been making Dom Pérignon since 1990 – told me his favourite food-and-wine match ever was 1959 Dom Pérignon with a virgin olive oil ice cream, which was served to him at elBulli restaurant. Classy.

FISH Oily fish may distort the flavour of wine, so a wine with a high acid content is best to cut through the oil. High-acid, gentle-flavoured wines are best. Try pairing mackerel or herring with Muscadet, or Gaillac, Soave, Trebbiano or Sauvignon Blanc, or even ice-cold Scandinavian eau de vie. Try Vinho Verde from northern Portugal with sardines grilled on the beach, or even the red Vinho Verdes. Oily fish are better suited to cooler climate, high-alcohol styles of red wine; try northern Italian reds made with varieties such as Schiava or Viosinho, which is used in Portugal for red Vinho Verde. I had one of the best seafood meals of my life in Portugal: oily sardines with a red Vinho Verde with rich red cranberry fruit and low tannins.

SMOKED FOODS These can be difficult to match with wine, depending on just how smoky we are talking. Manzanilla and Fino Sherries go well with smoked foods, as do Rieslings from Germany and Australia, with their high acidity and touch of sweetness. Smoked salmon is quite forgiving with wine, and is classically matched with Chablis or Champagne.

PICKLES & SAUCES When you are serving a food with a sharp, sweet, intense accompaniment such as chutney, cranberry sauce, or apple or mint sauces, to name a few, tread carefully. If you pair a roast leg of lamb with expensive Bordeaux, then throw vinegary mint sauce over the meat, it will kill the wine. Take care and use prudence with any high-sweetness vinegar flavours.

VINAIGRETTES When you are making a dressing for a dish to be paired with a good wine, consider using flavoured oils, or dressings made with lemon juice or wine. Use vinegar sparingly. Wines to go with vinaigrettes should be sharp whites and, even then, more mellow vinegars such as balsamic, Cabernet Sauvignon and Sherry can be more forgiving.

Desserts

CHOCOLATE Counterintuitively, the echoing chocolate flavour in ripe Shiraz, Merlot and Cabernet Sauvignon does not marry with the real thing. Instead, chocolate tends to make wines taste both stripped of flavour and tannic. And remember that bitter chocolate can be found in savoury foods, too, such as game dishes (see page 286).

With desserts, the problems are extreme sweetness and the tastebud-smothering texture of sauces. It does, however, very much depend on the dish. There is a world of difference between a light, frothy chocolate mousse and a thick, rich chocolate truffle cake. Muscat does work well with chocolate and comes in many different forms, from delicious Moscato d'Asti to Beaumes de Venise, Rivesaltes, Moscatels from Valencia, Málagas, or Australian liqueur muscats, to name but a few. Tawny Ports and Sauternes can also be good choices. Orange Muscats can be a revelation with chocolate-orange desserts. Or have a liqueur coffee instead!

ICE CREAM The cold, numbing effect of ice cream is its biggest problem, and only the heaviest, richest wines will match. Rich Pedro Ximénez Sherry is delicious poured over vanilla ice cream.

FRUIT-BASED DISHES It's a good rule of thumb, when in season, to serve a lot of apricot or peach dishes with *botrytis cinerea* sweet wines (see page 123), because they echo each other's flavours. Fruit is high in acidity, so German Riesling tends to work very well with fruit tarts and flans.

Cheese

Matching cheese with wine is not as simple as many people believe. We are in the habit of eating cheese with the wine we were drinking with the main course – often red – but white wine usually makes a far better accompaniment.

Firstly, consider what the rules of engagement with your cheese will be: do you want to showcase a good wine? If so, go for less assertive cheeses. Do you want to have just one cheese, an aged Parmesan or Comté for example? If so, look for a good wine from the same region. Do you want a big selection of different cheeses to enjoy as the end to a lively dinner with friends? If so, choose something simple, fruity and fun that's easy to drink (and that you have few bottles of). Do you want to show a serious selection of cheeses for serious people? Think of opening a selection, such as a Sauvignon Blanc to go with goat's cheese, oaked Chardonnay for hard and nutty cheeses, soft-tannined Merlot to pair with runny cheeses and dessert or fortified wines with blue cheeses.

Fine mature, complex wines are often overshadowed when paired with very powerful cheeses, such as Maroilles, Langres or Époisses. And runny cheese can be tricky to match with wine, because of its mouth-coating texture. Something like a ripe, runny Camembert works well with fairly youthful Loire Valley Cabernet Franc such as a Chinon or Bourgueil; the funky aromas and flavours of this cheese (that remind me of semi-decomposing grass cuttings in a compost bin) can be tamed by the bright acidity, pure berry fruit and farmyard aromas found in these wines. Similarly, youthful Beaujolais or village-level Bourgogne rouge would match well. Be careful not to choose anything too expensive or delicate, as its subtle flavour may well be overwhelmed.

Try aged Champagne with a good French soft cheese, such as Brie de Meaux, St Félicien, Chaource, or Brillat-Savarin, layered with black truffle slices or served with truffle honey.

Tannins in young red wines can clash with salty cheese and high-acid goat's cheese. To eat with a young red wine, it is best to go for a medium-fat hard cheese, such as Cheddar, Pecorino, Parmesan, Manchego or Mimolette. Or choose white wines instead, as the creamy lactic element in anything barrel-aged matches well with many types of cheese. Try a nutty hard cheese such as Beaufort, Grana Padano or Manchego with good oak-aged Chardonnay; the conversion of green malic acid into softer-flavoured lactic acid during the wine's malolactic fermentation, combined with oak ageing, make these a good match.

Many blue cheeses may be better matched with sweet dessert wines, or light fruity reds with low tannins. Here, the opposing flavours of salt and sugar help a lot, such as in the classic pairing of Sauternes with Roquefort, or Port with Stilton (see page 39 for more on pairing salty food with sweet wines).

Goat's cheese is a traditional match with Sauvignon Blanc, because of the high acidity in both. The Sauvignons of the central Loire have always gone well with the local goat's cheeses, and that is considered a classic partnership. The bistro classic *Salade de chèvre chaud* (warm goat's cheese salad) with rocket and walnut oil is perfect served with a glass of Sancerre.

Smoked cheeses can be challenging, but the flavour bombs of Oloroso Sherry, or dessert wine, can stand up to them.

Overall, when trying to match wine with cheese, it's best to take only one or two cheeses, rather than try to match a wine with a whole board containing many different kinds of cheese. However, if you have no choice but to serve an elaborate cheese course, go for a young wine, high in fruit, not too tannic and not too expensive.

The Bordelaise sometimes show some off their best old wines with cheese soufflés; even though eggs can be a problem with red wines, the dish matches very well, as here it is the cheese that predominates. These delicate flavours won't overpower a mature wine.

The rule of thumb is to go with wines from the same area as the cheese, as these matches and styles have been perfected over generations: classic examples are Comté and Château-Chalon from the Jura (see page 312); fresh goat's cheese with Sancerre or Pouilly-Fumé; or Munster from Alsace with Gewurztraminer.

Wine & food pairings

Some wine and food pairings are more successful than others. Red wine seldom drinks well with fish, for instance (though there are exceptions, see page 160). It's a complicated area, but hopefully this chart will help guide you through the maze. The largest circles indicate the best matches.

CANAPÉS		Nuts & olives
FISH 	Raw & cured	Sushi & smoked salmon
	Cooked	Grilled (with herbs & olive oil)
		Grilled (with cream &/or cheese)
		Tuna & salmon, or other oily fish
SHELLFISH 	Raw	Oysters & ceviché
	Cooked	Crab (plain)
		Lobster (with cream &/or butter)
PASTA	Dark sauces	With tomato & meat
	Light sauces	With cream or cheese
	Plain	With olive oil & herbs
EGG	Runny	Poached egg or hollandaise sauce
	Cooked or as soufflé	Omelette or cheese soufflé
COLD MEATS	Charcuterie	Spicy: peppered meats, chorizo or pepperoni
		Fatty: salami or saucisson
SOUPS 	Cold	Fresh: gazpacho
	Hot	Creamy (fish, chicken or vegetable)
		Dark (tomato or meat)
SPICE	Mild	Thai, Malasian, Chinese, or Indian korma
	Hot	Indian madras or vindaloo, Szechuan, Mexican
CHICKEN	Light	Simple roast with herbs
	Rich	With cream or cheese
GAME BIRDS/POULTRY	Light or fatty	Duck, goose or guinea fowl
	Rich or gamey	Partridge, pheasant or quail
TERRINES	Cold	Foie gras, game or other meats
MEAT 	Light meat	Rabbit & pork
	Beef, venison & lamb	Boeuf Bourguignon, heavy stews
	Grilled & barbecued	Steaks, smoked & charred
	Roasted joints	Simply roasted with cooking jus
DESSERT	Fruit	Fresh fruit, tarts or anything high in acidity
	Pastry	Rich, creamy or sweet
	Chocolate	Sponges, caramel & toffee, other heavy desserts
CHEESE 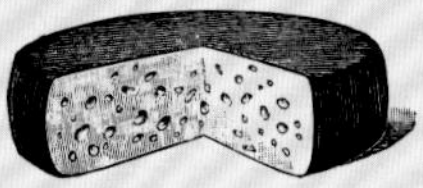	Fresh or salty	Feta, goat's cheese & halloumi
	Runny (pungent)	Camembert, Époisses & Maroilles
	Hard (nutty)	Cheddar, Manchego, Parmesan & Comté
	Blue	Stilton, Roquefort & Gorgonzola

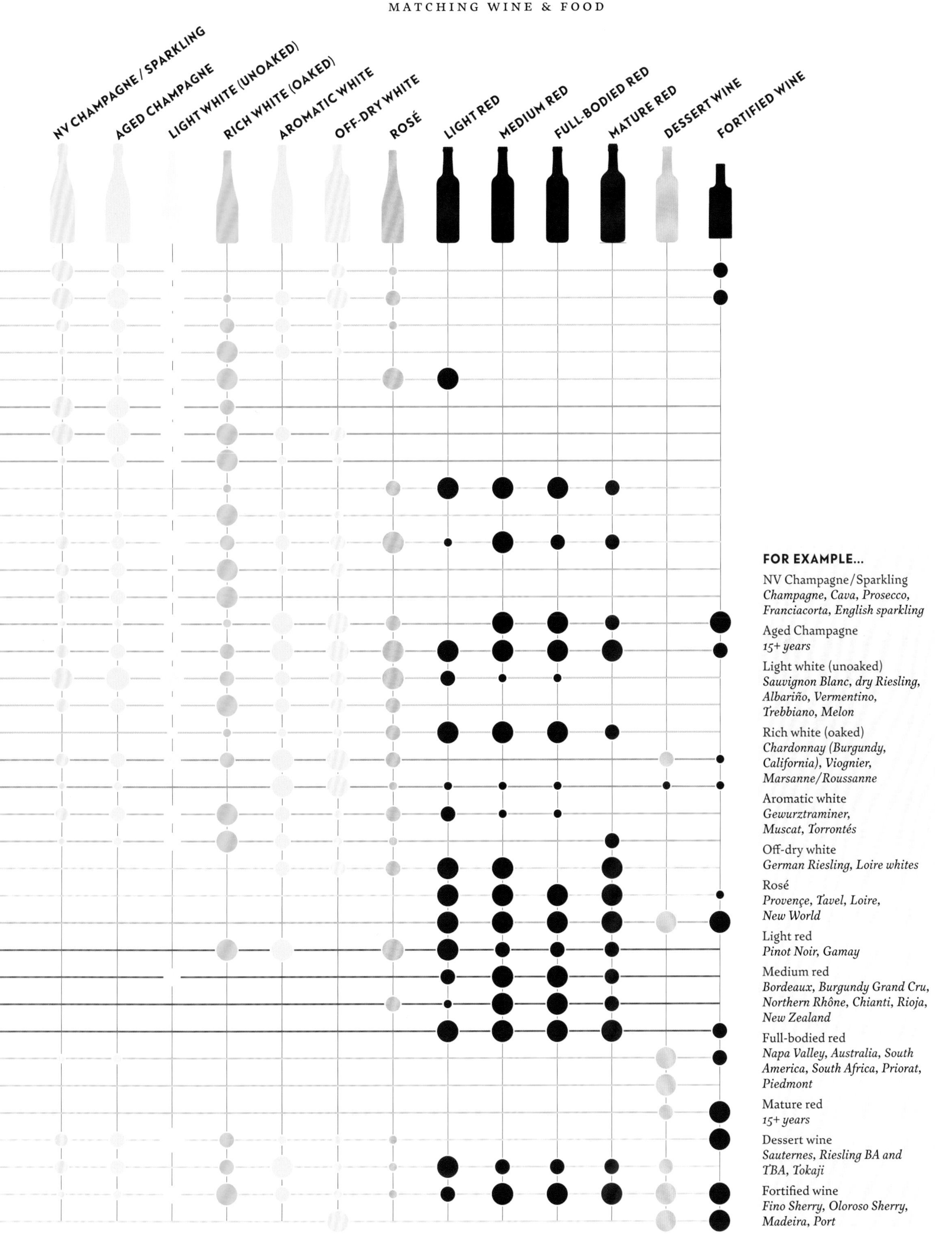

FOR EXAMPLE...

NV Champagne/Sparkling
Champagne, Cava, Prosecco, Franciacorta, English sparkling

Aged Champagne
15+ years

Light white (unoaked)
Sauvignon Blanc, dry Riesling, Albariño, Vermentino, Trebbiano, Melon

Rich white (oaked)
Chardonnay (Burgundy, California), Viognier, Marsanne/Roussanne

Aromatic white
Gewurztraminer, Muscat, Torrontés

Off-dry white
German Riesling, Loire whites

Rosé
Provençe, Tavel, Loire, New World

Light red
Pinot Noir, Gamay

Medium red
Bordeaux, Burgundy Grand Cru, Northern Rhône, Chianti, Rioja, New Zealand

Full-bodied red
Napa Valley, Australia, South America, South Africa, Priorat, Piedmont

Mature red
15+ years

Dessert wine
Sauternes, Riesling BA and TBA, Tokaji

Fortified wine
Fino Sherry, Oloroso Sherry, Madeira, Port

HOSTING A DINNER: PLANNING THE ORDER OF WINES

As a host, you should be guided by a general rule of moving from lighter to heavier styles of wine as you progress through a meal, and probably from younger to older wines, too.

Ideally, aim to begin with something high in acidity, so your guests start to salivate and become hungry: young dry white wines, or sparkling non-vintage wines and Champagnes, to go alongside something salty to nibble such as nuts, olives, or anchovy cheese straws, which will also stimulate the appetite.

If you're planning to serve multiple white wines, then consider their style. Lighter off-dry, low-alcohol styles such as Riesling are good to serve at the start of a meal, with foods such as pâtés, foie gras or terrines that work well with the wine's residual sugar.

Follow these with dryer, more full-bodied whites with no oak, or minimal amounts of oak. Sauvignon Blanc, or Italian whites that are crisp, lemony and fresh will work well with fish courses. After this, go for the fuller-bodied oakey whites, such as white Burgundy, or Chardonnay from anywhere in the world. These are good alongside pasta, egg, or richer seafood dishes with cream and cheese. (And remember that these styles of wine should be served at around 12°C and can be decanted before serving, see page 30.)

The last type of white wines are those very aromatic styles – Gewurztraminer, Viognier or Pinot Gris – from places such as the Rhône Valley and Alsace. These powerful wines can go with richer dishes and also cold terrines and foie gras.

As you can see, you are increasing alcohol, oak content and aromatics in the white wines as you progress through the meal, and at the same time decreasing acidity and freshness.

After white wines, move on to reds. Consider the softer, light reds first, such as Pinot Noir and Gamay, which can go with game birds. Next, you may want to try fuller-bodied reds from Europe, such as Bordeaux, Rhône Valley or Italian reds, with lamb or duck. Move on from there to heavier, full-bodied reds, richer in fruit and higher in alcohol, from places such as the USA, Australia or South America. These richer New World styles will suit beef, venison and heavier meats. But also consider the chosen sauce and its weight: light cooking juices, or heavily reduced and potently flavoured sauces, will require vastly different wines.

You could move to a dessert wine such as a Sauternes or a Tokaji with your pudding, or continue with your red wine with cheese. (Though I prefer most cheeses served with white wine; rich and nutty hard cheeses work especially well with oaky Chardonnay, that goes so brilliantly with all dairy.)

And if you are still thirsty, now is the time to be looking at fortified wines, such as sweet Sherries, Madeiras or Ports (see pages 125–127).

It's obviously important to consider serving temperatures (see page 30) and try to plan in advance what glassware you want to use and whether you will be using multiple glasses for the same dinner. Also consider, if it's a big party with lots of glasses, marking the glasses' bases with something to identify their contents. Pieces of tape can work, or Chinagraph crayons that you can use to number glasses, or to write the names of the wines on the glass.

Consider, too, which wines need to be decanted in advance; anything that can be done before you sit down at the table is going to cause you less stress as the host throughout the meal.

ABOVE The bar in the Members' Lounge at 67 Pall Mall in St James's, London

Seasonal menus

SPRING

APPETISER (see page 138)
Oyster tempura, green apple, wasabi & lime mayonnaise, shizo
Semillon 'Vat 1', Tyrrell's, Hunter Valley

STARTER (see page 310)
Chargrilled asparagus, romesco sauce, toasted almonds & fennel
Verdejo, Bodegas Naia, Rueda

MAIN COURSE (see page 251)
Roast cannon of lamb, chickpea salad, moutabel, pomegranate
Château Musar, Bekaa Valley

DESSERT (see page 326)
Pavlova, passion fruit cream & mango
Riesling TBA 'Forster Ungeheuer', Weingut Reichsrat von Buhl, Pfalz

SUMMER

APPETISER (see page 295)
Mini tomato bruschetta with baked bocconcini in prosciutto
Greco 'Mastro', Mastroberardino, Campania

STARTER (see page 130)
Scallop ceviche with peas, lime, dill & crisp pancetta
Riesling 'Polish Hill', Jeffrey Grosset, Clare Valley

MAIN COURSE (see page 255)
Lamb kleftiko with Greek salad
Xynomavro, Foundi Estate, Naoussa

DESSERT (see page 328)
Poached white peaches with zabaglione & amaretti
Zibibbo 'Ben Ryé', Donnafugata, Passito di Pantelleria, Sicily

SUMMER AL FRESCO

APPETISER (see page 193)
Salt cod croquetas, red pepper salsa
Godello 'Louro do Bolo', Rafael Palacios, Galicia

STARTER (see page 163)
Red snapper tacos, sweetcorn, avocado & lime salsa, chipotle mayonnaise
Riesling 'Bel Canto', Pegasus Bay, North Canterbury

MAIN COURSE (see page 280)
Barbecued beef skirt, stuffed green pepper with creamed sweetcorn, smoked bacon & merkén chilli
'Coyam', Emiliana, Colchagua

SALADS (see pages 318, 306 & 303):

Black rice & squash salad, quinoa, cumin, orange & pomegranate
Semillon 'La Colline', Raised by Wolves, Franschhoek

Superfood salad
Cinsault 'Pofadder', Sadie Family Wines, Swartland

Crisp spring vegetable salad with capers & preserved lemon
Picpoul de Pinet, Domaine Gaujal

DESSERT (see page 331)
Pannacotta with strawberries, lime & basil
Pink Moscato, Stella Bella, Margaret River

AUTUMN

APPETISER (see page 199)
Sticky chicken tulips, prunes, smoked bacon, toasted pecans, star anise
Sercial, Blandy's Vintage Madeira

STARTER (see page 144)
Lobster thermidor vol-au-vents
Meursault-Charmes 1er Cru, Domaine Guy Roulot

MAIN COURSE (see page 211)
Roast grouse with parsnip crisps
Bonnes-Mares Grand Cru, Domaine Dujac

DESSERT (see page 342)
Tarte Tatin with vanilla ice cream
'5 Puttonyos Aszú', Royal Tokaji Wine Company

WINTER

APPETISER (see page 293)
Cheese straw trio
NV Champagne 'Les Chétillons', Pierre Péters

STARTER (see page 220)
Pork & rabbit terrine, macerated apricots, toasted hazelnuts & yogurt dressing
Condrieu 'Coteau de Vernon', Georges Vernay

MAIN COURSE (see page 160)
Tranche of turbot braised in red wine with ceps & lardons
Chinon 'Clos de la Dioterie', Domaine Charles Joguet

DESSERT (see page 336)
Port-poached pear, whipped Stilton, honeyed walnuts
Quinta do Noval, 40-year Tawny Port

WINTER CELEBRATION

APPETISER (see page 294)
Gougères filled with Gruyère mornay
Chablis Grand Cru 'Grenouilles', Domaine Louis Michel

STARTER (see page 314)
Champagne & white Alba truffle risotto
Cuvée Dom Pérignon

MAIN COURSE (see page 266)
Fillet of beef Wellington
Grand Vin de Latour, Pauillac

DESSERT (see page 335)
Black Forest trifle
Tannat 'Alcyone', Viñedo de los Vientos, Uruguay

RIGHT A perfect way to begin your meal: Scallop ceviche with peas, lime, dill & crisp pancetta (see page 130) paired with the zingy Riesling 'Polish Hill', Jeffrey Grosset, South Australia

MIS EN BOUTEILLE AU CHATEAU
CHATEAU LAFITE ROTHSCHILD
1995
PAUILLAC

NOBLE GRAPES

1

RIESLING

RIESLING TENDS TO be the go-to choice of many people in the wine trade, as well as of sommeliers; more so than in the wine-drinking population as a whole. Unfortunately, too many older people remember this variety as that cheap off-dry wine that you took to a party when you were 16 years old, which is very unfair to this noble grape.

As a variety, Riesling can't be messed around with too much by a winemaker. It really doesn't work to age it in oak. Putting it through malolactic fermentation reduces the natural acidity that makes it so delicious, while lees ageing doesn't do much for it, either. It's a grape that truly expresses the terroir of where it's grown, which means that the winemaker's finesse is relatively more important when creating Riesling than it can be for some other varieties.

Riesling has to be grown in a relatively cool climate, in which it can develop and ripen slowly over a long period of time. The best Rieslings in the world can be found in Alsace, Germany, Austria, New Zealand and the cooler climate zones of Australia. It likes a long, cool growing season, so can be found close to the 50° lateral north and south; places such as Canada, the Finger Lakes in New York, Southern Chile and Tasmania are all making successful Riesling.

Depending on the local climate, the aromas and flavours of Riesling can run a fruity gauntlet from steely green apple skin, through to riper tropical passion fruit and mango. But all Rieslings will have a thread of citrus running through their flavour profiles. I find the German Rieslings of the Rheingau, Rheinhessen and Pfalz have a mandarin and tangerine orange character, while the wines of the Mosel boast a lighter lime green and lime blossom florality.

Rieslings from Alsace are very varied in flavour, because of the diverse soil types in this rift valley region (see page 15). Generally the wines are full-bodied, focused and elegant, with a lemony citrus flavour similar to that of the Rieslings of Austria. Australian Riesling tends to be very lime scented, with a lovely, lifted, fresh mint character that reminds me of mojito cocktails. The deep south of Chile, where vineyards almost meet glaciers, is making small quantities of excellent steely dry Rieslings.

OPPOSITE Shoots early in the growing season in Te Motu's vineyard on Waiheke Island, New Zealand

Riesling

ALSACE

STYLE & FLAVOUR Alsace has a diverse geology, due to the tectonic plate movement that created a rift valley (see page 11). The Northern Rhône Valley is also one, as is the Saône Valley (from the slope of the Côte d'Or to the Savoie mountains).

To the west in Alsace lie the Vosges mountains; to the east, over the Rhine, is Germany, the region of Baden, the Black Forest and the Kaiserstuhl mountains.

The point is this: the soil type of a region – its composition, density, nutrient levels and drainage capacity – all influence the flavours of a wine and how the grapes grow. Riesling is a variety that expresses its location more than any other. You don't mess with Riesling: it hates oak, you can't put it through malolactic fermentation, you can't leave it on its lees. So that leaves just soil and terroir as its major flavour influences. You could say it's a purist's grape.

In Alsace, there are sandstone, clay, alluvial deposits, limestone, volcanic and metamorphic soils, and therefore many different expressions of Riesling.

Alsace is privileged to enjoy some of the lowest rainfall in the whole of France, due to the rain shadow effect of the Vosges mountains. This means its grapes can grow undisturbed by heavy rains that often lead to rot. Also, the strong winds blowing down from the mountains mean the vineyards are relatively disease-free, making this region one of the best for growing organic and biodynamic grapes.

The Rieslings from here are focused, lean, intense and vibrant, with a textured mouthfeel and a steely minerality, with flavours of lemon rind and blossom. Other steely dry wines can be found in Alsace, made by grapes such as Sylvaner, Muscat, Pinot Blanc and Chasselas.

WHAT FOOD GOES WELL In Alsace, they eat fatty dishes such as goose or duck, charcuterie, the classic Choucroute Garnie (fermented cabbage with braised cuts of pork and smoked sausage), *tarte flambé* (a yeasted dough base with onions, bacon lardons and cheese), as well as oysters, shellfish and river fish.

RECOMMENDED PRODUCER

'Cuvée Ste Catherine', Domaine Weinbach

Other producers Ostertag; Schlumberger; Josmeyer; 'Clos Ste Hune', Trimbach; Kuentz-Bas; Kreydenweiss

RECIPE RECOMMENDATION

Choucroute garnie ☞ page 237

GERMANY (DRY & OFF-DRY)

STYLE & FLAVOUR The growing trend in Germany is to make dry Rieslings labelled as *Trocken*, and the very best of these are labelled *Grosses Gewachs* ('great growths') by *Verband Deutscher Prädikatsweingüter*, a group of Germany's finest winemakers. VDP wines are marked by the logo of an eagle clutching a bunch of grapes that appears on the neck foil.

The best off-dry styles of Riesling come from Germany (although New Zealand is increasingly doing a great job), with the two regions of the Mosel and the Rheingau producing many of the best.

Positioned at the upper limit of the grape-ripening climate in northern Europe, in Germany sugar is king. Its off-dry Rieslings have confusing labels for those not prepared to do a bit of study, moving up in sugar levels and price from Kabinett, to Spätlese, to Auslese and eventually to the dessert styles of Beerenauslese, Trockenbeerenauslese and Eiswein (see page 123).

Although many people are deterred by the memory of wines with a touch of sugar (again, teenage parties fuelled by sweet white wine are likely responsible), good off-dry Riesling should present a balance of natural sugars, juxtaposed with the natural acidity of this variety.

Riesling is the ballerina of the wine world: delicate and ethereal, graceful and elegant, but with a tremendous muscular tension, walking a finely judged tightrope between sugar and acid.

Maybe it's the connotations of the 1970s – flared trousers, bad haircuts and worse dinner parties – that have kept us from these wines. At that time, mass-produced cheap, one-dimensional wines paid for a lot of new Mercedes cars, but did irreparable damage to the German wine industry's reputation. (Ironically, most of the Liebfraumilch produced was made from the Müller-Thurgau grape rather than from Riesling, but Riesling's image was tarnished nevertheless.)

Off-dry Riesling can present aromas of apples, pears, stone fruits, yellow plums, lemons, limes and citrus blossom, with mineral and sulphurous undertones. In age, it can reveal hints of kerosene or petroleum, with dried fruits and quince.

Often these wines are low in alcohol, at 8–10%, so fit well into an evening where several wines are to be drunk. Serve them early at a dinner, to excite the tastebuds.

... Also, never trust a sommelier who does not like Riesling!

WHAT FOOD GOES WELL For Kabinett and Spätlese, try fish and seafood, deep-fried and crispy. Smoked or salted meats also work. Asian-style dishes flavoured with lemon grass, palm sugar and fish sauce match well, as do light Malaysian-style curries. Back to European flavours, try mild blue cheese with pears and walnuts, plus (of course) foie gras.

RECOMMENDED PRODUCERS

'Wehlener Sonnenuhr', Weingut Joh Jos Prüm (Mosel); 'Kiedricher Gräfenberg', Weingut Robert Weil (Rheingau)

Other producers Müller; Dönnhoff; Künstler; Karthäuserhof; Kesselstat; Thanisch; Keller; Bassermann-Jordan; Kessler; Von Winning; Wittmann

RECIPE RECOMMENDATIONS

Trout en papillote, orange & dill beurre blanc (Rheingau) ☞ *page 169*

Thai-baked sea bass, steamed coconut rice, fragrant herbs, coconut, lemon grass & lime dressing (Mosel) ☞ *page 179*

OPPOSITE 'Berncasteler Doctor', Weingut Dr H Thanisch, Mosel; 'Eitelsbacher Karthäuserhofberg', Weingut Karthäuserhof, Mosel; 'Clos Ste Hune', Maison Trimbach, Alsace; 'Isolation Ridge', Frankland Estate, Western Australia

Berncasteler Doctor
Riesling Auslese
2011
Mosel
KARTHÄUSERHOFBERG
ALSACE
APPELLATION ALSACE CONTRÔLÉE
FRANKLAND
ESTATE
2014
ISOLATION RIDGE VINEYARD
RIESLING

ABOVE: The Mosel river carves dramatic bends out of the slate hillsides, creating ideal amphitheatres for the Riesling vineyards, which, if facing south, are perfect sun traps in this marginal northern climate

Riesling

AUSTRALIA

STYLE & FLAVOUR Jeffrey Grosset is known as the 'King of Australian Riesling', a well-deserved title for several reasons. First, his 'Polish Hill' Riesling is the most revered in Australia. Second, when Riesling was a name used for any off-dry old rubbish made from Sultana or Pedro Ximénez grapes, or from Semillon grapes (when it was labelled simply 'Hunter Valley Riesling'), he pushed for anything labelled as Riesling to be made from Riesling grapes alone. Third, he kick-started the entire Oceania move to screwcapped wines.

The Yalumba winery had moved to bottling its wines under screwcap in the 1970s, but an overwhelmingly negative reaction from consumers forced them back to cork. Grosset knew that a screwcap was the right closure for the style of Riesling being made in the Clare Valley, so went to his fellow winemakers and persuaded them to convert, literally overnight. If he had done that as a sole producer, people would have stopped buying his wine, but because the entire community of Clare producers changed to screwcaps at the same time, the consumer attitude was forced to change: if they wanted the wine, they had to accept the screwcap. More than 95 per cent of Australian and New Zealand wines are now sold under a screwcap.

The Clare Valley lies north of Adelaide and the Barossa Valley, in an elevated series of parallel hills that get cold at night, helping to retain acidity in the grapes, and are hot during the day, producing both sugar and flavour. One of Australia's coolest wine regions, it is ideal for producing great Riesling.

These wines are intensely aromatic, with lime and fresh mint aromas. You can detect notes of Rose's lime cordial, green apple skin, white flowers, all clean and cool flavours, with even a touch of kerosene and a wash of green tropical fruits such as tart papaya and mango. Plus, it has a razor-sharp acidity that makes this a wine to be reckoned with.

The other emerging region producing really fantastic Rieslings in Australia is the Frankland River, south of Margaret River in Western Australia. These wines often have a few grams of residual sugar that just take the edge off the angular acidity found in very dry Riesling.

WHAT FOOD GOES WELL Fresh flavours that require high acidity, such as salads of finely sliced fennel, green mango and papaya. It's great with aromatic and spicy Asian flavours, such as Pad Thai noodles, coconut and lime leaf with red snapper, or Thai beef salad with soy. The cool notes balance well with shellfish and seafood, such as oysters with lime, mussels in white wine, scallop ceviche, fish tacos with lime and coriander, chilli crab, or sashimi.

RECOMMENDED PRODUCER

'Polish Hill', Jeffrey Grosset

Other producers Mount Horrocks; Tim Adams; Kilikanoon; Leasingham; Frankland Estate; Jim Barry

RECIPE RECOMMENDATION

Scallop ceviche with peas, lime, dill & crisp pancetta ☞ *page 130*

NEW ZEALAND

STYLE & FLAVOUR Riesling has become the fourth most-planted grape variety in New Zealand, but, at the time of writing, the country's vineyards still only cover less than 700 hectares, giving an idea of the dominance of Sauvignon Blanc here.

Riesling from New Zealand is racy, aromatic and fresh, with lemon and lime citrus, well-suited to the long growing season delivered by the maritime climate (see page 11). As with Riesling from all over the world, it's not aged in oak, and is naturally high in bright, piercing acidity.

The South Island is where 90 per cent of Riesling is found, in Marlborough and Canterbury. Dry and off-dry versions can be found here, which can cause confusion with consumers as to what they will get when opening the bottle. The alcohol levels will be a good indication; around 10 per cent or lower is likely to be off-dry, while above 12 per cent indicates a dry style of wine. The ever-pragmatic Nigel Greening of Felton Road in Central Otago labels his wines as 'Riesling' and 'Dry Riesling': problem solved.

One of the best Rieslings to be had outside Europe is the 'Bel Canto' Riesling produced by Pegasus Bay in Canterbury; it's made in a similar way to Smaragd wines (see page 81), the best wines of Austria's Wachau region. It takes on texture and richness as the grapes are allowed to develop a certain amount of *botrytis* rot before harvesting.

WHAT FOOD GOES WELL Mexican, Thai and Asian flavours, Japanese tempura, light chicken dishes, firm red snapper and the green-lipped mussels of New Zealand with coriander dressing.

RECOMMENDED PRODUCER

'Bel Canto', Pegasus Bay

Other producers Felton Road, Te Whare Ra, Wither Hills, Misha's Vineyard, Two Paddocks, Tongue in Groove

RECIPE RECOMMENDATION

Red snapper tacos, sweetcorn, avocado & lime salsa, chipotle mayonnaise ☞ *page 163*

NOBLE GRAPES

2

SAUVIGNON BLANC

SAUVIGNON BLANC MAY be the most popular grape variety in the UK and it can offer fresh, crisp, lemony, easy-drinking wine. At one point in the 1980s and 1990s the world was crazy for oaky Chardonnay, but the cheaper end of that scale can be pretty nasty, as it's made with oak chips (see page 23) and tastes of sweetcorn or cornflakes. Thankfully, wine-drinking trends have moved on to non-oaked, crisper styles of wine, which is where Sauvignon Blanc sits.

The grape is grown all over the world, but the six greatest areas making it now are the Loire Valley, Bordeaux, Marlborough in New Zealand, Chile, Styria in southern Austria and Friuli in northern Italy. Good wines are also coming from South Africa.

A common thread found in the flavours of all Sauvignon Blanc is a pyrazine note, which gives 'green' aromas of asparagus, peppers, pea shoots and cucumber skin. Some people find the New World style of Sauvignon Blanc – which is like a fruit salad bowl, with asparagus and green pepper thrown in – too intense. But while the green, grassy styles of Sauvignon Blanc are adored by some people and the more tropical fruit styles attract others, it's generally the high acidity along with the variety's freshness that is appealing to all.

Depending where it comes from, the characteristics of the wine will change. Sauvignon Blanc from the Loire Valley will have a stony minerality typical of the wines of Sancerre and Pouilly-Fumé. Chilean wines will possess ripe tropical mango and pineapple notes, while explosive fruit bombs can be found in New Zealand.

In Bordeaux or Styria, Sauvignon Blanc expresses itself as a gentle, elegant, oaked wine. When it is aged in oak, Sauvignon Blanc doesn't take on any vanilla or butterscotch characteristics – unlike Chardonnay – as it is unlikely to go through 100 per cent malolactic fermentation. When it is bottle-aged, Sauvignon Blanc tends to have more of a smoky, flinty, floral white lily character.

OPPOSITE Sauvignon Blanc grapes in the vineyards of Tohu, New Zealand's first 100 per cent Maori-owned vineyards

Sauvignon Blanc

ITALY

STYLE & FLAVOUR Italian white wine heaven lies in north-eastern Italy, especially in Friuli-Venezia Giulia, as you move to high-altitude vineyards in the Italian Alps south of Austria and to the east of Slovenia. This area is known for its indigenous white varieties, such as Picolit, Verduzzo and Friulano, but its Sauvignon Blanc is also stunning.

The flavours of the wine from here are not as intense as those of Marlborough Sauvignon Blanc. While they are richer and broader than the wines from the Loire Valley, they are still bright and acid-led, with power and focus. Chilly night-times in the Friuli region help build acid levels in the grapes, while warm and sunny days create intense fruit flavours of ripe pear, melon and yellow plum. There are other great Italian expressions of Sauvignon Blanc to be found in Piedmont, to the west.

WHAT FOOD GOES WELL With most Sauvignon Blanc, dishes that contain green herbaceous flavours and an element of tart acidity work well.

We chose to match it in this book with risotto primavera, because of cult winemaker Enzo Pontoni's (of Miani) Sauvignon Blanc, as his wine is so exceptional. The flavours of the risotto are a roll-call of great Sauvignon Blanc matches: goat's cheese, asparagus, green peppers, peas, mint and chervil.

RECOMMENDED PRODUCER
'Saurint' or 'Zitelle', Miani
Other producers Felluga; Gaja; San Leonardo; Ornellaia

RECIPE RECOMMENDATION
Risotto primavera with robiola cheese ☞ *page 317*

POUILLY-FUMÉ AND SANCERRE

STYLE & FLAVOUR The wines from this region may be compared to the wines of Chablis or, more accurately, to the wines of Saint-Bris, right next to Chablis, where the Sauvignon Blanc grape dominates over Chardonnay. Similar climates and limestone soils can be found in both regions, although many of Sancerre's greatest vineyards can be found in distinctive flinty (silex) soils. Both areas produce high acid levels in their grapes, bringing a certain minerality and tension to the wines.

These Sauvignon Blancs exemplify the notion of terroir (see pages 8–19), a combination of climate, soils, variety, winemaker and history.

As most producers here rarely use oak ageing, the wines remain grassy and herbaceous, with vegetal, green pepper and asparagus flavours and – in riper years – a lemony and grapefruit citrus palate that has tropical guava and passion fruit notes. However, even with these flavours, the wines should retain the freshness and minerality of cold river water running over pebbles.

WHAT FOOD GOES WELL A classic French bistro starter is a generous slice of baked Loire goat's cheese, served on a toasted croûte in a bed of rocket and drizzled with walnut oil. If you can find it, use Chavignol cheese, as this commune is considered a cru within the Sancerre appellation. It will also pair well with salmon, flat fish such as brill, oysters and freshwater river fish such as trout, grilled with a simple salsa verde made from green herbs and capers. With age, earthier flavours can be integrated, such as beetroot, or even beef Carpaccio with lemon juice squeezed over the top. Try to avoid cream-based sauces or hard Cheddar-like cheeses; save those for the barrel-aged Chardonnays, due to their lactic element. Sauvignon Blanc is better with foods that are tart and need a match that has freshness and acidity.

RECOMMENDED PRODUCERS
Domaine Vacheron (Sancerre); 'Silex', Didier Dagueneau (Pouilly-Fumé)
Other producers Bourgeois; Cotat; Mellot; Château de Tracy; Crochet

RECIPE RECOMMENDATIONS
Roast fillet of brill, cockles, ham hock & celery hearts (Sancerre) ☞ *page 158*
Herb-roasted fillet of salmon, fregola & summer vegetable salad, salmon 'crackling' (Pouilly-Fumé) ☞ *page 172*

OPPOSITE 'Cloudy Bay', Marlborough; 'Silex', Didier Dagueneau, Pouilly-Fumé; Château Smith Haut Lafitte, Bordeaux; 'Alteni di Brassica', Gaja, Piedmont

CLOUDY BAY
SiLEX
CHATEAV
SMITH HAVT LAFITTE
2011
ALTENI DI BRASSICA
Langhe
2016
GAJA

Sauvignon Blanc

BORDEAUX (OAKED)

STYLE & FLAVOUR The best Sauvignon Blancs from Bordeaux are aged in oak and found in the Graves appellation of Pessac-Léognan. These are made from a blend that is usually weighted higher in Sauvignon grapes, with the rest made up of Semillon (see page 72–74).

If you want to make these wines to age for as long as you would a good white Burgundy, this is a clever combination of grapes to choose. That is because, as a young wine, the Sauvignon flavours are more dominant, bursting with grassy, fresh green pepper and asparagus, with plenty of lemony citrus flavours, while Semillon is quite muted when young. Over time, as the Sauvignon character starts to die away, the Semillon begins to blossom into its rich honey, lanolin, waxy, chamomile-scented aromas.

Barrel-ageing Sauvignon does not impart the vanilla and butterscotch flavours found in oaked Chardonnay, but instead has a floral white lily and gunsmoke flint character. California followed the oaky Sauvignon Blanc style, most notably when Robert Mondavi created his Fumé Blanc wine. Cooler areas such as Washington are also making good wines.

WHAT FOOD GOES WELL Fish and shellfish, such as pan-fried scallops with bacon and peas, or fish ceviche with lime juice. Oysters from Arcachon is a classic pairing. Green herbs such as tarragon and dill work, as do salsa verde, pesto, asparagus, tomato dishes and those with green peppers, such as gazpacho. Also try it with goat's cheese, or chicken or fish cooked with preserved lemons.

RECOMMENDED PRODUCER

Château Smith Haut Lafitte

Other producers Domaine de Chevalier; Château Biac; Château Bauduc; Château Pape-Clément; Château de Fieuzal

RECIPE RECOMMENDATION

Fillet of wild sea bass, salsa verde & preserved lemon ☞ *page 181*

MARLBOROUGH, NEW ZEALAND

STYLE & FLAVOUR These are, quite simply, an explosion of flavour! A mix of tropical fruit notes – papaya, guava, nectarines, passion fruit and kiwi – as well as green peppers, asparagus, green peas, cucumber skins and citrusy lemon, lime and grapefruit. Sharp, fresh, with tangy acidity and usually no oak.

The Sauvignon variety of grape, both in its red Cabernet and white Blanc forms, is high in pyrazine, a component that gives 'green' aromas of peppers and asparagus spears. In New Zealand's Marlborough region, a combination of the cool maritime climate (see page 11) and the rainshadow effect of the huge Southern Alps (seen *The Lord of the Rings* movies?) causes the Sauvignon Blanc to develop methoxypyrazines, super-charged pyrazines that give these wines their intensity.

Some people in the wine world can be a bit sniffy about this full-on style, but these are the perfect bottles to choose when you are trying to get (or trying to get someone else) interested in wine, as their aromas and flavours are so apparent and easily understandable. It's hard to believe that Sauvignon Blanc only came to New Zealand in 1973, when the first vines were planted in Marlborough, as it has now become a must-have, distinctive wine on lists all over the world.

WHAT FOOD GOES WELL Seafood and shellfish, especially scallops and mussels, or gravadlax, or firm snapper with spices. Also Asian flavours of lemon grass and Thai basil, or Singapore chilli crab. And try it with goat's cheese, gazpacho, salads with tomato and vinaigrette, or a classic Waldorf salad.

RECOMMENDED PRODUCER
'Boundary Farm', Mahi
Other producers Cloudy Bay; Greywacke; Craggy Range; Dog Point; Clos Henri; Blind River; Amisfield

RECIPE RECOMMENDATION
Marinated snapper, green mango & fragrant herb salad, coconut, lemon grass & lime dressing ☞ *page 164*

BELOW Vines at Château Biac, overlooking the Garonne river, in the Graves appellation of Bordeaux

NOBLE GRAPES
3

CHENIN BLANC

CHENIN BLANC FINDS its home in the Loire Valley region of France, and in South Africa. Around the central part of the Loire Valley – scattered in the locality of the towns of Angers and Tours, as well as down the tributary river of the Layon – Chenin Blanc can be found in dry styles, or in lusciously sweet *botrytis*-affected versions. Maybe the greatest expression of Chenin Blanc is found in the vineyards of Savennières, where some *botrytis* can add richness and complexity to full-bodied dry white wines.

South Africa used to call Chenin Blanc *Steen* (which means 'stone' in Afrikaans), and it was made in a dry, steely-fresh style and kept shaded from the fierce winds of the country. But this name is seen less and less these days, and the Chenin Blanc made in South Africa now is exposed to the strong South African wind known as the Cape Doctor (so-called because, when it blows through the vineyards, it is pivotal in keeping the grapes dry and mould-free). The winds also thicken the skins of the fruit and thus allows this modern Chenin Blanc to be barrel-aged, giving the wine a structure and weight similar to that of a good Chardonnay.

Pockets of Chenin can be found planted in unexpected parts of the world. Due to its high acidity it has been used in India, Thailand and Israel as well as for bulk wine production in California. Outside of the Loire and South Africa, Millton Vineyards in New Zealand make a great example.

The underlying similarities common to all Chenin Blancs are their high acidity, along with the aromas and flavours of apple. Lighter styles give a green apple note, while the richer, fuller wines deliver riper yellow apples on the nose. When matured, Chenin Blanc has a distinctive, pleasantly oxidised apple fragrance.

The three famous 'blancs' of the Loire Valley start in the upper reaches of the river with Sauvignon Blanc (see page 56), the mid-section is where Chenin Blanc dominates, and at the mouth of the river by the coastal town of Nantes is where Melon Blanc (aka. Muscadet) is grown, the best between the rivers Sèvre and Maine, aged on its lees (*sur lie*).

OPPOSITE Old-vine Chenin Blanc in Stellenbosch, South Africa

Chenin Blanc

SAVENNIÈRES, LOIRE VALLEY

STYLE & FLAVOUR Chenin Blanc is a versatile grape and can be found in the Loire made as sparkling, teeth-rattlingly dry, semi-dry and sweet wines, but finds its greatest expression in the historic vineyards around Anjou, especially those of Savennières. Made famous by sweet *botrytis* ('noble rot') wines made during the Napoleonic era, the wines from here are more likely dry nowadays, but the light morning mists of the Loire can still help develop a touch of *botrytis*.

Chenin Blanc has a red or yellow apple quality and a tendency to develop bruised apple characteristics with age, due to oxidation, when it can also gain aromas such as wet wool, damp cloth or fragrant baked quince. A naturally high acidity gives a mineral, saline edge to the wine, while the hint of Loire *botrytis* lends a rich glycerol texture and yet another layer of complexity. High-acidity, off-dry styles here are known as *moelleux*, meaning 'creamy' (such as at Domaine Huet, see right).

Nicolas Joly was probably the world's first fervent biodynamic wine producer. His Savennières wine can be stunningly amazing or tragically disappointing, depending on the phases of the moon. That's biodynamics for you...

WHAT FOOD GOES WELL The impressive level of acidity makes this style of Chenin Blanc a perfect match for pork with apple sauce and crackling. Barrel-aged versions are great with pork fillet stuffed with dried stone fruits and pine nuts, or chicken with soft fruits and cream sauces. Light curry spices, especially turmeric and garam masala, work well, as do aged Loire Valley goat's cheeses such as Valençay or Chabichou du Poitou.

RECOMMENDED PRODUCER

'Coulée de Serrant', Nicolas Joly

Other producers Domaine des Baumard; Domaine du Closel; Château de Chamboureau; Domaine Huet; Ferme de la Sansonnière; Foreau; Chidaine; de Fesles

RECIPE RECOMMENDATION

Slow-roasted belly of Tamworth pork, autumn fruit & hazelnut compote ☞ *page 230*

SOUTH AFRICA

STYLE & FLAVOUR Chenin Blanc is South Africa's signature white variety, with close to one-fifth of the country's vineyards planted with the grape. The old style of these wines were sharp and steely, with teeth-grinding acidity and thin fruit. The grape bunches were kept shaded from the fierce sunshine and very intense Cape Doctor winds (see page 62).

Modern winemakers are embracing the winds of their location and leaving grapes exposed, which makes them develop thick skins that ultimately give the wines more weight, a more luxurious texture and greater density, along with the ability to hold new oak, which results in elegant and refined wines.

It is a very different expression of Chenin Blanc to that of the Loire Valley (see above), where Chenin Blanc can be slightly off-dry in places such as Vouvray, or possess a slight *botrytis*-like aroma as in Savennières. These South African expressions of the wine are broad-textured and weighty, carrying flavours of yellow apples and orchard fruits, similar in structure to southern Burgundy whites such as Mâcon or Pouilly-Fuissé.

Excellent Chenin Blanc can be found especially in the Swartland area of South Africa, on the region's decomposed granite schist soils.

WHAT FOOD GOES WELL Try seafood and shellfish such as lobster, with some spice, or sautéed scallops with a pumpkin or apple purée. Off-dry versions (Ken Forrester's 'The FMC' is best) go well with sweet-and-sour Asian dishes, Thai fishcakes or Indian kormas with coconut and mild spice. It is also a great festive white wine, to enjoy alongside the Christmas turkey.

RECOMMENDED PRODUCER

'The FMC', Ken Forrester

Other producers Mullineux & Leeu; Jean Daneel Wines; David & Nadia; Keermont; 'Palladius', Sadie Family; Mulderbosch

RECIPE RECOMMENDATION

Coronation chicken salad, apple, celery hearts & golden raisins ☞ *page 203*

OPPOSITE 'Clos du Bourg' Moelleux Première Trie Vouvray, Domaine Huet; 'La Lune', Domaine Mark Angeli, Ferme de la Sansonnière, Anjou; 'Hoë-Steen', David & Nadia, South Africa

1959
2017
La Lune
Vin de France
2017
Hoë-Steen
CHENIN BLANC · VINTAGE
David & Nadia

NOBLE GRAPES

4

CHARDONNAY

PROBABLY the world's most popular white grape, capable of making spectacular wines, or very dull and simple wines. It is to the wine world as a chicken is to a chef: a blank canvas. A chef with a chicken can cook a multitude of dishes; similarly, winemakers can manipulate Chardonnay to create the flavours they want. The most obvious way is by ageing it in oak, or allowing gentle oxidation.

Also, winemakers can put Chardonnay through malolactic fermentation (MLF), which softens its acidity and gives it a broader texture and mouth-feel and a certain creaminess, as the tart, 'green' malic acid converts into soft lactic acid (found in milk). They can age the wine on its lees and routinely stir it (Burgundian *battonage*), which gives yeasty characteristics, richness and texture.

In the same way that a chef can construct a great chicken dish, the finest wines depend on the skill of the best artisans.

For example, Burgundy is a cool climate region where grapes are acidic and benefit from MLF to soften the tart flavours. The same technique cannot be used in hot areas, where grapes already have softer acidity and very ripe fruit, as it would result in flabby, burningly alcoholic wines. Nowadays, in warmer climates, cutting back on MLF and oxidation in oak, along with a more restrained use of new oak, is producing streamlined, focused wines of great elegance that can mirror Burgundy's subtlety, while carving their own nuanced style based on their particular terroir.

It is Chardonnay's ability to thrive in all climates that accounts for its popularity. It's popular in California's coastal areas, especially Sonoma and Santa Barbara and in Chile by cool coastal areas or on patches of limestone in Limarí. Australia makes tight, reductive, struck-match styles around the Melbourne and Port Philip Bay areas of Geelong, Mornington Peninsula and Yarra Valley, and great Chardonnay from the gin-gin (aka Wente or Mendoza) clone in Margaret River. In New Zealand, riper, weighty Chardonnays are found in Hawke's Bay and leaner styles in Marlborough and Central Otago. Both Stellenbosch and Francshhoek in South Africa produce Chardonnay, while excellent wines are coming from Piedmont and Umbria in Italy and Penedès in Spain.

OPPOSITE Early morning mist in the vineyards of Puligny-Montrachet

Chardonnay

CHABLIS

STYLE & FLAVOUR The climate in Chablis is cold; it's closer to Champagne than it is to the rest of Burgundy. The limestone that covers northern France and southern England is prevalent here. Some areas in Chablis show the fossils of *Exogyra virgula* bivalves that point to the marine origins of these soils. Throughout most of the Jurassic period, northern Europe was a warm, shallow sea where many calcium-rich shell-covered creatures lived, from starfish to mussels. When they died, layers upon layers built up and were compacted into the limestone we see nowadays in Chablis, as well as in the cliffs of Dover, the South Downs and the Isle of Wight.

To get complexity into the wines of a cold northern region such as Champagne, winemakers can use autolytic flavours – that's when dead yeast from a secondary fermentation in the bottle (the Champagne method of making bubbles) causes cells to break down and release the delicious yeasty flavours of bread dough – but here they use other methods to give Chablis its unique characteristics.

First, they can choose the amount of malolactic fermentation allowed to occur. Winemakers who wish to keep the tart acidity will do minimal amounts. Second, ageing the wine on its lees, and stirring that lees, adds texture, a yeasty flavour or cream cheese character.

Third, maturing in old oak allows some oxidation, taking the edge off any harsh acidity and smoothing out the wine, without imparting a flavour of new oak. (New oak is rarely used, except in Grand Cru wines, or some Premiers Crus.)

Chablis is a result of climate, soil and technique. For me, the perfect Chablis is tart but balanced, with rounded flavours of apple, pear and dried straw, the fresh lactic character found in Brie rind and the impression of wet chalk.

On my first ever visit to Chablis, I was invited to lunch by the grandson of Louis Michel, Jean-Loup Michel, whose family have been making Chablis since 1850. As he spoke no English, I conversed with him in schoolboy French and asked him to order me a local speciality. He chose andouillette, a sausage made of (not very well cleaned) pig's intestine, of the highest grade, an AAAAA. Cutting into this sausage released an indescribable aroma. My saviour was a pot of Dijon mustard on the table that masked somewhat the tang of pig guts and stale urine, so I ate the entire pot. This caused an astonished Jean-Loup to exclaim '*Mon dieu! Tu aimes la moutarde!*'

Earlier in the day, we had eaten some incredible gougères (see page 294) with his 1971 'Les Clos' Grand Cru, so when matching a dish to this wine, I suggest choux pastry rather than pig's guts...

WHAT FOOD GOES WELL Andouillette anyone? Perhaps not. Instead choose crab, snails, mussels or oysters. Scallops with beurre blanc work well, as do sea bass, cod and salmon, steamed langoustines with lemon mayonnaise and sole Véronique (with grapes and a light cream sauce). Hard cheeses and cheese pastries match well with mature wines, while creamy cheeses such as Brie, Brillat-Savarin or goat's cheeses are best for younger wines.

RECOMMENDED PRODUCERS
'Grenouilles', Domaine Louis Michel & Fils;
'Valmur', Domaine François Raveneau
Other producers Fèvre; Dauvissat; Billaud-Simon; Defaix; Picq; Long-Depaquit

RECIPE RECOMENDATIONS
Gougères filled with Gruyère mornay (Grenouilles) ☞ *page 294*
Crab & samphire salad, grapes & soft herbs (Valmur) ☞ *page 134*

CÔTE D'OR

STYLE & FLAVOUR Chardonnay shows its best qualities in cooler areas and limestone soils, both found here.

Meursault, along with Chassagne-Montrachet and Puligny-Montrachet, are probably the three most famous wine villages for Chardonnay, making the benchmark wines that possess qualities any producer would dream of.

In Chassagne-Montrachet and Puligny-Montrachet, all the vineyards are Grand Cru: La Montrachet itself, Bâtard Montrachet, Bienvenues Bâtard-Montrachet, Criots-Bâtard-Montrachet and Chevalier-Montrachet.

These can be the most expensive white wines in the world, steeped in history. The wines of Puligny-Montrachet tend to be very linear and focused, with razor-sharp acidity, and are undoubtedly elegant. They can be matured for a long time, up to 30 years. I find Chassagne-Montrachet more rounded, less focused and, for me, more enjoyable.

The village of Meursault doesn't contain any Grands Crus, but many would say that Meursault Perrières should be elevated to a Grand Cru, as it lies in a similar place on the slope and can produce wines that are equally elegant.

The sign of a true great white Burgundy is a subtle mix of new top-quality French oak, bringing slight vanilla and hazelnut aromas, and a fine, taut, tropical fruit character. It will have a structured mineral-like acidity and a very long length: the flavours linger in the mouth for some time.

WHAT FOOD GOES WELL Something classy, rich and creamy, containing cheese, eggs and butter, works with the lactic qualities. Rich fish dishes: turbot with hollandaise, lobster thermidor, Dover sole with beurre noisette. Cheese soufflé and hard nutty cheeses work, as does Bresse chicken in butter with lemon.

RECOMMENDED PRODUCER
Meursault-Charmes 1er Cru, Domaine Roulot
Other producers Coche-Dury; Ente; Morey; Colin-Morey; du Prieuré; Gagnard; Boillot

RECIPE RECOMENDATION
Lobster thermidor vol-au-vent ☞ *page 144*

OPPOSITE 'Bannockburn', Felton Road, Central Otago; 'The Judge', John Kongsgaard, Napa; Pouilly-Fuissé, Domaine J A Ferret; Chablis Grand Cru 'Valmur', Domaine François Raveneau; Meursault-Charmes 1er Cru, Domaine Roulot

CHARDONNAY
CENTRAL OTAGO
2016
Cuvée Hors-Classe
VIN DE BOURGOGNE
Domaine J.A. Ferret
Fondé en 1840
APPELLATION D'ORIGINE CONTRÔLÉE
2016
2011
2009
Meursault-Charmes
Domaine ROULOT

Chardonnay

SOUTHERN BURGUNDY, MÂCON

STYLE & FLAVOUR As you travel south from Dijon, you trace the hillside all the way down the Côte d'Or, with a very pronounced limestone slope to your right. And this follows all the way down through Beaune and continues as you pass through the Chalonnaise region, then arrive at the Mâconnaise. The slope is starting to disappear now, the temperatures are warming up and you find a lot more fruit orchards. The limestone bedrock appears in certain areas, most famously where the Rock of Solutré sticks its head out.

The Chardonnay down here is always a great alternative to the Côte d'Or whites, usually far less expensive than they are, but at the same time maybe never reaching the exalted heights of its cousins further north. They are simpler and not as nuanced.

This region is also quite famous for wines from St-Véran, as well as for the three Pouillys: Fuissé, Loché and Vinzelles.

Because it is slightly warmer here, often the Chardonnays feel fuller and riper, with aromas and flavours of pineapples, yellow apples and plums, but since they are less expensive, they are probably produced using a more economical process, which means the winemakers don't put as much new oak in wine.

WHAT FOOD GOES WELL Classy, rich and creamy foods all work well with the lactic qualities of the wines, just keep it simple and delicious. Any type of seafood and shellfish is good, just plainly grilled fish with something rich, such as hollandaise sauce, or, in the same kind of combination, snails with a garlic butter. Hard, nutty cheeses also work.

RECOMMENDED PRODUCER
Pouilly-Loché 'No 2 Monopole', Clos des Rocs
Other producers Morat; de la Bongran; Ponsot; Pollier; des Héritiers du Comte Lafon; Ferret; Château-Fuissé

RECIPE RECOMMENDATION
Escargots à la Bourguignonne ☞ *page 223*

NEW ZEALAND

STYLE & FLAVOUR New Zealand is in a maritime climate (see page 11), surrounded by the Pacific Ocean, and, being quite far south on the globe, is a land of green, clean flavours. Traditional Burgundian winemaking is probably suited to the country because of this cooler weather. Chardonnay is grown all over New Zealand, but shows some of its best expression in Hawke's Bay. This is New Zealand's second biggest wine region, and lies on the east coast of the North Island. It's at the convergence of three rivers that run into the bay area, bringing huge amounts of alluvial deposits: gravel, sand and silt (which are also great for Bordeaux-style red grape varieties, making Hawke's Bay the Cabernet capital of New Zealand). The best Chardonnay generally comes from the coast, where the vineyards are cooled down by those ocean breezes, giving great acidity.

The wines give the impression of salinity, along with ripe pineapple fruit. Most producers go through a certain amount of malolactic fermentation, but they like to retain some freshness.

WHAT FOOD GOES WELL New Zealand's status as an island means that there's an abundant wealth of fantastic seafood. I had the local speciality abalone soup with pork and scallops in New Zealand once and really loved it with the local Chardonnay. Elsewhere, seafood is a good match, especially crab, in a sauce made of saline sea vegetables.

RECOMMENDED PRODUCER
'Block 5', Felton Road

Other producers 'Moutere' Neudorf; Pegasus Bay; Bell Hill; Pyramid Valley; 'Kidnapper Cliffs', Craggy Range; 'Matés Vineyard', Kumeu River; Tolpuddle; Greywacke

RECIPE RECOMMENDATION
Spicy crab linguine with *barbe di frate* ☞ *page 136*

LEFT Chardonnay vineyards cooled by the ocean breezes in Hawke's Bay, New Zealand. These vineyards produce ripe, tropical wines that are underscored by a beautiful saline and mineral acidity

CALIFORNIA

STYLE & FLAVOUR Chardonnay from California has definitely changed over the last 20 years. For many, the Californian Chardonnay style used to be rich, golden, oak-heavy butter monsters. But generally these days, Californian Chardonnay – and Pinot Noir, too (see page 90) – is embracing a 'less is more' quality, with winemakers looking for elegant, subtle flavours and reasonable alcohol levels.

I'm sure everyone remembers an age when Chardonnay was golden in texture, heavy and buttery, with bags of vanilla. They were fun wines for a certain amount of time. Some of that style may have been due to winemakers in California's hotter climates using a cooler-climate Burgundian model to make Chardonnay. However, in Burgundy, you have a very tart, thin grape juice to work with, so you want to put it through malolactic fermentation, to bring the acid down. You want to age it in barrels, to give texture and finesse. And you want lees ageing, too, which will start to add yet more complexity. If you are attempting these techniques in a hot climate, such as in California, your grapes are probably already lacking in acidity, as the sunshine has made them sweet, so malolactic fermentation just ends up making the wines flabby.

As that style of wine grew popular, though, winemakers on a budget took to adding oak in the form of chips, as a kind of 'teabag' thrown into the barrels (see page 23). It gave a vanilla and oak flavour, but not a very pleasant one! It was often quite nasty, in fact...

Thankfully, many of the producers in these warmer climates are now making Chardonnay with true Burgundian flavours. The most successful Californian Chardonnays come from the coast, or from high-altitude vineyards, where the climate is cooler and the grapes can retain freshness and acidity. Chardonnay makers all along the Sonoma Coast and down in Santa Barbara are currently at the top of their game. Napa Valley is still producing a small amount of Chardonnay, but in that region it is a case of the survival of the fittest: the best are still going; the worst have left.

Some extraordinary Chardonnay is also found in the coastal mountain ranges, some within a couple of kilometres of the Pacific and anything up to 200m in elevation. These are cool, foggy vineyards, producing wines with intense minerality and focus.

WHAT FOOD GOES WELL Due to the cold Pacific Ocean, California is likely to have plenty of great-quality seafood and shellfish. Look to pair the wines with buttery sauces, or with Californian sushi, which is usually quite heavy in crab and avocado, so it has a richness that is echoed in the wines.

RECOMMENDED PRODUCER

'The Judge', John Kongsgaard

Other producers Kutch; Sandhi; Failla; Hirsch; Montelena; Shafer; Arnot-Roberts; Peter Michael Winery

RECIPE RECOMMENDATION

Chargrilled spiny lobster, tarragon & shallot butter ☞ *page 147*

ABOVE Vineyards facing the Pacific Ocean in California's Sonoma region. They are shrouded in fog from San Pablo Bay first thing in the morning, cooling the vineyards and allowing the grapes to produce fantastic acidity

NOBLE GRAPES
5

SEMILLON

SEMILLON IS A variety of wine that is best known from one of two regions: Bordeaux, and Australia's Hunter Valley.

In Bordeaux, it is famously used as part of a blend with Sauvignon Blanc to make dry white wines. This is because Sauvignon Blanc is a very exuberant and aromatic variety when young and its flavours dominate the blend in the wine's youth, while young Semillon is relatively neutral. But, as the wine ages, the exuberance of Sauvignon Blanc starts to die away and the complexity of Semillon comes to the fore, bringing its flavours and aromas of beeswax, lanolin, chamomile and buttered toast that will carry the wine into its old age. This blend of wine, when married with ageing in new oak, will give wines of great longevity and lasting power. Obviously, Semillon is also the great dessert wine of Bordeaux, used to make sweet Sauternes (see page 124).

Semillon is also grown widely in the Hunter Valley, where the variety produces wines that are bone-dry, with a laser-like acidity and a fresh flavour of green apples. With some age, these wines develop beautiful lanolin and honeysuckle tones with, again, the aroma of hot buttered toast. As this region is warm and tropical, the grapes must be harvested early to retain their high acidity. But the early harvest also means also not much sugar has a chance to accumulate in the grapes, so, when fully fermented, these wines will never reach alcohol levels above around 11 per cent.

OPPOSITE Australia's Hunter Valley is a wet, semi-tropical region, but its flanking mountain ranges funnel cool Pacific breezes into the region. These Semillon grapes at Tyrrell's are picked early to retain acidity, meaning their sugars are low, so alcohol levels in the wine remain low, too

41

Semillon

SAUTERNES (DRY)

STYLE & FLAVOUR Due to the process that goes into making the sweet Bordeaux wines of Sauternes (see page 124), sometimes the Semillon and Sauvignon Blanc grapes never reach the levels of *botrytis cinerea* infection required to produce them. The grapes can hang in bunches side by side with *botrytis*-infected grapes, absorbing some of the flavours, or maybe becoming partially infected. These grapes are made into a dry white wine (labelled as Bordeaux Blanc, as a dry Sauternes appellation does not exist).

The aromas of these wines can also be similar to those of a Sauternes, displaying saffron and ginger biscuit, as well as ripe apricot, peach and quince, but on the palate they have a dry spice and mineral quality similar to Pessac-Léognan dry white wines.

The introduction of these wines has been a good move for Sauternes producers, as expensive sweet wines are a commodity drunk too infrequently to provide adequate sales. These dry white wines have allowed the makers here to move production into two styles of wines and save the best *botrytis* grapes for making exceptional sweet wines.

WHAT FOOD GOES WELL Richer types of fish and shellfish such as monkfish or lobster, and white meats such as chicken or pork. They could all be accompanied by cream sauces with saffron and some mild curry spices, or herbs such as tarragon or sage. Medallions of pork fillet cooked with paprika and finished with cream would also be delicious partnered with these wines.

RECOMMENDED PRODUCER
'G de Giraud', Château Giraud
Other producers 'Y' Ygrec de Château d'Yquem; 'R' de Château Rieussec; Clos des Lunes

RECIPE RECOMMENDATION
Chicken, girolle & tarragon pie ☞ *page 204*

HUNTER VALLEY, AUSTRALIA

STYLE & FLAVOUR This is a unique flavour and is definitely a style of wine that, as with Riesling in the Clare Valley (see page 55), is a particular expression of the Hunter Valley. Based two hours' drive north of a large city, the Hunter Valley is Sydney's equivalent of California's Napa Valley, and a hub destination for thirsty wine tourists.

The weather of a subtropical microclimate such as this creates the need to pick the thin-skinned Semillon grapes early, when the sugars in the fruit are low and the acidity high. This results in laser-sharp, crisp, clean and intense Semillon wines that are scented with lime juice, lime peel and apple blossom in their youth.

When young, this acidity tends to be teeth-shattering and almost impenetrable. The wines really need a few years (at least five, in my opinion) of ageing, to allow them to unwind and develop their mature aromas of hot buttered toast, lanolin floor polish, beeswax, lime cordial and honeysuckle and all-round deliciousness, plus a low alcohol level, never exceeding 11 per cent. They can age for up to 30 years.

The ageing brings out flavours that make you convinced that these wines have been aged in oak, when in fact they have not. And, as the wine really needs ageing before release, the advent of the screwcap has been described as the salvation of the variety by Hunter Valley grandee Bruce Tyrrell, as many bottles used to experience random oxidation under cork, and were returned to the winery before being drunk.

WHAT FOOD GOES WELL A saline and fresh lime juice quality make this wine a great match for something as simple as freshly shucked oysters (with coriander dressing rather than red wine vinegar and shallots), or even lightly cooked oysters with clean Japanese flavours. Seafood, shellfish, green herbs, salads and green papaya are also good, so you could choose south-east Asian food based on seafood, but without palm sugar added, which will strip the already delicate fruit and leave an acid bomb.

RECOMMENDED PRODUCER
Semillon 'Vat 1', Tyrrell's
Other producers 'ILR Reserve', Brokenwood; 'Lovedale', McWilliams

RECIPE RECOMMENDATION
Oyster tempura, green apple, wasabi & lime mayonnaise, shizo ☞ *page 138*

OPPOSITE Semillon 'Boekenhoutskloof', Sadie Family, South Africa; Château de Fargues, Sauternes; 'Vat 1', Tyrrell's, Hunter Valley; 'Y' Ygrec de Château d'Yquem, Bordeaux

2016
BOEKENHOUTSKLOOF
SEMILLON
APPELLATION SAUTERNES CONTROLÉE
CHATEAU DE FARGUES
Lur-Saluces
SAUTERNES
1990
MIS EN BOUTEILLE AU CHATEAU
Vat 1
2005
"Y"
2007
BORDEAUX BLANC

Semillon

SOUTH AFRICA

STYLE & FLAVOUR Originally planted here in the 1690s, by the 1820s as much as 90 per cent of grapes planted in the Cape were Semillon. However, *phylloxera* struck, and by 1995, it was only around one per cent, losing out to great plantings of Chenin Blanc, Chardonnay and Sauvignon Blanc. But the pockets of old-vine Semillon that remained are now being viewed in a new light, and making deep, rich and fat wines with Semillon's trademark bright acidity running through them. They also have great longevity for ageing, which brings out the honeysuckle and lanolin qualities of mature Semillon.

WHAT FOOD GOES WELL South African barbecue (*braai*) of snoek fish, or beer can chicken, or the subtle sweet and spice of a squash salad.

RECOMMENDED PRODUCER
'La Colline', Raised by Wolves, Franschhoek
Other producers Rupert & Rothschild; 'La Colline', Alheit; Boekenhoutskloof; Sadie Family; Vergelegen; Tokara

RECIPE RECOMMENDATION
Black rice & squash salad, quinoa, cumin, orange & pomegranate ☞ *page 318*

BELOW Plutons formed deep in the Earth's crust under immense pressure are responsible not only for South Africa's diamond industry, but also – after the surrounding landscape eroded away – the dramatic jagged mountain ranges that give the country its unique scenery

Gewurztraminer & Pinot Gris

GEWURZTRAMINER, ALSACE

STYLE & FLAVOUR Originally from northern Italy, the Traminer grape migrated into Germany and eventually to Alsace, where it found its home. The warm and dry climate of Alsace and its varied soils provide Gewurztraminer with the perfect environment to fully express itself, but this grape does provoke polarising reactions when first tasted. Gewürz is German for 'spice' and the aromas of this grape evoke just that – freshly warmed spices straight out of the grinder – turmeric, cardamom, anise, clove, garam masala… These spice aromas are usually mixed with those of ripe tropical fruits, especially mango and papaya, and often orchard fruits such as red apple or quince. The wines also have a strong aroma and flavour of roses or lychees, Turkish delight and talcum powder or, as wine writer Oz Clarke would say, dressing-room Nivea Creme.

Alsace Gewurztraminer can be found as a dry wine or as a *botrytis*-affected sweet wine, but I think is often at its best slightly off-dry.

The warming alcohol and soft acidity sometimes drives the spiciness and exotic flavour to levels that people dislike, and can make it tricky to match the wine with food, but well-thought-out dishes that connect with these flavours can produce something truly sublime.

WHAT FOOD GOES WELL Food with Asian ingredients, such as lemon grass, tamarind, galangal, chilli and palm sugar (for the off-dry styles), mango and other tropical fruits, even banana. The soft acidity makes it a good match to fattier meats, such as duck or goose, pork in various forms – cutlets, sausages or salamis – or foie gras or chicken liver parfait with quince paste or caramelised apples, or lobster with ginger, or octopus. Pair it with cheeses from its Alsace homeland, especially Munster. Avoid acidic foods with lots of citrus or vinegar.

RECOMMENDED PRODUCER
'Les Princes Abbés', Domaines Schlumberger
Other producers Boxler; Zind-Humbrecht; Hugel; Dirler-Cadé; Weinbach; Ostertag; Deiss; Bott-Geyl

RECIPE RECOMMENDATION
Thai octopus salad ☞ *page 150*

GEWURZTRAMINER, NEW ZEALAND

STYLE & FLAVOUR Outside of Alsace, one of the best places to find great Gewurztraminer is in New Zealand; they are doing a great job with aromatic, off-dry varieties such as Pinot Gris, Riesling and Gewurtztraminer. The cool maritime climate of the country (see page 11) causes a long growing season, where aromatic flavours can gently develop. For this reason, Gewurztraminer here is less pungent than it can be from Alsace. The lipstick and eyeliner notes are a bit less prominent; we still find aromas of mango and orchard fruits, but much less intense spice, and also a slight ginger hint. The acidity tends to be higher and the alcohol lower.

Nick Nobilo, whose family owned the brand White Cloud, set out on his own to make Gewurztraminer in the 1960s, after his father let him experiment with varieties. He fell in love with this spicy, complex variety and created Vinoptima in Gisborne. He says this variety should be treated like a red, and leaves the wine on its skins for up to 20 hours to help extract flavours and phenolics from under the skins. Whereas Riesling wine relies on acidity (see page 50), he believes that Gewurztraminer relies on the balance of these phenolics with alcohol and residual sugar to make interesting wines.

Pockets of Gewurztraminer can now be found all over the world, probably more as winemaker projects rather than commercial ventures, as some customers can have a love or hate relationship with this variety. Chile, Australia (notably S C Pannell), California, Washington and Moldova are all making good wines.

WHAT FOOD GOES WELL All the foods that match with Alsace Gewurztraminer (see left). And tender New Zealand lamb cutlets, because one of the most simple food and wine matching techniques is that 'it goes with where it grows' (see page 38).

RECOMMENDED PRODUCER
'Riverpoint', Millton
Other producers Te Whare Ra; Stonecroft; Vinoptima; Lawson's Dry Hills

RECIPE RECOMMENDATION
Tandoori-spiced lamb cutlets, spiced aubergine & tamarind yogurt ☞ *page 252*

PINOT GRIS, ALSACE

STYLE & FLAVOUR Alsace remains one of France's greatly under-appreciated wine regions, which is surprising as there is so much there to love; the cuisine and the food and wine combinations are some of the best in France. The vineyards lie on beautiful slopes in the foothills of the Vosges mountains, looking as pretty as the Côte d'Or. These same mountains provide a rain shadow, keeping the area dry, hot and sunny; the dry conditions preserve the old, brightly coloured townhouses in the villages, giving the area a picture postcard feel.

Pinot Gris (the French name, Pinot Grigio is the Italian rendering) from Alsace can be dry or sweet, but most commonly is a rich off-dry style with powerful flavours of over-ripe pear, mango, kumquat, honeysuckle, lemon grass and ginger.

These wines are generally soft in acidity and warm in alcohol and, due to the pink skins of the grapes, may appear slightly copper coloured. Hot, dry autumns in Alsace allow growers to leave the grapes hanging until they slightly shrivel and become concentrated in flavour and sugar. The best examples are from the 51 Grand Cru vineyard sites found spread throughout Alsace. Good examples can also be found in the North American states of Washington and Oregon, Canada and even New Zealand.

WHAT FOOD GOES WELL Alsatian *flammekueche*: a paper-thin pizza-like base topped with cheese, bacon and onions, is a delicious match. Many Asian dishes work, and sweet-and-sour flavours are good, as heat and chilli are tempered by the sweetness. Try Singapore crab with chilli, or octopus with Thai dressing, or rabbit with mustard and cream. It is good with fattier foods, such as foie gras, duck, goose or charcuterie.

RECOMMENDED PRODUCER
'Clos des Capucins', Domaine Weinbach
Other producers Schlumberger; Trimbach; Zind-Humbrecht; Deiss; Ostertag; Boxler; Dirler-Cadé; Josmeyer; Hugel; Greystone; Ata Rangi (NZ); Burrowing Owl (Canada); Simčič (Slovenia)

RECIPE RECOMMENDATIONS
Thai octopus salad ☞ *page 150*
Choucroute garnie ☞ *page 237*

Italian white wine grapes

Italians have told me in the past that white wines are 'something you drink before you get to the red wine'. This seems quite unfair, as Italy makes some superb white wines as well as a lot of very simple 'table' whites.

The most widely planted white variety in Italy is Trebbiano (aka Ugni Blanc *in France), a fairly neutral grape. But the coastal and mountain regions are home to some amazing wines made with esoteric indigenous varieties little known (and generally not grown) outside the country, such as the Cortese and Erbaluce of Piedmont; Fiano, Furore and Greco of Campania; Fruilano and Ribolla Gialla of Friuli; Garganega of Veneto; Filari of Tuscany; Grechetto of Umbria; Bosco of Cinqueterre; plus Verdicchios and Vermentinos found throughout Italy. And of course not forgetting the Carricante, Catarratto, Grillo, Insolia, Grecanico and Malvasia of Sicily. And many others. Italy is complicated.*

FIANO DI AVELLINO

Along with Greco di Tufo (see below), this is the other great Campanian white wine, made with the Fiano grape close to the town of Avellino, not far from Naples and Mount Vesuvius. Fiano is a variety similar to Assyrtiko (see page 80) that can hold its acidity even in a hot climate. It is thought to have been the ancient Roman wine *Apianum*, and this word appears on bottles of Fiano even now. Tastewise it can be similar to Albariño (see page 80), with floral, peachy, white almond aromas and a crisp, fine acidity; it is seldom aged in oak. It's proving popular in Australia, in areas such as McLaren Vale.

WHAT FOOD GOES WELL Seafood and shellfish from Naples, fresh green salads, fennel salads, or drink it as an aperitif with local olives and smoked almonds.

RECOMMENDED PRODUCER

Feudi di San Gregorio

Other producers Pietracupa; Caggiano; Mastroberardino; Molettieri; Montevetrano; Coriole (Australia)

RECIPE RECOMMENDATION

Panzanella with sardines ☞ *page 170*

FRIULANO, FRIULI

Friuli makes some of Italy's best white wines, including some sensational Sauvignon Blancs (see page 58). Friuli has become the home to many quite radical 'orange' winemakers, including Josko Gravner and Saša Radikon. They are making intensely coloured and flavoured skin-contact wines from the Ribolla Gialla grape variety. Other interesting white wine grape varieties found in this region include Picolit, as well as the red varieties Refosco and Schioppettino.

For me, the greatest producer in this region is Livio Felluga, who is making perhaps Italy's finest white wine, Terre Alte. It was first created in 1981, and is a blend of Friulano, Pinot Bianco and Sauvignon Blanc, with the Friulano being aged in oak casks. The wine is delicate in youth, but opens up with some ageing to become a seamlessly integrated white wine with a floral, honeyed melon character, and stone fruit, acacia and jasmine blossom on the nose.

WHAT FOOD GOES WELL Chicken, game and poultry with cream sauces, traditional Italian antipasti, as well as cheese-based pasta dishes.

RECOMMENDED PRODUCER

'Terre Alte', Livio Felluga

Other producers Gravner; Miani

RECIPE RECOMMENDATION

Vincisgrassi ☞ *page 234*

GRECO DI TUFO

This is located in Campania, close to the town of Avellino, which is also famous for its Fiano (see left). Greco di Tufo is thought to come from Greece, hence the name, and was used in the famous wine of the Roman Empire, *Falernia*.

The grapes can contain a lot of phenolic compounds, which explains the deep colour of the wines and their aromatic qualities, not dissimilar to those of Viognier, with its peachy stone fruit flavours and herbaceous, green hints.

The town of Tufo took its name from tuffa, a soil of volcanic ash and soft limestone, similar to the soils of Vouvray.

WHAT FOOD GOES WELL Pasta dishes from Naples, while this wine will cope with richer styles of sauce, too.

RECOMMENDED PRODUCER

Greco 'Mastro', Mastroberardino

Other producers Caggiano; Colli di Lapio; Montevetrano; Pietracupa

RECIPE RECOMMENDATION

Mini tomato bruschetta with baked bocconcini in prosciutto ☞ *page 295*

SOAVE

The wines of Soave in the Veneto region of north-east Italy can cause excitement or terror in the breasts of wine drinkers, as cheap Soave certainly doesn't excite anyone's senses, whereas Soave Classico from the original vineyard area, grown on volcanic soils, can produce some truly delicious wines.

The grape variety used is Garganega, with the addition of Trebbiano. This works well for many producers, notably Pieropan with its superb 'Calvarino', or 100 per cent Garganega 'La Rocca', although unfortunately Trebbiano is also used as a 'filler' grape by the cooperatives in the region, to make high volumes of lower-quality Soave. Winemaker Roberto Anselmi's protest against the addition of bland Trebbiano to the Soave blend caused him to quit the Soave DOC in 2000, and create his own superb Soave made from Garganega, with 10 per cent Chardonnay added, which he calls Capitel Croce. This only has an IGT Veneto classification, which is considered the second status appellation down from a DOC, however it is one of the best Soaves you can find.

WHAT FOOD GOES WELL Generally, Soave is a good match with rabbit, chicken and poultry, game birds such as pheasant and pigeon, and Italian sausage. It is also lovely with soft cream cheeses, dried fruits and nuts, and fresh pears.

RECOMMENDED PRODUCER

Capitel Croce, Anselmi

Other producers Pieropan; Inama; Prà; Coffele

RECIPE RECOMMENDATION

Chargrilled rabbit leg stuffed with cotechino, fried polenta & oven-dried cherry tomatoes ☞ *page 217*

TREBBIANO D'ABRUZZO

The Abruzzo region is on Italy's eastern coast, by the Adriatic. This mountainous region produces red wines from the Montepulciano grape, and whites from Trebbiano. (Though what the locals call 'Trebbiano' may actually be a variety called Bombino Bianco; as I've said, Italian wines take a lifetime of study…)

One of the oldest and greatest names in Italian winemaking, Valentini, makes Trebbiano here. As would be expected

from such a producer, his Trebbiano is not like any other. Only a small amount of the best grapes will ever go into making this wine. It has extraordinary ageability and its flavours can be of lemon and straw, with a hint of smokiness and a lovely, saline, oyster shell finish.

WHAT FOOD GOES WELL Generally, seafood and shellfish given the Adriatic treatment, such as *fritto misto*, or fried courgette; also green, herbal flavours.

RECOMMENDED PRODUCER

Valentini

Other producers Pepe; Masciarelli; Nicodemi

RECIPE RECOMMENDATION

Parmesan-battered courgette flower, courgette vinaigrette, anchovies & soft-boiled quail's eggs ☞ *page 301*

VERNACCIA DI SAN GIMIGNANO

Based around the Tuscan hill town of San Gimignano, this is considered to be one of Italy's finest white wines and is one of Tuscany's only white wines. The soils of this region are clay mixed with the seashell remnants of the ancient Ligurian Sea, and the mineral composition of this soil gives the wine its crisp, dry acidity and slightly bitter almond-like finish. The wine became famous after it was the first to be granted DOC status in 1966, after the DOC regulations were brought in.

WHAT FOOD GOES WELL Summery styles of food, fresh salads and light green vegetables such as broad beans and peas. Vernaccia and the foods that match it work as a good contrast to the meat dishes and their accompanying big reds found in Tuscany.

RECOMMENDED PRODUCER

Cesani

Other producers Teruzzi & Puthod; Selvabianca; Strozzi; Panizzi

RECIPE RECOMMENDATION

Orecchiette of summer vegetables, capers, preserved lemon & feta ☞ *page 309*

ABOVE Tuscan vineyards, with their iconic cypress and olive trees lining the roads and driveways to villas. The whole prospect turns a magnificent terracotta orange as the sun sets over the Mediterranean

Other white wine grapes

ALBARIÑO/ALVARINHO

STYLE & FLAVOUR From the north-west of Iberia (and known in Portugal as *Alvarinho,* where, with Loureiro, it makes Vinho Verde). The cool, wet climate makes this a green, fertile place.

The wines are usually unoaked, with high acidity and fresh orange and peach notes and honeysuckle and bergamot tones, or green apple. Many winemakers leave skins in contact with the juice, to bring a high phenolic flavour and a yeasty aroma, with crisp saline acidity.

The neighbouring region of Rueda also produces excellent dry, crisp wines from Verdejo; reminiscent of Sauvignon Blanc, they too match Atlantic seafood, while Galicia has its high-acid Godello.

Moving around Spain's coastline to the Basque country, they enjoy the seafood with the tart white wines of the Txakolí/Chacolí grape, poured from a height into glassware, to aerate them.

Great examples of Albariño can now be found in Uruguay and New Zealand.

WHAT FOOD GOES WELL Grilled Atlantic seafood, such as bass, cod, hake with butterbeans, shellfish and crustaceans.

RECOMMENDED PRODUCERS

Bodegas Naia; Pazo Señorans; Quinta da Soalheiro (Portugal)

Other producers Pérez; Valminor; Paco & Lola; Bouza; Pazo de Villerai; Mendoza; Neudorf

RECIPE RECOMMENDATIONS

Fillet of wild sea bass, warm salad of heritage tomatoes ☞ *page 182*

Piri piri tiger prawns ☞ *page 141*

Chargrilled asparagus, romesco sauce, toasted almonds & fennel ☞ *page 310*

ALIGOTÉ

STYLE & FLAVOUR The second main white variety in Burgundy. The grape was much more prevalent before *phylloxera* in the late 1800s (see page 10), found in famous vineyards such as Montrachet. Long considered to be the inferior grape, its wines produce tart, thin styles of wine; it is used to make a Kir cocktail where crème de Cassis is added to balance the acidity. Aligoté found fame again in 1997, when Bouzeron in the Côte Chalonnais was granted its own AOC for the grape; Aubert de Villaine and wife Pamela pushed for recognition for the variety. The Aligoté Doré grape, when yields are kept low, can make good wine.

WHAT FOOD GOES WELL Snails, roast Bresse chicken with tarragon, soft cheeses from the area, such as Charolais.

RECOMMENDED PRODUCER

Domaine A & P de Villaine

Other producers Coche-Dury; Mortet; Ponsot; Ramonet

RECIPE RECOMMENDATION

Escargots à la Bourguignonne

☞ *page 223*

ASSYRTIKO

STYLE & FLAVOUR A remarkable grape from Santorini, a remarkable place. It is a collection of islands formed as the result of a cataclysmic volcanic explosion.

The soil is based on volcanic ash with some limestone, low in organic matter. *Phylloxera* cannot thrive here, so some root systems are up to 400 years old.

The grape holds its acidity well in the fierce heat, helped by the extreme winds that blow across Santorini. These can be problematic at flowering time, so the vines are woven into nest-like baskets (see right). Vital moisture is collected when, after a cool night, condensation occurs in the baskets. It makes a focused, elegant, complex wine, crystal-clear with sharp acidity of lemon pith and fennel.

Assyrtiko can be unoaked, oaked or sun-dried to make delectably sweet Vin Santo or a historic wine, *Nychteri* ('picked at night'), which is slightly off-dry, usually oxidised and high in alcohol: a shock at first, but delicious and unique.

Greece provides a wealth of other exciting grapes such as Malagousia, Aithiri, Savatiano, Roditis and Vidiano.

WHAT FOOD GOES WELL Seafood, fennel, crunchy aromatic veg such as peppers.

RECOMMENDED PRODUCER

'Kavalieros', Domaine Sigalas (or his Nychteri)

Other producers Argyros; Hatzidakis; Vassaltis; Karamolegos; Attiki; Gerovassiliou; Jim Barry (Australia)

RECIPE RECOMMENDATION

Tempura squid, preserved lemon, marinated fennel & spicy tomato salsa

☞ *page 153*

BACCHUS

STYLE & FLAVOUR Created out of a cross of Sylvaner and Riesling grapes, further crossed with Müller-Thurgau. It's an early-ripening variety that produces fruit with good sugar, and keeps its acidity if picked slightly under-ripe. It wasn't commercially available until the 1970s, when it did well in Germany's cool climate, but plantings have decreased. England approved the variety in 1998 and it was subsequently mentioned by wine writer Oz Clarke as the UK's alternative to Sauvignon Blanc, due to its pungent, overly aromatic character. The aromas – green apple skin and freshly cut celery – may be too intense for some.

WHAT FOOD GOES WELL The apple and celery aromas make Bacchus a great accompaniment to a classic Waldorf salad, with celery, apples and grapes, as well as to other salads.

RECOMMENDED PRODUCER

Chapel Down

Other producers Camel Valley; Flint; 'Balfour', Hush Heath; Winbirri; Wirsching

RECIPE RECOMMENDATION

Waldorf salad ☞ *page 307*

ENCRUZADO

STYLE & FLAVOUR Portugal, like Greece or Italy, has a myriad of unusual and delicious indigenous grapes. The main white variety in the region of Dão is Encruzado, with 300 hectares planted on an elevated plateau surrounded by granite mountain ranges. Warm, long summers with cool nights develop fruit flavours in the day and acid at night.

Here, the wine takes well to lees stirring and barrel ageing, where its rich texture supports the oak well and it can make aromatic wines with the weight and elegance of fine white Burgundy. The historic Buçaco Palace hotel produces one of the country's classic white wines, Buçaco Branco Reservado, blended using Maria Gomes and Bical grapes from Bairrada with Encruzado from Dão. A stunning wine for long ageing.

WHAT FOOD GOES WELL Rich dishes work well, with nuts, or fatty pork.

RECOMMENDED PRODUCER

Quinta dos Roques, Dão

Other producers Quinta de Saes; Quinta dos Carvalhais; Filipa Pato

RECIPE RECOMMENDATION

Roast monkfish in pancetta, lamb's sweetbreads & peas ☞ *page 176*

Roast monkfish, arrocina beans, morcilla & clams ☞ *page 175*

FURMINT

STYLE & FLAVOUR First mentioned in the Tokaj region of Hungary in 1571. It is a high acid variety, susceptible to *botrytis*. The convergence of two rivers of different temperatures – Bogrod and Tisza – cause morning mist, responsible for the mould that makes the famous sweet Aszú wines (see page 124). Some partially botrytised grapes make full-bodied rich, dry wines called *Szamorodni* or 'as it comes'. The amount of sugar in the wine will depend how much *botrytis* there was in the bunch and defines the style as *édes* (sweet) or *száraz* (dry). It can be like a lighter Azsú and be similar in style to Sauternes. The dry style may be kept in barrel under a layer of *flor* similar to Fino Sherry (see page 125), giving complex flavours of nuts, apricots and dried figs. The wines are rich, full-bodied and ageable, with great acidity and length.

WHAT FOOD GOES WELL Rich chicken dishes and charcuterie, or creamy curries.

RECOMMENDED PRODUCER
'Szent Tamáz', István Szepsy
Other producers Disznókő; Royal Tokaji; Királyudvar; Dereszla; Tinon

RECIPE RECOMMENDATION
Chicken liver parfait, orchard fruit compote & toasted sourdough ☞ *page 200*

GRÜNER VELTLINER

STYLE & FLAVOUR The most widely planted variety found in Austria. Here it produces stunning wines, especially in the Wachau, Kamtal and Kremstal. Grüner has been trendy over the last decade, even earning the title 'Grü-Ve'.

The wines are exciting, often with a white radish spiciness and electrifying acidity if from the south-facing slopes of the Wachau. (They have a softer, broader texture if from the Kamtal and Kremstal.) The finest expression may be the top tier, Smaragd, where, to reach the alcohol levels required, it is left late on the vine to concentrate and catch a little *botrytis*. These wines are fermented dry and can reach alcohol levels of 14.5 per cent, but gain a rich texture and honeyed notes.

Grüner is also finding success across America from Oregon to California, as well as in Australia and New Zealand.

WHAT FOOD GOES WELL Austrian goose with spätzle, pork, trout, schnitzel.

RECOMMENDED PRODUCER
'Loibenberg', Weingut Emmerich Knoll
Other producers Schloss Gobelsburg; Hirtzberger; Domäne Wachau; Pichler; Bründlmayer; Prager

RECIPE RECOMMENDATION
Scotch Burford Brown eggs ☞ *page 224*

BELOW Due to arid ground and strong winds on Santorini, Assyrtiko vines are woven into a basket shape called a *kouloura*

KOSHU

STYLE & FLAVOUR This is considered an indigenous Japanese variety, though as it's a *Vitis vinifera* (or at least a *vinifera* cross, with indeterminate parentage) it must have come originally from Europe. As Japan's premier white grape, it accounts for 90 per cent of the 200 or so hectares of the country's small but dynamic wine industry. The grape itself is a pretty candy pink colour, thick-skinned and hardy against disease. It is grown on pergolas and, during the warm summer, the growers, in a meticulous Japanese manner, cover each bunch with a small paper disc that acts as a sunshade. These grapes in the warm Yamanashi Prefecture, surrounded by peach and cherry trees and in the gaze of Mount Fuji, give delicate flavours of yuzu citrus, lychee and peach.
WHAT FOOD GOES WELL Sushi, tempura, seafood and shellfish. Steamed dumplings of chicken and pork. Light salads and delicate Asian dishes containing lemongrass, miso or yuzu.
RECOMMENDED PRODUCER
'Cuvée Misawa', Grace Vineyards
Other producers Lumière, Haramo, Marufuji
RECIPE RECOMMENDATION
Herb-roasted fillet of salmon, fregola & summer vegetable salad ☞ *page 172*

MARSANNE/ROUSSANNE

STYLE & FLAVOUR The great double act of white grapes in the Rhône Valley – typically in the North – either made into a white wine, or blended into red wines in the more southerly appellations such as Hermitage and St-Joseph. At its best, it is a nutty, textured wine with marzipan-like qualities, honeysuckle and pear, but a firm mineral acidity; Robert Parker once wrote that Hermitage Blanc by Chave was like drinking liquid crystal.

In the Southern Rhône they are usually added to a blend, as they are naturally found scattered in vineyards and are collected as part of field blends. These can make the rare Châteauneuf-du-Pape Blanc. Some producers make wine from just Roussanne, as it can take oak well and produces full-bodied rich wines with weight, texture and longevity. Roussanne has more citrus, almost a verbena aroma, and a tauter acidity. Marsanne is also found in Switzerland, known as *Ermitage*. Both successfully make wines in Australia and California. The Southern Rhône valley white grapes stretch east into Provençe, west into the Languedoc/Roussillon and circle the Med. They include blends of Grenache Blanc, Marsanne, Roussanne, Viognier, Clairette and Rolle (Vermentino in Italy).
WHAT FOOD GOES WELL Roast chicken in cream with almonds, fish with butter.
RECOMMENDED PRODUCERS
Château de Beaucastel; 'Les Oliviers', Domaine Pierre Gonon
Other producers Rayas blanc; La Nerthe; Clos des Papes; Casèneuve; de la Source
RECIPE RECOMMENDATIONS
Dover sole meunière (Beaucastel) ☞ *page 156*
Pan-fried scallops, wild garlic mousseline potato (Gonon) ☞ *page 132*

PICPOUL

STYLE & FLAVOUR Ancient Languedoc variety that can be found as Picpoul Noir, Gris or Blanc, but is almost extinct in anything but the Blanc variety. Picpoul (*piquepoul* means 'lip-stinger') makes a light white wine with nervy and intense acidity. It can be used in the blend of grapes allowed for Châteauneuf-du-Pape, where it brings much-needed freshness.

The best is found in the AOC of Pinet, by the Thau lagoon close to Montpellier, where it provides a dry, citrussy wine to accompany Mediterranean seafood. Many of the grapes go to the local co-operative in Pinet, which does a good job producing this Muscadet of the Med.
WHAT FOOD GOES WELL Salads and shellfish with lemon, especially oysters.
RECOMMENDED PRODUCER
Domaine Gaujal
Other producers Pinet Co-operative; Genson
RECIPE RECOMMENDATION
Crisp spring vegetable salad with capers & preserved lemon ☞ *page 303*

RETSINA

STYLE & FLAVOUR Not actually a grape variety, but a style of wine famous in Greece. It is historically flavoured with resin from the Aleppo pine. Originally (2,000 years ago), the resin was used to seal amphorae and the flavour infused the wine. Made all over Greece, the best is from Attica, made mainly from the Savatiano, Assyrtito and Rhoditis grapes. It's a unique flavour: a strong resinous pine note, orange and lime peel with a saline tang.
WHAT FOOD GOES WELL Greek meze, or match it with seafood infused with pine.
RECOMMENDED PRODUCER
'Tear of the Pine', Kechris
Other producers Papagiannakos; Evinos; Tetramythos; Gaia
RECIPE RECOMMENDATION
Sea bream, Douglas Fir ☞ *page 185*

SAVAGNIN BLANC

STYLE & FLAVOUR A white variety of the Jura region in the French Alps. The pink version is found in Alsace as *Klevener de Heiligenstein* and the pink aromatic version as Traminer (latterly known as Gewurztraminer).

In the Jura it makes complex full-bodied wines, especially in *vin jaune* from Château-Chalon (not an estate, but an appellation for this style of wine). Here it is aged under a layer of *flor*, similar to Fino Sherry (see page 125), where it becomes nutty and rich, developing the flavour lactone sotolon, found in curry, fenugreek, walnuts and maple syrup (sounds odd, tastes delicious). In this time, it is said to evaporate by one sixth, so is put in a 62cl bottle called a *clavelin*.
WHAT FOOD GOES WELL Mature Comté cheese, or Morteau sausage and mustard.
RECOMMENDED PRODUCER
Château-Chalon, Domaine Berthet-Bondet
Other producers Tissot; Macle; Ganevat; Maire; Courbet
RECIPE RECOMMENDATION
Comté & walnut soufflé ☞ *page 312*

TORRONTÉS

STYLE & FLAVOUR I am not sure what vegetarians do in Argentina as the cuisine is based largely on huge portions of beef with plenty of fleshy Malbec. But when they must pause this diet, Torrontés Riojano is their white wine of choice. It's a cross of Criolla Chica and Muscat of Alexandria grapes and smells a lot like Gewurztraminer: orange peel, lychees, rose and jasmine; but is bone dry, high in acidity and doesn't have high alcohol or spicy richness. It would be great with seafood, but the vineyards are thousands of metres above sea level, so fish can't reach it. Cafayete in Salta and Catamarca produce the best. It makes a great aromatic aperitif before the steaks arrive.
WHAT FOOD GOES WELL Citrus salads, chicken, gazpacho, lighter Asian food.
RECOMMENDED PRODUCER
Bodega Colomé
Other producers El Esteco, Abel Mendoza, Etchart, Susana Balbo

RECIPE RECOMMENDATION
Coronation chicken salad, apple, celery hearts & golden raisins ☞ *page 203*

VIOGNIER

STYLE & FLAVOUR Condrieu, in the north of the Northern Rhône Valley, is a small (167 hectare) appellation, spiritual home to the Viognier grape. It is grown on steep-sided terraces made of granite, flint and mica (known locally as *arzelle*), overlooking the Rhône river. The grape became near-extinct when plantings decreased to less than 12 hectares in the 1960s. Legend Georges Vernay saved the appellation, and grape, by his dogged belief in this now-treasured variety.

Condrieu is often barrel-fermented and matured with plenty of lees stirring, to give richly textured, lactic-tasting wine. Fruit characteristics are rich peaches, apricots, tropical fruits and floral notes such as honeysuckle. The barrel-aged versions show slightly nutty, granola-like flavours. Acidity tends to be soft and the wine shows warming alcohol.

It takes well to oak, which can bring a silky, lactic, yogurt note to the wines. The exception that proves the rule are the wines of Château Grillet (a neighbouring property of only 3.8 hectares, which has its own AOC), that have a laser-like mineral acidity and are much less lactic. Viognier can be fussy and worry vineyard managers, as it develops for a long time with no flavour profile before bursting out in musky apricot-scented aromas.

The Languedoc is making plenty of vin de pays Viognier, and it is also grown in the Southern Rhône as a blending component, often paired with Marsanne, Roussanne, Bourboulenc and Picpoul.

California warmly embraced Viognier, especially makers passionate for Rhône varieties, such as Josh Jensen of Calera, John Alban and the Rhône Rangers.

Viognier can be found in Piedmont, with Ascheri making some of the best. Successful Viognier is also grown in New Zealand, Australia and South Africa, either used on its own or as part of the co-ferment with Syrah, a typical practice in Côte-Rôtie (see page 94).

WHAT FOOD GOES WELL Salads with citrus. Shellfish and firm white fish with cream sauces, or stone fruits.

RECOMMENDED PRODUCERS
'Coteau du Vernon', Georges Vernay; Tahbilk
Other producers Cuilleron; Montez; Guigal; Gaillard; Château-Grillet; d'Arenberg; Calera; Staete Landt; Alpha Domus; By Farr; Bosca

RECIPE RECOMMENDATIONS
Pork & rabbit terrine, apricots, hazelnuts & yogurt dressing (Vernay) ☞ *page 220*
Dukkah-encrusted cod, dried apricot falafel, sumac yogurt (Tahbilk) ☞ *page 188*

...AND ORANGE WINES

STYLE & FLAVOUR Orange wines have become mainstream and they provide interesting flavours, textures and food matching opportunities. Makers claim this is how white wines were once made, leaving the skins in contact with the must and allowing a long, cold fermentation of up to 12 months in amphorae buried in the ground. A long contact with the skins is how red wines are made and makes a quite different drink from the pale, limpid, clear white wines that became the norm 150 years ago, extracting phenolics from the skins to give a distinct orange colour. Extreme examples begin to resemble cider vinegar, but there are great orange wines. Georgia is leading the charge, and Pheasant's Tears, using the local Rkatsiteli grape, is excellent.

WHAT FOOD GOES WELL Salmon, tuna, roasted chicken and salads.

RECOMMENDED PRODUCERS
Pheasant's Tears; Millton; Raised by Wolves

RECIPE RECOMMENDATIONS
Black rice & squash salad, quinoa, cumin, orange & pomegranate ☞ *page 318*

ABOVE Steep terraces overlook the Danube in Austria's Wachau. Riesling prefers the *gneiss* rock faces, while Grüner Veltliner prefers the richer colluvial soil at the base of the hillsides

CHAMPAGNE
FREDERIC SAVART
L'OUVERTURE - PREMIER CRU
PETITE MONTAGNE · BRUT
VINS SINGULIERS, IDENTITAIRES
CHAMPAGNE VINTAGE
1982
KRUG
REIMS
GUSBOURNE
GUSBOURNE

Champagne & sparkling wines

Through the magical process of fermentation, yeast eats up sugar and excretes both carbon dioxide and alcohol, which it can tolerate up to a maximum of 15 per cent; more than that kills it. In sparkling winemaking, the process of autolysis means the dead yeast breaks down over time, adding a toasty, nutty, bready character to the wine. Think about this next time you are enjoying a nice glass of fizz...

YOUNG CHAMPAGNE

STYLE & FLAVOUR Champagne in its youth is the perfect aperitif wine, it is a celebratory drink and nothing starts off a party better. The appetite-stimulating crisp acid and lively bubbles, along with lemon, pear and toasted nut flavours, can be the perfect match to luxury foods such as caviar, smoked salmon and oysters, or to more humble, salty foods such as nuts and olives. Pastry canapés work well, as do bite-sized deep-fried items where richness is cut by the acidity. Young Champagnes are good with shellfish such as oysters, in the classic Valentine's Day aphrodisiac pairing. Avoid drinking them with anything sweet, as this accentuates the wine's acidity to unpleasant levels.

It is recommended to serve this style of Champagne quite cold, at around 8°C, whereas older Champagnes are better served, like white Burgundy, at 12°C.

RECOMMENDED PRODUCER

'Les Chétillons', Pierre Péters

Other producers Egly-Ouriet; Agrapart & Fils; Savart; Tarlant; Chartogne-Taillet; Lahaye

RECIPE RECOMMENDATION

Cheese straw trio ☞ *page 293*

AGED CHAMPAGNE

STYLE & FLAVOUR Champagne is a cold place for growing grapes; if the method of creating bubbles in the bottle had never been discovered, then Champagne may not even exist as a wine region, likely it would be a spirit-producing area instead. The grapes produce a thin, acidic juice, and it is unlikely that wines made from this juice would have become popular. However, this is precisely the kind of juice they need to make the base wine for Cognac or Armagnac.

The area became famous because many of France's kings and queens were crowned at the Notre Dame Cathedral in Reims before enjoying a hedonistic float back down the Marne River to Paris, while drinking the local wines.

Champagne gets its rich flavour from bottle ageing. The cold climate produces acidic, tart grapes that are turned into something magical by the addition of yeast, sugar and time. A second fermentation occurs in the bottle, and trapped carbon dioxide dissolves into the wine, creating bubbles. The dead yeast falls to the bottom of the bottle and, over time, imparts toasty, nutty, brioche-like flavours; this process is called autolysis.

Mature vintages will see the fruit character change from pear and citrus to dried mango and honeysuckle. With Champagnes more than 20 years old, mushroom and truffle aromas can develop, giving a sublime complexity.

WHAT FOOD GOES WELL River fish such as trout and perch with Champagne beurre blanc and girolles. Lobster or langoustine with mango and toasted nuts. Great-quality chickens, such as those from Bresse. Simple risotto with shaved white truffle. Or a good French soft cheese such as Brie de Meaux, layered with black truffle or served with truffle honey.

RECOMMENDED PRODUCER

Dom Pérignon (20 years +)

Other producers Bollinger RD; Krug; Collin; Dom Ruinart; Bouchard; Henriot Cuvée des Enchanteleurs; 'Vénus', Agrapart & Fils

RECIPE RECOMMENDATION

Champagne & white Alba truffle risotto ☞ *page 314*

SPARKLING WINE

STYLE & FLAVOUR Most wine-growing countries produce a sparkling wine, using the traditional Champagne process. The base for classic sparkling wine needs to be a tart, acidic wine, so warmer climate countries struggle to keep that acidity without actually acidifying the must. Certain cooler New World areas, such as the Californian Sonoma Coast, Tasmania, and Central Otago in New Zealand, are producing the most successful bottles.

In Spain, Cava is available in a whole range, from inexpensive up to the top level single-vineyard wines labelled as Cava de Paraje Calificado, the equivalent of a Grand Cru in the Cava world.

Over the last ten years, Prosecco has become amazingly popular and, as the second fermentation happens in sealed tanks rather than in the bottle, is also inexpensive. The best are found within the Valdobbiadene area of Veneto, but Italy's top sparkling wine can be found in Lombardy, in Franciacorta, and comes closer to Champagne in terms of quality.

But the real success story is the rise of English sparkling wines, many of which are planted in similar chalk soils to those of Champagne, and, in this cool northern European climate, produce a similar base wine, too. The climate of the English south east makes it a particularly popular region for growing vines, especially in the counties of Kent, Hampshire and Sussex.

WHAT FOOD GOES WELL Many things pair well with sparkling wines, due to the mouth-cleansing nature of acid and bubbles. They are great with fast food, as the acidity counterbalances the salt and fattiness of deep-fried foods.

Coming away from the high street and back to the dinner table, salty nuts and pastries, olives or seafood canapés can make a nice match before a meal. Try them with seafood, sashimi or tempura.

RECOMMENDED PRODUCER

Gusbourne (UK)

Other producers House of Arras (Tasmania); Quartz Reef (New Zealand); Roederer Estate (California); Nyetimber (UK); Ca' del Bosco (Franciacorta, Italy)

RECIPE RECOMMENDATION

Cheese straw trio ☞ *page 293*

OPPOSITE Frédéric Savart L'Ouverture 1er Cru; vintage Krug; Gusbourne Blanc de Blancs, England

NOBLE GRAPES

6

PINOT NOIR AND GAMAY

PINOT NOIR IS a difficult and capricious grape. It's thin-skinned. It's prone to rot and mildew. And it loses all its finesse if over-cropped at high yields. Its name is possibly derived from the French for 'pine' and 'black' ('pine' as its berries are tightly packed like a pine cone's scales). It favours cooler conditions; growing Pinot Noir in too hot a climate produces jammy, heavy flavours and – as it's naturally a warm alcohol grape – burning levels of alcohol. The berries are small, low in anthocyanins (due to thin skins) and make wines that are pale in colour.

Despite all these problems, Pinot Noir remains the Holy Grail grape to master for many winemakers. In fact, ask any wine lover which the first 'wow' wine was they tasted, and they'll often tell you it was a Pinot Noir from Burgundy. It has been said that Bordeaux is a wine that is enjoyed above the neck – an intellectual wine – whereas Burgundy is enjoyed below the waist. I won't explain further.

Pinot Noir has many different clones and mutates easily. Specific clones are used for high-quality wines, such as the Pinot Fin of Burgundy's best vineyards, or the Pinot Droit, which has bigger berries and produces less elegant wines. Famous clones came out of Burgundy in the 1970s, such as the Pommard and Dijon clones, along with the less romantically named 113, 114 and 777. With varying degrees of success, the grape continues to be planted around the world, with Burgundy remaining its home, though very successful Pinot Noir is coming from the Loire Valley around Sancerre, Germany (called Spätburgunder there), California's coastal regions, Chile, Australia and New Zealand, plus, of course, large amounts are used in sparkling wines, especially Champagne.

In the best wines, Pinot Noir's flavour is ethereal and delicate, with multi-layered flavours of red berries with leather, spice and bacon, a solid backbone of acidity and silky tannins, a grippy cranberry-like structure for Burgundian wines and dark cherry and less earthy flavours for those from warmer countries.

Gamay, the Beaujolais grape, is a close cousin flavour-wise to Pinot Noir, but was banned from Burgundy in 1395 when Philip the Bold, Duke of Burgundy, labelled it 'disloyal'. It's better suited to the granitic soils of Beaujolais anyway, and appears successfully in the Loire Valley, Oregon, Australia and Switzerland.

OPPOSITE Hundreds of years of observation by monastic orders, such as the monks of Cluny and Citeaux, have defined the Grands Crus in Burgundy. Here, from the Hill of Corton at the top of the Côte de Beaune, it was as simple as seeing where the snow melted first in spring; this identified the warmest areas, which would produce the ripest grapes

Pinot Noir

BURGUNDY CÔTE DE NUITS

STYLE & FLAVOUR This region is in the northern part of the Côte d'Or (the 'golden slope') or the Côte d'Orient (the 'slope that looks east'), and stretches from Dijon to Beaune. But, whereas the Côte d'Or is more famous for its white wines, the Côte de Nuits is famous for reds. It's home to some of the finest Pinot Noirs in the world. Driving south down the Côte d'Or is a must for every wine lover, as it's literally like driving through a wine list. The villages are spaced a few miles apart and are all famous: Gevrey-Chambertin, Morey-Saint-Denis, Chambolle-Musigny, Vosne-Romanée, Nuits-Saint-George, to name a few. The double-barrelled names often give an indication of that village's greatest vineyard, such as Le Chambertin in Gevrey, the Clos St-Denis in Morey and Musigny in Chambolle.

Generally, the reds here are heavier and richer than those of the Côte de Beaune (see below), with more muscular tannins and weight. All of the red Grands Crus are found in the Nuits, except one: Corton. The best vineyards lie mid-slope, where the limestone bedrock is exposed and where vines receive maximum sunlight; at the base of the slopes, more clay means less well-draining soils and lower-quality grapes.

Excluding Pauillac, perhaps the world's most prominent wine village is here too: Vosne-Romanée, home to the legendary Domaine de la Romanée-Conti and their numerous Grand Cru wines.

In general the wine of Nuits-Saint-George, Clos de Vougeot and Gevrey-Chambertin are the most robust and long-lived, Vosne-Romanée being silky and elegant and Chambolle-Musigny being floral and charming.

WHAT FOOD GOES WELL The strong flavours of game birds such as partridge, grouse and pheasant will work well with aged Burgundy; with younger wines try the French classics such as boeuf Bourguignon, *oeufs en meurette* and *coq au vin*, duck confit, rabbit, or rare-cooked Charolais beef. Charcuterie and *pâté de campagne* work well, as do veal chop with morel sauce, offal such as *tête de veau*, liver, kidney or sweetbreads, and Burgundian cheese such as Époisses, Chambertin or Citeaux.

RECOMMENDED PRODUCER

'Bonnes-Mares', Domaine Dujac

Other producers Domaine de la Romanée-Conti; Rousseau; Mortet; Domaine des Lambrays; Clos de Tart; Méo-Camuzet; Leroy; Mugnier; Comtes Georges de Vogüé; Cathiard; Roumier; Rouget; Dugat; Geantet-Pansiot; Groffier; Damoy; Fourrier; Hudelot-Noëllat; Gouges

RECIPE RECOMMENDATION

Roast grouse with parsnip crisps ☞ *page 211*

BURGUNDY CÔTE DE BEAUNE

STYLE & FLAVOUR Travelling south from Nuits-Saint-George, you pass the impressive Hill of Corton (see previous page) and arrive at the historic town of Beaune. A must-see stop for visitors is the Hospice de Beaune, a medieval hospital still run today as a charity.

Generally, in the Côte de Beaune, there is less of the red loam soil than in the Côte de Nuits and, for that reason, the red wines tend to be softer in general. The exception to this is Pommard (so named because the area used to be filled with apple orchards), which produces firm and full-bodied Pinot Noir. Pommard and Volnay are the two best reds from here; Volnay is a little lighter. The communes of Savigny, Chorey, Monthélie and Santenay are also producing very good wines.

Take note that when visiting producers in the Côte d'Or, get a taxi or use a designated driver, as you will be tasting a lot of wines. In Bordeaux, you may be offered a taste of just one or two wines of the current vintage, but in Burgundy you could easily be looking at tasting 20. Most producers will have a generic Bourgogne, three or four Villages wines, Premiers Crus and one or two Grands Crus, all in red and white. But they may only make a couple of barrels of each, due to the Napoleonic laws of inheritance which state that when a landowner dies, he must divide his land equally among his children. This has resulted in Burgundy's vineyards becoming dissected into micro-parcels, sometimes just a couple of rows owned by a single producer. This vastly adds to the enigma of Burgundy and makes it a lifetime's work to understand its complexities.

WHAT FOOD GOES WELL As for Côtes de Nuits (see above).

RECOMMENDED PRODUCER

Volnay 1er Cru 'Les Caillerets', Marquis d'Angerville

Other producers Lafarge; Domaine de Montille; Tollot-Beaut; Domaine de Courcel; Château de Pommard; Bouchard Aîné et Fils; Guillemot; Moreau; Arnoux; Delagrange; Bize; Drouhin; Rossignol; Lamy; Pavelot; Juillot

RECIPE RECOMMENDATION

Oeufs en meurette ☞ *page 196*

OPPOSITE Kutch, McDougall Ranch, Sonoma; Volnay 1er Cru 'Clos des Chênes', Domaine Michel Lafarge (Beaune); Gevrey-Chambertin 1er Cru 'Les Cazetiers', Domaine Armand Rousseau (Côte de Nuits); Fleurie 'Le Printemps' Gamay, Domaine Yvon Métras; Neudorf Moutere, Nelson

2016
Kutch
Volnay
Clos des Chênes
2013
2009
Gevrey-Chambertin
1er CRU "LES CAZETIERS"
GRAND VIN DE BOURGOGNE
DOMAINE ARMAND ROUSSEAU PÈRE & FILS
Fleurie
Le Printemps
NEUDORF
MOUTERE
PINOT NOIR
2015
WINE OF NEW ZEALAND

Pinot Noir

NEW WORLD

STYLE & FLAVOUR The first wine region outside of Burgundy to start making top-quality Pinot Noir was Oregon, when David Lett started The Eyrie Vineyards in the 1960s. Nowadays, great Pinot Noir is being made in America, Australia and New Zealand. A common practice for some winemakers is to ferment the grapes as a whole bunch without taking them off the stems (destemming), giving a herbaceous flavour to the wines and adding tannin, plus the stems will absorb some alcohol and colour, useful in warmer climates.

NEW ZEALAND New Zealand's success with Pinot Noir started with the arrival of the Abel clone, also known as the Ata Rangi clone, or Gumboot clone. There is a probably wildly exaggerated story regarding Malcolm Abel, a customs officer working at Wellington Airport. One day on duty, he discovered some Pinot Noir vine clippings that he couldn't allow into the country for quarantine reasons. But, as he had a vine nursery, he grew them and found them excellent. The story begins to lose credibility when apparently the clippings came from a famous vineyard in Burgundy and were carried on the 25-hour plane journey inside someone's gumboot. It loses even more credibility when that person is said to have been in the All Blacks.

The clone has since proved itself to be one of the best and most successful in New Zealand. The country's finest Pinot Noir can be found in Central Otago, Martinborough and Marlborough.

AUSTRALIA Great Pinot Noir is coming from the cooler climate areas such as the Yarra Valley, or Port Philip Bay close to Melbourne. Here, two big peninsulas reach out into the ocean – Mornington and Geelong peninsulas – where cool ocean breezes are perfect for Pinot Noir.

CALIFORNIA The American state turned a corner after the release of the movie *Sideways* in 2004. It can be said a lot of Californian Pinot Noir back then was deep-coloured, over-oaked, powerfully alcoholic and lacking elegance. (Of course there are exceptions; some makers have always produced more subtle styles.) But nowadays, coastal Sonoma County and Santa Barbara are both producing world-class Pinot Noir.

WHAT FOOD GOES WELL Duck works very well, as its fattiness is balanced by Pinot's acidity. Cherries and red fruits have a natural affinity, as do bacon and smoky flavours and, with maturity, the earthy taste of mushrooms. Young Pinot Noir would be my choice for Christmas turkey dinner. Salmon and tuna can also work, but with teriyaki sauces rather than cream. It's an all-round good cheese and charcuterie wine too; try it with Brie de Meaux, Camembert or Brillat-Savarin, layered with black truffle slices or served with truffle honey (see page 41 for more on matching wines with cheese).

RECOMMENDED PRODUCER

'La Côte', Domaine de la Côte, Santa Barbara

Other producers Hirsch; Kutch; Littorai; Radio Coteau; Calera; Williams Selyem; Lingua Franca; Eyrie; Antica Terra; Serene; Adelsheim; Peter Michael Winery (all USA). Felton Road; Bell Hill; Ata Rangi; Neudorf; Burn Cottage (all New Zealand). Mac Forbes; By Farr; Bass Phillip; Paringa Estate; Domaine A (all Australia). Hamilton Russell; Bouchard Finlayson (both SA). Viña Leyda (Chile)

RECIPE RECOMMENDATION

Spiced duck breast, stir-fried greens & cherry glaze ☞ *page 206*

ABOVE The setting sun over Los Carneros, an area that straddles both the Sonoma and Napa Valleys and enjoys the cooling effect of fog from San Pablo Bay

Gamay

BEAUJOLAIS

STYLE & FLAVOUR Gamay has had a bit of a chequered past. Originally banned from the region of Burgundy by the Dukes of Burgundy in the 14th century, for the sin of being considered inferior to the noble Pinot Noir, Gamay was sent down south to the granitic soils of Beaujolais. The region eventually became famous for Beaujolais Nouveau, which started a craze in the 1950s.

The idea was that, on the third Thursday in November at midnight, wineries could release their wines, and they actively encouraged consumers to race one another to get them back home and drunk. City boys of the 1980s probably remember drinking plenty of Georges DuBoeuf Beaujolais Nouveau with their bacon and eggs for breakfast. There were elaborate ways to transport the wine, including by hot air balloon, private jet, antique car… even elephant. This made the wines very famous, but killed a lot of their credibility.

And, as you can imagine, a wine that had only just finished its fermentation and had been recently bottled would not be showing at its best. It was generally dominated by tart cranberry notes and a grippy acidity, with the banana-like ester flavour of carbonic maceration that is used widely in Beaujolais.

But Beaujolais is definitely undergoing a renaissance. The ten cru villages are where the finest wines can be found, with the two most famous being Morgon and Fleurie. The best makers of Beaujolais can make some truly stunning wines. A lot of producers have started to make these styles of wine naturally, so have been boosted by the growth of the natural wine movement.

In the glass, Gamay has a distinctive purple colour and similar characteristics to those of Pinot Noir. It has fresh, defined, crunchy red fruits on the palate – raspberry, cranberry and cherry – is usually more gentle in alcohol than its cousin and is often oaked less, too.

WHAT FOOD GOES WELL Steak tartare, roast Bresse chicken with slivers of black truffle under the skin, charcuterie and pâtés, rabbit or duck rillettes, coq au vin, or salads with pomegranate or cranberry. Try duck with light Asian spices or confit duck leg on lentils and bacon lardons for something rustic but delicious.

RECOMMENDED PRODUCER
Morgon 'Côte du Py', Jean Foillard
Other producers Lapierre; Thévenet; Thivin; Liger-Belair; Breton; Rottiers; Yvon Métras

RECIPE RECOMMENDATION
Steak tartare ☞ *page 258*

BELOW Granitic soils create the bucolic rolling hillsides in Beaujolais

NOBLE GRAPES

7

SYRAH

THE SPIRITUAL HOME of good Syrah is the Northern Rhône region of France; wines from Hermitage and Côte-Rôtie excel. And when I travel around the world, bottles of Syrah are always standing empty on winery walls, because it's a variety that winemakers love to drink.

The best expressions of Syrah are silky-smooth with deep blackberry fruit, black pepper spice, a crisp acidity and an earthy gameyness. Bear with me on this: the very greatest Syrah is like roadkill: it's a mess of bloody fur and guts. It evolves into lovely truffley mushroom, damp forest floor gameyness with age.

The New World style of these wines is called 'Shiraz' (which has caused some confusion about its origins, because there is also a town in Iran called Shiraz). Shiraz was popularised by the Australians. And, usually, if you see the word 'Shiraz' on a label, it will indicate a richer style with very ripe blackberries and almost sweet mulberries (because of the sugar and the sun). It is usually aged in new oak and has smoke and leather under a meaty bacon character, so it still has a bestial quality even in its simplest expression. Imagine a sirloin steak covered in black pepper about to go on the barbecue… that's Syrah. The wine works particularly well with red meat, and of all the game to which it is suited, venison is its most natural accompaniment.

The DNA parentage of Syrah, surprisingly, shows the grape is a cross between Mondeuse Blanche and Dureza; one from the Savoie and the other from the Ardèche. And the most famous clone is found in the Northern Rhône: Sérine.

Syrah works well in blends, as it calms the jammy and fruity characteristics both of Grenache from the Southern Rhône and of Châteauneuf-du-Pape. Most notably, it is sublime in the famous combination of Syrah and Viognier, grapes traditionally co-fermented together in Côte-Rôtie (see overleaf). Syrah is now planted all over the world and seems to particularly like hillside sites and warm climates. Sonoma, Napa and the Central Coast in California, New Zealand's Hawke's Bay and the Swartland in South Africa are all making great Syrah, along with Australia and France, and even more surprising places such as the Judean Hills of Israel; Rhône star Alain Graillot also makes good Syrah in Morocco.

OPPOSITE Gnarled old-vine Syrah (see page 108) in the Eden Valley, Australia

Syrah

HERMITAGE

STYLE & FLAVOUR The Northern Rhône doesn't have a classification system, but if it did, Hermitage would definitely be a Grand Cru. It is located on a hillside opposite the town of Tain, at a pronounced bend in the Rhône river. As the Rhône travels south, its path curves around the village of Tain and the hill of Hermitage sits on the southern bank of the river. It has 120 hectares of vineyards, including such famous sites as La Chapelle, Les Bessards, Les Greffieux and Le Méal. The most famous site is still probably La Chapelle, where a tiny chapel overlooks the river, made famous by the winemaker Paul Jaboulet Aîné.

It got its name from a knight, Chevalier de Sterimberg, a nobleman from the region who went to fight in the Holy Wars, doing lots of plundering, raping and pillaging as knights on tour tended to do. Upon returning to Tain, he realised he was probably going to Hell after he died and wanted to repent of his sins. He gave away all his wealth, built a small church on the top of the hill and lived the rest of his life there as a recluse or hermit, which in turn gave the name to the hill of Hermitage.

The wines here are full-bodied and elegant expressions of Syrah, using the Sérine clone, and they really require some ageing, because they are big, full-bodied and tannic when young. The wines turn into beautiful leathery, mushroomy, elegant expressions of the grape after ageing. Imagine an antique chair made of walnut, covered in ageing leather: that's the image that come to mind when drinking old Hermitage.

Producers such as Chapoutier and Guigal make great wines, but the best is Chave. His ultra-rare 'Cuvée Cathelin' sells for crazy prices and is an exquisite treat.

WHAT FOOD GOES WELL Aged Hermitage can match with some very fine foods, as the bottle won't be cheap, so you might as well push the boat out. Try simply roasted venison, or other game dishes such as hare and wild boar, or lamb or duck. Think woodland flavours: truffles, chestnuts and mushrooms.

RECOMMENDED PRODUCER

Domaine Jean-Louis Chave

Other producers Chapoutier; Guigal; Paul Jaboulet Aîné; Ferraton Père & Fils; Graillot

RECIPE RECOMMENDATION

Parsnip-topped hare parmentier

☞ *page 218*

CÔTE-RÔTIE

STYLE & FLAVOUR The town of Ampuis played a part in ancient history, as the Romans had an outpost here, and, in this region, evidence of viticulture can be traced back to the 2nd century BC. The vineyards are located on a steep hillside of the Rhône river, where they are protected from the strong Mistral winds that blow down from the Savoie. As the vineyards are angled straight into the sun, the site received its name of the 'roasted slopes', which is what Côte-Rôtie literally means.

Syrah and Viognier are grown together here, usually occupying the same vineyards, and historically they have been picked together and co-fermented. Viognier ripens before Syrah, so when the Syrah grapes reach full maturity, the Viognier berries are over-ripe, slightly dessicated and packed full of sugar. So co-fermenting Viognier with Syrah acts as a natural chaptalisation (which is the process of adding sugar to increase alcohol levels).

This co-fermentation also stabilises the colour and brings some interesting aromatics to the blend, especially that of violet flowers. Up to 20 per cent Viognier is allowed to be added, but simply blending the two together will not cause the same result. These wines are fresh and focused with tart-but-dense blackberry fruit, earthy and leathery nuances with black pepper spice and purple (violet) flowers. Interestingly, the black pepper flavours are due to the presence of the aroma compound called sesquiterpene rotundone, which is found both in peppercorns and in the skin of Syrah grapes.

Côte-Rôtie became especially famous with Marcel Guigal's three 'La-La' wines: La Mouline, La Turque and La Landonne, all of which sell for large sums of money.

WHAT FOOD GOES WELL I roasted a venison loin with crushed black pepper and served it with a Port reduction, fresh blackberries and tuiles made from Parma ham and was quite pleased with the result when drinking it with Côte-Rôtie. Venison, lamb and peppered steak, all served on the bloody side and with sauces made from meat stocks, fresh berries and black olives, will work well. Also try garlic, thyme and rosemary, Provençal herbs and hard cheeses.

RECOMMENDED PRODUCER

'La Turque', Maison Guigal, or any of the 'Lala' wines, such as 'La Landonne' or 'La Mouline'

Other producers Gerin; Villard; Rostaing; Voge; Saint-Cosme; Tardieu-Laurent; Jamet; Montez, Domaine de Monteillet

RECIPE RECOMMENDATION

Peppered venison striploin, sprout tops & black pudding, blackcurrant jus

☞ *page 288*

OPPOSITE Ermitage 'Cuvée Cathelin', Domaine Jean-Louis Chave; Côte-Rôtie 'La Landonne', Maison Guigal; 'Le Sol', Craggy Range, Hawke's Bay; 'Hill of Grace', Henschke, South Australia

2009
ERMITAGE
DOMAINE
JEAN-LOUIS CHAVE
1997
LA LANDONNE
MCMXCVII
LA LANDONNE
CÔTE-RÔTIE
E. GUIGAL
LE SOL
GIMBLETT GRAVELS
2015
CRAGGY RANGE
HENSCHKE
Hill of Grace
2012
EDEN VALLEY

ANDRE ROCH

Syrah

NEW ZEALAND

STYLE & FLAVOUR Confusingly, the wine in this country is known as Syrah and not Shiraz. This is because winemakers globally use the names 'Syrah' and 'Shiraz' as a good indication stylistically of what you get in the bottle, prioritising style over geography: Old World earthiness and gameyness is labelled 'Syrah', while New World intensity and fruit annouces itself as 'Shiraz'. This is the former.

The cool climate of New Zealand makes wines from the Syrah grape that are more similar to those of the Rhône than those of Australia. At the moment, the production of Syrah in New Zealand is ridiculously tiny, but I wanted to include it here anyway, because these wines are world-class and show the perfect mix between the Old and New World styles.

Hawke's Bay is better known globally for its Chardonnay and its Cabernet-Merlot blends, but, to me, the Syrahs are the best wines from this region. They are usually grown on hillsides and are made according to a typical Côte-Rôtie model, often adding Viognier to the co-ferment (see page 94). These wines have ripe blackberry, mulberry and bramble fruit, with black pepper and that typical Syrah meatiness. They are riper than those from Côte-Rôtie. New Zealand's cool climate ensures structure, tannins and bright acidity, all in perfect balance.

WHAT FOOD GOES WELL New Zealand lamb, of course, with black olives and Provençal herbs, or try steak with black peppercorn sauce, or wild boar with the country's native sweet potato: kumara. Lightly spiced Indian foods also work well, as does barbecued pulled pork, or short ribs.

RECOMMENDED PRODUCER
'Le Sol', Craggy Range
Other producers 'Homage', Trinity Hill; 'Bullnose', Te Mata; 'Legacy', Vidal; Sileni

RECIPE RECOMMENDATION
Wild boar pie with kumara mash
☞ *page 238*

SOUTH AUSTRALIA

STYLE & FLAVOUR The Australians burst on to the international wine market in the 1980s, with their easy-to-read labels that were annotated by variety, which made them simple to understand. They looked fun, with images of kangaroos and surfboards rather then dusty old châteaux. Plus the wines were inexpensive and packed full of fruit, and you didn't have to wait ten years to drink them. Australia is a big country and there's lots of different styles of Shiraz. In the cooler climate areas such as Heathcote, The Grampians and the Adelaide Hills, the wines are fresh and herbaceous. But the iconic Aussie Shiraz is from the Barossa Valley, which has some of the oldest vines in the world. They were planted in the 1850s, when France was about to go through its *phylloxera* crisis (see page 10). These wines are typically full-bodied, jammy and rich, generous in alcohol, and often spend time ageing in American oak.

Although the diversity in Australian Shiraz makes it hard to categorise these wines as one style, Shiraz did prove a turning point for the Australian wine industry when Max Schubert, the head winemaker of Penfolds, travelled to France to look at vineyards in the 1940s. He was inspired by the vineyards of Hermitage, then returned home, excited about the prospect of making French-style wines with grapes from his mature vineyards. (Before that, the Australian wine industry was mostly concentrated on fortified Port and Sherry style wines.)

He called his wine Grange Hermitage: Grange is the outback name for a farm, and Hermitage as a salute to the French. His first vintage was in 1951, but it was not received well by the critics, who were used to a sweeter style; it was even said to have a taste like crushed ants. After some time in the bottle, the tannin, oak and fruit became more harmonised and open; retasting it, the critics hailed it as a work of genius. It turned a corner for the Australian wine industry, which realised it had the potential to make wines as great as those of France.

Incidentally, Penfolds is incredibly popular in China, as the lettering on the bottles is in red, which is considered lucky, while 'Penfolds' literally means 'running towards wealth' in Chinese.

WHAT FOOD GOES WELL Kangaroo, if you can find it (or even catch it!). Definitely garlic and roast beef, ox cheek, or barbecued meats, spicy sausages and smoked brisket. Think the bold flavours of roasted or flame-grilled meats, such as mutton, with cherries.

RECOMMENDED PRODUCER
'St Henri', Penfolds
Other producers 'Hill of Grace', Henschke; d'Arenberg; Clonakilla; Torbreck; Mount Mary; Jim Barry; Giaconda; Wendouree; Bird in Hand; Mitolo

RECIPE RECOMMENDATION
Confit shoulder of mutton, rosemary dauphinoise, buttered kale, sour cherries & Mum's mint relish ☞ *page 246*

LEFT The steep-sided and often terraced vineyards of Hermitage

NOBLE GRAPES

8

CABERNET SAUVIGNON

THIS IS THE famous grape of Bordeaux that, along with Burgundian Pinot Noir, has inspired more ambitious wines than any other grape... but there is one big difference. While Pinot is a fickle, fussy and capricious cat, Cabernet is a bouncy, eager-to-please dog. Pinot will only sleep on a silk cushion in a cool air-conditioned room, whereas Cabernet will kip on the porch, under the house or out by the bins, it's not picky.

The flavour profile of great Cabernet – inspired by the First Growth wines of the Médoc – has been attempted around the world. These efforts have produced some iconic wines: the great reds of Napa Valley, the Super-Tuscans of Italy, the wines of Australia's Coonawarra and Chile's Central Valley, as well as many of the reds from New Zealand's Hawke's Bay and Waiheke Island. The flavours are of streamlined blackcurrant fruit, freshly turned soil and a cedar cigar box note of elegant Havana tobacco. Plus, sometimes, the graphite, pencil-lead flavour of those deep gravel banks of the Médoc. Did you ever chew the end of your pencil through the wooden husk and down to the lead core when you were at school? If you did, I bet you love the flavour of Bordeaux wines.

The furious tail-wagging nature of Cabernet also means that it does not crave the luxuries of new French oak and gravel soils, but is happy wherever it's given a home, producing very decent wines from any type of soil or climate. As long as it's not too cold, it will be your friend. At the time of writing, the UK's biggest selling Cabernet is Casillero del Diablo ('the devil's cellar') from Concho y Toro in Chile, and it would be hard to find a more consistent, well-priced glass of wine in a last-minute dash to the corner shop.

Cabernet is popular because its flavours are pretty consistent, so consumers know what they're getting. And it's just as well, because, as China is becoming the world's second largest country under vine – and with 76 per cent of its plantings being Cabernet – there is going to be a lot of it around in future.

OPPOSITE Cabernet vines at Lokoya's Mount Veeder vineyard in Napa Valley

Cabernet Sauvignon

MÉDOC

STYLE & FLAVOUR The Médoc takes its name from the Latin *en medio* or 'in the middle', as the Médoc is a peninsula that points north from Bordeaux city out into the Atlantic Ocean to the west and the broad Garonne estuary (10km-wide at its mouth) to the east. It's almost like an island in the Atlantic. Originally, the Médoc was a wet, swampy area through which it was hard to pass; it was known mostly for raising (delicious) sheep on its salt marsh riverbanks.

In the 1600s, small streams, or *jalle*, were built through the Médoc as drainage channels by Dutch engineers. (The Dutch were important players in the history of Bordeaux, in fact Château Lafite was owned by the Dutch from 1797 to 1818.)

The Médoc is home to some of the world's most iconic wines – the First Growths – such as Châteaux Latour, Mouton Rothschild, Lafite-Rothschild, Margaux and Haut-Brion (which is actually in the Pessac-Léognan further south, but was included in the 1855 classification of Médoc wines by Napoleon III).

Its deep, free-draining, warm *croupes* (mounds) of *günzian* gravel, combined with its climate – which is moderated by the Atlantic influence – and especially its hot dry Septembers, allow the Cabernet here to develop tannins that are elegant and fine. I find Latour to be the most powerful and structured, Mouton more opulent and rounded and Lafite the most elegant and understated. In this region, the benchmark Cabernet flavour profile of blackcurrant, cedar wood and graphite is at its greatest.

In general, the wines of Saint-Estèphe, the most northerly commune, tend to be full-bodied, deep and tannic, requiring ageing before drinking, although more Merlot is being planted here recently, to be blended in to soften the wines (see page 114). The two most famous Saint-Estèphe wines are Châteaux Cos d'Estournel and Montrose, both of which are of Second Growth status. Montrose lies right on the edge of the Gironde in a similar position to Latour, albeit a few miles further north. Cos d'Estournel sits further inland, facing Lafite-Rothschild. Both properties are said to mirror their Pauillac equivalents in style.

Moving south past the two Second Growth Pichon châteaux of Baron and Longueville, the road dips and then rises as you move into Saint-Julien and on to a different gravel *croupe*. Again, the boundary is cut by a small stream, the Jalle de Juillac. Saint-Julien does not contain any First Growths, but for a small appellation it does contain the most classed growths, including the three Léovilles: Las Cases, Poyferré and Barton. The gravel mounds here are less defined than those of Pauillac and the wines slightly softer and more perfumed.

A five-mile gap lies between Saint-Julien and the commune of Margaux, the second biggest of the appellations (after Saint-Estèphe) and the most diverse in soil types, as well as the warmest area. There is one First Growth here, at the Palladian building of Château Margaux, whose wines show a floral character and a velvety mouth-feel.

WHAT FOOD GOES WELL Salt marsh lamb raised on the banks of the Gironde! Failing that, roast partridge is excellent, as is beef Wellington with mushroom duxelles and perhaps a little chopped truffle, or hard French cheeses such as Mimolette. It's best to keep the cooking simple, and let the wines do the talking.

RECOMMENDED PRODUCER

Château Latour

Other producers All Bordeaux First Growths including: Châteaux Haut-Brion; Pichon-Baron and Pichon-Longueville; Pédesclaux; Lynch-Bages; Mouton Rothschild; the three Léovilles; Cos d'Estournel; Montrose; Chasse-Spleen

RECIPE RECOMMENDATION

Fillet of beef Wellington ☞ *page 266*

MATURE

STYLE & FLAVOUR When Cabernet Sauvignon is aged, it loses most of its primary fruit characteristics and begins to show its tertiary flavours. These are autumnal flavours, quite earthy, smelling of freshly turned potting compost, wet leaves (the French call it *sous bois* 'under the wood'), truffle, leather, mushroom... Some of the primary characteristics stay around and reveal their country of origin, so, for example, old Bordeaux will probably still have a graphite pencil-shaving character, while New World Cabernet will probably retain its minty or eucalyptus freshness, overlying the mature tertiary flavours.

These wines throw off a sediment as they age, and, if not handled carefully when transporting from cellar to table and uncorking, the disturbed sediment will make the wine appear cloudy. So take great care when decanting (for more detailed advice, see page 30).

The question of when to decant depends on the age and vintage of a particular wine; usually a great classic can take several hours in a carafe. Michael Broadbent writes, of the legendary Mouton Rothschild 1945, that he would decant it four hours ahead of serving.

WHAT FOOD GOES WELL Generally, the older you get with wine, the higher the price; the wine definitely needs to be centre stage here. So keep the flavours simple. Stick with beef Wellington, or roasted meats with sauces made from the meat juices, though a little truffle may help, and keep garnishes simple, too.

CLASSIC MATURE BORDEAUX VINTAGES

1900, 1929, 1945, 1959, 1961, 1982, 1989, 1990

CLASSIC MATURE CALIFORNIAN VINTAGES

1936, 1941, 1970, 1974, 1978, 1987, 1997

RECIPE RECOMMENDATION

Fillet of beef Wellington ☞ *page 266*

OPPOSITE Sassicaia, Tuscany; Opus One, Napa Valley; 'Bin 707', Penfolds, Australia; Château Mouton Rothschild, Pauillac

ASSICAIA
2004
BOLGHERI SASSICAIA
Imbottigliato all'origine
Tenuta San Guido - Bolgheri - Italia
OPUS ONE
Penfolds.
BIN 707
CABERNET
SAUVIGNON
2009
42580
2002
toute la récolte a été mise
en bouteilles au Château
Château
Mouton Rothschild
PAUILLAC

Cabernet Sauvignon

TUSCANY

STYLE & FLAVOUR OK, so Cabernet Sauvignon is not a typical Tuscan variety, but that's the point. The landscape of Italian wines was changed forever in the late 1960s, with the commercial releaase of Sassicaia. It became one of the world's most iconic wines, creating the trend for Super-Tuscan wines (those that use grape varieties that are not indigenous) and the nonconformist Italians loved it.

Mario Incisa della Rocchetta came from the Italian nobility and had a love of horse racing. His travels took him to France in the 1920s, where he admired the wines of Bordeaux so much that he decided to plant Cabernet Sauvignon and Cabernet Franc close to the coastal Tuscan town of Bolgheri at his San Guido estate. Upon clearing the land for the vineyard, they found that the soils were so rocky that they gave it the name Sassicaia (*sasso* means 'stony'). Between 1948 and 1968, the wine was only made for family and friends, so with its commercial release it was classified as a lowly *vino di tavola* or table wine. As its fame and price grew, critics began to call it a *vino di favola* (a 'fairy' or mythical wine). This embarrassed the wine cognoscenti who controlled labelling regulations, so eventually, in 1994, a DOC for Bolgheri itself was created, followed in 2013 by a specific DOC for Bolgheri Sassicaia.

The wines Tignanello and Ornellaia soon followed, creating the unofficial Super-Tuscan category, where wines are often aged in small French barrels and usually include (but are not limited to) typical Bordeaux varieties.

Sassicaia now sits as a 75-hectare vineyard, planted with 85 per cent Cabernet Sauvignon vines, with the rest made up of Cabernet Franc.

WHAT FOOD GOES WELL Beef, veal and venison. Keep the flavours simple and enjoy the wine!

RECOMMENDED PRODUCER

Sassicaia, Tenuta San Guido

Other producers Ornellaia (and its excellent second wine, 'Le Serre Nuove'); Guado Al Tasso, Antinori; Tignanello

RECIPE RECOMMENDATION

Oxtail & celery ravioli, root vegetables

☞ *page 282*

AUSTRALIA

STYLE & FLAVOUR Australia has had great success with Cabernet Sauvignon, especially in the regions of Coonawarra and Margaret River. The early days of Australian Cabernet saw it often blended with Shiraz, taking the best red grapes of both Bordeaux and the Rhône to make a great wine. (Similarly, Chardonnay and Semillon blends were also popular.)

Now, although playing second fiddle to Shiraz, Australia loves Cabernet. However, as Australia is so big, there's plenty of different types of climate. Some Cabernets come from cooler areas, where they are more streamlined and structured as a result. Other, hotter regions produce fuller, riper and richer styles of wine.

These wines can have minty and lifted fresh aromas, with the underlying ripe Cabernet character. However, what singles out an Aussie Cabernet (or Shiraz, for that matter) is a whiff of eucalyptus. I have heard several stories about why this is detectable. Eucalyptus are arid soil-loving trees that grow to a great height, with huge foliage, and therefore have a gigantic root system that can often become entangled in the vine roots. Is there some transfer of flavour here? Also, it's thought that eucalyptus oils can blow from the trees and land on the grapes; does this impart its flavour into the wine? Who knows, but I'd love Aussie grape growers to get in touch and enlighten me with their theories or, indeed, facts...

WHAT FOOD GOES WELL Steaks on the barbecue, lamb or mutton with rosemary or with mint relish, or even venison.

RECOMMENDED PRODUCER

'Bin 707', Penfolds

Other producers 'John Riddoch', Wynns; 'Vanya', Cullen; 'Terra Rossa', Parker; Leeuwin Estate; Wendouree; Moss Wood; Yalumba

RECIPE RECOMMENDATION

Steak with peppercorn sauce

☞ *pages 276–279*

NAPA VALLEY

STYLE & FLAVOUR California has had an interesting wine history, following on from the Gold Rush, the *phylloxera* problem of the late 1800s (see page 10), and the Prohibition years of the early 1900s. Napa Valley was already an established producer of fine-quality wines when George de Latour – owner of Beaulieu Vineyards – employed André Tchelistcheff as his winemaker in 1938.

Called the 'Dean of American winemakers', noted Napa legends such as Robert Mondavi considered Tchelistcheff their mentor. He came from Russia and brought with him the concepts of ageing in French oak barrels, immaculate cellar hygiene, cold soaking of grapes and skins before ferment (to extract more flavour and colour) and malolactic fermentation in all reds. He is responsible for Napa eventually becoming a Cabernet region, as it was the Bordeaux variety in which most of his expertise lay. Also, the return of *phylloxera* in the 1990s saw a massive rethinking and replanting of vineyards, with Cabernet taking centre stage, as it was perfect for the soils and climate.

The Judgement of Paris in 1976 saw Californian Cabernet and Chardonnay beat the best of France's great wines in a blind tasting, which led to Bordeaux First Growth producer Mouton Rothschild creating a joint venture with Napa Valley winemaker Robert Mondavi: Opus One.

Then came the rise of mega-critic Robert Parker, eventually influencing the owners of the new-found wealth of the dotcom boom in Silicon Valley, who sought his guidance on what to buy, creating the cult Napa Cabernets such as Abreu, Bryant, Colgin, Dalle Valle, Harlan and Screaming Eagle along the way.

Napa Cabernet can be big, with ripe blackberry and sweet blackcurrant fruit, fine dusty tannins, judicious amounts of pricey French oak and generous alcohol, all balanced nicely together. These wines are expensive, often reaching or exceeding First Growth Bordeaux prices.

WHAT FOOD GOES WELL You want big, bold flavours with these: chargrilled meats, short ribs, chargrilled lamb with rosemary and garlic, hard mature and blue cheese… or a good American burger.

RECOMMENDED PRODUCER

'Martha's Vineyard', Heitz Cellar

Other producers Harlan; Opus One; Lokoya; Colgin; Dalla Valle; Scarecrow; Cain Five; Ridge; Dunn

RECIPE RECOMMENDATION

Roast fillet of beef, blue cheese-stuffed fig, Bourbon jus, collard greens ☞ *page 268*

ABOVE Cabernet vineyards on Howell Mountain, Napa Valley

NOBLE GRAPES

9

GRENACHE

GRENACHE, OR *Garnacha* as it's known in Spanish-speaking countries, likes to be in the heat. It is grown all around the Mediterranean in places such as the Southern Rhône, where it can be found making up most of the blend in Châteauneuf-du-Pape, Gigondas or Vaqueyras, or making rosé wines in Provençe or Tavel. It appears in many wines from the Languedoc area, too, such as Corbières, Faugères, Fitou and Minervois. Next to here, in the Roussillon, it is the variety used to make Banyuls, the French equivalent of Port (see page 127). The grape is also widespread in Spain, making wine in the southern region of Aragón, while it is also used as part of the blend in Rioja. Maybe its finest expression is in Priorat to the west of Barcelona (see overleaf), where it makes up the majority of the blend with *Cariñena* (Carignan, see page 120). Finally, and completing its Mediterranean circle, it's found in Sardinia, where it is locally known as *Cannonau*.

Grenache can also be found in the New World. Excellent wines are grown in the Paso Robles and Santa Cruz areas of California, as well as the Swartland in South Africa, where they are making similar styles to those found in the Rhône Valley. And, in Australia's McLaren Vale, close to Adelaide, the cool sandy soils are producing full-bodied but elegant Grenache from some very old vines (see page 108).

As it's a vigorous variety, it is quite often found in warm, dry vineyards and is trained short (canes are cut very short, with just two buds) in a bush or goblet style, to help control excessive growth.

OPPOSITE Old-vine Grenache basks in the hot Mediterranean sun of Châteauneuf-du-Pape

Grenache

SOUTHERN RHÔNE

STYLE & FLAVOUR Grenache is found down in the south of France in the Southern Rhône, concentrated around the appellations of Vaqueyras, Gigondas and Châteauneuf-du-Pape, which is the most well known by far. When the Papacy moved to Avignon (between 1309 and 1377), a 'new castle for the pope' was built, which became the centre of this large (3,100-hectare) appellation.

In the warm Mediterranean climate (it bathes in 2,800 hours of sunshine, as much as Los Angeles), wines made from the Grenache grape can become very high in alcohol with a low acidity, making for a flabby structure and a taste reminiscent of jammy strawberries and white pepper. This is why the blend for Châteauneuf-du-Pape is usually only around 70 per cent Grenache, with some Syrah and Mourvèdre added to the blend. The Syrah and Mourvèdre bring down the high alcohol levels and increase the acidity of the juice, which gives some firmer tannins and brings black fruit and black pepper flavours to the wine. The *Institut National des Appellation d'Origine* (INAO) lists 13 different varieties that may be allowed in the blend (it counts Grenache as one, but as this variety can be found in a Blanc, Gris and Noir version, really it's 15 varieties that are allowed... or, as Picpoul also comes in a Noir version, is it 16?).

In 1935, the French government created the INAO, and by 1936 the first AOC wine was created in the Southern Rhône. The purpose of the INAO was to regulate yields and the grape varieties used in different wines, as well as to monitor grape-growing and winemaking practices (it rules that, in order to be called Châteauneuf-du-Pape, a wine has to have a minimum of 12.5 per cent alcohol: the highest in France). The intention was to protect the consumer and give them a genuine product.

Châteauneuf-du-Pape can be a rich and heady mix of blackberry, plum, raspberry, liquorice and leather, plus white and black pepper. Ninety five per cent of production is red wine, but a tiny amount of white is also made here.

WHAT FOOD GOES WELL Rich and full autumnal beef stews with truffle, sweet potato or chestnuts with thyme, duck and orange, lamb tagine with prunes and star anise, slow-smoked beef brisket.

RECOMMENDED PRODUCER

Château Rayas (made from 100 per cent Grenache)

Other producers du Pégau; La Nerthe; Bonneau; de Beaucastel; du Vieux Télégraphe; Chêne Bleu

RECIPE RECOMMENDATION

Braised short ribs with thyme-roast sweet potato ☞ *page 271*

PRIORAT

STYLE & FLAVOUR Grapes have been grown in this part of Catalonia since the 12th century, when Carthusian monks occupied the monastery of Scala Dei (stairway to heaven).

Quality wines came to the region with the arrival of five growers who brought with them French varieties such as *Garnacha* (Grenache), *Cariñena* (Carignan) and Syrah. Each created an estate with the prefix of 'Clos': Clos Erasmus, Clos Mogador, Clos de l'Obac, Clos Martinet and Clos Dofi (later to be known as Finca Dofi and L'Ermita). Blending grapes, careful winemaking and ageing in French barrels were some of the keys to their success. This area of northern Spain is mountainous and the vineyards are at high altitudes, with little moisture retained by the unique friable schist soils found here, which are known locally as *llicorella*.

The wines are complex and elegant, but muscular and full-bodied when young. The *Garnacha* delivers strawberries and its distinct orange rind flavour, mixed with liquorice, spice and red berry fruit, while the *Cariñena* adds acidity while also toning down the warming alcohol of the *Garnacha*.

Great value, 'baby' Priorats can be found in neighbouring Montsant.

WHAT FOOD GOES WELL Steaks, Iberico pork, ribs with barbecue glaze, leg of lamb rubbed with garlic and anchovies, wild herbs such as thyme, fennel and lavender (the flavours of the *garrigue* in southern France), chorizo and lentils.

RECOMMENDED PRODUCER

Clos Erasmus

Other producers 'L'Ermita' and 'Finca Dofi', Palacios; Clos de l'Obac; Clos Mogador

RECIPE RECOMMENDATION

Chargrilled Ibérico presa, caramelised orange glaze, shaved fennel & orange salad ☞ *page 226*

OPPOSITE Clos Erasmus, Priorat; Châteauneuf-du-Pape 'Réserve des Célestins', Domaine Henri Bonneau; Grenache 'High Sands', Yangarra Estate, McLaren Vale; 'This is not an Exit', Sine Qua Non, California

CLOS ERASMUS
2016
PRIORAT
Propietària Daphne Glorian
PRODUCTE D'ESPANYA
2009
Châteauneuf-du-Pape
Réserve des Célestins
YANGARRA
High Sands
Grenache
2013
McLaren Vale
750ml
STA. RITA HILLS
SINE QUA NON
CONTAINS SULFITES

Grenache

CALIFORNIA

STYLE & FLAVOUR One of the main protagonists of the Californian move to grow Rhône varietals – and one of the creators of the 'Rhône Rangers' – was winemaker Randall Grahm. In the 1980s, a number of Rhône devotees created this group – presumably as a deliberate move away from Chardonnay and Cabernet Sauvignon – and began instead to plant principally Syrah, Grenache and Viognier. Some of the best areas in which to grow these wines are Santa Cruz, Ventura County and Paso Robles, and so wineries such as Qupé, Tablas Creek, Ridge, Alban and Sine Qua Non are great advocates of these varietals.

Randall owns the winery Bonny Doon, where he creates several wines in homage to their Rhône equivalents: Old Telegraph, named after Vieux Télégraphe in Châteauneuf-du-Pape, and Le Cigar Volant. This is a French term for a flying saucer and the label features a 'flying cigar', illuminating a rustic French vineyard with its red light. The tongue-in-cheek label refers to a bizarre bylaw from 1954 that disallows the landing of alien spacecraft in the vineyards of Châteauneuf-du-Pape. Presumably the wine authorities considered that extra-terrestrial intervention might risk giving some winemakers an unfair advantage...

WHAT FOOD GOES WELL Duck with hoisin sauce, pepperoni pizza, or braised or barbecued meat.

RECOMMENDED PRODUCER
Sine Qua Non
Other producers Bonny Doon; Qupé; Tablas Creek; Ridge; Alban

RECIPE RECOMMENDATION
Chargrilled Ibérico presa, caramelised orange glaze, shaved fennel & orange salad
☞ *page 226*

AUSTRALIA

STYLE & FLAVOUR Grenache originally came to Australia with Scotsman James Busby in 1832, along with many other vine clippings. Originally it was used as a big component in Australian 'Port', until the table-wine revolution started in the country during the 1950s. It is cultivated exclusively in South Australia, where it shows best in the Barossa Valley, Clare Valley, Langhorne Valley and the McLaren Vale.

Here it is made into popular GSM wines (a blend of Grenache, Shiraz and *Mataro*, the local name for Mourvèdre), replicating the classic blend found in the Southern Rhône. The Barossa Valley makes a legitimate claim to have the oldest Grenache vines in the world, planted in 1848, and have created the Old Vine Charter to recognise this: Grenache and Shiraz vines are labelled as Old Vine, Survivor, Centenarian or Ancestor depending if their age exceeds 35, 70, 100 or 125 years old respectively. The McLaren Vale has a huge diversity of soils and some of the best Grenache grows in the northern part, in sand over clay soils, at Blewitt Springs.

South Australia is generally *phylloxera* free (see page 10), as this pesky mite does not prosper well in sand, which would also explain why the vines can survive for so long. The mouth of the Vale is open to the sea and the influence of the Gulf of St Vincent, and the wines here generally show brighter acidity and less alcohol than those of Barossa, because of this cooling influence. The bright, dense notes of Australian Grenache show as an almost jammy, sweet, ripe flavour, but with a raspberry-pip tart acidity. With some age, it reveals layers of orange peel, tobacco, leather and liquorice.

If you are visiting the area, make sure you don't miss the d'Arenberg Cube restaurant and wine museum, which gives a crazy view into the mind of winemaker Chester Osborne.

WHAT FOOD GOES WELL Steak with a barbecued glaze, mutton or lamb rubbed with garlic and slowly braised with white wine and orange zest, an Aussie burger piled high with everything from cheese to pineapple and beetroot, lots of fun... and needs a big wine!

RECOMMENDED PRODUCER
'High Sands', Yangarra Estate
Other producers d'Arenberg; Reynella; Coriole; Kay Brothers; Noon Winery; Mitolo; Dandelion Vineyards

RECIPE RECOMMENDATION
Confit shoulder of mutton, rosemary dauphinoise, buttered kale, sour cherries & Mum's mint relish ☞ *page 246*

OPPOSITE TOP Grenache vineyards in Priorat. The unique schistous soil known as *llicorella* here – plus the steepness of the hillsides – demands the vines be grown in bush shapes, rather than in rows

OPPOSITE BOTTOM Pudding stones, or *galets roules*, in the vineyards of Châteauneuf-du-Pape

NOBLE GRAPES
10

NEBBIOLO AND SANGIOVESE

NEBBIOLO AND SANGIOVESE are the two pillars of great Italian red wines. Nebbiolo is the grape of Piedmont, found in Barolo and Barbaresco, while Sangiovese is the grape of Chianti and Tuscany. During a blind tasting, these Italian wines can give away their origin by a slightly lifted, volatile acidity found in Sangiovese and, less so, in Nebbiolo. Also, there's a type of aroma that I can only describe as 'Italian'! It's a certain type of elegance, almost a smell of history, dust and old wood. The French have a term for it: *vieux l'église* ('old church').

The vineyards of Piedmont lie in a basin famous for early morning mist known as *nebbia* (said to give its name to the grape). Nebbiolo can be a capricious vine, early budding and late ripening, so it needs a continental climate of hot summers with warm Septembers (see page 11). The patchwork of vineyards sit on a mixture of clay soils, but the best are on south-facing slopes angled into the sun.

These wines are light in colour, yet develop a mahogany rim quickly, giving the appearance of a 10-year-old (at least) Pinot Noir. But their pale colour betrays their very tannic, full-bodied nature. The aromas of Nebbiolo are often quite autumnal: dried rose petals, forest floors, tar and desiccated cherries.

In neighbouring Lombardy, excellent Nebbiolo (known here as *Chiavennasca*) is made in Valtellina, with the best an Amarone style, where the grapes are partially dried, known as *Sfursat* or *Sforzato*. It's well worth seeking out.

Sangiovese is found in Tuscany, where it produces a whole range of wines. The Sangiovese grape can mutate into various forms, from the top-quality Prugnolo Gentile of Brunello down to Sangiovese Piccolo.

The Chianti region was supposedly one of the first historically defined vineyard areas, created in 1716. The *consorzio* managing these 'Classico' wines comes under the banner of the Black Cockerel, or *Gallo Nero*.

Sangiovese, thought to be named for *sangius Jovis* (Jupiter's blood), has flavours of strawberries, sour cherries, plums and dried herbs, and a tart balsamic acidity that can be slightly lifted. Historically, it was used as the bulk blending variety of Chianti. Outside Italy the best Nebbiolo I have tasted has been from Australia in the higher Alpine and King Valleys or cool Yarra Valley.

OPPOSITE Brunello di Montalcino

Nebbiolo & Sangiovese

BAROLO (NEBBIOLO)

STYLE & FLAVOUR It has been suggested that, up until the mid-19th century, Barolo was a sweet wine, as the late-ripening variety would only be halfway through its fermentation before plunging November and December temperatures would cause fermentation to cease and leave a semi-sweet, low-alcohol red wine. With improved winemaking science, the wines were fermented dry, and found favour with the nobility of Turin and the House of Savoy, giving rise to the phrase 'the wine of kings and the king of wines'.

As wine consumption grew globally, especially during the 1970s, this style of heavily tannic, dried fruit-flavoured wine fell out of favour, and producers found their markets stagnating. A younger generation of winemakers began making wines in small French *barriques* with shorter maceration times, of days rather than weeks, in search of fruitier fresh flavours. These 'modernists', such as Altare, Voerzio, Scavino, Gaja and Sandrone, soon clashed with the older generation, who were shocked both by the use of new oak and by the break from previous methods, and publically objected, which led to the 'Barolo wars'. The modernists did put Barolo back on the map and their rising fame in the late 1990s led to high prices. The style has shifted back to a more traditional approach, with firm tannins and earthy flavours, as the fame of Barolo justifies 20 years of cellar ageing.

WHAT FOOD GOES WELL Meat, such as *bollito misto*, venison, pheasant, pigeon, hare and boar, or braised lamb shanks. Autumnal vegetable flavours, such as mushrooms and chestnuts, pumpkins and squashes, or risottos and polenta flavoured with wild mushrooms or herbs, and, of course, black and white truffles.

RECOMMENDED PRODUCER

'Cerequio', Roberto Voerzio

Other producers Giacomo Conterno; Aldo Conterno; Rinaldi; Mascarello; Giacosa; Sandrone; Vietti

RECIPE RECOMMENDATION

Rigatoni of braised venison shank ragù, sour cherries & chocolate ☞ *page 286*

BARBARESCO (NEBBIOLO)

STYLE & FLAVOUR If Barolo is the king of wines, then Barbaresco is their queen. These slightly lighter, elegant wines are grown in calcareous marl rather than clay and sandstone soils. They have gentler tannins, and the volume of production is only one-third that of their neighbour.

Angelo Gaja was mainly responsible for bringing fame back to this village in the 1960s, although his radical ideas upset a few locals. He created three single vineyard sites, introduced new French *barriques* and, worst of all, ripped out a Nebbiolo vineyard and planted it with Cabernet Sauvignon, giving it the name Darmagi, a local phrase meaning 'what a shame'. He followed this with plantings of Sauvignon Blanc and Chardonnay.

The co-operative *Produttori del Barbaresco* is based here, where around 50 families deliver grapes to what has been called one of the most successful co-ops in the world. Also at the centre of Barbaresco can be found the historic vineyard of Martinenga, belonging to the Marchesi di Grésy.

WHAT FOOD GOES WELL See above.

RECOMMENDED PRODUCER

'Rabajà', Bruno Rocca

Other producers Gaja; Marchesi di Grésy; Produttori de Barbaresco

RECIPE RECOMMENDATION

Penne of wild boar ragù ☞ *page 241*

CHIANTI (SANGIOVESE)

STYLE & FLAVOUR The Chianti Classico region, located at the heart of Chianti, is situated roughly between the three historic cities of Florence, Siena and Pisa. For those who love great food, wine, architecture, history, landscapes and amazing sunsets, there are few places as rich as Tuscany. In 1872 the Barone Ricasoli, at his Brolio Castle, invented the Chianti formula using a majority of Sangiovese grapes, some Canaiolo and some white Malvasia. Over time, the fame of Chianti wines grew and, to take advantage of the new, massive US market opening up after the Second World War, the production of cheap, uninteresting wine was inevitable.

Nowadays, Classico is extremely serious wine, which can be made with up to 100 per cent Sangiovese, or as a blend including Cabernet and Syrah, but with no white varieties. The top tier of wines – the Gran Selezione – are well worth seeking out. Outside of the Classico region, the vineyards rise in altitude as you venture into the Apennine spine of central Italy. The small region of Chianti Rúfina produces lightly coloured, tight red berry fruit wine with focused acidity and Pinot Noir-like characteristics.

WHAT FOOD GOES WELL Tuscan sausages with fennel braised with lentils, and meatballs with polenta. Tomato in all forms works with the bright acidity of Sangiovese. Or try a classic *bistecca alla Florentina* with olive oil and lemon juice.

RECOMMENDED PRODUCER

'Vigneto Bucerchiale', Selvapiana, Chianti Rúfina

Other producers Solaia; Fontodi; Sesti; Querciabella; Brancaia; Biondi-Santi; Castello di Brolio; Castello dei Rampolla; Argiano

RECIPE RECOMMENDATION

Braised Tuscan-style meatballs with rosemary-infused polenta ☞ *page 262*

OPPOSITE 'Sorì San Lorenzo', Gaja; Barolo Bartolo Mascarello; Brunello di Montalcino, Sesti

GAJA
SORÌ SAN LORENZO
2005
LANGHE
2004
BAROLO
SESTI
2011
CASTELLO DI ARGIANO
MONTALCINO - ITALIA
PRODOTTO IN ITALIA

NOBLE GRAPES

11

MERLOT

MERLOT IS PROBABLY most well known for the role that it plays in Bordeaux, where it accounts for about 60 per cent of the plantings of red grapes. However, it is mostly found here as a blend, particularly with Cabernet Sauvignon. The gravel-rich soils of Bordeaux's Left Bank tend to have blends that are more dominated by Cabernet Sauvignon, while the rest of Bordeaux sees higher percentages of Merlot mixed in.

So why is Merlot so often used as a blend? The answer is simple: Cabernet Sauvignon as a variety is all about black fruit and firm tannins, but the addition of Merlot brings red fruits, soft tannins and a more velvety texture. Plus, importantly, the different ripening times of the grapes can be an insurance policy in vintages that are climatically challenged (if it rains for the whole of September one year, for example). Merlot is an earlier-ripening variety, usually ready up to two weeks ahead of Cabernet Sauvignon. It tends to be fleshier and juicier than Cabernet Sauvignon, and the alcohol can be quite high too.

Generally, whereas Cabernet Sauvignon loves deep gravel soils that are warm and free-draining, Merlot doesn't mind cooler and wetter soils. For example, it does well in Pomerol (where there are very high levels of Merlot planted) and at Petrus, where the soils are particularly thick, rich in a blue clay and very cold and wet. Cabernet Sauvignon would absolutely hate it here, but obviously Merlot does just fine.

Merlot is planted all over the world, in Australia, New Zealand, Chile, California, or at the famous Tuscan Masseto vineyard, which has only seven hectares of Merlot. The Swiss canton of Ticino has adopted the grape as its own and its vineyards are 90 per cent Merlot. Everyone making a Bordeaux Médoc-style blend uses a percentage of Merlot grapes, maybe 10–15 per cent (see page 100).

I have spoken to growers in Bordeaux who foresee that, with global warming, alcohol levels in Merlot are going to start to get very high indeed, so many are starting to plant more Cabernet Franc than Merlot. (Cabernet Franc has more restrained alcohol levels.)

OPPOSITE In Pomerol, the church or l'église forms the centre of life in this tiny village

CHATEAU
St PIERRE DE POMEROL

Merlot

SAINT-EMILION

STYLE & FLAVOUR The town of Saint-Emilion has a medieval history and is a UNESCO world heritage site. The Romans are thought to have planted vines here around 48AD, and Roman poet Ausonius commented on the excellent wines. (The famous Château Ausone is named after him.)

Saint-Emilion is a large appellation for Bordeaux, of around 5,500 hectares. It has a complicated classification system, which starts with Grand Cru, then rises up to Grand Cru Classé, then up again to Premier Grand Cru A and B. At the top of the pyramid is A, consisting of four châteaux: Ausone, Cheval Blanc, Pavie and Angélus. This classification started in the 1950s and was supposed to be revised every decade, with the best-performing châteaux moving up a rank and poorly performing neighbours falling a grade. But, in 2006, four disgruntled producers challenged the classification and a legal battle ensued. Officially, the classification was suspended in 2006 and reinstated in 2012 in its current form.

The wines are predominantly made with Merlot, with some Cabernet Franc and very little Cabernet Sauvignon added. Three major soil types occur in Saint-Emilion: first, there's a limestone escarpment where Châteaux Pavie and Ausone sit. A second area of sandy vineyards at the base of the escarpment is home to châteaux such as Canon-la-Gaffelière. Meanwhile, the top of the plateau gently slopes down to Pomerol and, here, you find a mix of limestone, sand and patches of gravel. Some anomalies to the grape blend occur here, such as at Château Cheval Blanc, which uses two-thirds Cabernet Franc and one-third Merlot, and at Château Figeac, which blends equal parts of Cabernet Franc, Cabernet Sauvignon and Merlot. Saint-Emilion wines are elegant, silky, velvety, with red and dark berry flavours.

WHAT FOOD GOES WELL Obviously foods that work with Pomerol wines (see below), also try confit duck with lentils and bacon with a mature Saint-Emilion.

RECOMMENDED PRODUCER
Château Le Tertre Rôteboeuf
Other producers Angélus, Ausone; Pavie; Cheval Blanc; Figeac; Troplong Mondot; Valandraud; Canon; Clos Fortet

RECIPE RECOMMENDATION
Roast partridge, truffled celeriac purée, chestnuts & maple-cured bacon, cranberry jus ☞ *page 215*

POMEROL

STYLE & FLAVOUR Up until the 1950s, Pomerol wasn't a famous place for wines. Hence it has never been officially classified, as have Saint-Emilion or the Médoc. It has around 800 hectares of vines and there's not much to see in Pomerol except for the church. The soils are principally gravel and sand, with some red iron, known as *crasse de fer*. And famously there's a small button of blue clay known as the *boutonnière*, where Petrus sits. (Incidentally, Petrus is not 'Château Petrus', and neither does it have any accent on its 'e'. Petrus is Latin for Peter, and the name refers to St Peter, who is usually shown on the label.)

Even though it doesn't have any classification, wines from Pomerol such as Petrus and Le Pin are some of the most expensive in Bordeaux. I find many of the properties around the church to be my favourites, such as Château L'Église-Clinet and Clos L'Église.

The flavours of Pomerol wines tend to be soft, fleshy and plummy, with some liquorice characteristics and very silky, elegant tannins. If I were stranded on a desert island and had to choose which one case of wine would be washed up with me, it would probably be Pomerol.

WHAT FOOD GOES WELL Similar to the rest of Bordeaux, elegant French flavours with beef, truffle, bacon, game and lamb will make good pairings, but the wines of Pomerol will not be cheap, so try and reflect this expense when you choose what you want to eat with the wines.

RECOMMENDED PRODUCER
Château L'Église-Clinet
Other producers Petrus; Le Pin; Vieux-Château-Certan; Trotanoy; La Fleur-Pétrus; Hosanna

RECIPE RECOMMENDATION
Woodpigeon pithivier, truffled cep duxelles, Bordelaise sauce ☞ *page 209*

CALIFORNIA

STYLE & FLAVOUR Californian Merlot suffered a big blow on the release of the movie *Sideways*, which was very anti-Merlot. In California, Merlot is used as a component in a blend with Cabernet Sauvignon in Napa Valley, Dry Creek and Alexander Valley.

For a while, Californian Merlot looked as though it might become as popular as Cabernet Sauvignon, as it can be softer and fleshier, but these days, as a single variety, it is used in the cheaper styles of wine. Further north, in Washington State, Merlot is becoming an important variety, probably because it's grown in a cooler climate, so the wines become less alcoholic and jammy.

WHAT FOOD GOES WELL Steaks with a Bordeaux sauce, burgers, roast duck and veal, or tomato-based sauces.

RECOMMENDED PRODUCER
Pahlmeyer
Other producers Shafer; Cakebread Cellars; Trefethen; Vérité; Leonetti Cellar (Washington)

RECIPE RECOMMENDATION
67 burger with cheese & pancetta, with scrumpy-battered onion rings ☞ *page 259*

OPPOSITE Château Figeac, Saint-Emilion; Petrus, Pomerol; Pahlmeyer, California; 'Montevista', Emiliana, Chile

HATEAU-FIGEAC
REMIER GRAND CRU CLASSÉ
ST ÉMILION
2004
MIS EN BOUTEILLE AU CHATEAU
1979
PETRVS
POMEROL
Grand Vin
MIS EN BOUTEILLES AU CHATEAU
APPELLATION POMEROL CONTRÔLÉE
Pahlmeyer
2015.
Montevista
WINE OF CHILE
2013
MERLOT
VALLE DEL MAULE

Merlot

CHILE

STYLE & FLAVOUR Merlot came to Chile post-*phylloxera*, alongside Carmenere (see below) and, for a long time, Carmenere was called 'Merlot Chilean', until the 1990s, when its true identity was discovered. It remains an important part of the Bordeaux style of wines found in Chile's alluvial valleys between the coastal mountains and the Andes. Up to 15 per cent can be blended with the country's Cabernet. As with Carmenere, Chilean Merlot makes fruit-forward wines, but with great structure and acidity, due to the cool night-time temperatures in the vineyards.

WHAT FOOD GOES WELL Chileans are great barbecuers on *asados*, so any kind of grilled red meat will be great with the country's Merlot. It's good with the local spicy stew (*petaska*) and also Chilean *completos*: fancy hot dogs with lots of garnishes, salad and avocado.

RECOMMENDED PRODUCER
'Coyam' (blended), Emiliana
Other producers Montes; Lapostolle; Errázuriz; Viña Leyda

RECIPE RECOMMENDATION
Barbecued beef skirt, stuffed green pepper with creamed sweetcorn, smoked bacon & merkén chilli ☞ *page 280*

Other Bordeaux-type grapes

The grapes from the Bordeaux region have spread around the world, thanks to a tiny mite. The phylloxera *crisis (see page 10) led to Bordeaux's winemakers scattering to the four corners of the globe to find new homes for their grapes. Where they succeeded, the wines they created give the originals a run for their money. The Petit Verdot grape, often blended in quantities of about five per cent in many of Bordeaux's wines, does not get its own entry here, but watch this space: successful Petit Verdot is appearing in Spain, Italy and the New World.*

CABERNET FRANC

The daddy of Cabernet Sauvignon, (a cross of Cabernet Franc and Sauvignon Blanc), the son soon surpassed its father in plantings and popularity. However, Cabernet Franc is making a comeback as, increasingly, winemakers choose this variety. It's quite amenable, just doesn't like to be too cool, so will grow in similar conditions to Cabernet Sauvignon.

With global warming, Merlot may become too jammy and alcoholic in some sites, and Cabernet Sauvignon, unless blended, can taste a bit hollow. Cabernet Franc also ripens earlier than Cabernet Sauvignon and can produce sweeter, ripe raspberry and strawberry flavours, with herbal notes and tobacco with age, often showing similar green pepper pyrazine characteristics to Sauvignon Blanc.

However, in Bordeaux, Cabernet Franc is used mostly as a blending grape and famously makes up two-thirds of the blend at Cheval Blanc (see page 116).

Outside Bordeaux, Cabernet Franc does well in the Loire Valley, especially in wines from the appellations of Chinon, Saumur-Champigny and St Nicolas de Bourgueil. (It is originally thought to have been sent by Cardinal Richelieu to his Loire home from Bordeaux.) In these cool areas of the Loire, its expression can be of tart cranberry and pomegranate, with some blackcurrant fruit, fresh acidity and grippy tannins. With age, it can take on its lovely, heady, tertiary aromas of turned earth and animal farms.

WHAT FOOD GOES WELL Good, classic French bistro food, such as rack of lamb with redcurrant sauce, duck confit with lentils and bacon, or soft French cheeses such as goat's cheese salad. Try it with turbot, too, as a one-off (see below).

RECOMMENDED PRODUCERS
Clos Rougeard; Chinon 'Clos de la Dioterie', Charles Joguet
Other producers Filliatreau; Couly-Dutheil; Alliet; Amirault; de la Ermita

RECIPE RECOMMENDATIONS
Baked crottin de Chavignol en croute, beetroot, orange & watercress salad (Rougeard) ☞ *page 299*
Tranche of turbot braised in red wine with ceps & lardons (Joguet) ☞ *page 160*

CARMENERE, CHILE

Carmenere originally came from Bordeaux, where its cultivation can be traced back to Roman times. The Roman wine *Biturica* was thought to be made from Carmenere. It can be found in tiny quantities in Bordeaux still, with Château Clerc Milon and Château Brane-Cantenac having it added to the blend. A small amount can be found in Tuscany, where it is known as *Predicato di Biturica*.

The grape moved to South America after the *phylloxera* epidemic in France (see page 10). For many years it was thought to be Merlot, until 1996 when an ampelographer discovered it to be a distinct variety.

The typical flavours that you get from Carmenere are strong in pyrazines, giving the wine a distinctive vegetal green pepper character. Soft acidity can give the impression of sweet tannins and this, combined with dark blackberry, plum, coffee and savoury meaty flavours, make it great on its own, or a handy blending variety. The riper styles of this wine also take on roasted red pepper notes, so the classic Chilean dried chillies – used in small quantities, so as not to overpower the wines – are a great ingredient to serve with them.

WHAT FOOD GOES WELL Grilled meats with smoky flavours will work well, such as steaks, barbecued ribs, chimichurri sauces packed with green herbs and garlic, glazed chicken wings, or chorizo braised with meat in stews.

RECOMMENDED PRODUCER
'Coyam' (blended), Emiliana
Other producers Casa Silva; 'Purple Angel', Montes; De Martino; Antiyal; 'Cuvée Alexandre', Lapostolle; 'Milla Cala', VIK

RECIPE RECOMMENDATION
Barbecued beef skirt, stuffed green pepper with creamed sweetcorn, smoked bacon & merkén chilli ☞ *page 280*

MALBEC, ARGENTINA

Along with Sauvignon Blanc from Marlborough, Argentine Malbec has been a huge success story, as many drinkers love its dark berry, damson and violet aromas and chocolate-sweet tannins.

Malbec was originally found in Cahors in south-west France, halfway between Bordeaux and the Mediterranean, where it was somewhat romantically known as 'the black wine', as it was very dark and tannic. Eventually, the grape variety moved to Bordeaux, where it was known as *Pressac*. After the *phylloxera* crisis it migrated to Argentina and has been a phenomenal success.

In Argentina, the vineyards are up to 1,000 metres above sea level, and are arid, as the Andes mountains cast a rain shadow. Together, the height and aridity means the grapes receive an amazing amount of UV rays that thicken up the skins, giving the wines very deep colours, though they are not necessarily tannic.

The flavours are often of blackberry and blueberry, always with a distinctive scent of violets. The wines of Cahors tend to be more austere and tannic than their Andean relatives.

WHAT FOOD GOES WELL Beef! You get plenty of it in Argentina. Or sometimes spit-roasted goat. Chimichurri sauces (with green herbs and garlic), béarnaise sauce or peppercorn sauce (see page 279) all work well. Or try braised beef with black olives and prunes. For Cahors wines, try Cassoulet de Toulouse (see page 243), or duck confit.

RECOMMENDED PRODUCER

Bodega Noemia de Patagonia
Others Achaval-Ferrer; Catena; 'Eolo', Trivento; Familia Zuccardi; Bosca

RECIPE RECOMMENDATION

Steak with chimichurri ☞ *pages 276–278*

Spanish red wine grapes

RIOJA & TEMPRANILLO

Tempranillo is a grape variety found all over Spain. It can go by different names, such as *Tinto Fino*, *Cencibel* or *Aragonez*, depending which region it comes from, but it's all the same variety.

The name is derived from the Spanish word *temprano*, which means 'earlier', because it ripens before many other grapes. Its most famous expression is found in Rioja, a region in a broad valley based around the River Ebro on the southern side of the Cantabrian mountains. The mountains shelter it from the Atlantic weather on their other side, in San Sebastian and Bilbao.

The winemaking region of Rioja was really created as a consequence of the *phylloxera* crisis, when many winemakers from Bordeaux suffered the disastrous consequences of this mite. Some Spanish winemakers, such as the Marqués de Murrieta and the Marqués de Riscal, began using French techniques, including ageing wines in barrels. The difference was that they did so in American oak, which was cheaper than the French variety. American oak tends to impart more of a coconut or dill-like character (American sommeliers often refer to it, a little offputtingly, as 'pickle water').

Rioja producers place great emphasis on the *élevage* or ageing of the wine at the winery, and this means oak contact. The highest classification of Rioja wine is Gran Reserva, which indicates it has been aged for at least five years before release, with at least two of those years being in

oak barrels. So there is no real emphasis on terroir for the wines to hit the highest perceived quality level.

These days, more French oak is being used, with longer maceration times giving deeper wines of a more modern taste, more similar to Ribera de Douro wines than to traditional Rioja flavours. There is a bigger focus on single vineyards or single estates, rather than vast blends.

The wines of this region are a blend, with Tempranillo being the largest component at around 70 per cent, some *Garnacha* (Grenache, see page 104), Graciano and a small amount of *Mazuelo* (Carignan); a touch of Cabernet is sometimes tolerated, too. The flavours of Tempranillo hint at strawberry and cherry, but the dominant aroma is often oak; either French oak with its vanilla flavours, or sweet, coconutty American.

WHAT FOOD GOES WELL Lamb grilled on the *plancha* (a Spanish charcoal griddle), slow-roast pork or goat, all rubbed with light barbecue spices. Chorizo in a white bean stew with garlic, or a spread of jamón Ibérico and Manchego.

RECOMMENDED PRODUCERS

Gran Reserva 'Viña Tondonia', López de Heredia; Marqués de Murrieta
Other producers Muga; Roda; 'Aurus', Allende; Contino; La Rioja Alta; Artadi; Beronia; CVNE

RECIPE RECOMMENDATION

Chargrilled suckling lamb shoulder with Spanish tomato relish ☞ *page 248*

ABOVE Vineyards in Rioja Alavesa are protected from the cool Atlantic weather by the Cantabrian mountains, making the Ebro Valley a dry region for grape growing

Other red wine grapes

A NOTE ON ITALIAN REDS

Along with many European countries – such as Portugal, Spain and Greece – Italy has a wealth of indigenous varieties that make it a fascinating, though complex, country to study. It's not possible to cover all bases so I am just choosing my favourites; it is not possible to cover everything. Many Italian red varieties are discussed elsewhere in this section. Other varieties that produce red wines of note in Italy include Aglianico from Basilicata and Campania, Grignolino and Barbera from Piedmont, Aleatico from Puglia and Latium, Lambrusco Grasparossa from Emilia-Romagna, Lagrein and Schiava from Trentino, Sagrantino from Umbria and Negroamaro from Puglia.

BLAUFRÄNKISCH

STYLE & FLAVOUR The Austrian wine industry generally followed its German neighbours in wine styles and labelling laws (see page 52), with *Prädikat*-labelled wines, called Kabinett, Spätlese, Auslese and so on. In Germany, sugar is king, bringing richness and alcohol to the wines, so German drinkers were delighted to find cheap Auslese-style wines coming out of Austria. Until, that is, in 1985, when a German lab discovered that some producers had added toxic diethylene glycol (found in antifreeze) to replicate this sweetness and texture. This resulted in the overnight collapse of the Austrian wine industry, plus the problem of disposing of 36 million bottles (which ended up as coolant in a cement factory). Several arrests were made; one producer committed suicide. The long-term consequences were that Austrian wine laws were tightened up and now the country boasts some of the cleanest, most interesting wines in the world.

Austria's international wine reputation rests mostly on white wines (see page 82), but they also make world-quality red wines (see also St Laurent, right).

Blaufränkisch is Austria's second most-planted red grape, and is generally found in the Burgenland region. (Also, it can be found in Hungary, as *Kékfrankos*, where it is part of the blend in 1970s favourite Bull's Blood, or Egri Bikavér.)

The wines tend to be deep-coloured and full-bodied, with dark berry flavours and black olive characteristics. They have firm, grippy tannins that match well with the Austrian passion for game.

WHAT FOOD GOES WELL The bounty from hunting in the Austrian Alps: venison, wild berries such as bilberries, or wild mushrooms. Roast goose with braised red cabbage flavoured with juniper berries, and smoked meats such as speck.

RECOMMENDED PRODUCER

'Neckenmarkt', Weingut Moric

Other producers Umathum; Dorli Muhr; Uwe Schiefer; Wachter-Wiesler; Prieler; Tibor

RECIPE RECOMMENDATION

Roasted haunch of roe deer, braised cabbage, bilberries, spätzle ☞ *page 285*

CARIGNAN

STYLE & FLAVOUR This grape variety is fond of heat and can be found in the south of France and scattered throughout Spain, where it's known as *Mazuelo*, as well as on Sardinia, where it's called *carignano*. Recently, old-vine Carignan has made a comeback in Chile, where it's making some very good-quality wines in the Maule Valley. California has a bit, too, and, in the warm Central Valley, bulk producers love its naturally high yields, whereas Ridge Vineyards adds some credibility when it blends Carignan into wines such as Geyserville and Lytton Springs. It is also found as part of a blend in Lebanese wines of the Bekaa Valley.

In the 1960s, Carignan was one of the most-planted varieties in France, making up the bulk of rustic Languedoc red wines filling the European wine lake, until the late 1980s, when EU vine pull schemes meant there was more value in tearing up vines than in producing cheap grape juice. However, very good Carignan can be found in appellations such as Fitou, Corbières, St Chinian and Minervois, where older, lower-yielding vines produce really interesting aromas.

The grape has to be in a warm climate, as it ripens late and can be susceptible to rot. But it is considered a workhorse for everyday drinking wine, as its yields are high. If allowed to yield at its maximum, up to 200 litres per hectare (four times more than Cabernet Sauvignon), the wines can be very rustic and tannic.

WHAT FOOD GOES WELL If you go hunting in the South of France, you might be after wild boar, to make into daubes and eat with Carignan. It works with classic French cassoulet, or try the Lebanese wines with lamb and mild spices.

RECOMMENDED PRODUCERS

Château Musar; Grange des Pères

Other producers Bergé; de Lastours; Millegrand Minervois (all France); Fairview (South Africa); Vigno (Chile)

RECIPE RECOMMENDATIONS

Roast cannon of lamb, chickpea salad, moutabel, pomegranate (Musar) ☞ *page 251*

Cassoulet de Toulouse (Grange) ☞ *page 243*

CINSAULT

STYLE & FLAVOUR Another workhorse grape variety found in the Languedoc, usually used as part of a blend. It works well in rosé wine. Cinsault and Pinot Noir are the parents of the Pinotage variety.

Outside France, the Lebanon is producing nice Cinsaults. In South Africa, old vine Cinsault can be found in areas such as Swartland, where it makes interesting cranberry-like wines with fresh acidity and crunchy berry fruit.

WHAT FOOD GOES WELL Something with orange, maybe duck á l'orange, or a salad with an orange dressing. Rustic French food such as *bavette frites* for the Chilean styles, or a burger; you can get away with spice and chilli with those as well.

RECOMMENDED PRODUCER

'Pofadder', Sadie Family Wines (South Africa)

Other producers De Martino; Montes 'Outer Limits' (both Chile). Flotsam & Jetsam (South Africa). Terre Inconnue; de la Négly; Peyre Rose (all France)

RECIPE RECOMMENDATION

Superfood salad ☞ *page 306*

CORVINA

STYLE & FLAVOUR Corvina Veronese is a sizeable component of the trio of red grapes – along with Molinara and Rondinella – that make the wines of Valpolicella. Along with Soave, Bardolino and Prosecco, Veneto is Italy's largest wine-producing region. Valpolicella comes in many forms, from its most basic simple fruity style, through the Classico (original vineyard areas), Ripasso (used skins added back to the ferment) and quality sub-region of Valpentena. But its best wines are those made in the *apassimento* method, known as straw wine, *strohwein* or *vin de paille* in other countries. It's the process of leaving ripe grapes on straw mats to dry out. After several weeks, the grapes shrivel as they lose water content of up to 30 per cent. When pressed, they deliver a sweet, concentrated must that can be fully fermented to dryness, resulting in a wine easily more than 15 per cent alcohol and called *Amarone* ('bitter'). Or the must can be partially fermented to around 12 per cent alcohol, leaving some residual sugar, resulting in full-bodied, sweet red wine: *Recioto*. Both Amarone and Recioto della Valpolicella have concentrated espresso, date and prune-like aromas, with mocha and raisin-like flavours.

WHAT FOOD GOES WELL Recioto suits chocolate, date or prune desserts, pecan pie or tramisu. Amarone works with full wintry stews, venison and grilled meats.

RECOMMENDED PRODUCER

Giuseppe Quintarelli

Other producers Dal Forno Romano, Bertani, Masi, Tommasi, Allegrini

RECIPE RECOMMENDATION

Chocolate & honeycomb semifreddo ☞ *page 332*

MOURVÈDRE

STYLE & FLAVOUR Originally from Spain, where it is called *Monastrell* (it likely came out of a monastery).

It tends to like heat and is often used as part of a blend; especially, it can tame wildly alcoholic Grenache (see page 106).

Great-quality Mourvèdre is part of the blend of Châteauneuf-du-Pape, where it adds a wild *sauvage* and animal character. In California and Australia, it is known as *Mataro*. The flavours can be of blackberry and bramble and often take on a gamey sanguinity with age.

Provençe is a tourist destination for the French and produces vats of rosé for them, usually made with Grenache but, in Bandol, they use Mourvèdre in the blend, giving weight and depth.

WHAT FOOD GOES WELL Strongly flavoured fish, meats with Provençal herbs. Rosé works with bouillabaisse.

RECOMMENDED PRODUCER

Domaine Tempier

Other producers 'Grans Muralles', Torres (Spain). 'Château Romassan', Domaines Ott; Château de Pibarnon (France). Bonny Doon; Cline Cellars (both USA)

RECIPE RECOMMENDATIONS

Cassoulet de Toulouse ☞ *page 243*

Red mullet, braised fennel, orange & tapenade ☞ *page 166*

NERELLO MASCALESE

STYLE & FLAVOUR A surge of great wines are coming from the volcanic hillsides of Mount Etna on Sicily, made from indigenous grapes. Etna Rosso is made from Nerello Mascalese with Nerello Cappuccio, often biodynamically.

These can make fresh, tart cranberry-flavoured wines; rosés are deep-coloured and rich, with summer fruit and weighty body. Etna vineyards expose grapes to warm Mediterranean winds that thicken the skins and create interesting aromatic compounds. Along with the Cerasuolo ('cherry') grape of Vittoria (the first DOCG of Sicily) and Abruzzo, these are some of Italy's most interesting wines.

A wealth of other interesting red grapes are found on Sicily, such as Nero d'Avola (aka Calabrese) and Frappato. Its French-Italian neighbour Corsica makes powerful reds from Nielluccio (aka Sangiovese) or Sciaccarello.

WHAT FOOD GOES WELL Shellfish, Sicilian cheeses, Carpaccio and *salumi*.

RECOMMENDED PRODUCERS

Etna Rosato, Graci; Etna Rosso 'Feudo di Mezzo', Girolamo Russo

Other producers Pietradolce; Benanti; Abatucci; Masciarelli

RECIPE RECOMMENDATIONS

Fillet of beef Carpaccio, capers, rocket & croutons (Graci) ☞ *page 256*

Griddled giant puffball, sautéed wild mushrooms, spelt (Russo) ☞ *page 320*

ST LAURENT

STYLE & FLAVOUR This gets its name from St Laurentius, the patron saint of chefs, whose day falls on 10 August, which is when this variety begins to ripen.

The world's oldest winery and wine school, the 900-year-old Klosterneuberg, south-west of Vienna, has created many crosses, and St Laurent may have come from here, though direct evidence is lost.

St Laurent tastes like a cross between Pinot Noir and Syrah. In other words, it can have soft dark cherry and bergamot aromas, smoked meat and bloody spice, with rounded tannins and fresh acidity.

WHAT FOOD GOES WELL Game with berry sauce; smoky charred aubergine.

RECOMMENDED PRODUCER

'Jungle', Weingut Jurtschitsch

Other producers Pittnauer; Reinisch; Umathum; Schloss Gobelsberg

RECIPE RECOMMENDATION

Aubergine chickpea fritters ☞ *page 296*

TANNAT

STYLE & FLAVOUR Tannat originated close to Cahors producing big, deep, full-bodied and – as the name implies – tannic wines. The grape was taken to South America and is the variety of Uruguay. The wines are fresh, with dark berry, black olive and herb notes.

WHAT FOOD GOES WELL Beef, offal and punchy, robust flavours.

RECOMMENDED PRODUCER

'Montus', Alain Brumont

Other producers Viñedo de los Vientos; de Lucca; Garzón; Marichal (all Uruguay)

RECIPE RECOMMENDATION

Any steaks! ☞ *pages 268 and 276–281*

XINOMAVRO

STYLE & FLAVOUR Found in northern Greece, this is very similar to Nebbiolo, as it belies its pale colour by creating wines that are full-bodied and very tannic (though it bears no direct relationship to Nebbiolo). Those that love the wines of Piedmont will probably love Xinomavro.

Greece boasts other interesting indigenous red varieties, including Mavrodaphne and rare Mavrotragano.

WHAT FOOD GOES WELL Greek red meats.

RECOMMENDED PRODUCER

Foundi Estate

Other producers Thymiopoulos; Alpha Estate; Katsaros; Hatzidakis

RECIPE RECOMMENDATION

Lamb kleftiko with Greek salad ☞ *page 255*

ZINFANDEL

STYLE & FLAVOUR One of the flagship grapes of California, this is identical to Puglian Primitivo, but was originally from Croatia, where it's called *Tribidrag*.

Zinfandel can be full-bodied with jammy tones, soft tannins and high alcohol, which make it easy drinking.

WHAT FOOD GOES WELL Flavour bombs such as pepperoni pizza, or burgers. Cooler areas make structured, elegant wines that pair with beef, lamb or pork.

RECOMMENDED PRODUCER

Nalle, Dry Creek Valley

Other producers Edmeades; Ridge; Turley; Seghesio; Vineyard29

RECIPE RECOMMENDATION

67 burger with cheese & pancetta, with scrumpy-battered onion rings ☞ *page 259*

STANTON & KILLEEN
Rutherglen
WINE OF AUSTRALIA
SZEPSY
ASZÚ
TOKAJI 6 PUTTONYOS 2006
Riesling Auslese
2011
Mosel
DOCG

Sweet & fortified wines

There are two ways to make sweet wine.

The first method is through fortification, or mutage, *where you capture a grape's natural sweetness by allowing grape must to ferment to 5–7 per cent alcohol. Then you add a neutral grape spirit, which can bring the alcohol level up to 15–17 per cent; it will kill the yeast and stop fermentation, while leaving unfermented sugar still in the wine.*

The wines of Port, Banyuls and Muscat de Beaumes de Venise are made like this, as well as many other southern French dessert wines. They are known as vins doux naturel *(VDN), due to their natural sweetness.*

The second way to make dessert wine is by concentrating its sugars, drying grapes on the vine or as a cut bunch: passerillage *or* vin de paille *in France,* apassimento *in Italy,* strohwein *in Austria. Of note are sweet Jurançon made with the Manseng grape in SW France, the Recioto wines of Soave and Valpolicella and Pedro Ximénez in Sherry. Another way is by using those that are affected by* botrytis cinerea *mould ('noble rot'). Either will cause the grapes to become raisinated, losing water and concentrating acidity and sugar. The wines of Sauternes, Tokaji and German sweet Rieslings are all made in this way, as are some greats from the New World, notably De Bortoli's 'Noble One', a botrytis Semillon from Australia, and Vin de Constance. Since the fortification process helps preserve them over long sea voyages, these wines were developed on islands or close to ports and harbours. Madeira, Sherry and Port being the most famous but also Marsala from Sicily and Commandaria from Cyprus.*

The grape of choice for many sweet wines is Muscat. It is floral and aromatic and its family includes Ottonel (white), Hamburg (black) and Giallo (yellow).

RIESLING AUSLESE, BEERENAUSLESE, TROCKENBEERENAUSLESE

In Germany, sugar is king. Its vineyards are right on the northern limit of wine growing. Grapes produce a lot of acid, which is great for Riesling, but ripening grapes and getting sugar in fruit can be tricky. A way of developing sugar in their grapes is by late harvesting; as soon as a vine starts to feel winter coming, it puts energy into lignifying its shoots rather than ripening grapes. The grapes hang and start naturally to dehydrate.

In Germany, they call these Auslese or 'late harvested'. They're most successfully grown in a suitable microclimate, maybe a pocket of vines tucked at the base of a slope, or by a forest, or in a dip in the hills. These areas prone to more moisture and therefore the development of *botrytis*. The next stage on from Auslese is Beerenauslese (BA), which literally means 'late-harvested berries'. They will be individually picked from the bunches in the Sauternes style (see overleaf).

The next stage on again from this is Trockenbeerenauslese (TBA), which means 'dried late-harvested berries'. These are intensely botrytised, shrivelled and concentrated. These rare and precious liquids, from the best producers, demand prices of £1,000 per half-bottle.

The equivalent in Alsace of BA is *vendange tardive* (VT), and the equivalent of TBA is *Selection Grands Nobles* (SGN).

All these wines are intensely sweet, but retain a laser-like Riesling acidity.

WHAT FOOD GOES WELL Fruit-based desserts, especially if highly caramelised.

RECOMMENDED PRODUCER

TBA 'Forster Ungeheuer', Reichsrat von Buhl

Other producers Robert Weil; Egon Müller; JJ Prüm; Dönnhoff; Kracher; Fritz Haag

RECIPE RECOMMENDATION

Pavlova, passion fruit cream & mango ☞ *page 326*

MOSCATO

Moscato is grown all over the world, making light dessert styles of wine.

Its natural home is in Piedmont, close to Barolo and Barbaresco, and production is based around the town of Asti. The wines produced here are generally low in alcohol – 5.5 per cent by law – and contain the sweetness of residual sugar. The fermentation begins in sealed metal tanks, when carbon dioxide is produced, then absorbed into the liquid. Once alcohol levels reach 5.5 per cent, it is chilled, to stop fermentation, but the grape sugar remains. It is filtered under pressure, to remove yeasts, and bottled, again under pressure, to keep its sparkle. These are lemony, off-dry wines, not to be confused with Asti Spumante.

WHAT FOOD GOES WELL Delicious with lemon mousse, pannacotta and berries.

RECOMMENDED PRODUCER

Stella Bella, Margaret River

Other producers Vajra; Contero; Ascheri; La Spinetta (Italy). Innocent Bystander (Australia)

RECIPE RECOMMENDATION

Pannacotta with macerated strawberries, lime & basil ☞ *page 331*

RUTHERGLEN

The wonderful sweet Muscats of Australia's Rutherglen are the country's equivalent of sweet Madeira. Before the 1950s, the bulk of Australian wine was made in the style of Port or Sherry. In Victoria, Rutherglen and Glenrowan regions both became famous for these.

The wines are made from Muscat à Petits Grains grapes, which are left hanging on the vine to naturally dehydrate and shrivel up. The grapes are then picked and crushed and, halfway through fermentation, fortified with a neutral spirit in the classic Port style. They are *vins doux naturel* (see left).

The wines are aged with the Solera system (see overleaf) and become tawny in colour, oxidised and concentrated, with demerara and caramelised orange rind flavours. The wines are classified into a 40-year system based on age, sweetness and complexity, starting with the youngest Rutherglen Muscat, then Classic Muscat, then Grand Muscat, then Rare Muscat, whose residual sugar levels can reach up to 400g per litre and must be aged for a minimum of 20 years.

WHAT FOOD GOES WELL Dark, rich toffee, caramel, dates, chocolate, blue cheese.

RECOMMENDED PRODUCER

Stanton & Killeen

Other producers Seppelt; Campbells; Chambers Rosewood; Morris

RECIPE RECOMMENDATION

Sticky date pudding, salted toffee sauce, walnut praline & clotted cream ☞ *page 338*

OPPOSITE Rutherglen Muscat Stanton & Killeen, Australia; 'Aszú', István Szepsy, Tokaji; Château Coutet, Barsac; 'Berncastler Doctor', Weingut Dr H Thanisch, Mosel; Moscato d'Asti 'Bricco Quaglia', La Spinetta, Piedmont

SAUTERNES

When used to make dry wines, Semillon is part of a blend of grapes (see page 72). However, it is 100 per cent on its own in the sweet botrytis wines of Sauternes.

Thinner-skinned grape varieties such as Semillon are more susceptible to *botrytis*, which drinks the water content of a grape, leaving it raisinated, while also imparting a flavour of ginger, *pain d'épices* and orange marmalade. The lower juice content means less wine can be produced from a bunch of grapes. They say in Bordeaux that it takes one vine to make a bottle of wine, but in Sauternes it takes one vine to make a single glass of Sauternes… hence their price.

The vineyards of Sauternes are at the convergence of two rivers (the Garonne and the Ciron) and this position is key: one is warm and the other cold, and their collision creates early morning mist which encourages the growth of *botrytis*.

Botrytis mould doesn't develop in a uniform manner, so a whole bunch of grapes won't become botrytised, or at least not at the same time. Picking the whole bunch and pressing it would mean that the non-botrytised berries diluted the sweet juice of the botrytised berries.

Therefore, grape pickers pick off the botrytised berries up to ten times during the harvest season, from October to late November. They have to be skilled, which adds to the already high price.

In the neighbouring region of Bergerac lies Monbazillac, where they also make sweet wines from Semillon. These are sommeliers' favourites, as they are similar in style but great value for money.

WHAT FOOD GOES WELL All stone fruits, such as apricots and nectarines.

RECOMMENDED PRODUCER

Château d'Yquem

Other producers Climens; Rieussec; de Fargues; Suduiraut, Tirecul La Gravière

RECIPE RECOMMENDATION

Saffron-poached apricot & almond tart, Roquefort ice cream ☞ *page 344*

TOKAJI

One of the world's most famous dessert wines. It's thought some of the world's first *botrytis* wines were made here, in the north-east corner of Hungary, by Abbot Máté Szepsi in the 1630s.

The Turks were laying siege to one of the monasteries, which led to a delayed grape harvest. When finally picked, the fruits were highly botrytised, but made excellent wine. The vineyards of Tokaji were some of the first classified on the grounds of quality, in the 1730s.

The convergence of two rivers – the Bogrod and Tisza – one warm and the other cold, creates early morning mist, similar to the case in Sauternes (see left), which encourages *botrytis* mould growth.

The grape variety used here is Furmint (see page 81), which has a beautiful crisp acidity that balances with the rich, sweet, caramelised orange flavours of the wine. A range of complex wines are made here, from dry Szamorodni wines, which are slightly affected by *botrytis*, to sweet Aszú wines, to the ultimate nectar: Eszencia. This has sugar levels that can reach up to 700g per litre. It is sold in tiny bottles and tasted from a glass spoon.

WHAT FOOD GOES WELL Caramelised fruit, foie gras and blue cheeses.

RECOMMENDED PRODUCER

'5 Puttanyos Aszú', Royal Tokaji Wine Company

Other producers Királyudvar; Szepsy; Oremus; Disznókő; Pajzos

RECIPE RECOMMENDATION

Tarte Tatin with vanilla ice cream ☞ *page 342*

VIN DE CONSTANCE

This legendary wine, mentioned by both Dickens and Austen, is late-harvested and seldom becomes botrytised, and is a delicious, honeyed golden syrup. It has been made since 1685 (calling South African wine 'New World' may be a bit unfair, as many of Bordeaux's famous châteaux were either in their infancy or had not even been created at this time).

With the age of sea exploration and the spice trade in Asia and Europe, South Africa became an important stop-over, and the Dutch East India Company created an outpost close to Cape Town. In 1685, the Governor of the Cape, Simon van der Stel, created an estate at Constantia, where he grew the *Muscat de Frontignan* as a dessert wine. It became famous, drunk by kings and queens, and by Napoleon in exile on Saint Helena.

After *phylloxera* reached South Africa, the wines weren't made for nearly 200 years; production was resumed in 1986.

WHAT FOOD GOES WELL Fruit-based desserts and steamed puddings, or South African cheeses with dried fruit and nuts.

RECOMMENDED PRODUCER

Klein Constantia

RECIPE RECOMMENDATION

Malva pudding, Amarula sauce ☞ *page 324*

VIN SANTO

A disagreement here between the Italians and the Greeks. Vin Santo 'holy wine' has been made in Tuscany for generations, where it was often used at mass for its miraculous healing powers (or at least perking up the sick). Here it is made with Malvasia and Trebbiano or Sangiovese for the rosé version: *occhio di pernice* 'eye of partridge'. It is made by leaving the bunches to hang or rest on straw mats in ventilated lofts for several weeks to naturally dessicate and lose water content. After fermentation the wine is left to age in small chestnut or oak barrels. The Greeks would say the Santo name comes from the island of Santorini which has made sweet wines from sundried Assyrtiko grapes for hundreds of years and was used by both the Russians and the Italians in religious ceremonies.

WHAT FOOD GOES WELL Chocolate, sticky toffee pudding, tarte Tatin.

RECOMMENDED PRODUCER

Argyros Estate, Santorini

RECIPE RECOMMENDATION

Tarte Tatin with vanilla ice cream ☞ *page 342*

ZIBIBBO

A sweet muscat from the volcanic island of Pantellaria off the south coast of Sicily. One of the best makers is Donnafugata; he makes a wine called Ben Ryé that is one of my favourite dessert wines. The vines are trained close to the ground, to avoid the strong winds of the island.

In August, early-picked grapes are laid on racks to dry in the wind and sun. This creates a concentration of sugar and aromas. After September, fresh grapes are picked and made into a wine and the dried grapes are added to this fresh must, in a ratio of about 75kg of grapes for each 100 litres of must. This is left to macerate for weeks, to develop the wine's amazing aromas and maintain its freshness.

Its extraordinary aromas are definite: apricots, orange peel and a rich demerara-like caramelisation, counterbalanced by delicious bright acidity.

WHAT FOOD GOES WELL Stone fruit and almonds, salted pistachio gelato, sweet ravioli with ricotta, honey and nuts.

RECOMMENDED PRODUCER

'Ben Ryé', Donnafugata

Other producers Marco de Bartoli; Kamma

RECIPE RECOMMENDATION

Poached white peaches with zabaglione & amaretti ☞ *page 328*

SHERRY

To understand the wines of Jerez, you really should visit the region, to experience the sights and sample the local cuisine. Afterwards, you will have become a Sherry convert for life, because these are some of the most food-friendly and interesting wines on the planet. The vineyards of Jerez are only slightly larger than those of St-Emilion (see page 116), but despite their small size, they create some of the most complex wines in the world.

The Solera system is widely used, in which a multitude of casks from various years are fractionally blended and the resulting wines – labelled, for istance, '20 years' or '30 years' – are actually just an average of these dates. For instance, if a Sherry bottle is labelled '30 years old', some of the proportion of the blend might be a mere five years old; some might even be as old as half a century; but the average of everything that has gone into the blend is 30 years.

The town of Jerez has a large selection of fantastic tapas restaurants, and this style of eating small plates with strong flavours works perfectly with all the different styles of Sherry.

With the proximity of its vineyards to the Atlantic, Fino is the Sherry world's equivalent of a dry white wine and is enjoyed throughout a meal. The unique soils of the region grow the Palomino grape variety, which is used to make a dry white wine. This wine is held in cask with the hope that a thin layer of white *flor* (yeast) develops across its surface. Wines strong in this *flor* growth become classified as 'Fino' and are fortified up to a limit of 15.5 per cent alcohol. Those which attract little or no *flor* growth are classified as Oloroso, fortified up to the higher limit of 17 per cent and left to gently oxidise in the barrel without the protective layer of *flor*.

Flor feeds on the alcohol and glycerol found in the dry white Palomino grapes. The yeast brings a distinctive elderflower-like aroma to the wine and, as the glycerol diminishes with age, the Sherry will take on the general feeling of a very dry, nutty white wine.

Due to the fortification process, these wines are very adaptable to many types of food. So Fino Sherry should not just be pigeon-holed as an aperitif, as it tends to be outside Spain. *Fino en Rama* is literally taken straight from the cask and bottled with no filtering or fining; ideally, to capture their freshness, they should be drunk within six months. But aged *Fino en Rama* will take on more almondy nuttiness over time.

Oloroso ages in barrels, becoming dark brown and oxidised, and, over a period of many years, develops complex leathery, walnut, orange rind, Christmas cake spice characteristics. These wines are very high in savoury umami flavours, so the best dry styles make great complements to meat dishes.

One in 100 casks of Oloroso will develop to have the typical flavours of Oloroso but a more subtle nose, and these rarities are known as Palo Cortado.

WHAT FOOD GOES WELL Andalucian food, which contains a lot of seafood cooked outdoors. *Gambas à la plancha* with plenty of garlic, crayfish, langoustines, whelks, mussels and fish. Salty canapés, olives and smoked almonds are great with Fino-style Sherries. But with Oloroso and Palo Cortado, more savoury dishes can be chosen; the ideal match is aged *pata negra* ham, when the fat is brown and tastes nutty. The salty flavour of the ham with the Oloroso is a treat for the senses.

RECOMMENDED PRODUCERS

Fino en Rama Tío Pepe, González Byass; Palo Cortado, Bodegas Tradición

Other producers Equipo Navazos; Valdespino; Solear; Alvear; de Castilla; Emilio Hildago

RECIPE RECOMMENDATIONS

Baked salt cod, chorizo, tomatoes & chickpeas in Fino (Byass) ☞ *page 190*

Braised pork cheeks in Sherry with morcilla, orange, butter beans (Tradición) ☞ *page 232*

ABOVE Fino en Rama 'Saca de Mayo', Equipo Navazos

MADEIRA

Many fortified wines developed following the trade winds. In the days of the spice and slave trades, ships would visit the Ivory Coast to pick up slaves, then go on to Madeira, before putting up their sails and shooting over to the Caribbean. The fortification process that gave the wines their long life was also a massive boost to their popularity.

Madeira was the go-to drink of the Southern American slave plantation owners. In fact, the Declaration of Independence was signed over many bottles of Madeira and, famously, George Washington was supposed to drink a bottle of Madeira a day.

The first Portuguese settlers came to the volcanic island of Madeira in 1420, bringing winemaking with them. Simple Madeira is made from *tinta negra mole* (which is about 75 per cent of Madeira made), but four varieties make up the more interesting wines, which are, from sweetest to driest: Malvasia (Malmsy), Bual, Verdelho, and Sercial. Occasionally, you can find the rare Terrantez variety.

Winemaking in Madeira starts off by picking, crushing and fermenting the two dryer grapes, Verdelho and Sercial, which are separated from their skins and then fermented until their sugar turns into alcohol. The sweeter grapes, Malvasia and Bual, are left on their skins and, depending on the desired levels of sweetness, fermentation is halted by adding a neutral spirit. The wines will then go through the *Estufagem* process, literally baking them, to encourage heavy oxidation – aka Madeirisation – that is supposed to replicate a long journey inside a hot ship's hold. Cheaper Madeira is warmed in steel tanks to create these flavours, but the highest level is left in cask in warm rooms to be heated naturally by the sun: the *Canteiro* process.

There is another style of Madeira called 'Rainwater', which is slightly lighter, and this developed by accident: barrels of Madeira were left on a dock in the pouring rain, and the wine became slightly diluted.

Unlike Sherry, the best Madeira comes from single vintages, and the *Solera* system (see previous page) is rarely used.

WHAT FOOD GOES WELL The savoury umami flavours of drier styles of Madeira make them an excellent accompaniment to roasted meats, chicken and bacon, steaks with caramelised onions, well-hung game birds, hard nutty cheeses, or dried fruits and nuts. Sweeter styles are perfect with pecan pie with maple syrup and ice cream, or Tarte Tatin, or even sticky toffee pudding and other desserts with dried figs and prunes.

RECOMMENDED PRODUCER

Sercial, Blandy's Vintage

Other producers D'Oliveiras; Barbeito; Henriques & Henriques; Cossart Gordon

RECIPE RECOMMENDATION

Sticky chicken tulips, prunes, smoked bacon, toasted pecans, star anise ☞ *page 199*

SWEET TANNAT

I have chosen an unusual sweet, aromatic and fortified tannat to pair with the Black Forest trifle recipe in this book. Uruguay makes fantastic red wines from the Tannat grape (see page 121), which are normally deep, full-bodied and tannic, but this particular wine is unique. The winemaker aromatises it a bit like a vermouth, to a secret recipe, then he fortifies it in a similar manner to Marsala, in the way his Italian ancestors once did.

The wine has deep black kirsch cherry flavours, chocolate, coffee and vanilla bean. It would match very well with tiramisú, but the strong black cherry character makes it an ideal match to Black Forest flavours. The winemaker is called Pablo; he's an avid surfer and – along the Uruguayan coastline – has lots of opportunity for that when he's not busy with the wine.

WHAT FOOD GOES WELL Anything with cherries, or chocolate or coffee, tiramisú, even summer pudding.

RECOMMENDED PRODUCER

'Alcyone', Viñedo de los Vientos

RECIPE RECOMMENDATION

Black Forest trifle ☞ *page 335*

PORT

These historic vineyards were some of the first to be classified based on the quality of their wines, in 1756. The Methuen Treaty of 1703 brought favourable trading laws into effect between England and Portugal. (As the English tended to be at war with either France or Spain, or both at the same time, Portugal became a valuable source of wine.)

As trade with England developed, two English merchants were given a wine to taste. It was a total mistake: a winemaker had inadvertently added brandy to a semi-sweet red wine whose fermentation process hadn't yet finished. However, the English merchants liked the sugary result so much that they insisted on importing it, kicking off a trend for fortified Port as we know it today. It was also an extremely suitable drink for taking on long sea journeys, as it had a long and stable life.

Based in the northern part of Portugal, there are two distinct areas involved in the Port-making process. On the Atlantic coast at the mouth of the Douro river are the towns of Oporto and Villanova de Gaia, either side of the mouth of the river. This is where all the business of Port happens and where the offices and warehouses are located. But travelling up the Douro river and over the Montemuro mountains, you come into the Douro Valley, where the vineyards are situated. Here the land is hot, dry and arid, which makes a totally contrasting climate to the maritime mouth of the river (see page 11). The Douro river brings moisture and a cooling effect to the vineyards this far east in the region.

A whole selection of different grape varieties are planted here. The best are *Touriga Nacional*, *Tinta Roriz* (Tempranillo), *Tinta Barroca* and *Tinta Cão*, plus some white grapes such as *Gouvelo*, *Rabigato* and *Viosinho*. *Touriga Nacional* can be made into a dry wine, too. Portugal's finest red grape, it makes complicated, elegant wines, such as those from Barca Velha, Quinta do Côtto and Cedro do Noval.

The grapes grown in these hot conditions produce a full-bodied red wine that is traditionally crushed by foot in big stone *lagars* or troughs, to extract their maximum colour and flavour. They are then fortified by about one-fifth of their volume with a neutral grape spirit before fermentation has stopped, and so the neutral grape spirit still remains in the finished drink.

Port comes in several forms, from very simple ruby Port, to high-quality LBV (late bottled vintage). Single-vintage Port and single-estate Port are the top-quality wines, and these can be aged for decades. Deliberately oxidised Port – the process changes the colour as well as the flavour – falls under the Tawny Port category.

In the French region of Roussillon, they make sweet fortified Banyuls wine from Grenache using the same processes, and so this wine is often referred to as 'French Port'.

WHAT FOOD GOES WELL Salty-sweet combinations (see page 39), hence Port's fame with Stilton at Christmas. Try it with Welsh rarebit, or anchovy toasts with Parmesan custards. It is also famously paired with chocolate desserts and will also work extremely well with anything that contains darkly caramelised sweet elements.

RECOMMENDED PRODUCERS

Graham's Vintage; Quinta do Noval; Banyuls 'Quintessence', Coume del Mas (France); Blandy's Vintage

Other producers Taylor's; Churchill's; Dow's; Cockburn's; Delaforce; Sandeman, D'Oliveiras

RECIPE RECOMMENDATIONS

Fig galette with a blue cheese crust (Graham's) ☞ *page 340*

Port-poached pear, whipped Stilton, honeyed walnuts (Noval) ☞ *page 336*

Chocolate & honeycomb semifreddo (Banyuls) ☞ *page 332*

OPPOSITE 'Verdelho Solera 1880' Madeira, H M Borges; 'Terrantez 1971' Madeira, D'Oliveiras

ABOVE Quinta do Noval Port

Scallop ceviche with peas, lime, dill & crisp pancetta
Riesling 'Polish Hill', Jeffrey Grosset, Clare Valley

☞ page 55

SERVES 4 AS A STARTER

The scallops we use at the Club are hand-dived off the Isle of Mull by my friend Guy Grieve of The Ethical Shellfish Company. Guy likens himself to an 'ocean-going shepherd'. At the end of a dive, any small scallops are carefully redistributed in areas out of reach of destructive dredge boats, in places with a high tidal flow, where he knows they will flourish. This helps ensure stocks for the future.

Guy's scallops come to us live, so we serve them raw. At home, you will need either to shuck your own scallops (look online!) or get your fishmonger to do so in front of you as soon as possible before serving. (Ask them for 4 scallop shells, too.)

Clare Valley Riesling is a good match, as it has enough zing and acid to stand up to the lime in the ceviche.

ALTERNATIVE WINE MATCHES

Dry Riesling, Villa Bellangelo, Finger Lakes, New York ☞ *page 50*

Riesling 'Isolation Ridge', Frankland Estate, Western Australia ☞ *page 55*

Riesling 'Watervale', Mount Horrocks Wines, Clare Valley ☞ *page 55*

2 pancetta rashers, halved
150ml extra virgin olive oil
finely grated zest and juice of 5 limes
2 large mild green chillies, deseeded and finely chopped
1 small red onion, finely chopped
12 live scallops (see recipe introduction), without corals
150g frozen peas, defrosted and roughly chopped
1 tbsp chopped dill, any coarse stalks removed
salt and pepper
4 cleaned scallop shells, to serve
seaweed, or coarse sea salt, to serve

Place a large, heavy-based frying pan over a medium heat and cook the pancetta on both sides until crisp. Lay on kitchen paper and leave to cool.

In a bowl, mix together the oil, lime zest and juice, chillies and red onion. Allow to stand for 10 minutes, for the flavours to infuse.

Meanwhile, slice each scallop, horizontally, into 3 discs.

Once the lime marinade has had its infusing time, add the sliced scallops, mix to coat and allow to marinate for 3–4 minutes. During this time, the acidic lime juice will lightly 'cook' the scallops.

Stir in the chopped peas and dill just before serving (or they will discolour), then season well.

Place a scallop shell on each of 4 plates, arranging a little seaweed or coarse salt under each to hold them steady. Set the sliced scallops in each shell and spoon the marinade generously over the top. Crown each with a half rasher of crisp pancetta and serve immediately.

GROSSET
Polish Hill
2016

Pan-fried scallops, wild garlic mousseline potato, almond beurre noisette
St-Joseph Blanc 'Les Oliviers', Domaine Pierre Gonon

☞ page 82

SERVES 4 AS A STARTER

White St-Joseph from the Northern Rhône can have a marzipan richness, so the almond *beurre noisette* served with these scallops is a perfect match.

Wild garlic has a fairly short season at the beginning of spring. I know exactly when it's coming in, as it makes its appearance at the same time as daffodils peep out. If it's not the right time of year, or you can't manage to source it, the mousseline potato is also good with a little finely sliced spring onion stirred in instead.

ALTERNATIVE WINE MATCHES

Viognier-Marsanne 'The Hermit Crab', d'Arenberg, McLaren Vale ☞ page 83

Hermitage Blanc, Domaine Jean-Louis Chave ☞ page 82

80g blanched almonds
50ml vegetable oil
4 cleaned scallop shells, to serve
2 large potatoes (Maris Piper are best)
about 150ml full-fat milk
75ml double cream
about 150g unsalted butter
8 wild garlic leaves
12 large scallops (get the fishmonger to shuck them in front of you as soon as possible before cooking)
juice of ¼ lemon
1 tbsp chopped parsley leaves
salt and pepper
lemon wedges, to serve

Preheat the oven to 170°C. On a small baking tray, toast the blanched almonds for about 7 minutes in the oven with a little salt and a light drizzle of oil. They should only be toasted lightly, to bring out the oils and flavour. Once cooked, remove them from the oven and, when they're cool enough to handle, chop them roughly.

Place the shells in the oven, switch it off and leave them to keep warm.

Peel and quarter the potatoes. Place them in a saucepan, cover with cold water, add a little salt and bring to the boil. After 15–20 minutes, once the potatoes are soft, drain them in a colander. Allow to stand for a couple of minutes so they release steam and dry out.

Meanwhile, bring the milk, cream and 100g of the butter to the boil in a small saucepan, then remove from the heat. Once the potatoes have rested but are still hot, press them through a potato ricer back into the pan. Fold in the hot milk mixture until you reach the desired consistency. Season with salt. Stir in the wild garlic, remove from the heat and cover to keep warm.

Heat a large heavy-based frying pan over a high heat. Place the scallops in a bowl, season, then coat with the remaining oil. It's better to oil the scallops than the pan, so you use minimal oil and the scallops sear rather than boil.

Carefully place each scallop into the hot pan. Scallops must be cooked quickly so they caramelise but don't overcook. Sear the scallops until caramelised on one side, then turn over. Don't be tempted to shake the pan, as this will only cool it down. After a few seconds, add the remaining 50g butter and the chopped almonds, then season. Now you can move the pan around so the butter browns evenly. Once the butter smells nutty and is a brown colour, squeeze in the lemon juice. This will arrest the cooking, stopping the butter from burning. Finish with the chopped parsley.

Put a warm scallop shell on each of 4 warmed plates. Spoon warm potato mousseline into each shell, followed by 3 scallops and a spoonful of almond butter. Serve with lemon wedges.

Crab & samphire salad, grapes & soft herbs
Chablis Grand Cru 'Valmur', Domaine Raveneau

☞ page 68

SERVES 6 AS A STARTER

Chablis has a natural affinity with anything from the sea. Its high acidity and mineral qualities make it great for shellfish, plus it grows in the fossils of old mussel shells, so perhaps there is some respect to pay there! We have chosen a Grand Cru that would also work with rich brown crab, so if you'd like that, mix it with a little mayo and serve it on the side. Or choose a Village- or Premier Cru-level Chablis.

Choose the grape to go into the salad wisely. A ripe grape with more sugar is better for older Chablis, but a sharper grape is better with a younger, unoaked wine of higher acidity.

I always have this versatile lemon dressing in the fridge. Use it to dress a salad, shaved raw summer vegetables, or grilled fish. It's hard to buy chervil, but it is delicious here, so if you grow your own, use it, or just leave it out.

ALTERNATIVE WINE MATCHES

Chablis, Domaine Gilbert Picq ☞ *page 68*

Chablis 1er Cru 'Les Vaillons', Domaine Bernard Defaix ☞ *page 68*

Chablis 1er Cru 'Montmain', Domaine Louis Michel & Fils ☞ *page 68*

FOR THE LEMON DRESSING (MAKES 500ML)

- 2 garlic cloves
- a few tarragon sprigs
- 80ml Chardonnay vinegar, or good white wine vinegar
- juice of 1 lemon
- 300ml extra virgin olive oil
- 100ml sunflower oil
- salt and pepper

FOR THE SALAD

- 300g samphire, all woody stems removed
- 300g white crab meat
- 120ml Lemon dressing (see left)
- juice of ½ lemon
- small pinch of cayenne pepper
- 150g seedless white grapes, halved, or quartered if large
- 1 shallot, finely chopped and rinsed in a sieve under cold water
- 1 tbsp chopped chervil leaves (optional)
- ½ tbsp chopped dill, any coarse stalks removed

Start by making the dressing; it's best to do this the night before, if you can. Crush the garlic with the flat side of a knife and bruise the tarragon with the back of a spoon to release its flavours. Whisk all the ingredients together, season generously and allow to infuse overnight. Strain and decant into a bottle, so you can give it a good shake before using.

Fill a saucepan with water and bring it to the boil. Blanch the samphire in the boiling water for 30 seconds, strain it through a sieve and plunge it straight into iced water to arrest the cooking and keep it a vibrant green. Remove the samphire from the iced water and drain it on kitchen paper.

Place the samphire in a mixing bowl and add the white crab meat. Give the bottle of lemon dressing a good shake and add 4 tbsp to the samphire and crab. Squeeze in the lemon juice, add the cayenne and fold together gently. Taste and add a little salt if you feel it needs it. Scatter the crab meat and samphire evenly between 6 plates.

Place the grapes, shallot, chervil (if using) and dill in a mixing bowl and fold in the remaining lemon dressing, then scatter over the crab and samphire.

Spicy crab linguine with barbe di frate
Chardonnay 'Block 5', Felton Road, Central Otago

☞ page 70

SERVES 4–5

This Chardonnay is one of the best wines from Central Otago, and is owned by a Club supporter: Nigel Greening. Like a good Burgundy, it is broad and rich in the mouth and tails off to a beautiful, long, saline finish.

Crab linguine has proved the most popular pasta dish at the Club, making a regular appearance on the menu. We source our crab from Alan and Shaun Henderson in Devon. It's all lovingly picked by hand and an absolute pleasure to work with. This dish uses both white meat from the claws and the richer, full-flavoured brown meat.

Barbe di frate, also known as monk's beard, is a succulent that grows in coastal areas of the Mediterranean. It is now cultivated and sold in good food markets. If you can't find it, samphire makes a great substitute.

ALTERNATIVE WINE MATCHES

Chardonnay, Tolpuddle Vineyard, Tasmania ☞ page 70

Chardonnay, Ataraxia, Hemel-en-Aarde, South Africa ☞ page 66

'Cervaro della Sala', Marchesi Antinori, Umbria ☞ page 66

100ml fish stock
150g brown crab meat
100g shallots, finely chopped
2 red chillies, deseeded and finely chopped
250g unsalted butter, chilled and chopped
50ml white wine
2 tbsp Sherry
40ml double cream
juice of ½ lemon
pinch of cayenne pepper
500g dried linguine
150g *barbe di frate*
150g white crab meat
2 tbsp chopped chives
salt

Bring the stock to the boil in a saucepan. Stir in the brown crab meat and return to the boil, then pour into a blender and blitz until smooth. Strain through a sieve, pushing it through with the back of a spoon.

In a clean pan over a low heat, sauté the shallots and chillies in 40g of the butter with a pinch of salt, cooking gently until the shallots are soft and translucent. Add the wine and Sherry and reduce the liquor by half, then pour in the blended stock and crab mixture and return the sauce to the boil. Add the cream. Now, gradually, over a medium heat, whisk in the remaining chilled butter to form an emulsion. Once it has been incorporated, add the lemon juice. Season the sauce with salt and cayenne pepper to taste, then remove from the heat until you're ready to add the cooked pasta.

Bring a large pan of water to the boil and season it liberally with salt.

If you've chosen to make your own pasta (see page 234) it will cook in a matter of seconds, so make sure you have everything ready to go before it hits the water. If you're using dried pasta, use the timings specified on the packet as a guide, but check it a couple of minutes before it's supposed to be ready, as they can be inaccurate.

While the pasta is cooking, pick off and discard the roots from the *barbe di frate* and give it a good wash in cold water. Drop the *barbe di frate* into the boiling pasta water for the last 30 seconds, then strain in a colander.

Gently reheat the sauce, but do not boil it or it will split. Add the white crab meat and chives, then toss the pasta through the sauce.

Serve immediately on warmed plates or pasta bowls.

FELTON

Oyster tempura, green apple, wasabi & lime mayonnaise, shizo
Semillon 'Vat 1', Tyrrell's, Hunter Valley

☞ page 74

SERVES 4 AS AN APPETISER

Soon after leaving Tyrrell's winery in the Hunter Valley, just north of Sydney, Ronan emailed me to explain the flavours in the wine and to say that it would be perfect by the glass with a bar snack, with its flavours of lime and green apple with an oyster minerality. This is what I came up with as a match.

Before opening the Club in 2015, we tasted many oysters. Carlingford rocks from north-east Ireland shone head and shoulders above the rest. Like wine, oysters gain much of their flavour from their environment; each can filter 55 litres of water a day, so nature determines how they taste. Carlingford has a huge exchange of water with each tide, with fresh water also flowing in from the mountains, giving the oysters a creamy richness and subtle mineral freshness.

ALTERNATIVE WINE MATCHES

Albariño, Neudorf Vineyards, Nelson ☞ page 80

Sylvaner VV 'Rosenberg', Domaine Barmès-Buecher, Alsace ☞ page 52

'Minéral' Blanc de Blancs, Agrapart & Fils ☞ page 85

1 quantity Tempura batter (see page 153), plus 100g tempura flour, to coat
1 tbsp wasabi paste
2 tbsp lime juice
150g Mayonnaise (see page 307)
vegetable oil, to deep-fry
12 live rock oysters
1 Granny Smith apple
rock salt, to serve
1 punnet purple shizo cress, to serve (optional)

Start by making the batter, then leave it to rest for 30 minutes.

In a mixing bowl, whisk the wasabi and lime juice into the mayonnaise. Don't adjust the seasoning yet, as you will add some of the salty oyster juice.

Once the batter has rested, set a deep-fat fryer to 170°C. If you don't have a fryer, place the oil in a large, deep saucepan, leaving enough room at the top to allow for rapid boiling when the oysters are added. Place over a high heat, but be careful it doesn't get too hot. If you have a cooking thermometer, use it to regulate the temperature. If not, test the heat by dropping in a cube of bread; it should bubble on entry and start to brown after 15 seconds.

Have to hand some kitchen paper and a slotted spoon to remove the oysters from the hot oil. (Don't try to use spring-loaded tongs; this can be very dangerous, for obvious reasons.)

Shuck the oysters (find a guide online, if you need it), taking care to protect your hands, then tip off the juices and reserve. Place the oysters into a colander and wash the bowl-shaped shells (discard the flatter half of the shells). Fill a serving platter with rock salt and sit the shells on the salt.

Strain the reserved oyster juice to remove any fragments of shell. Add enough of it to the mayonnaise to give a loose salad cream consistency.

If you have a mandolin, use it to cut the apple into thin batons. If not, do so with a knife. Dress immediately with mayonnaise, to prevent discolouration. Place a little apple into each shell, being generous with the dressing.

Place the tempura flour into a bowl, and, one by one, coat the oysters with the flour, shaking off excess. Drop the floured oysters into the batter.

When you're ready to cook the oysters, lift them out one at a time, placing them carefully into the fryer with a spoon. Hold the oyster in the spoon submerged in the oil for a few seconds to allow the batter to set, before letting it go. (This will stop it sticking to the bottom.) Cook 6 at a time, or they will stick together. Deep-fry for about 2 minutes, until golden and crisp. Drain on kitchen paper to soak up any oil, before placing them on the dressed apple in the shells. You shouldn't need to season them. Pick a few purple shizo tips, if you like, and place them on top of each oyster to serve.

TYRRELL'S WINES
Vat 1

Soalheiro
ALVARINHO

Piri piri tiger prawns
Alvarinho, Quinta da Soalheiro, Vinho Verde

☞ *page 80*

SERVES 4 AS A STARTER

At the Club we skewer these prawns and cook them quickly in the Josper grill (see page 277) before tossing them through the piri piri sauce. You could do the same at home on a barbecue if you wish, as they benefit from the flavour that charcoal adds.

In the small fishing villages of the Algarve, each restaurant has a chef out the front cooking fish on a huge barbecue made from a 200-litre oil drum split down the middle, filled with hot coals, with a wire rack perched on top. The smell is paradise.

Alvarinho's zesty acidity and citrus flavours make it a superb seafood wine. I couldn't think of anything better than enjoying a glass with this dish on a hot day in the Algarve.

You only need half the piri piri sauce for this recipe. Try the leftovers with chargrilled sardines, or chicken.

ALTERNATIVE WINE MATCHES

Albariño, Pazo de Villarei, Rías Baixas ☞ *page 80*

'K-Naia', Bodegas Naia, Rueda ☞ *page 80*

Sauvignon Blanc 'Amayna', Garcés Silva, Leyda ☞ *page 56*

- 200ml extra virgin olive oil, plus 50ml more to fry the prawns
- 1 red pepper, deseeded and chopped
- 2 shallots, chopped
- 4 red chillies, chopped
- 2 large garlic cloves, chopped
- 1 tsp sweet smoked paprika
- 1 tbsp Lingham's sweet chilli sauce
- 1 tsp Tabasco sauce, or to taste
- 1 tbsp red wine vinegar
- finely grated zest and juice of 1 lime, plus lime wedges to serve
- 16 tiger prawns (heads on, tails on, shells removed)
- salt

To make the piri piri sauce, set a heavy-based saucepan over a medium heat. Add 50ml of the oil and cook the red pepper, shallots, chillies and garlic for a few minutes until soft. Season with salt, add the smoked paprika and continue to cook for a minute or so. Remove from the heat and allow to cool. Once cool, tip into a blender and add the sweet chilli sauce, Tabasco, vinegar, lime zest and juice and the remaining 150ml oil. Blend until the consistency is smooth and the sauce has emulsified. Have a taste and add more salt and Tabasco if you feel it's needed. Store in a sealed jar in the fridge until ready to use; it will keep for a few weeks.

To cook the prawns, preheat a large non-stick frying pan over a high heat. Season the prawns liberally with salt. Drizzle about 50ml olive oil into the pan and add the prawns. Allow them to cook on one side for 45 seconds, before carefully turning them over. Pour half the piri piri sauce into the hot pan over the prawns. (You don't need the other half of the sauce.)

Allow the prawns to cook for another 30–40 seconds, or until they are done; they will be pink on all sides.

Place 4 prawns on each of 4 warm plates and spoon the sauce over the top. Serve with lime wedges.

Lobster thermidor vol-au-vents
Meursault-Charmes 1er Cru, Domaine Roulot

☞ page 68

SERVES 6 AS A STARTER

See previous page for picture

Vol-au-vents are certainly a retro classic, but I can't get enough of them. What could be better than buttery puff pastry filled with a rich, unctuous sauce? This version came from a menu we served at the Club for François Audouze, one of the world's best-known wine collectors. We matched it with a very old white Burgundy, which proved to be a perfect combination with the rich creamy sauce, crisp buttery pastry and sweet lobster.

As the name implies, the Charmes vineyard in Meursault produces wine that is forward, open and – yes – charming. With age it is opulent and full and a great match for rich cream, cheese and lobster.

FOR THE HOLLANDAISE SAUCE

80ml white wine vinegar
2 small shallots, chopped
a few tarragon sprigs
6 black peppercorns
250g unsalted butter
3 egg yolks
salt and pepper

FOR THE VOL-AU-VENTS

plain flour, to dust
600g all-butter puff pastry
5 egg yolks
2 x 600g live lobsters
300ml double cream
100g Gruyère cheese, grated
150g Hollandaise sauce (see left)
1 tsp English mustard
1 tsp Worcestershire sauce
20ml brandy
2 tbsp chopped tarragon leaves

Start with the hollandaise. Place the vinegar, shallots, tarragon and peppercorns in a saucepan over a medium heat and boil until reduced to about 2 tbsp. Strain and set aside.

Melt the butter in a saucepan, then simmer over a low heat for 5–10 minutes until it separates. Allow to cool for a few minutes; the whey solids will settle on the bottom. Pour off the warm clarified butter and discard the whey.

Put the egg yolks into a heatproof bowl with half the vinegar reduction. Place over a pan of barely simmering water, making sure the base of the bowl does not touch the water, and whisk until light and fluffy. Be careful not to heat the mixture too much, or the eggs may scramble; remove the pan from the heat if necessary. Slowly drizzle the warm clarified butter into the eggs, whisking to form an emulsion. You may need to add up to 3 tbsp of warm water if it gets too thick, before continuing with the butter. Season and taste to see if you want to add more vinegar reduction. Keep warm.

Preheat the oven to 180°C.

Dust a work surface and a rolling pin with flour. Roll out half the pastry to a thickness of about 5mm. Take a fork and prick the pastry all over at close intervals. This is known as docking and stops the pastry from rising so much as it cooks. From the docked pastry, using a 9cm pastry cutter, cut 6 discs. You can use a fluted cutter, but even for me that's taking retro a bit too far...

Place the discs on an oven tray lined with baking parchment. Repeat the process with the remaining pastry, but this time do not dock it. This second sheet is for the edges of the vol-au-vents and you need them to rise high to create the sides of the tart case. Once you have cut your 9cm discs, cut the centre out of each to make rings, using an 8cm cutter.

Mix the 5 egg yolks in a small bowl. Using a pastry brush, brush the docked pastry disks with the yolk, right to the edge. Stick the pastry rings on to the discs, then brush on more egg yolk to glaze. Bake in the middle of the oven

ALTERNATIVE WINE MATCHES

Pouilly-Fuissé Vieilles Vignes, Château-Fuissé ☞ *page 70*

Chassagne-Montrachet 1er Cru 'Les Caillerets', Jean Nöel Gagnard ☞ *page 68*

Chardonnay, Château Montelena, Napa Valley ☞ *page 71*

for 15–18 minutes, until the layers of pastry have risen high and are crisp and golden. Allow them to cool enough to handle.

Once cool enough, with a small sharp knife, carefully cut through the layer of risen pastry all the way around the inside of the frame, then push the centre of the vol-au-vent down to its base, creating a cavity for the filling.

Fill a large stockpot with water, season it heavily with salt and bring to a rapid boil. Before you cook the lobsters, you will need to dispatch them. The most humane and quickest way to do this is by plunging the tip of a heavy cook's knife through the middle of the lobster's head, about 2.5cm back from its eyes. It will still be moving after this, sometimes quite violently, but this is only the nerves reacting. If this is a bit much for you, just put the lobsters into the freezer 45 minutes before boiling them. This will make them docile and the process will be a lot less stressful, not just for the lobster but also for the faint-hearted cook. Boil the lobsters for 8 minutes, then remove them from the water using sturdy tongs.

Allow the lobsters to cool enough to handle, but not too much, as it's easier to extract the meat from the shell when they are still warm. First, remove the whole tail by pulling and twisting it from the head. Then remove the claws from the head in the same way. Using pliers or nutcrackers, crack all the sections of each claw and remove the meat, keeping it as intact as possible. To extract the tail meat, (assuming you're right-handed) hold the tail in your left hand with the underside facing up and the tail pointing away from you. Using sturdy kitchen scissors, cut through the softer underside, snipping through each hard, calcified joint until you reach the tail. Prise the shell open and remove the tail meat in a single piece. Slice the tail meat into 1cm medallions and store in the fridge with the claw meat until needed.

The heads and broken shells will keep in the freezer for 3 months and are ideal for a soup or lobster bisque for another occasion.

In a heavy-based saucepan over a medium heat, bring the cream to the boil, and reduce to 150ml, stirring regularly so it does not catch. Whisk in the cheese until melted and well incorporated.

Remove the sauce from the heat and fold in the hollandaise, mustard, Worcestershire sauce, brandy and tarragon. Season, fold in the lobster meat and fill each vol-au-vent case evenly.

Bake on the middle shelf of the oven for 10 minutes, until the filling has a golden glaze. Test the centre is hot by inserting a small knife; it should emerge hot. Serve immediately on warmed plates.

Chargrilled spiny lobster, tarragon & shallot butter Chardonnay 'The Judge', John Kongsgaard, Napa Valley

☞ page 71

SERVES 6

Spiny lobsters are common in New Zealand and Australia, and my friend Guy Grieve, up in the Isle of Mull, now and then comes across one and sends it down to me. They are few and far between and a real treat. The sweet tail flesh is to die for... If you can't find them, native UK lobsters are also good, but boil the claws separately, as they don't cook well on a barbecue.

Warmer regions such as Napa give round, rich tropical fruit flavours to Chardonnay, and it is this richness that matches both the butter and the sweet lobster flesh so well.

A rich herb butter basted over the lobster as it cooks is also key, as, just like lobster, Chardonnay loves butter!

ALTERNATIVE WINE MATCHES

Chardonnay, Greywacke, Marlborough ☞ page 70

Chardonnay 'Red Shoulder Ranch', Shafer, Napa Valley ☞ page 71

Puligny-Montrachet 1er Cru 'La Truffière', Domaine Jean-Marc Boillot ☞ page 68

- 4 large shallots, finely chopped
- 350g unsalted butter, softened
- 200ml dry white wine
- 3 tsp Dijon mustard
- 3 tbsp chopped tarragon leaves
- 6 x 500–600g spiny lobsters
- salt and pepper
- lemon wedges, chips and green salad, to serve

Prepare a barbecue and let it burn down until the coals are glowing.

In a heavy-based saucepan over a medium heat, cook the shallots gently in a knob of the butter until soft and translucent. Add the wine, increase the heat, then reduce until it has completely evaporated. Let it cool. In a mixing bowl, mix the cooled shallots, mustard and tarragon into the remaining softened butter until incorporated. Season and set aside, but do not chill.

Before you cook the lobsters, you will need to dispatch them and split them in half down the middle (see page 145). Scoop out the green tomalley, and also the bright orange roe if you were lucky enough to get a female. (The roe of a spiny lobster is bright orange, but that of a native UK lobster is deep green, only turning orange when cooked.)

Mix all the tomalley and the roe into the butter. This imparts great flavour into the lobster as the butter bastes the meat.

Once the barbecue is nice and hot, season the flesh of the lobsters. Smear a little of the butter on the flesh and place them on the barbecue, flesh side down. Don't be alarmed if they twitch as they cook, this is just nerves.

Cook the lobsters for a minute or so before turning over on to their shell sides for another 3 minutes. Baste the flesh with the tarragon butter, using a pastry brush, as they cook. Once they are done, plate the lobster halves back to back on 6 plates. Melt the remaining butter in a saucepan and pour it over the top. Serve with lemon wedges, chips and a green salad.

Moules marinières
Muscadet Sèvre & Maine sur lie 'Excelsior', Domaine Pierre Luneau-Papin

☞ page 62

SERVES 4 AS A STARTER

Moules marinières is the classic food pairing with bone-dry Muscadet from the Loire Valley. Muscadet has a saline-like quality, especially in wines from those vineyards closer to the sea that experience salty sea breezes, which makes it perfect with bivalves such as mussels or oysters.

Muscadet that is aged on its lees (*sur lie*) develops a creamy texture, and the longer on the lees, the richer the texture. This works well with the light creamy broth that needs mopping up with crusty baguette once all the mussels are gone.

ALTERNATIVE WINE MATCHES

Muscadet 'Terre de Gneiss', Christelle Guibert, Domaine Le Fay d'Homme ☞ page 62

Bizkaiko Txakolina, Gorka Izagirre, Txakolí ☞ page 80

Vouvray Sec, Domaine du Clos Naudin, Philippe Foreau ☞ page 64

1 garlic bulb
250ml double cream
2kg plump live mussels
150ml Muscadet
3 large shallots, finely chopped
4 tbsp chopped parsley leaves
juice of ½ lemon
salt and pepper
crusty baguette, to serve

Separate the garlic cloves and crush them one at a time with the flat side of a cook's knife under the heel of your hand.

Place the crushed garlic, skin and all, into a small saucepan and pour over the cream. Set over a medium heat, bring to the boil, then remove from the heat. Leave to infuse for 30 minutes, then strain through a sieve into a bowl.

Remove the beard from each mussel and, using a blunt knife, scrape off any barnacles or white worm growing on the shells. Give them a quick rinse to remove grit. If any shells are open, give them a firm tap on a work surface. If they don't close, discard them, along with any that are cracked or broken.

Preheat a large saucepan over a high heat and add the mussels, Muscadet, shallots, parsley and garlic-infused cream. Season with salt and pepper. Place a tight lid over the pan and allow the mussels to steam open, giving the pan a shake from time to time. This should only take a minute or so. Discard any mussels that do not open, or warn your diners to do so.

Once the mussels are open, squeeze in the lemon juice and serve immediately, discarding any that have failed to open, with more crusty baguette than you think you will need. Mopping up the sauce is the highlight of this dish!

Zalto

Thai octopus salad
Gewurztraminer 'Les Princes Abbés', Domaines Schlumberger

☞ page 77

SERVES 6 AS A STARTER

Ask your fishmonger to order the octopus in advance, as they are readily available frozen, and freezing helps to tenderise them. Fishermen in Greece bash octopus on the rocks instead to tenderise them and I've even heard talk of cement mixers being used!

I won my job as Club head chef partly on the back of this dish. After a phone chat about the flavours in the off-dry Alsatian Gewurztraminer we match it with, I added lemon grass, lime, ginger and sugar, contrasted with salty fish sauce. Gewurztraminer is great with exotic foods, due to its spicy character and tropical fruit aromas. South-east Asian seafood dishes are a particularly good match. You could even add shredded green mango or papaya here and it would further complement the wine.

ALTERNATIVE WINE MATCHES

Gewurztraminer 'Gimblett Gravels', Stonecroft, Hawke's Bay ☞ page 77

Pinot Gris 'Sand Dollar', Greystone, North Canterbury ☞ page 77

Gewurztraminer 'Sonnenglanz', Domaine Bott-Geyl, Alsace ☞ page 77

TO PREPARE THE OCTOPUS

1.5kg whole octopus
4 lemon grass stalks, bruised
2.5cm fresh root ginger, chopped
4 garlic cloves, crushed
10 fresh lime leaves, bruised
80ml fish sauce
2 limes, halved
80ml white wine vinegar
½ tbsp fennel seeds
2 star anise
10 peppercorns
1 large onion, roughly chopped

FOR THE THAI DRESSING

250ml groundnut oil
4 garlic cloves, finely chopped
250ml lime juice
125ml fish sauce (Squid brand is good)
125g caster sugar
15 fresh lime leaves, stalks removed

FOR THE SALAD

2 ripe tomatoes, deseeded and sliced
½ small red onion, finely sliced
3 red chillies, finely sliced
30g coriander cress, or regular coriander leaves, finely sliced
30g Thai basil cress, or regular Thai basil leaves, finely sliced
30g purple shizo cress, or regular purple shizo leaves, finely sliced
30g green shizo cress, or regular green shizo leaves, finely sliced
150ml Thai dressing (see left)

Place the octopus into a large saucepan and cover with cold water. Over a high heat, bring to the boil. Once boiling, strain the octopus through a colander over the sink, discarding the water. In a clean saucepan, bring all the remaining ingredients for the octopus to the boil in 2 litres of water. Add the octopus, reduce the heat and simmer for 45–50 minutes.

Meanwhile, make the dressing. Place the oil in a small saucepan and add the garlic. Place over a medium heat, stirring; the garlic will start to bubble and slowly turn light gold. Strain over a bowl to catch the oil, then allow to cool.

In a separate mixing bowl, stir together the lime juice, fish sauce and caster sugar until the sugar dissolves. Slice the lime leaves into fine strips and add to the dressing to infuse. Once the groundnut oil and garlic have cooled down, whisk them into the dressing. Taste: it should have a harmonious balance of acid from lime, salt from fish sauce and sweetness from sugar.

Once the octopus is tender, remove from the heat and cool for 45 minutes in the cooking liquor. Clean it (there's instructions online) and slice the tentacles on an angle into 2.5cm pieces. Do the same with the head. Use half the dressing to marinate the octopus at room temperature for 1 hour.

Place the tomatoes into a large bowl with the red onion and chillies. Drain the octopus of its marinade and add to the salad. Finally add the fragrant micro cresses or regular herbs and toss the salad together with the dressing.

Serve immediately.

DOMAINES
SCHLUMBERGER
GEWURZTRAMINER

Tempura squid, preserved lemon, marinated fennel & spicy tomato salsa
Assyrtiko 'Kavalieros', Domaine Sigalas, Santorini

☞ page 80

SERVES 6 AS A STARTER

Paris Sigalas is definitely a star on Santorini and Ronan has loved his wines for a long while. He was serving them by the glass in 2001 in a three-star restaurant back when people had never heard of Greek wine, except Retsina. The 'Kavalieros' (knight) is Sigalas's crowning glory. Assyrtiko, from Santorini, is a remarkable grape, which holds its acidity well in the heat of the island and has fennel and grapefruit notes that work well with seafood, and reflect the flavours here.

Although preserved lemons are readily available, you can make your own at home. They are such a good addition to so many dishes.

This fresh, lightly pickled fennel is sublime. Please take care using a mandolin and always use the hand guard; if you think it would be quicker and easier without it, then that is a mistake I've also made. Only once...

ALTERNATIVE WINE MATCHES

Assyrtiko, Domaine Papagiannakos, Attiki ☞ page 80 and 82

Assyrtiko de Mylos Vielles Vignes, Hatzidakis Winery, Santorini ☞ page 80

FOR THE FENNEL

2 fennel bulbs
50ml Chardonnay vinegar, or other white wine vinegar
50ml extra virgin olive oil
1 tbsp icing sugar
2 medium chillies, deseeded and finely chopped
1 tbsp chopped dill or fennel tops
salt and freshly ground white pepper

FOR THE SALSA

6 ripe tomatoes
2 shallots, finely chopped
2 tbsp Lingham's sweet chilli sauce
1 tbsp white balsamic vinegar
80ml extra virgin olive oil
2 tbsp finely chopped parsley leaves

FOR THE SQUID

600g squid, cleaned
vegetable oil, to deep-fry
couple of pinches of cayenne pepper
300g Spicy tomato salsa (see left)
1 tbsp shredded Preserved lemon rind (see page 181)

FOR THE TEMPURA BATTER

300ml sparkling water, chilled
1 ice cube
150g tempura flour, plus more to dust

Cut the fennel bulbs in half and remove the cores. Using a mandolin, shave them finely. Place in a bowl, add the vinegar, oil, icing sugar and chillies and season with salt and white pepper. Leave at room temperature for 1 hour, stirring every so often. Just before serving, add the chopped herbs.

Make the salsa fresh, so the flavours are lively. Quarter each tomato, discard the seeds and cut the tomato into small dice. Put the shallots in a sieve and rinse well, to reduce their heat. Put the tomato and shallots in a bowl with the chilli sauce, white balsamic and olive oil. Fold in the parsley and season.

Slice the squid tubes into rings about 1cm thick. Chill with the tentacles.

When making tempura batter, it's important the sparkling water is chilled. To keep it cold, slide an ice cube inside the whisk. Place the flour in a bowl. Slowly whisk in the sparkling water a little at a time. The consistency should be light enough to just coat the squid. Chill until ready to use. Once the batter has rested, set a deep-fat fryer to 190°C, or use a saucepan, taking the same precautions and care as usual (see page 138).

Tip some tempura flour into a bowl and coat the squid with it, shaking off excess. Drop the floured squid into the batter. When you're ready to fry the squid, lift it out of the batter a couple of pieces at a time and allow excess batter to drain off before carefully dropping it into the oil. (Don't try to fry it all at once; you'll end up with single mass of squid all stuck together.) Deep-fry for 2 minutes, until golden and crispy. Drain on kitchen paper to soak up any oil, then dust sparingly with cayenne pepper and salt.

Serve on warmed plates with the marinated fennel and spicy tomato salsa, sprinkling over the preserved lemon.

Dover sole meunière with capers
Châteauneuf-du-Pape blanc, Château de Beaucastel

☞ page 82

SERVES 4

See previous page for picture

Counterintuitively, Dover sole do not cook well on the bone if they are too fresh; the flesh can be tough and the fish are harder to fillet. They are best a day or two after being pulled from the water. Ask your fishmonger to remove the dark skins.

Beaucastel Blanc is produced from old vines, 80 per cent of which are Roussanne and about 5 per cent Grenache (see pages 82 and 106). The rest come from a blend of grapes that fare well in the hot Southern Rhône climate. This wine is rich, golden and full-bodied and often has a nutty, buttery characteristic, which complements the burned butter here. Try not to be too heavy-handed with the capers; the acidity of Roussanne can cope with them, but be judicious.

ALTERNATIVE WINE MATCHES

St-Joseph Blanc 'Les Oliviers', Domaine Pierre Gonon ☞ *page 82*

Chardonnay, Hamilton Russell Vineyards, Hemel-en-Aarde, South Africa ☞ *page 66*

- 4 x 400g Dover soles, dark skins removed
- plain flour, to dust
- 250g unsalted butter, softened
- juice of ½ lemon, plus lemon wedges, to serve
- 40g salted capers, rinsed and soaked for 3 hours
- 2 tbsp chopped parsley leaves
- salt and pepper
- boiled new potatoes and green beans, to serve

Preheat the oven to 180°C.

Using sturdy kitchen scissors, trim off the fins running the length of the fish on each side and then remove the tails. Place some flour on a tray and lay the skinned sides of the fish, one at a time, in the flour. Lift them out and pat to remove excess flour. Place on a work surface and rub a generous layer of the butter over the floured surface of each fish, then season.

Preheat a non-stick frying pan large enough to hold 2 fish over a medium heat. Place 2 of the soles buttered sides down in the dry pan. As they hit the pan, the butter will sizzle and the fish will begin to caramelise. As the cooking progresses, the milk solids in the butter will begin to separate from the fat and turn golden brown, giving off a toasted nutty aroma. Once the fish have caramelised nicely on one side, using a pair of tongs, turn them one at a time by lifting them by the head. Add a little more butter to the pan and allow it to bubble away for a minute or so. Lift the first 2 fish from the pan and place them on a large oven tray. Repeat with the last 2 fish.

Place in the oven for 6 minutes. Once the fish is cooked, allow it to rest on 4 warmed serving plates for a couple of minutes.

Meanwhile, wash out the frying pan and place it over a medium heat. Put about 150g of the butter into the pan and season it with salt and pepper. Keep the butter moving in the pan, swirling it to allow it to brown evenly. In the early stages of cooking the butter will be noisily bubbling away, but as the whey separates from the fat, the bubbles will reduce in size to almost a foam and the sizzling will subside. The butter at this stage will have turned a golden nutty brown. This is when you should turn off the heat and quickly squeeze in the lemon juice to arrest the cooking. Be careful though: when the juice hits the pan it will spit.

Give the pan a good shake to incorporate the lemon juice and add the capers and parsley. Pour the caper butter over each fish and serve immediately, with lemon wedges, boiled new potatoes and green beans.

012
ILLE PERRIN
de Beaucastel
ATEAUNEUF-DU-PAPE
EAUNEUF-DU-PAPE CONTROLÉE

Roast fillet of brill, cockles, ham hock & celery hearts Sancerre, Domaine Vacheron

☞ page 58

SERVES 6

Many people consider brill an inferior fish to turbot. I beg to differ. Turbot has always been put on a pedestal, but I prefer the slightly lighter, more delicate brill. The two are very similar in appearance and are related so closely that they can interbreed.

In the UK, brill is in season from October to March. Avoid them during the late spring and summer, so they can get on and procreate. Besides, the female will be carrying roe and putting her energy into making eggs, leaving the flesh of relatively inferior quality.

We have chosen Sancerre to pair with this dish. Ideally, find a Sancerre that has developed complexity with age, not one that is too young and fresh. Some time in oak is also important, so it can handle the rich, buttery sauce here. The celery hearts in this dish complement the vegetal notes typical of Sauvignon Blanc.

ALTERNATIVE WINE MATCHES

Sancerre 'Les Perrois' Domaine François Crochet
☞ page 58

Pouilly-Fumé 'Pur Sang', Didier Dagueneau
☞ page 58

- 1 green (unsmoked) ham hock, soaked overnight
- 1 carrot, quartered
- 1 onion, halved
- 1 leek, white part only
- 2 hearts of celery
- 1 bay leaf
- 5 thyme sprigs
- about 30 plump live cockles, tightly closed
- 6 x 160g brill fillets, skinned
- 50ml sunflower oil
- 100ml dry white wine
- 150g unsalted butter, chopped and chilled
- salt and pepper

Place the soaked ham hock into a large saucepan with the carrot, onion, leek, 2 chopped celery sticks, the bay leaf and thyme. Cover with cold water and bring to the boil over a high heat, then reduce the heat to a simmer. Simmer for 2½ hours, topping up with water as required to keep the hock covered. It is ready once the meat is falling from the bone. Lift the ham out of the stock with a slotted spoon and strain the stock through a sieve. Skim off any fat from the surface, allow to cool, then chill until needed.

Once the ham is cool enough to handle, discard the skin and fat and flake the meat into small pieces, removing any gristle.

Place the cockles in a colander and run under cold water for around 10 minutes, agitating regularly to release any sand or grit they may be holding. They should be tightly closed. If any open cockles don't close when tapped on a work surface, discard them. Drain.

Remove the light central stems from the hearts of celery (keep the remaining stalks for stock). Pick the light-coloured leaves and slice the stems finely.

Place a non-stick frying pan over a medium-high heat. Season the brill fillets and fry them in the sunflower oil, cooking them until golden on one side, then turn them and reduce the heat to low. Cook for 1 minute on the other side, then turn the heat off. The residual heat will finish off the fillets gently.

Put a large saucepan over a high heat. Drop in the cockles, wine and 100ml of ham stock and cover to steam open the cockles. Once the cockles are all open, add the ham, sliced celery hearts and butter. As the butter melts, it will emulsify with the wine and stock to create a light buttery broth.

Serve the cockles, ham and celery evenly between 6 warmed serving bowls, discarding any cockles that have failed to open. Ladle the sauce over the cockles and place a portion of brill on top. Scatter with a few crisp celery leaves to serve.

Tranche of turbot braised in red wine with ceps & lardons
Chinon 'Clos de la Dioterie', Charles Joguet

☞ page 118

SERVES 4

Turbot is the most revered fish caught around the UK and it comes with a hefty price tag. You can occasionally find wild turbot caught from boats by rod and line, but, sadly, much of the wild turbot available is caught by trawling boats that indiscriminately destroy the seabed. Farmed turbot is much more sustainable. As with brill, avoid turbot in the warmer months.

Turbot are a robust firm-fleshed fish that can handle being braised in red wine. And with a garnish of smoky lardons and ceps, the most revered of mushrooms, what could be better than a Chinon from the Loire Valley. It has high acidity to cut through the fish and spicy notes to suit the star anise, fennel and pepper in the braising liquor. The king of fish served with the king of mushrooms. How regal...

ALTERNATIVE WINE MATCHES

Saumur-Champigny 'Filliatreau', Domaine Filliatreau ☞ page 118

Gamay Noir, Brick House, Oregon ☞ page 86

- 750ml red wine
- 4 thyme sprigs
- 1 bay leaf
- ½ star anise
- 1 tsp fennel seeds
- 10 black peppercorns
- 200g unsalted butter
- 2 large shallots, finely sliced
- 2 garlic cloves, finely chopped
- 2 tbsp caster sugar
- 4 tbsp red wine vinegar
- 400ml beef or veal stock
- 250g ceps
- plain flour, to dust
- 4 x 250g turbot tranches, cut from a large fish
- 50ml sunflower oil
- 120g smoked bacon lardons
- 2 tbsp chopped parsley leaves
- salt and pepper

Pour the wine into a large saucepan and add 3 of the thyme sprigs, the bay, star anise, fennel seeds and peppercorns. Season with salt and bring to the boil over high heat, then leave to infuse. Strain through a sieve. Set aside.

To make the sauce, preheat a heavy-based saucepan over a medium heat. Put in a little of the butter and cook the shallots and garlic with the sugar, stirring until well caramelised. Add the remaining thyme and the vinegar and reduce by half. Add 200ml of the infused wine, return to the boil, then reduce until you have a rich 'jam'. Add the stock and return to a simmer. Reduce the sauce, skimming off any impurities on the surface, until it coats the back of a spoon; you should have about 200ml. Strain and set aside.

If the ceps are dirty, give the stalks a good scrape and rub off any dirt with a clean damp cloth. Cut into large pieces and set aside.

Place some plain flour on a tray and lay in the turbot tranches, turning to coat both sides. Lift them out, patting to remove any excess flour. Place the fish on a work surface with the dark skin facing upwards. Rub a generous layer of butter over the dark-skinned side and season.

Preheat a large non-stick frying pan over a medium heat. Add about 2 tbsp of the sunflower oil and place the turbot, buttered sides down, in the pan. As it hits the pan, it will sizzle. Caramelise well on one side, then turn, cook for a minute, and pour over the remaining infused wine. Bring to a simmer and cook for a couple of minutes. Cover and remove from the heat to cook through; this should take 2–3 minutes, depending on thickness.

Meanwhile, set a separate frying pan over a medium heat. Cook the lardons in the remaining sunflower oil until they are just beginning to caramelise. Add the ceps with a generous knob of butter, season and sauté for a few minutes until caramelised and cooked though. Toss in the parsley.

Return the sauce to the boil and whisk in a small knob of butter to give it a shine. Carefully lift the turbot out of the braising liquor and allow to drain on kitchen paper. Place a portion of fish on each of 4 warmed serving plates, with a pile of ceps and lardons. Spoon the sauce generously over and serve.

CHINON
Clos de la Dioterie
MONOPOLE
2015
CABERNET FRANC
JOGUET

Red snapper tacos, sweetcorn, avocado & lime salsa, chipotle mayonnaise
Riesling 'Bel Canto', Pegasus Bay, North Canterbury

☞ page 55

SERVES 4 AS A STARTER

You could serve these with all the ingredients and condiments at the table so your guests can build the tacos themselves. Or assemble them in the kitchen and serve them ready to go. The choice is yours!

I chose red snapper but, if you're having trouble sourcing it, sea bream is an ideal substitute.

This off-dry Riesling from New Zealand's Canterbury region is an ideal pairing for this exotic dish. 'Bel Canto' is one of my favourite Rieslings, and one of the finest outside Europe. In an Austrian Wachau Smaragd style (see page 82), it is slightly botrytised to give it richness, depth and texture, preparing it for the avalanche of sweet, citrus, spice and smoke in these delicious tacos.

ALTERNATIVE WINE MATCHES

Torrontés, Abel Mendoza, Argentina
☞ page 82

Riesling 'Block 1', Felton Road, Central Otago
☞ page 55

Riesling Spätlese, Weingut Robert Weil, Rheingau
☞ page 52

FOR THE CHIPOTLE MAYONNAISE

- 100ml Mayonnaise (see page 307)
- 50g soured cream
- ½ tsp chipotle chilli powder
- ½ tsp smoked paprika
- 1 tbsp chopped deseeded chipotle in adobo, plus 1 tsp adobo sauce
- juice of ½ lime, plus lime wedges, to serve
- 2 tbsp cold water, or as needed
- salt

FOR THE SALSA

- 3 ears of sweetcorn, husks and silks removed
- ½ small red onion, finely chopped
- ½ red pepper, finely chopped
- 1 avocado, peeled, stoned and finely chopped
- 1 tbsp deseeded and finely chopped pickled jalapeño peppers
- 2 tbsp chopped coriander leaves
- 1 tsp smoked paprika
- juice of 2 limes
- 2 tbsp extra virgin olive oil
- pepper

FOR THE TACOS

- 8 mini tortillas (12–14cm)
- 200g plain flour
- 1 tbsp ground cumin
- 1 tsp cayenne pepper
- 4 x 180–200g red snapper fillets, skinned and pin boned
- a little sunflower oil
- 2 Baby Gem lettuces, shredded
- 1 small red onion, finely sliced
- ½ green pepper, finely sliced
- 50g coriander sprigs, plus more to serve
- 2 ripe tomatoes, chopped

To make the mayonnaise, mix all the ingredients together in a bowl and season with salt. The consistency should be that of a loose salad cream, so add a touch more water if necessary. Store in a squeezy bottle in the fridge.

For the salsa, stand each ear of corn on end. Run a knife down the cob, slicing off the kernels. Scrape out all the juices and any pulp left in the cob carefully, using the sharp edge of the knife, and place in a mixing bowl. Fold in all the other ingredients for the salsa and season.

Preheat the oven to 100°C. In a large dry frying pan over a medium-high heat, cook the tortillas on each side until they colour slightly and start to crisp on the edges but are still soft enough to fold. Keep warm in the oven.

Place the flour, cumin and cayenne into a mixing bowl. Slice each fish fillet into 4, season with salt and coat in the flour. Set a large frying pan over a high heat and fry the snapper in the oil until crisp and just cooked through.

You can take all the components to the tables in bowls for your guests to assemble their own tacos. Or, to plate it yourself, lay the warm tortillas on a work surface. Place shredded lettuce on each tortilla, followed by red onion, green pepper, coriander and chopped tomatoes. Squeeze a generous amount of chipotle mayonnaise over each, adding a couple of slices of snapper.

Squeeze on a little more chipotle mayonnaise and a generous spoon of salsa. Fold the tacos and serve with more coriander sprigs and lime wedges.

Marinated snapper, green mango & fragrant herb salad, coconut, lemon grass & lime dressing Sauvignon Blanc 'Boundary Farm', Mahi, Marlborough

☞ page 61

SERVES 6 AS A STARTER

We have no boundaries for the food at the Club, so we are not restricted to cooking the cuisine of a certain culture. Our driving philosophy is only that whatever is on the menu must work alongside wine. Marlborough Sauvignon Blanc is an explosion of tropical and citrus fruits, pairing well with this fresh, zingy salad.

If you have trouble finding snapper, sea bream or sea bass would make a fine substitute. As it's eaten raw, you must ensure the fish is at its freshest. As with most south-east Asian food, you have to make sure this dish is a harmonious balance of heat, salt, sour and sweet. It's important you find a good-quality coconut milk; the best south-east Asian brands separate in the can, with the solids setting on top and the liquid collecting underneath.

ALTERNATIVE WINE MATCHES

Riesling 'The Florita' Jim Barry, Clare Valley ☞ *page 55*

Sauvignon Blanc, Outer Limits, Montes, Zapallar Coast ☞ *page 56*

Sauvignon Blanc 'Section 94', Dog Point Vineyard, Marlborough ☞ *page 61*

FOR THE COCONUT, LEMON GRASS & LIME DRESSING (MAKES 500ML)

200g palm sugar, crushed
100ml lime juice
25g fresh root ginger, peeled and finely chopped
1 lemon grass stalk, trimmed of hard outer leaves and finely chopped
70ml fish sauce
130ml solids from the top of a can of good-quality coconut milk
¼ tsp ground turmeric
3 medium red chillies, deseeded and finely chopped
10 fresh lime leaves, stalks removed, finely sliced

FOR THE SALAD

2 Thai green (unripe) mangos
2 ripe plum tomatoes
¼ red onion
2 red chillies
100g beansprouts
30g coriander cress, or regular coriander leaves, finely chopped
30g Thai basil cress, or regular coriander leaves, finely chopped
30g purple shizo cress, or regular purple shizo leaves, finely chopped
30g green shizo cress, or regular green shizo leaves, finely chopped
4 x 180–200g skin-on fillets of red snapper, scaled and pin-boned
300ml Coconut, lemon grass & lime dressing (see left)

Start with the dressing. Place the palm sugar, lime juice, ginger, lemon grass, fish sauce, the solids from the top of the coconut milk (the coconut cream) and turmeric into a blender and blend at high speed for a minute or so. Pour into a bowl and stir in the chillies and lime leaves. Allow to infuse for an hour or so. (Keep it covered in the fridge and it will last for a week.)

Peel the mangos. They have a large flat stone, so take this into account when slicing. Using a mandolin, slice long thin strips of mango. If you don't have a mandolin, proceed carefully with a knife. Place in a large salad bowl. Quarter the tomatoes lengthways, discard the seeds, slice the tomatoes into long thin strips and add to the mango. Slice the red onion into very thin strips and rinse under cold water to mellow its raw heat. Dry on kitchen paper, then add to the salad. Cut off the stalk end of each chilli, deseed and slice into thin crescents. Add to the salad with the beansprouts and all the cresses, or regular herbs.

Using a very sharp knife with a long thin blade, cut thin sashimi-style slices of the snapper, working from the tail towards the head of the fillets. Place the sliced fish into a separate bowl and pour over the dressing. Fold the dressing through the fish to coat, then allow to marinate for 3–5 minutes, as you would for ceviche. The acid in the lime juice will partially cook the fish.

Finally, add the marinated snapper to the rest of the salad along with all the dressing. Toss and serve immediately.

Mahi

Red mullet, braised fennel, orange & tapenade
Bandol Rosé, Domaine Tempier, Provençe

☞ page 121

SERVES 6 AS A STARTER

Provençe on a plate! The light tannins from the Provençal rosé skin-contact wine pair well with the strong flavours of olive tapenade. There is no precise recipe for this Provençal spread, so the proportions can be adjusted to taste.

Red mullet are fairly easy fish to fillet, so if you're feeling confident you could buy whole fish and do it yourself, but you must ensure all the small pinbones are removed; the best way to do this is with tweezers.

If you buy whole fish, it's easier to assess their freshness: the eyes should be bright and clear, the gills vibrant red and it should smell of the sea. The general rule is that about half a fish's weight will be waste (head and bones). So, to yield 6 x 100–120g fillets, a suitable size for a starter, you will need to buy 3 x 200–250g fish. Ask your fishmonger to gut and scale them, to save the mess at home.

ALTERNATIVE WINE MATCHES

Clos Ste-Magdeleine Rosé, Cassis, Provençe
☞ page 104

Château Simone Rosé, Palette, Provençe
☞ page 104

FOR THE TAPENADE (MAKES 400G)

1 garlic clove
2 tbsp capers in brine, drained
350g pitted Kalamata olives
6 anchovy fillets
100ml extra virgin olive oil, plus more (optional) to store
pepper

FOR THE DISH

1½ large fennel bulbs, plus a few fennel fronds
75ml extra virgin olive oil
3 oranges, 2 segmented
4 tbsp sunflower oil
6 x 100–120g red mullet fillets, scaled and pin-boned
90g Tapenade (see left)
salt

Start with the tapenade. I like to blanch the garlic in a small saucepan of boiling water for 4–5 minutes to reduce its raw strength, but this is optional. Either way, chop the garlic finely and squeeze the brine from the capers to ensure they are dry. Place everything except the oil into a food processor and blend at full speed while pouring in the olive oil, until you have a thick coarse paste. Season with a few twists of pepper; no salt will be needed. Store in a jar in the fridge covered with a thin film of olive oil. It will keep for about 1 month. Pull the tapenade out of the fridge so it comes to room temperature when you start making the dish.

Preheat the oven to 180°C.

Quarter the fennel bulbs and slice out most of the cores, leaving just enough to hold the quarters together. Place in a mixing bowl and add the olive oil and the juice and grated zest of 1 orange. Season well, then toss so it is well coated in the oil and juice. Tip into a small baking dish and cover with foil. Bake for 30 minutes, or until cooked through. Remove the foil and scatter the orange segments and fennel fronds over, then fold the foil back to cover, so the segments warm though.

Heat a large non-stick frying pan with the sunflower oil over a medium-high heat. Season the red mullet fillets and fry them, skin-side down. When the fillets hit the pan, the skin will contract and it may curl up, so press down on them gently with a palette knife to keep them flat so the skin crisps evenly. Once the skin is golden and crisp, turn each fillet over and turn off the heat. Allow the fillets to finish cooking in the residual heat from the pan. Red mullet fillets are fairly thin, so this only takes a minute or so.

Put a piece of fennel on each of 6 warmed plates, along with a few orange segments and fennel fronds. Drizzle any of the orangey braising juices over the fennel and lean a fillet of red mullet against each.

Using 2 spoons, form quenelles of tapenade, place one on top of each fillet and serve.

Domaine
BANDOL
2018

Trout en papillote, orange & dill beurre blanc
Riesling Trocken Kiedricher Gräfenberg, Weingut Robert Weil, Rheingau

☞ page 52

SERVES 6

When matching food with wine, it's important to look at the cuisine from the region where the wine is produced. The Mosel and Rheingau regions are both on the banks of their namesake rivers, which provide freshwater fish to match the wines. Weingut Robert Weil in Rheingau is one of the greatest estates in Germany; this Riesling has depth, power and intensity with elegance and grace. Riesling has citrus: lime in Clare Valley and Mosel; orange in Rheingau, Rheinhessen and Pfalz.

The best way to cook river trout is baked whole in a parchment envelope. The fish cooks in its own steam, with the parchment sealing in the goodness until it's torn open at the table, unleashing delicious aromas. This is best served with boiled new potatoes and white asparagus, as in Germany.

ALTERNATIVE WINE MATCHES

Riesling, Pegasus Bay, North Canterbury ☞ *page 55*

Riesling 'Hochheimer Kirchenstück', Weingut Künstler, Rheingau ☞ *page 52*

Riesling 'G-Max', Weingut Keller, Rheinhessen ☞ *page 52*

FOR THE FISH

6 x 700–800g brown trout, scaled and gutted, fins and tail trimmed
a few dill sprigs
2 oranges
240g unsalted butter
salt and pepper

FOR THE BEURRE BLANC

finely grated zest of ½ orange and juice of 3 oranges
1 large shallot, finely chopped
180ml dry white wine
250g chilled unsalted butter, chopped into 1cm cubes
1 tbsp chopped dill
freshly ground white pepper

Preheat the oven to 190°C.

There are more ways than one to fold an envelope for baking fish. The simplest and most effective is to take a 50cm sheet of baking parchment cut from a standard-sized roll. Fold it in half to form a square, then open it again. To season the underside of the fish, sprinkle a little salt and pepper in the middle of the paper where you are going to rest your fish. Place the fish with its backbone against the creased centre fold and season the top side. Place a few dill sprigs on each fish. Slice each orange into 6 thin discs, and place 2 discs on top of each fish. Place 40g of the butter on each fish and fold the paper over so the 2 sides meet. Starting from one end of the crease, make small overlapping diagonal folds, working your way around the fish from its head to tail. You should finish with a well-sealed crescent-shaped parcel resembling a Cornish pasty. Repeat to prepare all 6 fish.

(If you want to prepare the parcels in advance, don't season the fish directly. Place all the salt and pepper on the butter and put it on the fish between the dill and the orange discs. As it melts in the oven, the seasoning will be distributed over the fish.)

Bake for 18 minutes, then let it rest for 3 minutes or so.

Meanwhile, prepare the sauce. Put the orange zest and juice in a saucepan with the shallot and wine. Over a medium-high heat, reduce the wine and juice to a syrup. Reduce the heat and whisk in the chilled butter a few cubes at a time, forming an emulsion. (It's important the butter is chilled, as this gives you more control. If you use soft butter it will melt too quickly and the beurre blanc might split.) The butter is the only emulsifier in this recipe, so it's important not let the sauce boil or, again, it might split. Season with salt and white pepper. Add the chopped dill just before serving.

Serve the sauce at the table with the fish, allowing each guest to unwrap their own parcel to get the full benefit of the aromas.

Panzanella with sardines
Fiano di Avellino, Feudi di San Gregorio, Campania

☞ page 78

SERVES 6

This Tuscan bread salad is one of my favourite summer dishes. Traditionally made with stale ciabatta, I prefer focaccia, which is lighter and has the added flavour of rosemary. At the Club, rather than wait for focaccia to go stale, we bake it in the oven with garlic until golden. The idea of panzanella is to soften the croutons with the juices from tomatoes and roasted pepper. The anchovies and sardines are optional if you have vegetarian guests, but they do add another dimension.

Feel free to play around with the ingredients here. It's great with chargrilled courgette ribbons, or peas with mint and preserved lemon.

The Fiano grape, of southern Italy's Campania region, has the assertive acidity to cut through the oily fish and stand up to fresh tomatoes. A few minutes aeration in the glass will open the wine and add to your experience.

ALTERNATIVE WINE MATCHES

Vernaccia di San Gimignano, Teruzzi & Puthod, Tuscany ☞ page 79

Toscana Bianco, Ornellaia, Tuscany ☞ page 58

300g rosemary focaccia
6 garlic cloves, skin on
150ml extra virgin olive oil
40g Parmesan cheese, finely grated
1 red pepper
350g cherry tomatoes on the vine
½ small red onion
2 tbsp capers in brine, drained
15 black olives, pitted and halved
1 tbsp red wine vinegar
8 salted anchovies, chopped
3–4 basil sprigs, leaves torn
9 sardines, scaled and filleted
salt and pepper

Preheat the oven to 180°C.

Tear the focaccia into rough 3cm pieces and lay on a large baking tray. Using a skewer or toothpick, prick a few holes into each garlic clove and add to the focaccia. Drizzle generously with olive oil and bake for 5–7 minutes, until golden. While still hot, sprinkle with the Parmesan, giving the tray a good shake so it coats the croutons, melting into them.

To roast the pepper, it's best to use a naked flame. If you don't have a barbecue, you can achieve a similar result over the naked flame of a gas hob. Blacken the skin of the pepper, turning it regularly so it chars evenly. Place in a small bowl and cover. As it cools, the steam it releases will help lift the burned skin, so it can be easily removed.

Cut the tomatoes in half and place into a sieve sitting over a bowl. Season with a little salt. This will draw some of the juices out, which you will need to make the dressing. Allow to rest for 1 hour.

Once the red pepper has cooled, remove its burned skin, stem and seeds. There will be a little pepper juice left in the bottom of the bowl; reserve this for the dressing. Slice the pepper flesh into thin strips and place them in a large mixing bowl. Thinly slice the red onion and rinse it under cold water for a minute to tone down its raw heat, then pat dry. Add the onion to the bowl with the pepper, along with the capers, olives and tomatoes.

To make the dressing, in a large mixing bowl, mix the tomato juices with the pepper juices and the red wine vinegar. Add the anchovies and 3 tbsp olive oil. Whisk the dressing, pulverising the anchovies as you go. Toss the croutons through the dressing to absorb it, then add to the salad. Add the basil, bruising the leaves to release their scent.

Change the oven setting to grill and place the sardine fillets skin side up on an oiled oven tray. Season and grill at a high temperature, so the skins crisp.

Meanwhile, season the salad with a few twists of pepper and toss together. It shouldn't need any salt, as the anchovies in the dressing should suffice, but have a taste just in case. Distribute evenly between 6 serving bowls, lay 3 grilled sardine fillets on top of each and serve.

2017

Herb-roasted fillet of salmon, fregola & summer vegetable salad, salmon 'crackling'
Blanc Fumé de Pouilly 'Silex', Didier Dagueneau

☞ page 58

SERVES 6

A few years back when I was visiting my family in New Zealand, I noticed large schools of krill in the harbour, so I took my dad's rod down to the jetty. I ended up with a 4.5kg sea trout. My dad was a little on the envious side...

I prepared it like this, with wafer-thin fish 'crackling' that snaps between your fingers. There's nothing like preparing a fish that was swimming hours ago, especially if you caught it.

We have chosen Pouilly Fumé (called Blanc Fumé de Pouilly by this producer), for its bracing acidity and bright citrus flavours. The acidity cuts through the oily salmon and the citrus notes complement the lemon dressing. The preserved lemon rind here has a certain minerality. The wine also has a mineral character, from the limestone and flinty soil in which the vines grow.

ALTERNATIVE WINE MATCHES

Sauvignon Blanc, Klein Constantia, South Africa
☞ *page 56*

Semillon, Vergelegen Estate, Stellenbosch
☞ *page 76*

Koshu 'Cuvée Misawa', Grace Winery, Japan
☞ *page 82*

6 x 180g salmon fillets, scaled and skinned, skin retained
100ml extra virgin olive oil
6 asparagus spears
80g fine green beans
80g sugar snap peas
300g broad beans, in their pods (to yield about 80g of podded broad beans), podded
200g peas, in their pods (to yield about 80g of podded peas), podded
300g fregola
5 tbsp chopped chervil or parsley leaves
5 tbsp chopped dill, any coarse stalks removed
5 tbsp chopped chives
50g capers in brine, drained
4 Preserved lemons (see page 181), flesh discarded, rind shredded
100ml Lemon dressing (see page 134)
salt and pepper
a few pea shoots, to serve (optional)

Preheat the oven to 180°C.

Lay each piece of salmon skin flat on a chopping board and scrape a sharp knife across it to remove any remaining flesh. Line an oven tray with baking parchment and lay out the skin with the outside facing upwards. Season with a generous sprinkling of salt and drizzle with olive oil. Place another sheet of baking parchment over and put another oven tray on top. Bake for 15–20 minutes, until crispy. (Do not refrigerate, or it will lose its 'crack'.)

To prepare the vegetables, remove the woody ends from the asparagus spears and cut each into 2.5cm batons. Top and tail the fine green beans and do the same with those. Cut the sugar snaps in half. Blanch the asparagus, green beans, broad beans and peas for 1 minute in boiling water, then refresh in iced water. Do the same with the sugar snaps, but for only 30 seconds. Once the vegetables are cold, remove them from the water. Sort through them, popping the broad beans out of their bitter skins.

To cook the fregola, fill a large saucepan with water and a good handful of salt. Bring to the boil, drop in the fregola and cook it according to the packet instructions. Once al dente, strain through a sieve and allow it to drain. Toss a little olive oil through the grains to keep them separate and set aside.

Mix all the herbs in a bowl, then spread half out on a tray. Season the salmon, then lay it in the herbs, turning to coat both sides.

Heat a large non-stick frying pan over a medium-high heat and add the remaining olive oil. Lay the salmon in the pan and cook for 2 minutes, then turn and cook for a further 2 minutes. Transfer to an oven tray to rest.

Place the vegetables in a bowl with the fregola, capers, remaining herbs and preserved lemon rind. Give the lemon dressing a good shake and toss it through the salad with salt and pepper. Divide between 6 warmed serving bowls. Flake each salmon fillet into chunks and place on the fregola, adding shards of the crispy skin to serve, and some pea shoots, if using.

DAGUENEAU
SILEX

Roast monkfish, arrocina beans, morcilla & clams
Rioja Blanco 'Cappellania', Marqués di Murrieta

☞ page 119

SERVES 6

There are two key styles of white Rioja, differentiated by a difference in ageing. When young, these wines tend to taste fresh with zingy acidity, citrus notes and melon aromas. As they age, white Riojas develop richer nutty characteristics, more body and depth. I advise choosing the richer of the two styles for this unctuous dish, to match the creamy beans, rich morcilla and meaty roasted monkfish.

When buying monkfish fillets, ask the fishmonger to cut them from a thick tail and trim the membrane.

You'll find morcilla (my favourite of all blood sausages) at a good Spanish delicatessen, though any good-quality black pudding would work.

ALTERNATIVE WINE MATCHES

Rioja Blanco 'Viña Tondonia', López di Heredia
☞ page 119

Buçaco Branco Reservado, Portugal
☞ page 81

1 onion, finely chopped
1 garlic clove, finely chopped
1 tbsp chopped rosemary leaves
50ml extra virgin olive oil
250g arrocina beans, soaked overnight
1 bay leaf
1.2 litres chicken stock
30 plump live clams, tightly closed
6 x 150g monkfish fillets, cut from a large tail
50ml sunflower oil
150ml dry white wine
40g unsalted butter
200g morcilla, cut into 2cm lozenges
1 tbsp chopped parsley leaves
salt and pepper

In a large heavy-based saucepan set over a medium heat, cook the onion, garlic and rosemary in the olive oil until the onion is soft and translucent. Add the drained beans, bay leaf and stock. Bring to the boil, then reduce the heat to a simmer. Season and cook for 1 hour, or until the beans are tender.

Remove one-fifth of the beans with a little of their cooking liquid. Using a blender, blend them to a smooth paste. Add this paste back to the saucepan of beans to thicken and enrich the sauce, giving it a creamy consistency. Season to taste and set aside.

Place the clams in a container and rinse under cold water for 10 minutes or so, agitating regularly to release any sand or grit they may be holding. They should be tightly closed. If any open clams don't close when tapped on a work surface, discard them. Drain.

Preheat the oven to 180°C.

Place a non-stick frying pan over a medium-high heat. Season the monkfish fillets and fry them in the sunflower oil, turning to caramelise them on all sides. Once properly sealed, transfer to an ovenproof dish and put them in the oven for 5 minutes.

Meanwhile, place a large saucepan over a high heat. Drop in the clams and white wine and cover, to steam open the clams. Once they are all open, add the butter and braised beans. Bring to the boil, then add the morcilla and allow it to heat though. Morcilla is very soft and a few pieces may disintegrate, but don't worry, as they'll add great flavour to the beans.

Stir in the parsley and serve the beans, clams and morcilla evenly between 6 warmed bowls, discarding any clams that have failed to open. Remove the monkfish from the oven and serve on top.

Roast monkfish in pancetta, lamb's sweetbreads & peas Encruzado Quinta dos Roques, Dão

☞ page 81

SERVES 6

Sweetbreads are delicious, with a luxurious creamy texture. There are two common types available, so ask your butcher for 'heart' sweetbreads as opposed to 'throat'. These are plumper and go particularly well with the meaty monkfish. Not your typical surf-and-turf, but effective none the less.

Indigenous to Portugal, Encruzado is a voluptuous-textured wine, pairing well with meaty fish, so monkfish is perfect. When fermented in oak, it holds up well with a creamy sauce, and is also complemented by the smoky pancetta that wraps the monkfish.

Fish velouté is an important base sauce for so many great fish dishes. Being creamy, it's best served with white wines aged in oak that have undergone malolactic fermentation, such as Chardonnay, Viognier or this Encruzado.

ALTERNATIVE WINE MATCHES

Loureiro 'Dócil', Niepoort, Vinho Verde
☞ page 80

Chardonnay, Morganhof Estate, Stellenbosch
☞ page 66

FOR THE FISH VELOUTÉ (MAKES ABOUT 300ML)

1 large shallot, finely chopped
2 thyme sprigs
1 bay leaf
30g unsalted butter
100ml white wine
200ml fish stock
250ml double cream
juice of ½ lemon
salt and pepper

FOR THE DISH

350g lamb's sweetbreads
400ml whole milk
1 celery stick, finely chopped
½ onion, finely chopped
½ carrot, finely chopped
2 thyme sprigs
1 bay leaf
12 rashers of thinly sliced pancetta
6 x 130g monkfish fillets, cut from a large tail, membrane trimmed
100ml sunflower oil
100g plain flour, to dust
50g unsalted butter
300ml Fish velouté (see left)
200g frozen peas, defrosted
a few pea shoots, optional
60ml Lemon dressing (see page 134)

Make the velouté. In a heavy-based saucepan over a medium heat, cook the shallot, thyme and bay leaf in the butter until soft but not coloured. Pour in the wine and increase the heat, reducing it to 50ml. Add the stock and reduce to 150ml. Add the cream and return to the boil, then reduce the heat to a simmer and reduce to a light sauce consistency. Season and squeeze in the lemon juice. Pass through a sieve and allow to cool, then chill.

Soak the sweetbreads in the milk overnight. Rinse the milk off and place in a saucepan with the celery, onion, carrot, thyme and bay and just cover with cold water. Season with salt and bring to the boil. Remove from the heat and rest for 1 minute, then strain the sweetbreads. It is important not to overcook them, or they will be tough and lose their soft, creamy texture. Once they are cool enough to handle, use a knife to peel the membranes from the outsides while they are still warm, as it's much easier. Chill.

Preheat the oven to 180°C. On a work surface, stretch the pancetta rashers out flat. Roll 2 around each monkfish fillet, ideally so they criss-cross, as a ribbon wraps a gift. Heat a non-stick frying pan over a medium-high heat. Season the monkfish and fry in half the sunflower oil, sealing on all sides, then transfer to an ovenproof dish and place in the oven for 5 minutes.

Meanwhile, finish the sweetbreads. Season them, roll them in the flour and shake off excess. Place a non-stick frying pan over a medium heat. Heat the remaining oil and the butter and fry until golden and crispy. The key is not to move them around too much; let them crisp on one side, then turn them over and crisp the other side. Drain on absorbent kitchen paper.

In a saucepan over a medium heat, bring the velouté to the boil and add the peas. Divide between 4 warmed bowls and add the fish, sweetbreads and pea shoots, if using. Finally, drizzle the dressing over, for a boost of acidity.

Joh. Jos. Prüm
2016
Sonnenuhr
Spätlese

Thai-baked sea bass, steamed coconut rice, fragrant herbs, coconut, lemon grass & lime dressing
Riesling Spätlese 'Wehlener Sonnenuhr', Weingut Joh Jos Prüm ☞ page 52

SERVES 6

The first thing that springs to mind when I think about Thai food is the delicate balance between sweet, sour, salt and spice. The same applies to off-dry German Riesling from the banks of the Mosel river. Their high acidity levels are perfectly balanced out by their sweetness. They are a joy, with flavours of lime, apple blossom and honey dancing on your palate and that tell-tale aroma – similar to petroleum wax – unique to Riesling. The acidity and sweetness makes it perfect with spicy food, and the balance of lime and sugar in the dressing mirrors the wine.

If you don't have a rice cooker, you should invest in one! They make life so much easier. But for those who don't, I've explained how to cook the rice using the absorption technique. Don't be tempted to remove the lid at any stage though, or it's likely to fail.

ALTERNATIVE WINE MATCHES

Riesling 'Isolation Ridge', Frankland Estate, Western Australia ☞ *page 55*

Riesling 'Scharzhofberger Kabinett', Weingut Egon Müller, Mosel ☞ *page 52*

2 garlic cloves, finely chopped
1 lemon grass stalk, trimmed of hard outer leaves and finely chopped
3 fresh lime leaves, stalks discarded, finely chopped
1 chilli, deseeded and finely chopped
30g galangal, peeled and finely chopped
2 tbsp vegetable oil
100g Thai basil leaves
50g coriander leaves
2 tbsp sweet soy sauce (*kecap manis*)
2 tbsp sesame oil
6 x 170g skin-on sea bass fillets, scaled and pin-boned
6 x 20cm square sheets of banana leaf
500g jasmine rice
275ml water
350ml coconut milk, well shaken
½ tbsp salt
30g purple shizo cress
30g Thai basil cress
30g coriander cress
150ml Coconut, lemon grass & lime dressing (see page 164)

To prepare the marinade for the sea bass, place a saucepan over a low heat and sauté the garlic, lemon grass, lime leaves, chilli and galangal in the vegetable oil for a few minutes until soft. Remove from the pan and allow to cool. Once completely cool, place in a food processor with the Thai basil, coriander, *kecap manis* and sesame oil and blend to a paste.

Smear the marinade generously over both sides of each fillet of sea bass. Wrap each fillet in a sheet of banana leaf. Chill until ready to cook.

Preheat the oven to 180°C.

Tip the rice into a large sieve and wash it thoroughly under a cold tap until the water runs clear, which means the excess starch has been rinsed off and helps stop it from sticking together in lumps. Drain it well.

Place the rice into a saucepan with the measured water, coconut milk and salt. Cover the pan with a tightly sealed lid so no steam escapes. Bring to the boil over a high heat, then reduce the heat to the gentlest of simmers. Cook for 6–8 minutes, or until all the liquid has been absorbed. Do not remove the lid at any stage. Remove from the heat and allow to stand for at least 10 minutes, still covered.

Meanwhile, place the wrapped sea bass into the oven on a baking tray. The fillets are thin, so should only take 10 minutes to cook. Remove them from the oven and allow them to rest for a couple of minutes.

Place the sea bass on warmed serving plates and tear back the banana leaves to expose the fish. For a clean presentation, pack individual portions of rice into a small teacup or pudding basin and turn them out on to each plate.

In a salad bowl, toss the fragrant cresses in half the dressing. Place the fragrant herbs on the plates and drizzle the remaining dressing over the fish.

LAFITTE
2014

Fillet of wild sea bass, salsa verde & preserved lemon
Château Smith Haut Lafitte, Pessac-Léognan

☞ page 60

SERVES 4 AS A STARTER

More often than not, simplicity is the key when pairing wine with food. This dish is the perfect example. The simple herb sauce complements the herbaceous character of the white Bordeaux to which we matched it.

Barrel-aged Sauvignon Blanc such as this takes on a wonderful gunsmoke and white lily aroma, while retaining its grassy Sauvignon character.

With such a simple dish, what is most important is that the ingredients are as good as they can be and, with this dish, that means the freshest fish.

This recipe makes about 500ml of salsa verde. It will keep in the fridge for a week and is also great with lamb.

ALTERNATIVE WINE MATCHES

Sauvignon Blanc 'Clos Henri', Clos Henri Vineyard, Marlborough *☞ page 61*

Sauvignon Blanc 'Ried Zieregg', Weingut Tement, Styria *☞ page 56*

Château de Fieuzal, Pessac-Léognan *☞ page 60*

- 50g mint leaves
- 50g parsley leaves
- 50g basil leaves
- 100g capers in brine, drained
- 20g salted anchovies
- 2 garlic cloves, finely chopped
- 400ml extra virgin olive oil
- 50ml sunflower oil
- 1 x 800g–1kg piece of wild sea bass fillet, skin on, scaled and pin-boned, cut into 4 portions
- 50g unsalted butter
- 4 Preserved lemons (see below)
- Jersey Royal potatoes, to serve
- salt and pepper

FOR THE PRESERVED LEMONS

- 8 unwaxed lemons, plus the juice of 4 lemons
- 2.5cm cinnamon stick
- a few saffron threads
- 2 star anise
- 100g caster sugar
- 150g sea salt

Preserved lemons will keep for months, so you can make them well ahead of time, and they are excellent to keep in the pantry. If you can't manage to find unwaxed lemons, just give them a good scrub. Make a criss-cross cut into the top of each lemon to about halfway though.

Crush the cinnamon, saffron and star anise in a mortar and pestle and mix with the sugar and salt. Stuff the mixture into the cuts in the lemons and push the lemons into a sterilised jar just large enough to hold them. Add the remaining curing mixture and pour in the lemon juice. Top up with enough cold water to just cover. Screw the lid on tightly and store in a cool dark place for 2–3 months. The curing mixture will draw the juice out of the lemons, creating a brine as it mixes with the salt and sugar. Give the jar a good shake once a week, but make sure the lemons stay submerged or they may develop a white mould, which doesn't look great, but is harmless.

To make the salsa verde, place the herbs, capers, anchovies, garlic and olive oil into a food processor and blend until it reaches the consistency of pesto. Be careful not to over-blend; you are not making a smooth purée. Also, if blended for too long, the friction creates heat which means you will lose the freshness that makes this simple sauce so good.

Score the fish filets (see page 182). Heat a non-stick frying pan with the sunflower oil over a medium–high heat. Season the sea bass and fry, skin-side down. When the fish hits the pan, the skin will contract and it may curl up. Using a palette knife, press down gently on the fillets, keeping them flat so the skin crisps evenly. Once the skin is golden and crispy, add the butter to the pan and turn each fillet over, reducing the heat to finish cooking the fish gently. As the fillets are cooking, spoon the melted butter over them.

Once the sea bass is cooked, cut the preserved lemons in half and rub the flesh of one half on the skin of each fish fillet.

Serve the other half of the preserved lemons on the plate with the salsa verde and some boiled Jersey Royal new potatoes.

Fillet of wild sea bass, warm salad of heritage tomatoes, anchovies, capers & basil
Albariño, Pazo Señorans, Rías Biaxas

☞ page 80

SERVES 6

Heritage tomatoes are increasingly popular and more available in recent years. They are old varieties, grown with seed in a traditional manner, with open pollination and no hybridisation. The range is seemingly endless and diverse, and you get an interesting mix of colours, textures, acidity and sweetness. This simple, easy-to-make dish is a delight, with summer flavours of the Mediterranean.

Albariño is definitely a seafood lover's wine. It has a delicate saltiness about it and good lemony acidity, appealing flavours that pair well with fish. It should be served cold, but, if left in the glass, as it increases in temperature its flavours change from citrus and minerally to the richer notes of apple, pear and even stone fruits such as peaches and apricots.

ALTERNATIVE WINE MATCHES

Sauvignon Blanc, Blind River, Awatere Valley, Marlborough ☞ *page 61*

Chenin Blanc 'Steen op Hout', Mulderbosch Vineyards, Stellenbosch ☞ *page 64*

Chasselas 'Les Terrasses', Domaine Jean-René Germanier, Switzerland ☞ *page 52*

1kg heritage tomatoes
18 salted anchovies, chopped
50g capers in brine, drained
150ml Lemon dressing (see page 134)
2 x 800g fillets of wild sea bass, skin on, scaled and pin-boned
a little sunflower oil
24 basil leaves
salt and pepper

Using a paring knife, remove the core from each tomato, quarter them, then cut each quarter in half. If you have a few cherry tomatoes in the mix, just halve them. Place in a large bowl. Add the anchovies, capers and lemon dressing. Season the tomatoes, bearing in mind that the anchovies are salty, so you will need less salt than usual.

Place a fillet of sea bass skin-side down on a chopping board and, using a sharp knife, remove any belly still attached and the last 5cm of the thin tail end of the fillet. Cut each fillet into 3 even portions. Turn them over so the skin is facing you. Cut 4–5 score marks into the skin across each portion, no more than 5mm (¼in) deep, being careful not to score too deeply into the flesh. The easiest way to achieve this is to hold the top and bottom of the portion between your fingers and thumb and squeeze the fillet gently so the skin arches upwards before making the cuts. Scoring the skin helps the fish to cook through evenly, and it will also curl up less in the pan while frying.

Heat a large non-stick frying pan with a little sunflower oil over a medium–high heat. Season the sea bass portions and fry the fish, skin-side down. When the fillets hit the pan, although you have scored them, the skin will contract and may still curl up a little. Using a palette knife, press down gently on the fillets, keeping them flat so the skin crisps evenly. Once the skin of the fish is golden and crispy (this should take 2–3 minutes), turn each fillet over and reduce the heat to its lowest for 1 minute, then switch it off. Allow the fillets to finish cooking gently in the residual heat of the pan.

Meannwhile, heat a large saucepan over a medium heat. Drop in the tomato mixture and warm it through, stirring gently. This should be a quick process, as you don't want the tomatoes to break down too much. Once the tomatoes have warmed through and are releasing their juices, tear up the basil leaves, bruising them as you go so they release their flavour. Fold the basil through the tomatoes. Have a taste and adjust the seasoning if required.

Spoon the tomatoes into 6 warmed bowls, place the fish on top and serve.

Sea bream en papillote, Douglas Fir needles
Retsina 'Tear of the Pine', Kechris, Thessaloniki

☞ page 82

SERVES 6

When Ronan first introduced me to Retsina, I thought he was winding me up! It instantly took me back to my Norsca 'Forest Fresh' deodorant-wearing days as a teenager. Funny how your senses do that to you. After half a glass, though, I began to understand.

The dish we chose for this had to reflect the pine resin fragrance in the wine. Straight away I thought of Douglas Fir needles. It took ages to crack this dish, with unsucessful forays into fir-infused oil and salt...

Finally, I figured it out. Cooked this way, there is just enough fir fragrance to complement the wine, while not overpowering the delicate fish. I chose sea bream, as they are plentiful in Greece from the Mediterranean. Another way of capturing the flavour would be to barbecue the fish over green pinecones instead of charcoal, so don't be afraid to experiment!

You will need 6 x 20cm squares of muslin.

6 x 500–600g whole sea bream, gutted and scaled, heads and tailed removed
Douglas Fir sprigs
200ml extra virgin olive oil
3 lemons, halved
boiled new potatoes and chopped salad, to serve
salt and pepper

Preheat the oven to 200°C.

Using a pair of sturdy kitchen scissors, trim off and discard all the fins of the fish and give them a good rinse. Dry with kitchen paper.

Run 6 x 20cm muslin squares under a cold tap and wring out the excess water. Season the fish well and wrap each of them in a muslin square. Take a 40cm sheet of baking parchment cut from a standard-sized roll. Fold it in half to form a square, then open it again. Give the Douglas Fir sprigs a rinse under a cold tap, then bruise them using the back of a pan. Lay a good nest of sprigs just south of the crease where you are going to rest your fish. Place the muslin-wrapped fish with its backbone against the creased centrefold and place a layer of more fir sprigs on each fish. Give the lot a generous drizzle of olive oil and fold the paper over so the 2 sides meet. Starting from one end of the crease, make small overlapping diagonal folds, working your way around the fish from its head to tail. You should finish with a well-sealed crescent-shaped parcel resembling a Cornish pasty. Repeat to prepare all 6 fish.

Bake the fish for 18 minutes, then rest for 3 minutes or so before serving.

Serve the fish inside its envelope at the table, so as your guests tear them open they are met with the smell of pine to match that of the retsina.

Serve with boiled new potatoes and a simple chopped salad of cucumber, tomato and red onion dressed with olive oil. And, of course, half a lemon.

Dukkah-encrusted cod, dried apricot falafel, sumac yogurt & pomegranate
Viognier, Tahbilk, Victoria

☞ page 83

SERVES 6

See previous page for picture

Started in 1860, Tahbilk is one of Australia's oldest family-run wineries. This Viognier is packed with juicy apricot flavours and spice, making it perfect for the flavours in this dish.

This North African-inspired recipe mirrors many flavours in the wine. The nuts in the dukkah, the apricots in the falafel and the creamy-sharp sumac yogurt that echoes the Viognier's malolactic fermentation in oak. It is one of my favourite summer fish dishes at the Club: light and healthy, with unusual flavour combinations and textures coming together wonderfully with the wine, while the colours look beautiful on the plate.

I find much of the pomegranate molasses on sale is of poor quality, over-reduced and too caramelised. The one we use is made by Belazu. Go to the effort of sourcing this one, as you can really taste the fruit and it has a little sharpness about it, a bit like a good aged balsamic vinegar.

FOR THE DUKKAH

70g blanched hazelnuts
70g blanched almonds
100g sesame seeds
15g coriander seeds
20g cumin seeds
½ tbsp sumac
1 tsp pepper
½ tbsp sea salt

FOR THE FALAFEL

2 garlic cloves, peeled but left whole
200g (7oz) dried chickpeas, soaked overnight
1 small onion, finely chopped)
2 tbsp chopped parsley leaves
3 tbsp chickpea flour (gram flour)
1 tsp sea salt
½ tsp bicarbonate of soda
1 tbsp ground cumin
1 tbsp ground coriander
generous pinch of cayenne pepper
juice of ½ lemon
80g dried apricots, finely chopped

FOR THE REST

180g Greek yogurt
1 tbsp sumac
1 pomegranate
50ml sunflower oil, plus more to deep-fry
150g Dukkah (see left)
6 x 180g thick cod fillets, skin on and scaled
120ml pomegranate molasses
coriander cress, to serve (optional)

First make the dukkah. Preheat the oven to 170°C.

Spread the hazelnuts and almonds over a baking tray and toast them in the oven for 10 minutes until golden. Place in a food processor and pulse until coarsely chopped. Transfer to a large bowl. Spread the sesame seeds over a baking tray and toast them at the same temperature for 6–7 minutes, until golden. Add them to the bowl with the nuts. Place the coriander and cumin seeds in a dry frying pan over a medium heat. Toast the spices, stirring frequently, for 2 minutes or so, until they begin to pop and give off their toasted aromas. Transfer to a mortar and pestle and grind them until they are finely crushed. Add the crushed spices, sumac, pepper and salt to the nuts and sesame seeds and mix well. (This recipe makes twice the amount you will need for this dish, but it will store well for a month or so in a sealed jar in a dark, cool cupboard.)

For the falafel, blanch the garlic cloves in boiling water for 5 minutes, then peel and chop them finely.

Rinse the soaked chickpeas under cold water and drain them well. Pour them into a food processor with the garlic and all the other ingredients for the falafel except the dried apricots. Pulse all the ingredients together to form a coarse meal. Scrape the sides of the processor with a spatula as you go to gain an even consistency and be careful not to over-process the mixture; you don't want a paste.

Pour it out into a large mixing bowl, add the apricots and give it a good stir with a fork so the consistency is even throughout. Cover and chill for 1 hour.

ALTERNATIVE WINE MATCHES

Viognier 'Mount Harlan', Calera Winery, Monterey, USA ☞ *page 83*

Viognier 'State of Surrender', Staete Landt, Marlborough ☞ *page 83*

Mix the yogurt with the sumac and chill until required.

Cut the pomegranate in half and, one half at a time, hold over a bowl and bash the hard outside skin with the back of a ladle or heavy spoon. The juicy red seeds will fall through your fingers into the bowl. Pick out and discard any white membrane that may also have fallen through.

With wet hands, roll the falafel into tight 30g balls and place them on a tray in the fridge to set for 30 minutes.

Preheat the oven to 180°C.

Set your deep fryer to 170°C, or use a saucepan, taking the same precautions and care as usual (see page 138).

Cook the falafel a few at a time. When they are a light shade of brown, lift them out gently with a slotted spoon. They should only take a minute or 2. Drain them of any excess oil on kitchen paper. Once the falafel are all cooked, place them on an oven tray.

Spread the dukkah out on a tray. Season the portions of cod, then lay each in the dukkah, turning them to coat all sides generously.

Heat a large non-stick frying pan over a medium-high heat and add the 50ml of sunflower oil. Lay the cod portions gently in the pan skin side down and cook for 2 minutes until lightly browned before turning over. Cook for a further 2 minutes, then transfer to an oven tray. Sprinkle any dukkah left on the tray over the cod and place in the oven with the falafel. After a couple of minutes, remove the cod and allow it to rest and cook through gently.

Drag a spoon of sumac yogurt across each plate, then drizzle with a little pomegranate molasses. Remove the falafel from the oven and break them in half. Place 4 falafel halves on each plate. Arrange a cod fillet on each plate, leaning it against the falafel.

Scatter a few pomegranate seeds over the top and garnish with the coriander cress, if using.

Baked salt cod, chorizo, tomatoes & chickpeas in Fino
Fino en Rama Tío Pepe, González Byass

☞ *page 125*

SERVES 4

Salt cod is available ready prepared from good European delicatessens, but is also easy to make at home, as we do here. All you need is cod, a lot of sea salt and time (if making it yourself, you'll need to start about 10 days in advance).

Fino en Rama is a celebration of *flor*, a film of yeast that forms on the surface of the Sherry while it is in the barrel. It's bottled without filtering or fining, and takes on an almondy nuttiness over time. It should not be pigeon-holed as an aperitif; in Jerez and all across its Spanish homeland, it is treated as a dry white wine and enjoyed throughout the meal.

Using sherry in the cooking with the tomatoes, chorizo and chickpeas adds a deep richness to the sauce and an authentic taste of Spain.

ALTERNATIVE WINE MATCHES

Solear Manzanilla, Bodegas Barbadillo ☞ *page 125*

La Bota 68 de Fino, 'Macharnudo Alto', Equipo Navazos ☞ *page 125*

Fino Tradición, Bodegas Tradición ☞ *page 125*

1kg boneless, skinless thick cod fillet
750g coarse sea salt
4 large ripe vine tomatoes
150g cooking chorizo, cut into 1cm lozenges
50ml extra virgin olive oil
1 red onion, finely chopped
2 garlic cloves, very finely chopped
1 bay leaf
1 tsp smoked paprika
150ml Fino Sherry
150ml tomato passata
20g capers in brine, drained
400g can of chickpeas in brine, drained and rinsed
1 tbsp chopped parsley leaves
salt and pepper

Rinse the cod and pat dry. Sprinkle a generous layer of sea salt into a baking dish large enough to fit the cod. Lay the cod on the salt. Pack the remaining salt over, completely encasing the fish. Place in the fridge for 24 hours.

Rinse the fish to remove the salt and dry well. It will have shrunk and feel much firmer, having had its water content drawn out. Wrap in muslin and place on a wire rack over a tray in the fridge. The wire rack is important to allow air circulation, so the cod dries effectively. Allow to dry out for a week, then store in an airtight container in the fridge (it will keep for 3–4 weeks).

Before cooking the cod, soak it in a generous amount of water for 48 hours, changing the water 2–3 times.

Preheat the oven to 150°C. Cut the salt cod into 4 even-sized portions and place in a baking dish.

To peel the tomatoes, bring a large saucepan of water to the boil. With a small pointed knife, remove the core of each tomato and cut a shallow cross into the skin on top. Prepare a bowl of iced water and have a slotted spoon to hand. Place the tomatoes into the boiling water for 30 seconds until the skins start to split, then lift out with the slotted spoon and plunge into the iced water. Allow to cool for a minute, then lift them out, peel, then chop.

In a large heavy-based saucepan over a medium heat, cook the chorizo in the olive oil, rendering out the bright orange fat. Remove the chorizo from the pan and reserve, leaving the tasty fat behind. Put the red onion in the pan with the garlic and bay leaf and cook until the onions are soft and translucent. Stir in the smoked paprika and cook for a further minute. Deglaze the pan with the Sherry and allow it to boil for a minute or so, to evaporate the alcohol. Return the chorizo to the pan with the chopped tomatoes, passata, capers and chickpeas. Bring to a simmer and allow to bubble gently for 3–4 minutes. Season with a few twists of pepper.

Pour the sauce over the fish, cover with foil and bake for 15–20 minutes, or until the fish is cooked through. Lift the fillets out carefully into warmed serving bowls. Pour the sauce back into a saucepan, taste and adjust the seasoning if needed. Add the parsley, then spoon generously over the fish.

LOURO

Salt cod croquetas, red pepper salsa
Godello 'Louro do Bolo', Rafael Palacios, Galicia

☞ page 80

SERVES 10–12 AS AN APPETISER (MAKES ABOUT 25)

This tapa can be served in a smaller format as a canapé, or in larger pieces as an appetiser. It's great at the start of a meal, as the explosion of salty cod really gets your mouth watering.

The region of Valdeorras lies in north-west Spain, close to Galicia, so the cuisine is fish- or seafood-based. Godello is found only in this region. It's dry, fresh, with ripe tropical fruit and citrus and works like a squeeze of lime juice across the croquetas.

At the Club we make large batches of this filling and roll it into long cling-filmed logs, freezing them ready to be cut and crumbed. There's nothing stopping you doubling this recipe at home and doing the same. (They are also easier to crumb from frozen.) Just remove all the cling film first!

ALTERNATIVE WINE MATCHES

Albariño, Maior de Mendoza, Rías Biaxas
☞ *page 80*

Chardonnay 'Talinay', Viña Tabalí, Limarí
☞ *page 66*

Sauvignon Blanc, Tokara, Stellenbosch
☞ *page 56*

FOR THE CROQUETAS

300g salted cod, soaked for 48 hours (see page 190 for home-made)
1 onion, sliced
1 bay leaf
400ml whole milk
2 garlic cloves, very finely chopped
40g unsalted butter
40g plain flour
250g potatoes, cooked and riced
1½ tbsp chopped parsley leaves
2 litres vegetable oil, to deep-fry
salt and pepper

FOR THE SALSA

100ml extra virgin olive oil
3 large shallots, finely chopped
1 large red chilli, deseeded and finely chopped
6 red peppers, deseeded and finely chopped
finely grated zest and juice of 2 limes
2 tbsp Lingham's sweet chilli sauce
1½ tbsp chopped mint leaves

FOR THE COATING

200g plain flour, plus more to dust
3 eggs, lightly beaten
200g panko crumbs

Put the salt cod in a saucepan with the onion and bay leaf and pour over the milk. Set over a medium heat and bring to the boil. Remove from the heat and set aside for 10 minutes, then lift the cod out and strain the milk through a sieve, reserving it. Flake the cod between your fingers.

Place a large heavy-based saucepan over a low heat and cook the garlic in the butter for a minute or so, then stir in the flour. Cook for a minute or so, then slowly add the warm milk, stirring to avoid lumps. Cook over a low heat, stirring, until the raw flour flavour has gone. Add the potatoes, then the cod. Taste and adjust the seasoning. Stir in the parsley and spread the mixture out on a tray. Cover with cling film so a skin doesn't form, and chill.

For the salsa, heat the oil over a medium heat in a heavy-based saucepan and gently cook the shallots and chilli until soft. Add the peppers and lime zest, season and cook for a few minutes until the peppers soften. Remove from the heat, add the chilli sauce, lime juice and mint and adjust the seasoning.

To coat the croquetas, put the 200g of flour into a shallow bowl, the eggs in a second and the panko in a third. Set a deep-fat fryer to 190°C, or use a saucepan, taking the same precautions and care as usual (see page 138).

Once chilled and set, roll the croqueta mixture into 40g logs. (You may find this easier with a little flour on your hands.) Coat the croquetas in flour and shake off any excess, then dip into the beaten eggs, a few at a time, and finally roll them in the panko crumbs. If you want a thicker coat, dip them back into the egg, then again into the crumbs for a second coating.

Deep-fry the croquetas for a couple of minutes until golden and crispy. You will need to do this in batches, so as not to over-crowd the fryer. Once ready, drain on kitchen paper to soak up any oil. They won't need any salt as the béchamel has already been seasoned. Serve with the salsa.

hand

Oeufs en meurette
Volnay 1er Cru 'Les Caillerets', Marquis d'Angerville

☞ page 88

SERVES 4 AS A STARTER

This started off as peasant food, but has become a Burgundian classic. It's a pretty easy choice to go with a red Pinot Noir, and a softer style such as the wines from the Côte de Beaune (see page 88) – including this Volnay – is perfect.

The recipe is one of the grand classics of Burgundian country cooking. Just like *coq au vin* or *boeuf Bourguinon*, *oeufs en meurette* is served in a rich red wine sauce layered with the flavours of bacon lardons, earthy mushrooms and sweet caramelised onions. What is unique about it is that the eggs are poached in red wine, which forms the base of the rich sauce.

ALTERNATIVE WINE MATCHES

Mercurey Rouge, Domaine Michel Juillot ☞ page 88

Savigny-Lès-Beaune 1er Cru 'La Dominode', Domaine Jean Marc Pavelot ☞ page 88

Clos des Lambrays Grand Cru, Domaine des Lambrays ☞ page 88

500ml light Pinot Noir
1 tbsp red wine vinegar
500ml Demi-glace (see page 279)
4 eggs
2 large shallots, finely chopped
1 small garlic clove, finely chopped
a few thyme sprigs
½ bay leaf
100g softened unsalted butter
1 tbsp plain flour
100g unsmoked bacon lardons
1 tbsp sunflower oil
100g cocktail onions
100g small button mushrooms, halved
50g clarified unsalted butter
4 x 2cm-thick slices of baguette
1 tbsp chopped parsley leaves
salt and pepper

In a heavy-based saucepan over a high heat, bring the wine, vinegar and demi-glace to the boil, then reduce the heat to a simmer. Crack the eggs into 4 cups and slip them one at a time into the liquor. Poach for 3 minutes, until the whites are set but the yolks still runny. Using a slotted spoon, carefully lift from the liquor and rest on kitchen paper. Snip off any straggly bits of white to tidy them up, then set aside. Reserve the poaching liquor.

In a separate saucepan over a medium heat, gently cook the shallots, garlic, thyme and bay in 1 tbsp of the butter. Once the shallots have lightly caramelised, add 600ml of the egg poaching liquor and bring it to a simmer. Reduce by half, skimming off any impurities from the surface. To thicken the sauce, in a small bowl, mix the flour with 1 tbsp more of the butter to form a paste. Add half, a little at a time, to the simmering liquor and simmer for a few minutes to cook out the raw flour. If the sauce needs thickening further, add some more, until you reached the desired consistency.

In a separate saucepan, over a medium heat, cook the lardons in the sunflower oil until caramelised and the fat has rendered out. Remove the lardons from the pan on to kitchen paper with a slotted spoon and add the cocktail onions to the pan. Caramelise the onions gently, then remove from the pan, placing them with the lardons. Finally, add the mushrooms and cook them until they soften. Carefully drain any remaining fat and oil from the mushrooms. Place a sieve over the saucepan containing the mushrooms and strain the sauce over them, pushing it all through. Return the lardons and onions, taste and season.

Melt the clarified butter in a small frying pan over a medium heat and fry the baguette slices, turning, until golden and crisp. Drain on kitchen paper.

Reheat the remaining 400ml of poaching liquor in a small saucepan until it simmers. Carefully add the poached eggs for 2 minutes, to warm through.

Place a warm crouton on each warmed serving bowl and set an egg on top. Spoon the rich sauce generously around the bowl. Finally, sprinkle with a little chopped parsley and serve.

OLNAY
AILLERETS
2005

968
ERCIAL

Sticky chicken tulips, prunes, smoked bacon, toasted pecans, star anise
Sercial, Blandy's Vintage Madeira

☞ *page 126*

SERVES 4 AS AN APPETISER

Madeira is one of the most wonderfully complex wines you will ever taste, but it's often left to the end of the meal, or served with cheese. We wanted to do something different with it. This sticky chicken dish works very well, as the intense flavours in the Madeira need to be paired with punchy ingredients. It's a fun bar snack or pre-dinner nibble.

The sticky glaze is infused with the most prominent flavours present in aged Madeira, such as smoky bacon, prunes, honey and nuts, with the complementary spices of star anise and cinnamon. This is the perfect example of what we endeavour to achieve at the Club: to create dishes to match the flavour notes of a certain wine, resulting in a memorable synergy between the two.

ALTERNATIVE WINE MATCHES

Sercial, D'Oliveiras Vintage ☞ *page 126*

Verdelho Terrantez, Blandy's ☞ *page 126*

16 chicken wing 'drumsticks', ordered from the butcher
600ml chicken stock
8 star anise
2.5cm cinnamon stick
50g pitted prunes
40g pecans
1 tbsp honey
4 smoked pancetta rashers, finely chopped
2 tbsp groundnut oil
80ml Madeira
1 tbsp soft brown sugar
salt

To prepare the chicken tulips, using the heel of a heavy cook's knife, assertively chop the small knuckle off the end of each wing drumstick to reveal the bone. Pull back the flesh from the drumsticks, turning it inside out to reveal the bone in its entirety.

Place the chicken tulips into a small saucepan and cover with the stock. Add the star anise and cinnamon and season well with salt. Over a medium heat, bring to the boil, skimming off any impurities that collect on the surface with a ladle. Once it is boiling, drop in the prunes and remove from the heat. Allow to cool and infuse for 30–40 minutes.

Meanwhile, preheat the oven to 170°C.

Place the pecans on a small oven tray and toast for 5 minutes or so. Remove the tray from the oven, drizzle over the honey and mix, coating the nuts in the honey, then return to the oven for a final 2–3 minutes. Remove from the oven, mix them again, then allow to cool.

Once the stock has cooled, strain the chicken through a sieve over a bowl to collect the cooking liquor. Remove and discard the star anise and cinnamon; they have done their job.

Place the chicken tulips on kitchen paper to dry. Chop the softened prunes very finely to create a paste.

To finish the chicken, preheat a non-stick frying pan over a medium heat. Fry the chicken tulips and pancetta in the groundnut oil until the pancetta is crispy. Deglaze the pan with the Madeira and add the brown sugar and prune paste. Toss the tulips in the pan to coat, then pour in 150ml of the reserved stock. Stirring regularly, reduce the stock to a sticky caramelised glaze, with a consistency that coats the chicken. Place the tulips on a serving platter and coat with the glaze.

Roughly chop the honey-roasted pecans and sprinkle them over the top. Serve with a finger bowl and plenty of napkins.

Chicken liver parfait, orchard fruit compote & toasted sourdough
Furmint 'Szent Tamás', István Szepsy

☞ *page 81*

MAKES 18 SLICES

The word parfait means 'perfect', and in this case is truly fitting. This makes a whole 32cm terrine, but halve it if you have a smaller terrine to set it in.

Speak to your butcher ahead about the marrow bones and ask them to cut the bones into 2.5cm rings. If you can't get it, don't worry, but it does enhance the velvety smooth texture.

Furmint is the primary grape used in Hungary's iconic sweet wine, Royal Tokaji. When used to make dry wines (see page 81), it has the aromatics of Sauvignon Blanc, the rich mouth-feel of Chardonnay and the vibrant acidity of Riesling. The whole package!

The orchard fruits in the compote reflect the flavours in Furmint. This is more compote than you need, but it keeps for a week and is great for breakfast with yogurt and granola.

ALTERNATIVE WINE MATCHES

Pinot Gris, Burrowing Owl Estate Winery, Okanagan Valley, Canada ☞ *page 77*

'Bonnezeaux', Château de Fesles, Loire ☞ *page 64*

Monbazillac 'Madame du Château', Château Tirecul La Gravière, France ☞ *page 124*

FOR THE COMPOTE

350g caster sugar
300ml water
1 lemon
1 quince
2 pears
2 peaches
30g unsalted butter
2 large Bramley apples, peeled, cored and chopped

FOR THE PARFAIT

5 shallots, chopped
1 garlic clove, chopped
a few thyme sprigs
1 bay leaf
450g unsalted butter
150ml Port
150ml Madeira
150ml red wine
2 tbsp double cream
1kg chicken livers, trimmed
5 medium eggs
100g bone marrow (from 400g of 2.5cm-thick marrow bone rings)
2 tsp white truffle oil
½ nutmeg, grated
salt and pepper
toasted sourdough, to serve

Make the compote as on page 230, omitting the hazelnuts and poaching the peaches for 5 minutes after the quince, then peeling and chopping them.

In a heavy-based saucepan over a medium heat, gently cook the shallots, garlic, thyme and bay in 50g of the butter until the shallots are soft and translucent. Add the Port, Madeira and red wine, increase the heat and boil until the liquor reduces almost entirely. Stir in the cream and leave to cool. Mix with the livers and marinate for 30 minutes. Preheat the oven to 140°C.

Place the livers in a blender with the eggs, marrow, truffle oil and nutmeg. Melt the remaining butter. Liquidise the livers and other ingredients on the highest speed of your blender. After a minute or so, pour in the hot butter slowly to emulsify and season liberally. The parfait will take more salt than you think, so don't be shy. Pass the mixture through a very fine sieve.

Cut a long strip of baking parchment to 3 times the length of a terrine and the same width as its base. Line the base of the terrine with the parchment so it overhangs both ends. Pour in the parfait and fold the parchment over the surface. Cover and place in a deep roasting tin. Fill the tin with boiling water to 2.5cm below the level of the terrine. Cook for 25–30 minutes. To check if it's cooked, carefully lift the lid. The parfait should be very slightly risen and a little wobbly. If it's still slightly liquid, give it another 5 minutes. Remove from the oven and lift the terrine from the water. Allow to cool for 30 minutes at room temperature, then chill to set. It will take a few hours.

To remove the parfait from the terrine, sit it in a sink of hot water for a minute. Run a knife down each side. Peel the parchment back and turn upside down on to a board. If it doesn't release, give the parchment a tug. Cut the parfait with a hot knife just before serving as it will oxidise quickly. Serve with the fruit compote and toasted sourdough. Any remaining parfait will keep, rewrapped, covered and refrigerated, for about 5 days.

SZEPSY
SZENT

THE
FMC

Coronation chicken salad, apple, celery hearts & golden raisins
Chenin Blanc 'The FMC', Ken Forrester, Stellenbosch

☞ page 64

SERVES 6 AS A STARTER

Chenin Blanc is the signature white wine variety of South Africa and this FMC is a classic. Made in a Loire style, Chenin's natural high acidity is offset by a little residual sugar. It also has flavours of green apple. This dish, with its lovely balanced tandoori spice flavours, mango chutney, marinated golden raisins and Granny Smith apples all work in perfect harmony.

At the Club we use chicken oysters supplied by one of our butchers, but they are very difficult to source, so here we're using breast instead.

Thanks to my brother-in-law Andy Aitken for the inspiration for the versatile tandoori-spiced butter. He uses it to cook gurnard fillets, as it's not just great with chicken but also with fish, or light game birds such as partridge or pheasant.

ALTERNATIVE WINE MATCHES

Torrontés, Bodega Colomé, Argentina ☞ page 82

Chenin Blanc 'Te Arai Vineyard', Millton, Gisborne ☞ page 62

Riesling 'Bel Canto', Pegasus Bay, North Canterbury ☞ page 55

FOR THE CORONATION DRESSING

50ml vegetable oil
1 onion, finely chopped
1 garlic clove, finely chopped
20g fresh root ginger, peeled and finely chopped
1 tsp ground turmeric
5 cardamon pods
1 tsp fenugreek seeds
1 tsp ground cumin
1 red chilli, deseeded and finely chopped
250g Greek-style yogurt
50ml whole milk
1 tbsp mango chutney
salt and pepper

FOR THE TANDOORI-SPICED BUTTER

4 green chillies, deseeded and finely chopped
1 tsp salt
2 tsp black mustard seeds
10 fresh curry leaves, finely chopped
2 tsp ground turmeric
1 tsp garam masala
1 tsp ground cumin
1 garlic clove, finely chopped
3 tbsp finely chopped coriander leaves, plus more to serve
2 large shallots, finely chopped
500g softened unsalted butter

FOR THE SALAD

3 large chicken breasts, skin on
50ml sunflower oil
10 fresh curry leaves
3 small celery sticks, plus the leaves from a heart of celery
30g coriander cress, or regular coriander leaves
1 Granny Smith apple
1 tbsp olive oil
100ml Coronation dressing (see left)
50g golden raisins, soaked overnight, then drained

For the dressing, heat the oil in a saucepan over a medium heat. Add the onion, garlic and ginger and stir until the onion is soft. Add the spices and chilli and stir for 2–3 minutes. Put the yogurt, milk and chutney into a liquidizer and blend with the contents of the pan until smooth. Season, pass through a sieve and chill. It will keep for the same shelf life as the milk in it.

For the butter, fold all the ingredients into the softened butter until well incorporated. Keep covered in the fridge; it will last about 3 weeks.

Skin the chicken. Heat the oil in a frying pan over a medium-high heat. Season the chicken skin with salt and fry until crisp. Add 30g of the spiced butter, to impart the spices, then place on kitchen paper to drain. Slice the chicken into 1cm medallions and season. Melt the remaining spiced butter in a large frying pan. Add the curry leaves and chicken and cook gently.

Slice the celery sticks about 3mm thick. Place in a bowl with the celery leaves and coriander cress. Slice the apple into thin half-moons. Place in the bowl and dress with the olive oil, to give the leaves a sheen.

Squirt a generous amount of dressing and using the back of a spoon, drag it across each plate. Place a little apple and celery salad on the plate, then the chicken, spooning a small amount of spiced butter over. Finish with a little more salad and a few plump raisins. Garnish with the crispy skin and serve.

Chicken, girolle & tarragon pie 'G' de Guiraud, Château Guiraud

☞ page 74

SERVES 6

For this recipe, you can either choose to prepare individual pies, as we do at the Club, or, for a family dish, fill a baking dish with the pie filling and lay a sheet of pastry over the top. (If you choose this option, reduce the pastry to 400g. You will need a pie bird to lift the pastry off the filling to ensure it cooks. Brush a little beaten egg on the rim of the dish and fold the pastry over it, sticking it fast to the egg, or the pastry top will shrink.)

The pie moulds we use in the Club are heavy cast iron, which cook the pastry effectively on the inside. Stoneware works just as well.

We chose this pie to match with Semillon because of the buttery pie crust flavours in the wine, due to its time spent in oak. It also works well with poultry, herbs and cream.

ALTERNATIVE WINE MATCHES

Sauvignon Blanc, Seven Hills Winery, Washington State ☞ *page 60*

'Director's Reserve white', Tokara, Stellenbosch ☞ *page 76*

'Alteni di Brassica', Gaja, Langhe ☞ *page 58*

- 200g fresh girolle mushrooms
- 100g unsalted butter, plus more for the pie dishes
- 12 skinless boneless chicken thighs
- 500ml chicken stock
- 5 thyme sprigs
- 1 bay leaf
- 1 onion, finely chopped
- 60g plain flour, plus more to dust
- 150ml white wine
- 100ml double cream
- 1 tbsp Dijon mustard
- 3 tbsp chopped tarragon leaves
- 1kg all-butter puff pastry
- 2 eggs, lightly beaten
- salt and pepper
- mashed potato, to serve

Brush leaves or grit from the girolles with a damp cloth. In a small frying pan, cook them gently in 40g of the butter and season. Set aside to cool.

Place the chicken into a large pan with the stock, thyme and bay leaf. Season well with salt and bring to the boil. Reduce the heat to a simmer and cook for 10 minutes, skimming off any scum that gathers on the surface. Remove from the heat and strain, keeping both the stock and the chicken.

In a separate pan over a medium heat, cook the onion in the remaining butter with no colour until soft. Add the flour and cook for 2 minutes, stirring regularly. Slowly add the wine to the roux and continue stirring for a minute. Stir in the hot stock and bring to the boil. Reduce the heat and simmer until the taste of raw flour has gone. Add the cream and reduce until the desired flavour and consistency (of a thick gravy) is reached. Stir in the mustard and taste for seasoning. Cut the cooked chicken into 2.5cm pieces and add them to the sauce with the tarragon and girolles. Set aside to cool.

If making individual pies, divide the pastry into 6 slabs. From each slab, cut away one-quarter of the pastry to be used for a lid. Dust a work surface with flour and roll the pastry lids first. They will need to be about 5mm thick and the perfect size to fit just inside each pie dish, so use the dish as a stencil. Using a small cookie cutter, cut a 2cm hole into the centre of each lid, so, as the pies cook, they can release steam. Dust the lids lightly with flour.

Lightly butter the pie dishes. Place a disc of baking parchment in the base of each. Roll the pastry cases out, making sure they're large enough to line the pie dishes with a 2.5cm overhang. Lay the pastry into the dishes, trimming the edges so they only overlap the sides by 2.5cm. Fill each almost to the top with the filling, then cover with a lid. Using a pastry brush, lightly brush egg around the edge of each lid and fold over the overlapping pastry, pinching it all the way around to seal. Brush the top with more beaten egg and chill until ready to bake. These can be prepared a few hours in advance.

Preheat the oven to 200°C. Bake the pies on the middle shelf of the oven for 25–30 minutes until golden brown, then rest them for a couple of minutes. Carefully run a knife around the sides of the dishes to make sure they aren't stuck, turn them out on to warmed plates and serve with mashed potato.

G
CHÂTEAU GUIRAUD

Spiced duck breast, stir-fried greens & cherry glaze
Pinot Noir 'La Côte', Domaine de la Côte, Santa Barbara

☞ page 90

SERVES 6

We usually serve this dish with an orange glaze, but cherries also work with duck and are complementary to the Californian Pinot Noir, which is strong in ripe red fruit flavours.

For me, the hero in this dish is the spice rub. It really packs a savoury punch and not only is it suitable for duck, it's also a great seasoning for pork. The recipe here makes about a kilo, but it will keep for six months or so in an airtight container in a dark, cool cupboard. I use it often.

ALTERNATIVE WINE MATCHES

Pinot Noir 'Las Brisas', Viña Leyda, Leyda ☞ page 90

Pinot Noir 'McDougall Ranch', Kutch Wines, Sonoma ☞ page 90

Pinot Noir 'Ma Danseuse', Peter Michael Winery, Sonoma ☞ page 90

FOR THE SPICE RUB

50g cardamon pods
25g star anise
75g cumin seeds
60g black peppercorns
40g cinnamon sticks
50g mustard seeds
400g sea salt
125g paprika

FOR THE DUCK

100ml red wine
50g dried Morello cherries
2 tsp sesame seeds
6 duck breasts
100g duck spice rub
150ml Red wine jus (see page 209)
2 heads *gai lan* (Chinese broccoli)
2 heads choy sum
1 head pak choy, quartered
1 head bok choy, quartered
20ml sesame oil
20ml groundnut oil
1 large garlic clove, finely chopped
1 tsp peeled and finely chopped fresh root ginger
1 red chilli, deseeded and finely chopped
50ml soy sauce
50ml clear honey
handful of coriander sprigs, plus coriander cress, to serve (optional)

Preheat the oven to 170°C. For the spice rub, spread the first 6 ingredients out on a baking tray and toast in the oven for 10 minutes, stirring occasionally to ensure they toast evenly. They'll darken by a couple of shades, but don't let them burn. Grind the toasted spices thoroughly, in a coffee grinder set aside for the purpose, then add the sea salt and paprika.

Increase the oven temperature to 180°C. In a saucepan, bring the wine to the boil, then add the cherries. Remove from the heat and steep for 2 hours. Toast the sesame seeds in the oven on a tray for 5 minutes, to lightly brown.

Score the duck fat in a criss-cross pattern. Place the spice rub on a plate and roll the duck breasts in it, coating each excessively and rubbing it into the score marks. Lay skin side down in a large dry frying pan, then place over a medium heat. As the pan heats up, the fat will render out; as it slowly fills the pan, tip it off. If the skin caramelises too quickly, reduce the heat, or you will burn the spices. It should take about 5 minutes. Once you're satisfied enough fat has been released, turn them to seal the other side. To cook them pink, roast in the oven for 3–4 minutes, then rest for 5 minutes.

Meanwhile, bring the red wine jus to the boil and add the cherries, along with a couple of tbsp of the wine. Reduce the sauce to a glazing consistency.

Cut the *gai lan* and choy sum to a manageable size. In a wok or large frying pan over a high heat, stir-fry all the greens in both the oils. Toss through the garlic, ginger and chilli and cook until the greens have slightly wilted. Add the soy, honey, coriander sprigs and sesame seeds and cook for a minute.

Slice each duck breast. Serve the greens and duck on warmed plates with the cherry glaze. Scatter with coriander cress, if using.

Côte
PINOT NOIR
BOTTLED BY
DE LA CÔTE
CALIFORNIA

HATEAU
LISE CLINET
OMEROL

Woodpigeon pithivier, truffled cep duxelles, Bordelaise sauce
Château L'Église-Clinet, Pomerol

☞ *page 116*

SERVES 4

We match this dish with a beautiful mature Pomerol, whose earthy and gamey flavours and soft tannins work beautifully with the woodpigeon, bacon and mushroom duxelles.

This is a complex dish with precise timings, but it's well worth the effort to impress your dinner guests. Give yourself plenty of time to make it. The pithivier can be prepared a day in advance to make life easier on the day.

You will only need the pigeon breasts for this dish, so I suggest when making your red wine jus (which can also be made a day in advance), that you substitute pigeon legs and carcasses for the chicken wings. This will result in a gamier-flavoured sauce more suited to the dish.

You will need: a truffle slicer, a digital temperature probe and 10cm and 12cm circular pastry cutters (preferably fluted).

FOR THE RED WINE JUS

500g chicken wings
50ml vegetable oil
2 carrots, chopped
3 large shallots, chopped
½ leek, white part only, chopped
3 celery sticks, chopped
1 garlic clove, crushed
1 bay leaf
3 thyme sprigs
10 peppercorns
500ml red wine
1 litre chicken stock
1 litre Demi-glace (see page 279)

FOR THE PITHIVIERS

8 woodpigeon breasts, plus their carcasses (order from your butcher in advance)
50ml vegetable oil
300g spinach, coarse stalks removed
plain flour, to dust
600g all-butter puff pastry
¼ quantity Mushroom duxelles (see page 266, substitute ceps for the button mushrooms there)
white truffle oil, plus more to serve
6 egg yolks, lightly beaten
frisée lettuce, to serve
25g white or black truffle (depending on budget or love for your guests)
salt and pepper

FOR THE SAUCE

a little vegetable oil
100g smoked bacon lardons
100g frozen cocktail onions
150g ceps, cut into 1cm pieces
200ml Red wine jus (see left), to serve
1 tbsp chopped parsley leaves

Using the heel of a heavy knife, chop the chicken wings each into 3 pieces, opening the bones. In a heavy-based saucepan set over a high heat, brown the chicken in the oil, stirring. Once golden and crisp, remove from the pan. Add the carrots to the same pan. Once they have browned, reduce the heat slightly and add the shallots. When they, too, have browned, add the leek, celery, garlic, bay, thyme and peppercorns. Cook until soft, stirring. Return the chicken wings and deglaze with the red wine. Reduce until the wine has disappeared, then pour in the stock.

As the chicken stock comes to the boil, skim thoroughly and reduce it by half. Add the demi-glace and, as it comes to the boil, once again skim thoroughly. Reduce the heat slightly so it's not boiling too rapidly. Continue to reduce, skimming regularly, until it has reached a light sauce consistency.

Strain the jus through a sieve. At the Club we strain all our jus through muslin to extract the finest of impurities. If you don't have muslin, a clean pair of tights will do the trick, but make sure you get permission! Allow to set in the fridge. It will keep chilled for 2 weeks, or frozen for 3 months.

Peel off and discard the skin from each pigeon breast and season liberally. Heat the vegetable oil in a large frying pan over a high heat and, when it begins to smoke, add the breasts, lightly browning each side. Remove and place on a plate to cool quickly in the fridge, so they don't overcook.

continued overleaf ☞

☚ *continued from previous page*

ALTERNATIVE WINE MATCHES

Ronan by Clinet, Bordeaux ☞ *page 100*

Cabernet Sauvignon Shiraz 'The Signature', Yalumba ☞ *page 102*

Cos d'Estournel, Château Cos d'Estournel, St-Estèphe ☞ *page 100*

Bring a large pan of lightly salted water to the boil and blanch the spinach for a few seconds before plunging it into iced water. Drain in a colander, then lay it out in an even layer on a clean tea towel to dry.

To build the pithiviers, dust a work top with flour and, using a rolling pin, roll out half the pastry into a rectangle. It needs to be large enough to cut out 4 x 10cm discs. Using a 10cm pastry cutter, cut out the discs. These will be the pithivier bases. For the lids, repeat with the remaining pastry, using a 12cm cutter. Cover the discs with cling film so they don't dry out.

Place the cooked spinach in a bowl and season it. Pile a small, even layer of spinach into the middle of each base disc, keeping 1.5cm around the edge free from spinach, so you can stick the top layer of pastry to it. Next, place on 2 pigeon breasts on top of each other, topping and tailing them.

Place the duxelles into a mixing bowl and add a few drops of truffle oil. (Go easy on this, a little goes a long way.) Place a tidy pile of duxelles over each pair of pigeon breasts, using a cupped hand to press it neatly into place.

With a pastry brush, brush egg yolk around the clean edges of pastry. Gently stretch the pastry lids over the top, sticking them to the edges and pushing out as much air as possible. To tidy up the shape, using the blunt side of a smaller pastry cutter, place it over the dome, pressing down gently to seal. Pick up each pithivier and carefully squeeze the seal tighter, flattening the rim further. Place on a heavy baking tray lined with baking parchment.

Brush the pithiviers with a generous coat of egg yolk and chill until it dries (a couple of hours). Once dry, with the tip of a knife, score the egg yolk from the middle of the dome to the rim, being careful not to cut the pastry, curving the cut as you go for the characteristic swirling starburst pithivier pattern. An hour before serving, preheat the oven to 185°C. Place the pithiviers in the middle of the oven, baking for 20–25 minutes until golden.

While the pithiviers are baking, complete the sauce. Preheat a large saucepan over a medium heat. Add a little vegetable oil and caramelise the lardons until crispy. Add the onions and ceps and sauté gently for a couple of minutes until cooked through. Add the red wine jus and bring to a simmer. Skim any fat from the surface and stir in the parsley.

To check the pithiviers are done, test the core temperature with a digital probe: it should read 35°C. Or use the blade of a knife: place it in the centre of a pithivier for a few seconds, then remove and place it on the inside of your wrist: it should feel just warm. Rest the pithiviers for 8–10 minutes.

Place the pithiviers in the centre of 8 plates and scatter the Bordelaise garnish and sauce generously around. Dress the frisée lightly with truffle oil, place a few leaves around each plate and shave the truffle over the top.

Roast grouse with parsnip crisps 'Bonnes-Mares' Grand Cru, Domaine Dujac

☞ page 88

SERVES 6

See overleaf for picture

Red Burgundy is a very classic match with game birds, as aged Burgundy starts to take on gamey farmyard and bacon-like characteristics.

The 'Glorious Twelfth' of August marks the beginning of an exciting time in the British culinary calendar. It's the first day of grouse shooting, which kicks off the game season for another year. One of the most poignant moments in the kitchen for me is the distinctive smell of the first grouse being pulled from the oven. It means that summer is coming to an end and autumn, with its bounty of interesting ingredients, is just around the corner.

It's best to hang grouse for a few days to allow the flavour to mature and the meat to tenderise. The length of hanging time is entirely down to personal preference. The meat on a young bird is already tender so, for my taste, only needs hanging with the viscera left inside for 4–5 days to develop the flavour.

ALTERNATIVE WINE MATCHES

Pinot Noir 'Stoney Vineyard', Domaine A, Tasmania ☞ *page 90*

Pinot Noir 'San Andreas Fault', Hirsch Vineyards, Sonoma ☞ *page 90*

Chambertin Grand Cru 'Clos de Bèze', Domaine Armand Rousseau ☞ *page 88*

- 2 litres vegetable oil, to deep-fry, plus more for the birds and offal
- 3 large parsnips, peeled
- 6 oven-ready grouse, plus their hearts and livers (optional)
- 6 thyme sprigs
- 150g unsalted butter
- 6 x 2.5cm-thick slices of crusty bread
- 1 large banana shallot, finely chopped
- 1 small garlic clove, finely chopped
- 100g chicken livers, cleaned and patted dry
- 150ml Port
- 80ml double cream
- salt and pepper
- 300ml hot Red wine jus (see previous page), to serve
- rowanberry jelly, or redcurrant jelly, to serve
- bread sauce, to serve

Start by making the parsnip crisps. Set a deep-fat fryer to 150°C, or use a saucepan, taking the same precautions and care as usual (see page 138). Using a peeler, shave the parsnips into strips until you are left with only the core. Test the oil with a shaving: it should boil on entry and gradually turn golden. Drop in half the shavings and move them around gently with a slotted spoon. Once they are an even gold (about 90 seconds), remove with the slotted spoon and drain on kitchen paper. Repeat with the rest of the parsnips. Season with salt.

Preheat the oven to 190°C. Remove the wishbone from each bird for ease of carving and place a thyme sprig inside the cavities. Season liberally. In a large frying pan over a medium-high heat, fry the birds in vegetable oil to seal all over, then add 100g of the butter. Place the bread slices in a roasting tin and a bird, on its back, on top of each. Pour the melted butter over.

Roast for 6–8 minutes, depending on size, if you like them nice and pink, spooning the butter over a few times. Halfway, turn each slice of bread over so both sides become crispy. As the grouse roast, the juices soak into the bread 'trencher', packing it full of flavour. Remove from the oven and rest for 6 minutes. (Turn the birds on to their breasts, to retain their juices.)

Work quickly now so the chicken livers and grouse offal (if using) don't overcook and your grouse don't cool too much. Heat the remaining butter in a small frying pan over a medium heat and cook the shallot and garlic until soft. Remove from the pan. Increase the heat to high. Season the grouse offal and chicken livers and coat them in a couple of tbsp vegetable oil. Place into the pan with the garlic and shallots and seal on all sides. Add the Port carefully, as it may spit, and boil until there is virtually no liquid left. Add the cream and reduce to coat the offal. Using a slotted spoon, lift the offal out on to a board and chop, then return it to the pan. Check the seasoning.

Spread the offal liberally on each trencher and serve with the grouse and parsnip crisps. Offer the jus, rowanberry jelly and bread sauce on the side.

MARES
DUJAC

Roast partridge, truffled celeriac purée, chestnuts & maple-cured bacon, cranberry jus Château Le Tertre Rôteboeuf, St-Emilion

☞ *page 116*

SERVES 4

If you're not used to game birds, partridge are a good starting point, as they are one of the mildest types. However, any stronger flavoured birds would also work here, as the wine will hold its own.

This dish has been created to pair with older red Bordeaux. As this wine matures, it develops flavour notes of earthy undergrowth, truffle, leather and gamey, meaty flavours. This is where the truffled celeriac, roasted chestnuts and smoked pancetta come into play. And, finally, dried cranberries, to match the berry fruit flavours typical of Bordeaux.

This purée is great with game, chicken and firm fish such as halibut. It will keep in the fridge for 4–5 days.

ALTERNATIVE WINE MATCHES

'Geyserville', Ridge Vineyards, Alexander Valley, USA ☞ *page 103*

Roc des Cambes, Côte de Bourg, Bordeaux ☞ *page 100*

Château La Fleur-Pétrus, Pomerol ☞ *page 116*

FOR THE PARTRIDGES

150ml red wine
40g dried cranberries
8 smoked pancetta rashers
50ml maple syrup
12 fresh chestnuts
4 thyme sprigs
4 oven-ready partridges, wishbones removed
50ml sunflower oil
100g unsalted butter
200g kale sprouts
200ml Red wine jus (see page 209)

FOR THE TRUFFLED CELERIAC PURÉE

500g celeriac, peeled and cut into 2.5cm cubes
3 thyme sprigs
1 bay leaf
600ml whole milk, or as needed
30g softened unsalted butter
1 tsp celery salt
2 tsp white truffle oil
salt and pepper

Pour the wine into a small saucepan and bring to the boil over a high heat. Add the cranberries. Remove from the heat and leave to swell for 2 hours.

For the purée, put the celeriac, thyme and bay leaf in a saucepan and cover with the milk. Cover and bring to the boil over a medium heat, then reduce to a gentle simmer. Cook for 10–15 minutes until the celeriac is very soft. Strain through a colander, reserving the milk. Tip the celeriac into a blender with the butter, celery salt and truffle oil. Blend to a very smooth purée, then adjust the consistency with a little reserved milk if required. Season.

Preheat the oven to 180°C. Lay the pancetta on a tray and brush with the syrup. Bake for 5–7 minutes or until crisp. Score a cross in the pointed ends of the chestnuts and roast for 10–15 minutes, or until the ends splay open. Remove the shells and membranes, break each in quarters and set aside.

Place a thyme sprig inside each partridge, then season liberally. In a large frying pan over a medium-high heat, fry the birds in the oil to seal. Add half the butter, then transfer to a roasting dish and put in the oven. Roast for 6–8 minutes if you like them nice and pink, spooning the butter over a few times to keep them moist. Turn the birds over on to their breasts to rest.

While the birds rest, bring a large saucepan of salted water to the boil. Blanch the kale sprouts for a couple of minutes, then strain. Return them to the pan with the remaining butter and season well.

In a small saucepan over a medium heat, bring the red wine jus to the boil. Add the chestnuts and the strained cranberries with a couple of tbsp of their soaking red wine. Reheat the celeriac purée, if needed.

Once the partridges have rested, remove the legs and breasts from each bird. Spread a little truffled celeriac purée on each of 4 warmed plates. Place a few buttered kale spouts on each, then the partridges. Top with a couple of rashers of pancetta and finish with the chestnut and cranberry jus.

Roast rabbit leg stuffed with cotechino, fried polenta & oven-dried cherry tomatoes
Capitel Croce, Alselmi, Veneto

☞ *page 78*

SERVES 4

To all intents and purpose, this wine is a Soave (see page 78), and a great one. Rich in body and texture, it is perfect with the rabbit, sausage stuffing and nutty polenta here.

It's best to use farmed rabbits for this dish, as they are generally larger and more tender. Wild rabbits get more exercise, so their legs tend to be tougher and more suited to slow braising. You'll need your butcher to tunnel-bone the legs, leaving only the small shank bone in place, as it's a tricky and time-consuming task.

Caul fat is a great tool for a chef. Here, it's used to wrap the rabbit legs to keep the stuffing in place. A good butcher should stock it, but order it ahead of when you need it.

ALTERNATIVE WINE MATCHES

Soave Classico 'Calvarino', Pieropan, Veneto ☞ *page 78*

Furore Bianco 'Fiorduva', Marisa Cuomo, Campania ☞ *page 78*

Chardonnay 'Gaia & Rey', Gaja, Langhe ☞ *page 66*

FOR THE POLENTA

1 quantity polenta (see pages 262–263), plus more to coat
50ml olive oil

FOR THE COTECHINO STUFFING

1 onion, finely chopped
2 garlic cloves, finely chopped
1 carrot, finely chopped
2 celery sticks, peeled and finely chopped
2 tbsp chopped oregano leaves
100g unsalted butter
500g cotechino sausage, finely chopped, with its jelly (but not its fat)
150g fresh breadcrumbs
2 tbsp chopped parsley leaves
salt and pepper

FOR THE SAUCE

12 cherry tomatoes, halved
2 tbsp extra virgin olive oil, plus more for the tomatoes
1 small onion, finely chopped
1 garlic clove, very finely chopped
1 tsp chopped oregano leaves
100ml white wine
200ml Demi-glace (see page 279)
300ml tomato passata

FOR THE RABBIT

200g pig's caul fat
200g Cotechino stuffing (see left)
4 farmed rabbit legs, tunnel-boned by the butcher
50ml sunflower oil

Make the polenta as on pages 262–263. Pour it into a rectangular container or tray to a depth of 5cm, smooth the surface and place in the fridge to set for a few hours. Once set firm, cut into bricks about 2cm thick.

Now the stuffing. In a heavy-based saucepan, gently cook the onion, garlic, carrot, celery and oregano in the butter until soft. Add the cotechino jelly. Remove from the heat, add the crumbs, cotechino and parsley and season.

For the sauce, preheat the oven to 130°C. Lay the tomatoes on a tray, drizzle with oil and season. Roast for 30 minutes, then cool. In a heavy-based saucepan over a low heat, gently cook the onion, garlic and oregano in the oil until soft. Add the wine and increase the heat, reducing the wine until it evaporates. Add the demi-glace and passata, then return to the boil and reduce the heat to a simmer. Cook for 20 minutes, stirring, until rich in consistency. Add the tomatoes, adjust the seasoning and set aside.

To prepare the rabbit, place the caul fat in a bowl in the sink. Rinse under running water for 10 minutes. Preheat the oven to 150°C. Roll the stuffing into 4 balls and stuff inside each rabbit leg. Cut a piece of caul the size of A4 paper and lay it on a work surface. Place a rabbit leg in the middle and wrap the corners over tightly to encase. Repeat with the remaining legs. Season.

In a large frying pan over medium-high heat, fry the legs in the oil until browned. Put in a dish, roast for 20–25 minutes, then rest for 6 minutes. Coat each polenta brick with dry polenta to stop it sticking and add a crisp texture. In a heavy-based, non-stick frying pan over a medium heat, fry in the olive oil until golden. Serve with the rabbit and reheated tomato sauce.

Parsnip-topped hare parmentier
Hermitage, Domaine Jean-Louis Chave

☞ page 94

SERVES 6

This classic dish is named after Antoine-Augustin Parmentier, who made an important contribution to nutrition and health in the late 16th century by promoting the potato as a staple food throughout Europe. There are many versions of parmentier, including our humble shepherd's pie.

Hare is amazing with the Northern Rhône Syrah. It is one of the strongest game meats and Syrah has a distinct whiff of bloody game, or wet dog, on the nose. For this very reason, I've added offal to this dish, to give it that extra gamey punch. It's optional, though, if it's not to your taste. If you struggle to find hare, substitute haunch of venison.

ALTERNATIVE WINE MATCHES

Crozes-Hermitage, Domaine Alain Graillot ☞ page 94

Cornas 'Les Vieilles Fontaines', Alain Voge ☞ page 94

Côte-Rôtie 'Les Grandes Places', Domaine Jean-Michel Gerin ☞ page 94

FOR THE HARE SAUCE

50ml vegetable oil
1kg hare, in 1cm cubes (1 medium hare), plus offal (optional) of 1 hare (liver, heart, kidneys), finely chopped
50g unsalted butter
1 large onion, finely chopped
2 garlic cloves, very finely chopped
4 juniper berries, finely ground
2 tsp chopped thyme leaves
3 tbsp plain flour
1 tbsp tomato purée
300ml red wine
800ml Demi-glace (see page 279)
1 tbsp redcurrant jelly
salt and pepper
buttered winter greens, to serve

FOR THE PARSNIP TOPPING

3 large parsnips, roughly chopped
2 floury potatoes (such as Maris Piper), quartered
80g unsalted butter
100g Tomme de Savoie, grated, or Gruyère
80g fresh breadcrumbs

Heat the vegetable oil in a large saucepan over a high heat until very hot. Season the hare (not the offal) and fry it in 2 batches until lightly browned. Remove the meat from the pan and place it in a sieve to drain any excess fat.

Heat the butter in the same pan over a medium heat and cook the onion, garlic, juniper and thyme for about 5 minutes, until soft. Add the flour and stir well, then stir in the tomato purée. Gradually add the wine, stirring to avoid lumps. Add the demi-glace and redcurrant jelly, then return the hare meat. Bring to the boil, then reduce the heat to a simmer. Season and simmer gently for 45 minutes, stirring occasionally. The final consistency should be that of a rich Bolognese sauce. Fold in the offal, if using, and adjust the seasoning if necessary. Fill a baking dish with the ragù, leaving enough room for the layer of parsnip. Chill so it sets before you attempt to add the mashed parsnip.

Place the parsnips and potatoes in a saucepan of lightly salted cold water and bring to the boil. The parsnips cook slightly faster, so once they are cooked, remove them with a slotted spoon to drain. Rest the parsnips for a couple of minutes in a colander to dry out, then blend to a purée in a food processor. If there are lumps, rub it through a sieve with a rubber spatula.

Preheat the oven to 180°C. Drain the potatoes in the colander and allow to sit to release their steam and dry out. Mash using a ricer or masher. Add the parsnip purée and the butter and mix well. Taste for seasoning and add salt if required. While still hot, spread it on the hare evenly in a layer about 2.5cm thick. (If you have a piping bag, it's easier to get even coverage.)

Bake on the middle oven shelf for 25 minutes. Mix the grated cheese and breadcrumbs in a bowl and sprinkle on top. Bake for a final 10–15 minutes until golden and crisp and the sauce is hot in the middle (test it with the tip of a knife). Serve with buttered winter greens.

Pork & rabbit terrine, macerated apricots, toasted hazelnuts & yogurt dressing
Condrieu 'Coteau de Vernon', Georges Vernay

☞ page 83

MAKES 16 SLICES

This was a dish we created for a dinner with Michel Roux Jr and he loved it. Condrieu is normally aged in new oak and, even though it's generally low in acidity, the malolactic fermentation derived from the oak ageing gives it a lovely, creamy-yogurty and nutty character. Viognier smells and tastes of ripe peaches and apricots, so this terrine with apricots, hazelnuts and yogurt touches perfectly on all the flavour elements in the wine.

Building a terrine requires time and patience. Don't be put off, as the rewards greatly outweigh the labour. It's great when you slice it to reveal a mosaic masterpiece!

This recipe is designed to fill a 32cm Le Creuset terrine, so it's best saved for a big occasion when you have many mouths to feed.

ALTERNATIVE WINE MATCHES

Viognier 'State of Surrender', Staete Landt, Marlborough ☞ page 83

Viognier, By Farr, Geelong, Victoria ☞ page 83

Condrieu 'La Doriane', Maison Guigal ☞ page 83

FOR THE TERRINE

- 2 tbsp vegetable oil
- 8 rabbit loins, trimmed of sinew
- 4 shallots, finely chopped
- 1 large fennel bulb, finely chopped
- 1 garlic clove, finely chopped
- leaves from 5 thyme sprigs, chopped
- 30g unsalted butter
- 500ml cider (we use Burrow Hill)
- 1kg 30% fat minced pork
- 300g pork liver, trimmed and chopped
- 1 tbsp chopped tarragon leaves
- 1 tbsp toasted fennel seeds, ground
- 300g dried apricots, soaked in dry white wine overnight
- 300g pancetta rashers
- 8 rabbit kidneys, any fat removed
- 100g toasted hazelnuts, chopped
- salt and pepper

FOR THE YOGURT DRESSING

- 200g Greek-style yogurt
- 50ml liquor from the macerated apricots, plus more if needed
- 50ml extra virgin olive oil
- 2 tbsp chopped dill, any coarse stalks removed

Preheat the oven to 150°C. Place a frying pan with the vegetable oil over a high heat. Season the rabbit liberally, Once the oil lightly smokes, sear the rabbit on all sides, then place straight in the fridge to cool.

Place a saucepan over a low heat and sauté the shallots, fennel, garlic and thyme in the butter until soft. Pour in the cider, increase the heat and reduce down to a 'jam'. Remove from the pan and chill in the fridge.

In a large bowl, mix the minced pork and liver with the chilled cider jam, then add the tarragon and ground fennel seeds. Season generously. (Always slightly over-season a terrine.) Make a small patty of this and fry it so you can taste and adjust the seasoning. Drain the apricots, reserving the wine.

Line the terrine mould with pancetta, leaving lengths draped over the side. Wet your fingers. Form a thin layer of pork mixture, then a line of rabbit loin. Between each line of rabbit, press a thin layer of pork to hold everything in place. As you build it, distribute one-third of the apricots and all the kidneys throughout, thinking about how it will appear once sliced. Fold over the ends of the pancetta tightly, cover and place in a roasting tin. Fill the tin with boiling water to 2.5cm below the top of the terrine.

Bake for 40–50 minutes or until a probe inserted into the centre reads 55°C. Or check the temperature with a small knife: the blade should feel lukewarm when touched on the inside of your wrist. Carefully remove from the water bath and rest for 30 minutes. Place a piece of cling film over the terrine, then cover with a piece of heavy card. Put a couple of tins of baked beans or the like on the card to press the terrine and chill for 24 hours. (Pressing the terrine ensures it retains density and forces out any air pockets.) Whisk all the ingredients for the yogurt dressing in a bowl, season and chill.

Cut the terrine just before serving. Serve with the yogurt dressing, a few apricots and the toasted hazelnuts.

Coteau de

Escargots à la Bourguignonne
Pouilly-Loché 'N°2 Monopole', Clos des Rocs

☞ page 70

SERVES 4 AS A STARTER

Buy good-quality prepared snails in a tin or jar, as snails take a lot of preparation when cooked from fresh. A good French deli or butcher will sell the shells, or you can buy them online; they can be reused.

Those working in vineyards, either picking, pruning or leaf plucking, often carry net bags and collect snails as they move through the vines.

Make sure the snails are served with lots of crusty bread, to mop up that lovely butter. The buttery element of the dish means that it's a good complement to Chardonnay, which, together with snails, is a classic pairing in Burgundy.

ALTERNATIVE WINE MATCHES

Aligoté, Bouzeron, Domaine A & P de Villaine, Côte Chalonnaise ☞ *page 80*

St-Aubin 'Le Banc', Domaine Pierre-Yves Colin-Morey ☞ *page 68*

Puligny-Montrachet 1er Cru 'Les Referts', Domaine Arnaud Ente ☞ *page 68*

300ml white Burgundy
1 bay leaf
2 thyme sprigs
2 shallots, finely chopped
3 garlic cloves, 1 crushed, 2 finely chopped
48 prepared snails and 48 snail shells
200g unsalted butter, softened
pinch of freshly grated nutmeg
3 tbsp finely chopped parsley leaves
splash of Cognac (optional)
50g breadcrumbs (optional)
salt and pepper
rock salt, to serve (optional)
crusty bread, to serve

In a small saucepan over a high heat, bring the wine to the boil with the bay leaf, thyme, half the shallots and the crushed garlic clove. Season and, once boiling, add the snails. Return to the boil, then reduce the heat to a simmer and remove the bay leaf, or its flavour will become too intense. Using a small ladle, skim off any scum on the surface. Simmer for 5 minutes.

Lift the snails out with slotted spoon and place them in a bowl. Reduce the wine by half, then strain it over the snails through a sieve. Allow to cool.

Place the softened butter in a mixing bowl. Add the remaining shallot, the chopped garlic, grated nutmeg and parsley. Some people like to add a tiny splash of Cognac at this stage, I'll leave that up to you. Season and mix well until combined.

Place a little butter into each shell, followed by a snail. Fill the rest of the shell with more butter. Once all the shells have been filled, chill until ready to cook. They will keep overnight, if you'd rather prepare them in advance.

If you don't have an escargot dish, lay a generous layer of rock salt in a baking dish and rest the shells in it to hold them steady.

Preheat the oven to 220°C.

Sprinkle a few breadcrumbs on top of each snail if you fancy it and put them in the oven. Bake for 5–7 minutes, until the butter is bubbling in the shells.

Remove from the oven and serve with plenty of crusty bread.

Scotch Burford Brown eggs with haggis & piccalilli
Grüner Veltliner 'Loibenberg', Weingut Emmerich Knoll

☞ page 81

SERVES 6 AS A SNACK OR LIGHT LUNCH

The famous London department store Fortnum & Mason claims to have invented Scotch eggs in 1738. Being five minutes walk from the Club, it is apt that this is one of our most celebrated dishes. To take it off the menu would be a travesty, I think we'd have members picketing the building!

Always use good free-range eggs. We use Clarence Court Burford Brown eggs for their rich, bright orange yolks. The haggis is made by Macsween.

This wasn't an easy dish to pair with wine, as egg yolk coats your mouth, making it harder to taste nuances in wine. But as one of our biggest sellers, it had to go in... We chose a Grüner Veltliner from Austria's finest region, the Wachau, as it is high in acidity to meet the piccalilli head-on, and has texture and spice to match the haggis.

ALTERNATIVE WINE MATCHES

Pinot Gris 'Lismore', Ata Rangi, Martinborough ☞ page 77

'Ktima' Malagousia, Gerovassiliou, Epanomi, Greece ☞ page 80

Riesling 'Bel Canto', Pegasus Bay, North Canterbury ☞ page 55

FOR THE SCOTCH EGGS

120g haggis
420g sausagemeat
6 medium eggs, plus 2 eggs, lightly beaten
plain flour
panko crumbs
sunflower oil, to deep-fry
salt
mustard cress, to serve
200g Piccalilli, preferably home-made (see right), to serve

FOR THE PICCALILLI (MAKES 1KG)

1 cucumber
½ large cauliflower
1 large onion
2 large shallots
2–3 tbsp salt
150g caster sugar
60g English mustard
10g ground turmeric
1 small chilli, deseeded and finely chopped
150ml malt vinegar
250ml white wine vinegar
40g cornflour

For the piccalilli, cut the cucumber in half lengthways and scoop out the seeds with a spoon. Slice each half into 3 lengths, then cut across into 1cm pieces. Separate the cauliflower into 1–2cm florets. Cut the onion and shallots into 1cm pieces. Toss all the vegetables except the chilli in a colander with the salt, then chill for 4 hours, with a bowl underneath to catch any water. Wash in cold water to remove the salt, then drain.

In a saucepan, mix the sugar, mustard, turmeric, chilli and the 2 vinegars. Over a high heat, bring to the boil, then reduce the heat to a simmer for 2–3 minutes. Mix the cornflour in small bowl with 100ml cold water, then whisk it slowly into the vinegar mixture. Simmer for another 5 minutes until the sauce thickens. Add the well-drained vegetables to the hot sauce, heat the piccalilli for a minute or so, stirring, then preserve in hot, sterilised jars.

To make the Scotch eggs, mix the haggis and sausagemeat in a bowl. Bring a saucepan of water to the boil. Boil the 6 eggs for 5½ minutes (you need to be precise). Remove with a slotted spoon and plunge into iced water to arrest the cooking. Once they are cool, peel, starting at the rounded end.

Split the sausagemeat mixture into 6 even balls, then roll each out between 2 sheets of baking parchment to 1cm thick. Wrap a portion of meat around each egg, making sure they still resemble the shape of the egg. To crumb the eggs, set up a bowl each of flour, beaten eggs and crumbs. Roll them one at a time in the flour, then into the eggs, then coat generously with the crumbs.

Preheat the oven to 180°C. Set your deep fryer to 190°C, or use a saucepan, taking the same precautions and care as usual (see page 138). Deep-fry the Scotch eggs for a couple of minutes until golden and crispy. Remove from the oil and place in the oven on a tray for 3 minutes, so the yolks warm through. Rest them on kitchen paper to soak up any oil, then season lightly with salt. Carve the eggs in half, being careful not to spill the yolk, and serve on a nest of mustard cress with the piccalilli on the side.

Chargrilled Ibérico presa, caramelised orange glaze, shaved fennel & orange salad
Clos Erasmus, Priorat

☞ *page 106*

SERVES 6

Priorat is grown in relatively high altitude, cool vineyards. The wines are deep and concentrated, with black fruits and a hint of orange citrus.

The Iberian pig is found in herds clustered in central and southern Portugal and Spain. It is thought they first arrived with Phoenicians from the Eastern Mediterranean coast (present-day Lebanon), where they'd interbred with wild boar. They have insatiable appetites and a great capacity to accumulate fat, which produces the marbling typical of the breed. This, together with feeding on acorns, is what makes the meat so special. Grilled medium-rare, it's juicy and tender with a full flavour.

I served this to our Club managers without telling them what it was. They were convinced it was well-aged steak.

ALTERNATIVE WINE MATCHES

Montsant 'El Brindis', Franck Massard, Spain ☞ *page 106*

Grenache, David & Nadia, Swartland ☞ *page 104*

Clos Mogador, Priorat ☞ *page 106*

1 tbsp fennel seeds
3 star anise
1 tbsp chopped rosemary leaves
80ml extra virgin olive oil
1.2kg Ibérico presa
8 oranges
3 tbsp caster sugar
3 fennel bulbs
80ml Lemon dressing (see page 134)
salt and pepper

Preheat the oven to 170°C.

To make a marinade for the pork, place the fennel seeds and star anise on a baking tray and toast in the oven for 10 minutes, shaking from time to time so they cook evenly. They will darken by a couple of shades, but don't allow them to burn. Grind to a powder in a mortar and pestle, or a coffee grinder set aside for the purpose. Place the ground spices in a bowl and add the rosemary and oil. Mix thoroughly and rub it on the pork. Rest at room temperature for 1 hour, to take on the flavour of the spices.

Meanwhile, make the orange glaze. Using a vegetable peeler, shave the zest from 2 of the oranges, leaving the bitter white pith behind. Cut the 2 peeled oranges in half along with 3 more of the oranges and juice all 5 into a small saucepan, making sure no seeds fall in. Using a small knife, remove any pith from the peel shavings and slice it into thin strips. Add to the juice with the sugar. Bring to a simmer over a medium-high heat. Simmer gently for a few minutes until reduced to a light syrupy marmalade, then set aside.

Segment the remaining 3 oranges using a sharp knife. Place the segments in a small bowl and squeeze any juice left in the shells over them.

Cut the fennel bulbs in half and remove the cores. Using a mandolin, carefully shave it very finely. Plunge it into a bowl of iced water, to crisp it up, leaving it for 30 seconds only. Drain, then pat dry with kitchen paper.

Season the pork liberally. Preheat a griddle pan, or a barbecue to the point that the charcoals are glowing. Seal the pork over a high heat and, when it has caramelised, place it over a lower heat to cook more slowly. Once it is cooked medium-rare, brush it with the orange glaze and return it to a high heat to caramelise. Keep turning the meat and brushing on more glaze. Remember, you want it to caramelise, not burn. Leave to rest for 8 minutes.

Meanwhile, in a large salad bowl, toss the shaved fennel with the orange segments, juice and lemon dressing and season.

Slice the Ibérico presa 1cm thick against the grain. In carving against the grain, the knife is doing the work, so your jaw doesn't have to. It can make the difference between a successful meal and a disaster.

Divide the meat between 6 warmed plates, or a board to share, with the candied zest on top, and add a pile of fennel salad, or serve it on the side.

ERASMUS
2016

CLOS
SAVENNIERES-COULEE DE SERRANT CONTROLEE

Slow-roasted belly of Tamworth pork, autumn fruit & hazelnut compote
Savennières 'Coulée de Serrant', Nicolas Joly

☞ *page 64*

SERVES 8

See previous page for picture

When we tried this Loire Chenin Blanc, we were overwhelmed by the intensity of its ripe autumn fruits. Usually, I'd serve roast pork with a simple Bramley apple sauce, but it wasn't just apple we were tasting in the wine, we were also getting the distinct floral fragrance of quince, so we had to add that. The compote makes more than you need for this dish, but keeps for a week in the fridge and is great over muesli with yogurt for breakfast.

A dry Chenin Blanc such as this has a crisp acidity which cuts through the pork fat and crackling. In the gravy I've used cider rather than wine, which is great with pork and enhances those orchard fruit flavours. Serve with roast potatoes.

FOR THE COMPOTE

100g blanched hazelnuts
360g caster sugar, or to taste
300ml water
1 lemon
2 quinces
2 pears
50g unsalted butter
3 large Bramley apples, peeled, cored and chopped

FOR THE PORK

4kg boneless pork belly, rind scored by your butcher
15 sage leaves, chopped
3 garlic cloves, chopped
vegetable oil
1 carrot, chopped
1 celery stick, chopped
½ leek, chopped
1 onion, chopped
200ml dry cider
2 tbsp plain flour
1 bay leaf
2 thyme sprigs
600ml hot Demi-glace (see page 279)
salt and pepper
roast potatoes, to serve

Start with the compote. Preheat the oven to 170°C. Toast the hazelnuts in the oven on a small tray for 7 minutes. Remove from the oven and chop. Place 300g of the sugar, the measured water and the juice of ½ lemon in a saucepan. Peel the quinces and pears and submerge in the liquid. Over a medium heat, poach at a simmer. The pears should take 10–15 minutes and the quince twice as long. Once each is cooked, remove with a slotted spoon. Slice the flesh from the cores and cut into 1cm cubes. Melt the butter in a pan over a medium heat. Add the apples and the remaining lemon juice and sugar. Add the nuts and cook, stirring regularly, until soft. This should only take 8–10 minutes. Once they're soft, add the pears and quince. Taste and add sugar if you find it too tart, but it shouldn't be too sweet as it needs to cut through the fatty pork. Cool, cover and store in the fridge.

For the pork, preheat the oven to 220°C. Turn the belly flesh-side up and season its underside, then evenly scatter over the sage and garlic. Roll up lengthways and tie it with butcher's string. Place it on a wire rack over the sink. Pour over a large kettle of boiling water; the skin will tighten up and the pores will open, allowing heat and salt to penetrate, enhancing the crackling. Pat dry and rub it with vegetable oil and sea salt. Place on a wire rack in a roasting tray in the oven. After 45 minutes, the skin should be crackled. Reduce the oven temperature to 160°C and roast for 1 more hour.

Lift out the rack with the pork. Scatter the chopped vegetables into the roasting tray, mixing them with the fat. Place the rack with the pork back over the vegetables. Roast for a final 1 hour, until the pork is tender. Remove the pork from the oven and rest for at least 20 minutes.

For the gravy, transfer the vegetables from the tray to a saucepan using a slotted spoon. Skim off all the fat left in the tray, but leave behind any meat juices. Place the tray over a medium heat and pour in the cider to loosen the flavoursome morsels, helping it along by scraping with a wooden spoon.

ALTERNATIVE WINE MATCHES

Vouvray 'Le Haut-Lieu', Domaine Huet, Loire ☞ *page 64*

Vouvray 'Baudoin', Domaine François Chidaine, Loire ☞ *page 64*

Chenin Blanc 'The FMC', Ken Forrester, Stellenbosch ☞ *page 64*

Place the saucepan containing the vegetables over a medium heat and add the flour. Cook gently, stirring regularly, for 2 minutes. Add the cider and deglazed roasting juices and stir for 2 minutes to evaporate any remaining alcohol and thicken the gravy. Add the bay and thyme and gradually pour in the hot demi-glace, stirring. Bring to the boil, giving it a thorough skim with a ladle to remove any fat on the surface. Reduce the heat to a simmer and reduce the sauce, skimming regularly, until it reaches a gravy consistency. Taste to check the seasoning and adjust accordingly.

When ready to serve, remove the string from the pork belly and carve it into thick slices, using a large serrated knife to saw through the crackling. Warm the compote and serve it at the table with the meat, with roast potatoes.

Braised pork cheeks in Sherry with morcilla, orange & butter beans Palo Cortado, Bodegas Tradición

☞ page 125

SERVES 6

Madeira, Oloroso and Palo Cortado are some of the most complex wines you can get, with layers of flavour such as walnuts, leather, lanolin, demerara sugar, orange rind and aldehydes derived from the breakdown of wood over many years. They go well with almost any full-bodied meat dish and definitely should not be saved just for cheese. (Palo Cortado is a rare and special type of Oloroso, see page 125.)

Pork cheeks are the best braising cut from a pig, broken up by several thin layers of sinew running through them. When slow-cooked, this sinew breaks down into the most divine jelly that melts in your mouth. However, pork cheeks are still under-used and it may be an idea to give your butcher advance warning.

ALTERNATIVE WINE MATCHES

Rainwater Reserva, Vinhos Barbeito, Madeira ☞ page 126

Oloroso, 'La Bota 78', Equipo Navazos, Jerez ☞ page 125

Rioja Gran Reserva 'Viña Tondonia', López de Heredia ☞ page 119

200g dried butter beans
18 pork cheeks, trimmed of outer fat
100g plain flour
4 tbsp sunflower oil
50g unsalted butter
2 onions, chopped
2 carrots, chopped
2 celery sticks, chopped
4 garlic cloves, chopped
6 thyme sprigs
1 bay leaf
2 tbsp tomato purée
500ml good-quality dry Sherry
1 litre chicken stock
1 litre Demi-glace (see page 279)
2 oranges, halved
40g dried porcini mushrooms
300g miniature tapas-style morcilla
3 tbsp chopped parsley leaves
salt and pepper
crusty sourdough bread, to serve

In a large bowl, cover the butter beans with 3 times their volume of water, as they will swell substantially. Leave overnight.

Preheat the oven to 150°C. Season the pork cheeks and place in a large plastic bag. Add the flour and, holding the bag closed, shake to coat the meat with the flour. Remove the cheeks from the bag; reserve the flour.

Heat a large saucepan over a high heat. Pour in the sunflower oil and fry the floured pork until evenly browned. (You may need to do this in 2 batches so as not to overcrowd your pan.) Transfer to a braising dish or casserole dish.

Reduce the heat under the saucepan to medium and add the butter, onions, carrots, celery, garlic, thyme and bay leaf. Cook for 4–5 minutes, stirring to release any tasty pork morsels, until soft and slightly caramelised.

Stir in the reserved flour and tomato purée and cook for another minute, stirring so they don't catch. Stir in the Sherry, a little at a time, so that lumps don't form. Once all the Sherry has been added, pour in the stock and demi-glace, add the orange halves and dried porcini and bring to the boil.

Pour the liquid and vegetables over the pork, then cover. Place in the oven for 2 hours, or until tender. Lift the pork out and set aside.

Meanwhile, drain and rinse the beans. Place in a saucepan and cover with fresh, lightly salted water. Bring to the boil, then reduce the heat to a simmer. Cook for 45 minutes or until soft, topping up with water as required. Once cooked, drain and set aside.

Strain the pork braising sauce through a sieve into a large saucepan. Bring to the boil over a medium heat, then reduce to a simmer. Skim to remove any fat on the surface. If the sauce appears a little thin, reduce it slightly until it has reached the desired consistency. Taste and season. Add the butter beans, pork cheeks and morcilla. Allow the morcilla to cook for 5 minutes. This is enough time for it to impart flavour to the sauce but not so long that it bursts. Add the parsley and serve with crusty sourdough bread.

PALO CORTADO
TRADICION
30 YEARS
BODEGAS TRADICION

Vincisgrassi
'Terre Alte', Livio Felluga, Friuli

☞ page 78

SERVES 8

Vincisgrassi is a traditional dish of the Marches region of Italy, and this delicious variant of lasagne is believed to have been created especially for the Austrian army general – Windisch Graetz – who fought against Napoleon during the siege of Ancona in 1799.

At the Club we make it with fresh pasta. However, you can buy pasta sheets from an Italian delicatessen. You need to blanch them first though, and they will take more time to cook in the water than fresh pasta. Some purists insist on making pasta dough by hand, but I've never seen the point: it's messy, takes three times as long and you can achieve exactly the same results in a food processor. You'll need a pasta roller.

This Terre Alte is one of the best white wines found in Friuli, Italy, a blend of Sauvignon Blanc, Pinot Bianco and Friulano with some time spent in oak. With five years age, the wine becomes rich and complex with layers of tropical fruit, earthiness and a silky texture; a great combination with truffle and porcini.

FOR THE PASTA

370g '00' pasta flour, plus more to dust
1 tsp fine sea salt
1 tbsp extra virgin olive oil
3 medium eggs, plus 4 egg yolks

FOR THE VINCISGRASSI

750ml whole milk
400ml single cream
1 large onion, finely chopped
100g unsalted butter
250g sliced prosciutto, cut across in 1cm strips
100g plain flour
500g fresh porcini mushrooms
50ml extra virgin olive oil, plus more for the pasta, dish, and to serve
4 tbsp chopped parsley leaves
120g Parmesan cheese, finely grated
salt and pepper
white truffle oil, to serve
shaved truffle, to serve

Place the flour and salt in a food mixer fitted with a blade. Turn it on to full speed and slowly add the oil, followed by the eggs and yolks. The dough should come together in a ball. Knead for 10 minutes, until it softens and springs back when you press it. Wrap in cling film and chill for 2 hours.

In a heavy-based saucepan over a medium heat, bring the milk and cream to the boil, then pour into a jug. In a large clean saucepan over a medium heat, sauté the onion gently in the butter until soft and translucent. Add the prosciutto and cook for a couple of minutes, then stir in the flour to form a roux. Slowly whisk in the hot milk and cream a little at a time, so no lumps form. Cook over a gentle heat for a few minutes, stirring regularly so it doesn't catch, until you can no longer taste the flour. Season and set aside.

Clean the porcini with a damp cloth, carefully brushing away dirt or sand. If they are really dirty, you may need to use a small knife to scrape them, but don't dunk them into water. (Mushrooms are like sponges, and will take on too much water.) Once they are clean, slice them finely. Place a frying pan over a medium-high heat and sauté the mushrooms in the olive oil. Depending on the size of your pan this may need to be done in batches, seasoning as you go. Once cooked, fold into the béchamel with the parsley.

To roll the pasta, cut off 80g of dough and shape it to fit the pasta roller. Keep the remaining dough wrapped so it doesn't dry out while you are rolling. Set the pasta roller to its thickest setting. Sprinkle a little flour over the machine and your work surface. Roll the dough through the machine 3 times, reducing the thickness by 2 settings each time. Fold the length of dough into 3 and set the machine back to the thickest setting. Feed the dough through again and keep rolling, reducing the thickness a setting each time, until you have reached the thinnest setting. You may need to sprinkle more flour over the machine and your work surface as you go so the pasta doesn't stick. Cut the pasta into large but manageable sheets.

To blanch the pasta, bring a large pan of water to the boil and season it liberally with salt, adding a little olive oil to stop the sheets from sticking

ALTERNATIVE WINE MATCHES

Fiano 'Rubato', Coriole, McLaren Vale
☞ *page 78*

Filari di Timorasso, Luigi Boveri, Tuscany
☞ *page 78*

Verdicchio dei Castelli di Jesi Classico Riserva 'Il Cantico della Figura', Andrea Felici, Marches
☞ *page 78*

together. Get a large container of iced water to cool the pasta sheets after blanching. Blanch the fresh pasta sheets in the boiling water in 2–3 batches, so you don't overload the pan. After a minute or so, remove the pasta sheets with a large skimmer and a pair of tongs and plunge them into the iced water. This can be a juggling act as the sheets are slippery. Don't leave the pasta in the water for too long or it will swell. Lay the pasta out on sheets of greaseproof paper drizzled with olive oil so they don't stick together. You will need enough pasta sheets to build 4 layers in your chosen baking dish.

Oil a 30 x 25cm baking dish lightly. Lay in an even layer of pasta, then one-quarter of the béchamel, sprinkled with a little Parmesan. Repeat to make 4 layers, using the last of the sauce on the final layer. It should be about 5cm deep. Sprinkle with Parmesan and chill until ready to cook.

Preheat the oven to 150°C. Cover the vincisgrassi with foil and place it on the middle oven shelf. After 15 minutes, increase the oven temperature to 180°C and remove the foil. Bake for 20 minutes, until golden brown. Test the middle is hot with the tip of a small knife, then remove from the oven and rest it on a cooling rack for 5–8 minutes.

Drizzle a little white truffle oil over and shave truffle over the top, to serve.

Choucroute garnie
Riesling 'Cuvée Ste Catherine' Grand Cru Schlossberg, Domaine Weinbach

☞ page 52

SERVES 8

Alsace is amazing for gastronomy: *flammekuchen* with Pinot Gris or Munster with Gewurztraminer are world-class wine and food matches. Choucroute, with the acidity in the fermented cabbage, is amazing with Riesling. There is no fixed recipe for this Alsatian dish. Any combination of sauerkraut, smoked sausages and pork with potatoes would qualify.

As Alsace is on the German border, you can feel the German influence in this dish. Sauerkraut, traditionally a German and Eastern European dish, has been adopted in Alsace to create this famous classic. The sausages I've used are produced in their namesake Alsatian cities and towns. Find them online, or substitute German sausages. Your guests may want to wear loose trousers, as this is a substantial meal…

ALTERNATIVE WINE MATCHES

Riesling 'Lago Ranco', Casa Silva, Patagonia ☞ page 50

Gewurztraminer 'Clos Windsbuhl', Domaine Zind-Humbrecht, Alsace ☞ page 77

Riesling 'Clos Ste-Hune', Maison Trimbach, Alsace ☞ page 52

1 ham knuckle
3 litres chicken stock
2 Morteau sausages
2 Montbeliard sausages
4 Strasbourg sausages
800g sauerkraut
1 bay leaf
5 juniper berries
2 cloves
1 large onion, finely sliced
2 garlic cloves, finely chopped
60g duck or goose fat
1 Granny Smith apple
400g smoked streaky bacon, in a single piece
400ml Riesling, ideally from Alsace
600g Charlotte potatoes, peeled
salt and pepper

Place the ham knuckle in a large saucepan, pour over the stock and set over a high heat. Bring to the boil, then reduce the heat to a simmer, partially cover and cook for 2½–3 hours, skimming off fat. As the stock evaporates, top up with water from time to time, to keep the ham just covered.

After 2 hours, add the sausages and reduce the heat to just below a simmer. Poach for 20 minutes, being sure not to boil the sausages or the skins will split. Remove the sausages and ham knuckle and strain the cooking liquor through a sieve. Reserve the liquor. Allow the meats to cool slightly.

Place the sauerkraut into a colander and rinse briefly under cold water. Squeeze out all the water and set aside.

Make a muslin pouch containing the bay leaf, juniper berries and cloves and tie it at the top with string.

Preheat the oven to 150°C.

In a large heavy-based saucepan over a low heat, cook the onion and garlic in the duck or goose fat until soft and translucent. Add the onion to the sauerkraut and mix well. Peel the apple and coarsely grate it in.

In a large casserole or lidded baking dish, place half the sauerkraut in an even layer. Remove the fat and skin from the ham knuckle and flake the meat into large pieces. Scatter it into the casserole over the sauerkraut. Cut each of the Morteau and Montbeliard sausages into 4 pieces and add them to the casserole. Cut the Strasbourg sausages in half and add these, too. Cut the smoked streaky bacon into 4 thick slices, cut each slice in half and add to the casserole with the muslin pouch. Cover evenly with the remaining sauerkraut and pour in the wine, then enough reserved cooking liquor to just cover. Cover with the lid and cook in the oven for 1½ hours.

Meanwhile, cook the Charlotte potatoes in any remaining stock, topped up with a little water if needed. Once ready, remove the choucroute garnie from the oven and taste it, adjusting the seasoning if necessary.

To serve, distribute the choucroute garnie evenly between 8 warmed bowls, pour over some of the liquor and add the potatoes.

Wild boar pie with kumara mash
Syrah 'Le Sol', Craggy Range, Hawke's Bay

☞ page 97

MAKES 6

Kiwis just love pies! Syrah from Hawke's Bay is delicious and only made in tiny quantities at the moment. It has ripe dark blackberry and liquorice notes and a firm, structured palate; great to pair with something full-flavoured such as braised wild boar.

You can prepare individual pies as we do at the Club, or make a big pie as a family dish (see recipe introduction, page 204, for how to assemble and cook a larger pie).

Orange kumara (New Zealand sweet potato) is my choice for mashing.

FOR THE RAGÙ

1 tsp fennel seeds
30g dried porcini mushrooms
50ml sunflower oil
1kg wild boar shoulder, sinew removed, cut into 2.5cm cubes
100g unsalted butter
1 large onion, finely chopped
1 large carrot, finely chopped
2 celery sticks, finely chopped
3 garlic cloves, finely chopped
1 tbsp chopped thyme leaves
1 bay leaf
40g tomato purée
70g plain flour
500ml red wine
800ml Demi-glace (see page 279)
1 tbsp redcurrant jelly
salt and pepper

FOR THE PIES

1kg all-butter puff pastry
plain flour, to dust
unsalted butter, for the dishes
2 eggs, lightly beaten

FOR THE MASH

rock salt
1kg large orange-skinned kumara sweet potatoes
50g unsalted butter

Preheat the oven to 150°C. Toast the fennel seeds on a tray for 8 minutes, then set aside.

Soak the dried porcini in 200ml warm water for 20 minutes, then strain and reserve the water. Squeeze all the water out of the porcini and chop finely.

In a large heavy-based saucepan over a high heat, heat the sunflower oil to smoking point. Add the wild boar and season well. As the wild boar cooks, it will release its juices. These will gradually evaporate and the meat will begin to caramelise. Lightly brown on all sides and set aside.

Add the butter to the pan and reduce the heat to medium. Cook the vegetables, garlic, toasted fennel seeds, thyme, bay leaf and porcini until soft. As the vegetables cook, scrape the pan with the wooden spoon to dislodge any tasty morsels that have stuck while the boar was caramelising. Once the vegetables soften, add the tomato purée and flour, reduce the temperature to low and stir for a minute. Increase the temperature to medium and slowly add the wine, stirring to avoid any lumps forming.

Add the wild boar, demi-glace, the porcini soaking water and the redcurrant jelly. Season and bring to the boil, stirring regularly. Reduce the heat right down to a gentle simmer and cook, stirring often, so it doesn't catch on the pan. Every so often, skim off any fat and impurities that collect on the surface. Cook gently for 1 hour, or until the meat is very soft. As it cooks, the stock will reduce, and the sauce will slowly thicken. Cool, then chill.

continued overleaf ☞

☜ *continued from previous page*

ALTERNATIVE WINE MATCHES

Shiraz, Bird in Hand Winery, Adelaide Hills, South Australia ☞ *page 97*

Syrah, Wind Gap Wines, Sonoma ☞ *page 92*

Syrah 'Homage', Trinity Hill, Hawke's Bay ☞ *page 97*

If making individual pies, divide the pastry into 6 even slabs. From each slab, cut away one-quarter of the pastry to be used for a lid. Dust the work surface and rolling pin liberally with flour and roll the pastry lids first. They need to be about 5mm thick and the perfect size to fit just inside the rim of each pie dish, so use the rim of the dish as a stencil, trimming around it with a small knife. Using a small round cookie cutter, cut a 2cm hole into the centre of each lid, so that as the pies cook, they can release steam. Dust the lids lightly with flour and set aside.

Lightly butter the pie dishes. Place a disc of baking parchment in the base of each, so the pies can be easily turned out. Roll the pastry cases out one at a time, making sure they're large enough to line the pie dishes with a 2.5cm overhang. Lay the rolled pastry sheets into each of the pie dishes, trimming the edges of the pastry so they only overlap the sides by 2.5cm.

Fill each dish almost to the top with the chilled filling, then cover with a lid. Using a pastry brush, lightly brush a little beaten egg around the edge of each lid and fold over the overlapping pastry, pinching it all the way around to seal. Brush the top with more egg and chill until ready to bake. The pies can be prepared a few hours in advance. Refrigerate any ragù you have left. It's delicious reheated and tossed through some pasta for a hearty lunch (see right).

Now make the mash. Preheat the oven to 180°C.

Scatter a little rock salt into a baking dish and rest the kumara on the salt to hold them steady. Bake for 45 minutes to 1 hour. When they offer no resistance to a knife, they are ready. Halve lengthways and scoop out the flesh. Melt the butter in a small saucepan, then remove from the heat. While the kumara is still hot, place it in a food processor, add the butter, season, then blend into a smooth mash. Push through a sieve using a spatula, to free it from any lumps. Keep it warm.

Increase the oven temperature to 200°C.

Bake the pies on the middle shelf for 25–30 minutes, until golden brown, then rest them for a couple of minutes before attempting to turn them out. Carefully run a small knife around the sides of the dishes to make sure they aren't stuck, then turn them out and serve with the mashed kumara.

Penne of wild boar ragù
Barbaresco 'Rabajà', Bruno Rocca

☞ page 112

SERVES 4

This is a lighter, more subtle ragù than my rigatoni of venison (see page 286). We are going to pair the venison ragù with a Barolo, which, although it is made using the Nebbiolo grape, tends to be a more massive, tannic and rich expression of the variety. This Barbaresco, considered more elegant and approachable, is therefore the choice for this lighter of the two ragùs. Nebbiolo often has liquorice flavour notes, which is where the fennel seeds in the ragù come in helpful...

ALTERNATIVE WINE MATCHES

Nebbiolo 'Martinenga', Marchesi di Grésy, Langhe ☞ *page 112*

Barolo 'Cerequio', Roberto Voerzio, Piedmont ☞ *page 112*

Barolo 'Monfortino', Giacomo Conterno, Piedmont ☞ *page 112*

15 cherry tomatoes
extra virgin olive oil
500g dried penne
1 quantity wild boar Ragù
(see page 238), but tweaked:
* meat cut into 1.5cm cubes
* 50g plain flour
* cooked for only 45 minutes
1 tbsp chopped parsley leaves
50g Parmesan cheese, finely grated
salt and pepper

Preheat the oven to 130°C.

Halve the cherry tomatoes and lay them out on a baking tray, seeds showing. Drizzle a little extra virgin olive oil over them and season lightly. Dry the tomatoes in the oven for 30 minutes until they start to shrivel.

Meanwhile, fill a large saucepan with water and bring it to the boil. Season generously with salt. Once boiling, add the penne and cook to al dente. You can follow the time on the packet, but I never trust it. Strain the pasta.

Fold the cooked penne through the ragù with the oven-dried tomatoes and parsley. Serve immediately, topped with a generous sprinkling of Parmesan.

DE LA
DES PÈRES
2016

Cassoulet de Toulouse
Domaine de la Grange des Pères, Pays d'Hérault

☞ page 120

SERVES 6

While writing this book, we have had lots of fun inventing new dishes to go with wines. But the classics are classics for a reason, and should be celebrated. This is a winter dish, or it's for those working in fields: it's not calorie light! A full-bodied southern French red is needed for its warmth and depth of flavour with these earthy ingredients.

Cassoulet is the quintessence of classic French cookery. There are many provincial variations using lamb or mutton, so feel free to mix it up. This, however, is a traditional recipe. If you can't find smoked Toulouse sausages, go with fresh unsmoked and use smoked bacon, as smokiness should permeate the braise, flavouring the creamy beans and enriching the sauce.

You'll need to soak the beans and salt the duck for 24 hours.

ALTERNATIVE WINE MATCHES

Château Millegrand Minervois, Languedoc ☞ page 120

'Léonie', Domaine Terre Inconnue, Languedoc ☞ page 121

'Clos des Truffiers', Château de la Négly, Languedoc ☞ page 121

300g dried coco or haricot beans
3 duck legs, separated into thighs and drumsticks by your butcher
1kg duck or goose fat
a few thyme sprigs, plus 1 tbsp finely chopped thyme leaves
1 bay leaf
200g streaky bacon, in a single piece
3 smoked Toulouse sausages
2 red onions, finely chopped
3 garlic cloves, finely chopped
1 tbsp finely chopped rosemary leaves
750ml Demi-glace (see page 279)
750ml chicken stock
salt and pepper

FOR THE HERB CRUST

2 large shallots, finely chopped
50g unsalted butter
150g fresh breadcrumbs
3 tbsp chopped parsley leaves

Soak the beans in water for 24 hours. Season the legs liberally with sea salt and chill overnight.

Preheat the oven to 140°C. Place the duck legs in a deep ovenproof dish. In a saucepan, melt the duck or goose fat. Gently pour the fat over the duck, to completely submerge. Add the thyme sprigs and bay, cover and place on the middle oven shelf. Cook for 3 hours. To test them, carefully lift out a thigh to check if the meat is just coming away from the bone when you press it. Remove the duck from the fat and place on kitchen paper, skin side up, to cool. Strain the fat through a sieve and reserve it in the fridge. It can be used again and again for the same purpose, or for roasting potatoes.

Drain the beans and rinse. In a large saucepan, cover the beans with water and season well with salt. Simmer for 20 minutes to par-cook, then drain.

Preheat the oven to 180°C. Cut the streaky bacon into 3 thick rashers and remove the rind. Cut each rasher in half. Cut the smoked sausages in half crossways. Place the duck, sausages and bacon on an oven tray and cook on the middle oven shelf for 25–30 minutes until lightly browned.

Place a cast-iron casserole over a medium heat. Add 80ml of the reserved fat and gently cook the onions, garlic, the 1 tbsp of thyme and the rosemary until the onions are soft and translucent. Add the demi-glace, stock and beans. Season and bring to the boil, then reduce to a gentle simmer. Add the meat and simmer until the beans are cooked (about 30 minutes).

Meanwhile, in a saucepan over a low heat, cook the shallots in the butter until soft, then add the breadcrumbs and parsley. Remove from the heat and mix well so the breadcrumbs soak up the butter.

Remove a couple of ladles of beans with a little of their stock and blend to a smooth, thick paste. Return to the casserole to thicken the sauce, then taste and season. Sprinkle the crumb over the cassoulet. Turn the oven to the grill setting and brown the crumbs, to form a toasted crust. Serve.

Zalto
DENK'ART

Confit shoulder of mutton, rosemary dauphinoise, buttered kale, sour cherries & Mum's mint relish
Shiraz 'St Henri', Penfolds, South Australia

☞ page 97

SERVES 8

See previous page for picture

This makes an impressive spread, set down in the middle of a table. Mutton cooked in this manner takes on all the flavour of the spices with which it has shared the goose fat, and the meat pulls easily from the bone, so no fancy carving technique is required.

The South Australian Shiraz we have developed this dish around has bold red and black fruit and spice, with the interesting addition of the eucalyptus that grows so abundantly all over Australia. My mother's mint relish is the obvious condiment with mutton, but also complements the minty, lifted flavours in the Shiraz; when I was a child, we always had a few jars around. Some mint sauces are too vinegary to serve with wine. This one, however, is well-balanced with sweet honey and other ingredients.

FOR MUM'S MINT RELISH (MAKES 2 X 500G JARS)
300g ripe tomatoes
5 shallots, finely chopped
50g raisins, roughly chopped
100g mint leaves, chopped
300g Granny Smith apples, grated
375ml apple cider vinegar
1 tsp wholegrain mustard
250g clear honey
1 tsp sea salt

FOR THE MUTTON
1 mutton shoulder on the bone, about 2.5kg
1 cinnamon stick
8 star anise
1 tbsp cumin seeds
1 tbsp coriander seeds
1 tbsp black peppercorns
3 bay leaves
2kg goose or duck fat
50g dried Morello cherries
100ml red wine
300ml Red wine jus (see page 209)
800g curly kale, stalks removed, leaves shredded
100g unsalted butter
salt and pepper

FOR THE DAUPHINOISE POTATOES
6 garlic cloves
6 rosemary sprigs
600ml double cream
1½ tbsp sea salt
1.5kg potatoes (Maris Piper or King Edward are good for this)

Start with the relish. To blanch the tomatoes, bring a large saucepan of water to the boil. Have to hand a large bowl of iced water and a slotted spoon. With a small paring knife, remove the core of the tomatoes and, at the opposite end, make a small, shallow cross cut. Plunge them into the boiling water and leave until the skin begins to come away from the flesh at the cross cut. This will only take a few seconds, especially if the tomatoes are very ripe. Remove from the boiling water with the slotted spoon and refresh briefly in the iced water. Carefully peel the tomatoes, cut them into quarters, then deseed and chop them finely. Mix with the shallots, raisins, mint and apples in a large bowl. In a saucepan, bring the vinegar, mustard, honey and salt to the boil, then pour over the rest of the ingredients. The final consistency will be a chunky relish in a loose liquid. If you wish to preserve the relish, bring it back to the boil once all ingredients are added, then decant into hot sterilised jars and seal with the lids immediately. Otherwise, keep refrigerated; it will be good for about 3 months.

Season the mutton shoulder on all sides generously with sea salt. Cover and place it in the fridge overnight.

The following morning, preheat the oven to 140°C.

Place the cinnamon, star anise, cumin and coriander seeds, peppercorns and bay leaves into a muslin bag. In a large heavy-based saucepan over a medium heat, melt the goose or duck fat. Remove the mutton shoulder from the fridge and rinse it under a cold tap to remove any salt flakes. Pat dry with kitchen paper and place it into a large, deep roasting dish. Carefully pour the hot fat

ALTERNATIVE WINE MATCHES

'Woodcutter's Shiraz', Torbreck Vintners, Barossa Valley ☞ *page 97*

Shiraz 'Savitar', Mitolo Wines, Barossa Valley ☞ *page 97*

'Grange', Penfolds, South Australia ☞ *page 97*

over, submerging it completely. Add the spice bag and cover with a lid or foil. Bake for 4 hours, until the meat easily pulls away from the bone. Allow it to cool to room temperature, still submerged in the fat.

Place the dried cherries into a small container and bring the red wine to the boil in a small saucepan. Pour the wine over the cherries and set aside.

While the mutton is cooling, prepare the dauphinoise potatoes. Preheat the oven to 180°C.

Crush the garlic and bruise the rosemary with the back of a small pan. In a large heavy-based saucepan over a medium heat, bring the cream to the boil with the crushed garlic and bruised rosemary. Season with the salt and a few good twists from the peppermill. The amount of salt may seem excessive, but this needs to be generously seasoned. Once the cream has boiled, remove from the heat and allow to infuse for 1 hour.

Peel the potatoes and slice them about 2mm thick with a mandolin. Lay the potatoes in even layers into a baking dish that is at least 5cm deep. Strain the cream infusion through a sieve and pour it over the potatoes.

Cover with baking parchment, then with foil. Place into the oven and bake for 45 minutes, then remove the foil and parchment and return it to the oven to caramelise on the surface. After about 15 minutes, it should be golden brown. Remove from the oven and test the middle with a small knife to make sure the potatoes are cooked through: it should pierce with no resistance. Serve at the table in the dish it was cooked in. Any leftovers will keep covered in the fridge for 3 days and can be reheated in the oven.

When the dauphinoise has about 30 minutes cooking time left, carefully lift the mutton shoulder out of the fat, so it stays intact. Place it into a roasting dish and slide it into the oven above the dauphinoise. Allow to roast for 20–30 minutes, until it has crisped and caramelised nicely on the outside.

Pour the red wine jus into a saucepan, place over a medium heat and bring to the boil. Add the cherries and 2 tbsp of the wine they were steeping in.

In a large pan of well-salted boiling water, cook the kale for 2 minutes or so until tender. Drain well in a colander, giving it a good shake to allow the water to escape. Place the butter into the same saucepan and melt it over a medium heat. Return the kale to the pan, adjust the seasoning and stir well to flavour it with the butter.

Serve the mutton with the buttered kale, dauphinoise potatoes, a sauceboat of cherry jus and Mum's mint relish.

Chargrilled suckling lamb shoulder with Spanish tomato relish
Rioja Gran Reserva 'Viña Tondonia', López de Heredia

☞ page 119

SERVES 2

The classification system in Rioja is based on the time a wine has spent in an oak barrel. The highest level, Gran Reserva, will have spent a few years in the barrel, softening the tannins and giving gentle toasted coconut flavours if aged in American oak. A delicate meat is perfect with this, while the tomato relish here matches the bright acidity of the Tempranillo grape.

One of our Spanish suppliers sent me a suckling lamb shoulder from Segovia, a picturesque town perched in the mountains just north of Madrid. It is so small, it doesn't take long to cook, and the meat is pale, tender and delicate. (It can be bought online.)

This relish is versatile and will keep for a couple of years. Add the smoked paprika if you're drinking older Rioja, or Tempranillo that has spent time in American oak, getting smoky notes.

ALTERNATIVE WINE MATCHES

Rioja Reserva, Bodegas Beronia, Rioja ☞ page 119

Rioja Imperial 'Gran Reserva', CVNE, Rioja ☞ page 119

Rioja 'Viña El Pisón', Artadi, Rioja ☞ page 119

FOR THE RELISH

50ml extra virgin olive oil
2 tsp mustard seeds
1 red onion, finely chopped
1 celery stick, peeled and finely chopped
1 green pepper, finely chopped
1 red pepper, finely chopped
1 garlic clove, very finely chopped
1 tsp tomato purée
1 tsp smoked paprika (optional)
8 ripe vine tomatoes, peeled (see page 246) and chopped
4 tbsp Sherry vinegar
2 tsp sugar
salt and pepper

FOR THE LAMB

1 tbsp chopped oregano leaves, plus more sprigs, to use as a brush
1 tbsp chopped rosemary leaves, plus more sprigs, to use as a brush
extra virgin olive oil
1 suckling lamb shoulder on the bone

Heat the olive oil in a small saucepan over a medium-high heat. Add the mustard seeds and keep them moving around the pan gently. As they begin to pop, add the onion, celery, both peppers and garlic. Reduce the heat to medium and cook, stirring regularly, until the onion is soft and translucent. Stir in the tomato purée and the paprika, if using, and cook for a minute or so before adding the tomatoes, vinegar and sugar. Reduce the heat and simmer gently, stirring regularly, for 30–40 minutes, or until the relish has a rich consistency. Season well.

If preserving the relish, sterilise the jars and make sure they're still hot. Pour in the hot relish and seal. If you are just making a small batch, it will keep in an airtight container in the fridge for 2–3 weeks.

As the lamb is so young, it has developed little fat, so tie a small faggot of oregano and rosemary sprigs together and use this as a basting brush.

Get a barbecue prepared to a low temperature. In a small bowl, mix the chopped oregano and rosemary with a couple of tbsp of olive oil. Rub this into the shoulder and season well. Place the shoulder on the grill and close the lid of the barbecue so it acts as an oven. The thermostat should fluctuate between 130 and 150°C. Cook for 30–40 minutes, turning and basting regularly, until nicely caramelised; the foreshank muscle should be starting to retract from the bone. Wrap in foil and rest for at least 15 minutes.

Serve with the room temperature relish.

RIOJA
VIÑA
COSECHA DE

Musar

Roast cannon of lamb, chickpea salad, moutabel, pomegranate Château Musar, Bekaa Valley

☞ page 120

SERVES 4

Château Musar sits 1,000m above sea level in the fertile Bekaa Valley. As legend goes, winemaker Serge Hochar managed to call a ceasefire during the Lebanese civil war just long enough to bring truckloads of grapes to his winery during a period of heavy fighting. The Middle Eastern flavours in this dish are well matched to the rustic, smoky and earthy flavours of the wine, while the light acidity in the yogurt cuts through the lamb fat.

A cannon of lamb is one of the most prized cuts, and there are 2 cannons (loins) on each animal, either side of the saddle. Ask your butcher to leave a clean strip of fat on them, so it can be rendered until crispy; the caramelised fat has so much flavour.

Moutabel is also good with lamb chops rubbed with dukkah (page 188).

ALTERNATIVE WINE MATCHES

Syrah du Maroc 'Tandem', Alain Graillot, Morocco ☞ *page 92*

'Clos des Cistes', Domaine Peyre Rose, Languedoc ☞ *page 121*

'Misty Hills', Tzora Vineyards, Judean Hills, Israel ☞ *page 92*

FOR THE MOUTABEL (MAKES ABOUT 500G)

4 aubergines
2 garlic cloves, very finely chopped
2 tbsp extra virgin olive oil
150g Greek yogurt
juice of ½ lemon
salt and pepper

FOR THE LAMB AND SALAD

280g canned chickpeas, drained and rinsed
½ medium red onion, finely chopped
1 red chilli, deseeded and finely chopped
2 ripe tomatoes, deseeded and chopped
2 Preserved lemons (for home-made, see page 181), pulp discarded, rind shredded
2 tbsp chopped coriander leaves, plus coriander sprigs to serve
2 x 350–400g lamb cannons, fat on
50ml extra virgin olive oil
juice of 1 lemon
40ml pomegranate molasses
seeds of ½ pomegranate

Start with the moutabel. Charring aubergine skin is best achieved over hot charcoal. What you are trying to harness is that intense smoky flavour, produced by the blackened skins, that permeates into the flesh as they burn. If you don't have a barbecue, char them in the direct flame of a gas stove. When charring the skin, don't be afraid of burning it: the aubergines should look shrivelled, even cremated. Allow to cool enough to handle, then remove and discard the skins and tops. Hang the pulp in the fridge in a bag of muslin overnight, with a bowl underneath to catch the unwanted liquid.

Cook the garlic in the oil over a low heat until it starts to turn light golden. Meanwhile, run your knife through the aubergine pulp a few times. Add the aubergine pulp to the garlic and increase the heat slightly. Season and cook, stirring, for 3–4 minutes, then remove and place in a bowl. Fold in the yogurt and adjust the seasoning, adding lemon juice to taste. Allow to cool.

Tip the chickpeas into a large bowl. Add the red onion, chilli, tomatoes, preserved lemon rind and chopped coriander.

Preheat the oven to 200°C. Score the fat on the lamb cannons in a criss-cross pattern. Cut each cannon in half and season well. Place fat sides down in a cool, dry frying pan over a medium heat. As the pan heats up, the fat will render. Tip it off every now and then. Once the fat has rendered, turn the lamb to seal the other sides. Once sealed, roast for 6–7 minutes, then rest for 5 minutes.

Meanwhile, season the salad, add the oil and squeeze in the lemon juice.

To dress the plates, drizzle a little pomegranate molasses on each. Place a pile of chickpea salad on, along with a generous dollop of moutabel. Slice each cannon and sit them below the salad. Sprinkle pomegranate seeds over the top and add the coriander sprigs.

Tandoori-spiced lamb cutlets, spiced aubergine & tamarind yogurt
Gewurztraminer 'Riverpoint', Millton, Gisborne

☞ page 77

SERVES 6

James Millton was the first biodynamic producer in the Southern Hemisphere, starting Millton Vineyards in Gisborne with wife Annie in 1984. He is passionate about his wines; he should be, they are intense and focused. His Gewurztraminer bursts with lychees and tropical fruit; a great match to spices and yogurt. Gewurztraminer, if slightly off-dry, can cope with chilli, ginger, garam masala and tamarind.

Lamb cutlets are best cooked on a barbecue, preferably over charcoal to replicate the flavour of a tandoor oven. They make great finger food, using the tamarind yogurt as a dipping sauce.

For a less formal barbecue, chops are great, or less expensive neck fillet. If you're using neck fillet, allow 2–3 hours marinating, cook for longer, then rest for 6 minutes before serving.

ALTERNATIVE WINE MATCHES

'Aromatico', SC Pannell, Adelaide Hills ☞ page 77

'Vinoptima Reserve', Vinoptima, Gisborne ☞ page 77

Gewurztraminer 'Clos des Capucins, Cuvée Théo', Domaine Weinbach, Alsace ☞ page 77

FOR THE LAMB

400g Greek-style yogurt
2 tsp caster sugar
1 tsp salt
50ml sunflower oil
2 tsp black mustard seeds
10 fresh curry leaves
4 green chillies, deseeded and finely chopped
2cm piece of fresh root ginger, peeled and finely grated
2 tsp ground turmeric
1 tsp garam masala
18 French-trimmed lamb cutlets

FOR THE TAMARIND YOGURT

200g tamarind pulp
200ml boiling water
120g Greek-style yogurt

FOR THE SPICED AUBERGINE

2 aubergines
150ml sunflower oil
2 tsp black mustard seeds
1 large red onion, finely chopped
2 garlic cloves, finely chopped
2 red chillies, deseeded and finely chopped
10g fresh root ginger, peeled and finely grated
1 tsp ground turmeric
1 tsp garam masala
1 tsp ground cumin
½ tsp ground coriander
4 large ripe vine tomatoes, chopped
1 tbsp chopped coriander leaves, plus coriander cress to serve (optional)
salt

Place the yogurt, sugar and salt in a large mixing bowl. Set a small saucepan over a medium heat and heat the oil until smoking point is just reached. Add the mustard seeds and cover immediately. Once they stop popping, add the curry leaves for a couple of seconds, then the chillies, ginger, turmeric and garam masala. Remove from the heat, stir for 30 seconds, then mix into the yogurt. Add the lamb, mix to coat, then cover and chill for 1 hour.

Place the tamarind in a bowl, pour the measured water over and leave for 10 minutes. Mix with your hands until the pulp dissolves. Over another bowl, push the tamarind through a sieve, then whisk into the yogurt. Chill.

Cut the aubergines into 2.5cm cubes, season well with salt, then leave in a colander for 30 minutes. Rinse, then dry very well. In a large frying pan over a medium-high heat, fry the aubergine in half the oil, allowing it to brown; do this in 2–3 batches. Drain on kitchen paper to soak up excess oil.

In a large saucepan over a medium heat, heat the remaining oil to smoking. Add the mustard seeds, cover until they stop popping, then add the onion, garlic, chillies and ginger. Cook until the onions are translucent. Add the remaining ground spices and cook for 2 minutes, stirring. Add the tomatoes and their juices and cook for a further 2 minutes, then fold in the aubergine and coriander. Season with salt to taste. Cover and keep warm.

Season the cutlets with salt, leaving as much yogurt on them as possible, then place on a glowing barbecue. Char on one side, then turn and char the other side. Once caramelised, pull them off and rest them for a couple of minutes. Serve with the aubergine, yogurt and coriander cress, if using.

ΚΤΗΜΑ
2011

Lamb kleftiko with Greek salad
Xinomavro, Foundi Estate, Naoussa

☞ *page 121*

SERVES 5

Xinomavro is the great red grape of Greece, with a flavour profile and colour almost indistinguishable from Piedmontese Nebbiolo, though they are not related. The similar earthy, dried berry fruit, high acidity and firm tannins make a fine match to this dish.

This is one of my favourite lamb recipes and so easy to prepare. You will need to talk to your butcher about portioning the shoulder into 5 even-sized pieces on the bone. Greeks have the best dried oregano and use it a lot in their cooking. If you manage to find it, great! But if not, I'd suggest using fresh. Anchovies aren't to everyone's taste, but I think they are wonderful with lamb: a bold Mediterranean seasoning. For best results, marinate the lamb overnight to allow the meat to absorb the wonderful flavours.

ALTERNATIVE WINE MATCHES

Nebbiolo 'Perbacco', Vietti, Langhe ☞ *page 112*

Xinomavro 'Uranos', Thymiopoulos Vineyards, Naoussa ☞ *page 121*

Mavrotragano, Hatzidakis Winery, Cyclades, Greece ☞ *page 121*

FOR THE LAMB

10 large garlic cloves, unpeeled
2 unwaxed lemons
1 tbsp dried oregano, or 2 tbsp chopped fresh oregano leaves
150ml extra virgin olive oil
10 salted anchovies (optional)
1 lamb shoulder on the bone, cut into 5 pieces by the butcher
1kg waxy potatoes, Charlottes are ideal
20 cherry tomatoes, halved
1 red pepper, deseeded and thickly sliced
1 red onion, cut into wedges
100ml chicken stock
salt and pepper

FOR THE SALAD

½ cucumber, cut into bite-sized pieces
50g Kalamata olives
15 cherry tomatoes, halved
½ small red onion, thinly sliced
1 Preserved lemon (for home-made, see page 181), pulp discarded, rind shredded
30g capers in brine, drained
100g feta cheese, crumbled
10 mint leaves, finely shredded
1 tbsp chopped oregano leaves
80ml extra virgin olive oil
juice of ½ lemon

The evening before you serve your kleftiko, pierce each garlic clove a few times with a knife. Cut a lemon into 6 wedges and place in a large bowl with the garlic, oregano, olive oil, anchovies and the juice from the other lemon. Add the lamb, season liberally, mix, then cover and chill overnight. A few hours before cooking, remove the lamb from the fridge, so it comes to room temperature.

When you're ready to cook, preheat the oven to 180°C. Remove the lamb from the bowl, leaving the marinade behind, and set aside. Peel the potatoes and cut into large pieces, or halves if they are small. Add to the bowl of marinade with the tomatoes, red pepper and red onion. Season with more salt and pepper, then toss all the ingredients together to coat.

Line a large oven tray with 3 layers of baking parchment, to overhang the tray. Scatter the vegetables and marinade into the tray and place the lamb on top. Pour in the stock and gather the corners of the parchment together, tying them at the top with string. Bake in the oven for 2 hours.

Carefully open the parchment, folding the edges back to expose the lamb and vegetables: the aroma is magnificent! Increase the oven temperature to 220°C, then return it to the oven for 20–30 minutes to crisp the potatoes.

Meanwhile, prepare a simple Greek salad, tossing all the ingredients together in a bowl and seasoning well.

Once you are satisfied the lamb has enough colour and the potatoes have crisped up on the surface, serve the whole tray in the centre of the table as a centrepiece. What a show!

Fillet of beef Carpaccio, capers, rocket & croutons
Etna Rosato, Graci, Sicily

☞ page 121

SERVES 6 AS A STARTER

Etna Rosato, made with Nerello Mascalese grapes, is a rosé of great personality, with a raspberry and wild strawberry character; perfect with raw beef. These vineyards are definitely volcanic, as they are 600m up the side of Mount Etna in Sicily.

This famous dish was first served at Harry's Bar in Venice in the 1950s. It was named after Vittore Carpaccio, the Venetian Renaissance painter known for his use of brilliant reds and whites, the colours that define this dish, though 'Carpaccio' has now become a catch-all term for 'thinly sliced'.

It's a simple but delicious starter for a lunch on a hot summer's day. I like to serve it with Caesar dressing, as it's great with the anchovies, Parmesan and Worcestershire sauce.

ALTERNATIVE WINE MATCHES

Cerasuolo d'Abruzzo Rosato, Masciarelli Wine Company, Abruzzo ☞ *page 121*

Gran Reserva Rosé 'Viña Tondonia', López de Heredia, Rioja ☞ *page 119*

Château Musar Rosé, Bekaa Valley, Lebanon ☞ *page 120*

FOR THE CAESAR DRESSING (MAKES 700ML)

50ml white wine vinegar
2 eggs
1 garlic clove, chopped
2 tbsp wholegrain mustard
10 salted anchovies
juice of 1 lemon
1½ tbsp Worcestershire sauce
60g Parmesan cheese, finely grated
½ tsp caster sugar
250ml sunflower oil
250ml olive oil

FOR THE CARPACCIO

800g beef fillet, fully trimmed of sinew
50ml sunflower oil
1 ciabatta loaf
50ml extra virgin olive oil
60g capers in brine, drained
100g rocket
120g Parmesan cheese
salt and pepper

Make the dressing. Bring a small saucepan of water up to the boil over a high heat and add the vinegar. Poach the eggs until the whites have just set on the outside; this should take about 45 seconds. Carefully lift the eggs out of the water with a slotted spoon and place into a blender. Add all the remaining ingredients except the oils. Blend on a high speed until smooth, then, still blending, slowly drizzle in both oils. The dressing should have a loose creamy consistency, so you may need to loosen it with a little water. It shouldn't need any seasoning.

Place a large, heavy-based frying pan over a high heat. Sprinkle a generous layer of salt and twists of pepper on a work surface. Roll the beef fillet evenly in the seasoning. Pour the sunflower oil into the hot pan and sear the beef evenly on all sides, then immediately chill for 20 minutes or so.

Preheat the oven to 180°C.

Shave a few slices from the ciabatta as thinly as possible. Lay on a baking tray, season with salt and drizzle with olive oil. Bake for 5–8 minutes, until golden and crisp, depending on thickness, then allow to cool.

By this stage, the beef should be sufficiently chilled. In order to slice it thinly, it will have to be wrapped tightly in cling film. Roll the cling film out on a work surface. Place the beef on the film and roll it away from you, wrapping tightly as you go. Roll numerous layers until you are satisfied the beef is tightly packed. Chill for a couple of hours to allow it to set.

When you are ready to serve, remove the beef from the fridge and, using a very sharp carving knife, slice as thinly as you can, keeping the cling film on so it holds its density. Remove the cling film from each slice as you carve.

Lay the slices on 6 plates and season them. Drizzle a generous serving of Caesar dressing over and scatter with a few capers. Place a small pile of rocket in the middle of the plates and shave the Parmesan over with a vegetable peeler. Serve with the crispy ciabatta wafers.

GRACI

Steak tartare
Morgon 'Côte du Py', Jean Foillard

☞ page 91

SERVES 4 AS A STARTER

I'm a great fan of steak tartare, it's one of those simple dishes that I tend to judge the quality of a restaurant on. Well executed, it's a great pleasure.

Sadly, over the last few years, it's been dropped from menus because of strict preparation guidelines for raw meat. Food safety bosses are asking chefs to sear a large joint of meat, chill it, then trim off the cooked outside before dicing. Meanwhile the French are sitting back at home, eating steak tartare and sniggering, 'These *rosbifs*, they are so paranoid!'

Cru Beaujolais has gone through a revival in recent years, as the world moves away from oaky, warm alcohol wines towards brighter, high-acidity fruit flavours. The tart elements of this dish – capers, gherkins and ketchup – are well matched with the fresh acidity found in the Morgon.

ALTERNATIVE WINE MATCHES

'Moulin-à-Vent' Vielles Vignes, Thibault Liger-Belair, Beaujolais ☞ *page 91*

Gamay Noir, Brick House Wines, Oregon ☞ *page 86*

Fleurie, Yvon Métras, Beaujolais ☞ *page 91*

400g beef topside
2 tbsp drained, chopped capers
2 tbsp finely chopped shallots
2 tbsp finely chopped gherkins
1 tsp Dijon mustard, or to taste
2 egg yolks
1 tbsp Worcestershire sauce
1 tbsp tomato ketchup, or to taste
1 tbsp extra virgin olive oil
1 tsp Tabasco sauce, or to taste
1 tbsp chopped parsley leaves
2 anchovy fillets, finely chopped (optional)
salt and pepper
toasted baguette slices, frites and dressed green salad, to serve

Using a sharp knife, dice the beef into 5mm cubes. I prefer hand-dicing the beef to mincing it, because it makes for a better texture. Place in a large mixing bowl and add all the other ingredients, with the anchovies, if you like them. Season well. Mix until it's all thoroughly amalgamated, then taste. Steak tartare is a personal taste and this recipe is more guide than gospel. If you like it spicier, add a little more Tabasco or mustard; sweeter, add more ketchup. Keep adjusting until you've found your perfect balance.

Serve with toasted baguette slices, frites and a dressed green salad.

burger with cheese & pancetta, with scrumpy-battered onion rings Zinfandel Nalle, Dry Creek Valley, Sonoma

☞ page 121

SERVES 6

See overleaf for picture

We just had to pair our classic burger with American wine, and the obvious choice was Californian Zinfandel, which complements anything cooked on the barbecue. Zinfandel is perfect with smoked foods. The barbecue spice rub we use contains smoked paprika and brown sugar, which caramelises over the coals, echoing the sweetness of the wine.

This rub is not only great for burgers. If you make up a batch and store it in a sealed jar in a cool dark cupboard, it will keep for a year and you can pull it out when you're having a barbecue and use it for dusting chicken wings or seasoning steaks.

A few years ago, I had a coeliac friend over for dinner. I wanted to prepare steak with battered onion rings, so I tried making the batter with Doves Farm gluten- and wheat-free self-raising flour. I couldn't believe how long the batter held its crunch! Sometimes great discoveries happen just by chance.

FOR THE BARBECUE SPICE RUB
4 tbsp soft light brown sugar
1 tbsp caster sugar
3 tbsp smoked paprika
1 tbsp sweet paprika
2 tsp freshly ground black pepper
4 tbsp sea salt
1 tbsp fine table salt
1 tbsp garlic salt
1 tbsp onion salt
1 tbsp celery salt
2 tsp ground cumin
2 tsp ground cinnamon
½ tsp cayenne pepper

FOR THE BURGER SAUCE
70g tomato ketchup
30g American-style mustard

FOR THE ONION RINGS
3 large onions, peeled, centres removed, cut into 1cm rings
300g gluten-free self-raising flour, plus more to dust
500–600ml Scrumpy Jack cider, plus more if needed
2 litres vegetable oil

FOR THE BURGERS
6 x 225g beef burgers, 30% fat (ask your butcher about this)
12 smoked pancetta rashers
6 brioche burger buns
80g Mayonnaise (for home-made, see page 307)
2 Baby Gem lettuces, shredded
6 thick slices of mild Cheddar cheese
3 large ripe tomatoes, sliced
3 large gherkins, sliced
½ small red onion, cut into fine rings

Mix all the ingredients for the spice rub together.

For the sauce, mix the ketchup and mustard in a bowl.

Bring a large pan of lightly salted water up to a rolling boil. Add the onion rings and blanch for 30 seconds to soften them and mellow that raw onion heat. Plunge into iced water to cool, then lay on kitchen paper to dry.

Make the batter by placing the flour in a large mixing bowl. Whisk in the cider to form a loose batter, then leave to rest for 30 minutes.

Set your deep-fat fryer to 190°C, or use a saucepan, taking the same precautions and care as usual (see page 138).

To test the batter, place some more gluten-free self-raising flour in a bowl and add an onion ring, coating it with flour so the batter has something to stick to. Dip the ring in the batter, then gently lower it into the oil. It will float to the top and need turning halfway through, to cook the other side. If the onion emerges with a good covering of crispy batter that is not too thick, then start frying the rest of the rings in small batches, being careful not to overload the fryer. If the batter doesn't coat the test ring, add a little more flour, or if it is too thick, add some more cider. Fry the onions until golden brown, then drain on kitchen paper. Season with salt and serve hot.

continued overleaf ☞

☜ *continued from previous page*

ALTERNATIVE WINE MATCHES

Primitivo di Manduria, Feudi di San Gregorio, Puglia ☞ *page 121*

'The Chocolate Block', Boekenhoutskloof, Franschhoek ☞ *page 92*

'Finca Piedra Infinita', Familia Zuccardi, Altamira ☞ *page 119*

Meanwhile, preheat the oven grill to high. Heat a large griddle pan over a high heat. Season the burgers liberally with the barbecue spice seasoning and place them carefully in the hot dry pan. You won't need to use any oil, as the fat in the burgers will gradually release. Seal the burgers until well caramelised on both sides, then reduce the heat to low. If you like your burgers medium-rare, allow them to cook for 2 more minutes, turning them a couple of times so they cook evenly. For well-done, add another 3 minutes to the cooking time. Remove from the heat and allow the burgers to rest in the pan.

While the burgers are resting, place the pancetta on a rack under the grill for a couple of minutes until crispy. Slice the burger buns in half horizontally, then toast them lightly under the grill. Mix the mayonnaise with the shredded lettuces and distribute evenly between the bases of the buns.

Place the cheese on the burgers and put them under the grill until the cheese melts, then place the burgers on top of the lettuce. Place the sliced tomatoes on next, followed by the sliced gherkins, red onion rings and crisp pancetta. Pour over a little burger sauce and place the bun lid on top. Enjoy your burger with the scrumpy-battered onion rings.

Braised Tuscan-style meatballs with rosemary-infused polenta 'Vigneto Bucerchiale', Selvapiana, Chianti Rúfina

☞ page 112

SERVES 6

A simple classic and one of our most popular lunch dishes, this was one of our first (and favourite) pairings when we opened the Club. The acidity of the tomato matches well with lean Chianti Rúfina, which retains acidity at high altitude in its Apennine mountain vineyards.

Sangiovese pairs with a wide range of foods, from roast pork to pizza to hard cheeses, due to its medium weighted body and savoury character. We chose this dish because of the savoury-flavoured meatballs and the rich tomato sauce with plenty of oregano, two flavours often apparent in Sangiovese. You could serve it with spaghetti, but we went with cheesy, rosemary-infused polenta, as the Parmesan and herbs complement the wine. A little sage in the meatballs would work well, too.

FOR THE MEATBALLS

1 large onion, finely chopped
1 garlic clove, very finely chopped
1 tbsp chopped oregano leaves
50ml extra virgin olive oil, plus more to fry the meatballs
100g fresh white breadcrumbs
500g minced beef
500g minced pork
50g Parmesan cheese, finely grated
salt and pepper

FOR THE SAUCE

2 large onions, finely chopped
3 garlic cloves, very finely chopped
1 tbsp chopped oregano leaves
2 red chillies, deseeded and finely chopped
50ml extra virgin olive oil
1 tbsp tomato purée
250ml dry red wine
800ml beef stock
600g canned chopped tomatoes
15 basil leaves, chopped, plus basil tips to serve

FOR THE POLENTA

1 large onion, sliced
2 garlic cloves, crushed
5 rosemary sprigs
900ml whole milk, plus more if needed
300g instant polenta, plus more if needed
30g unsalted butter
100g Parmesan cheese, finely grated

Start by making the meatballs. In a heavy-based saucepan over a medium heat, sauté the onion, garlic and oregano in the olive oil until soft, but not coloured. Remove from the pan and allow to cool. In a large mixing bowl, mix all the ingredients for the meatballs together and season. To test the meat mixture for seasoning, make a small burger and fry it in a little olive oil. Taste it, then adjust the seasoning. With wet hands, roll the mixture tightly into 30g balls (roughly 5 per portion). Rest the meatballs uncovered on a tray in the fridge for 1 hour to set, allowing space between each for air to circulate. (This helps them to hold together when frying.)

Meanwhile, make the sauce. In a large heavy-based saucepan over a low heat, gently cook the onions, garlic, oregano and chillies in the olive oil until soft but not coloured. Spoon in the tomato purée and cook, stirring constantly, for another minute or so. Add the red wine and increase the heat, reducing the wine until it has completely evaporated. Pour in the stock and reduce by half, then add the tomatoes, return the sauce to the boil, then reduce the heat to a simmer. Cook for 30–40 minutes, stirring regularly, until it has a rich consistency. Season.

In a large frying pan, fry the meatballs in batches in extra virgin olive oil. Once they are browned on all sides, drain on kitchen paper to soak up any excess oil, then add them to the sauce. Simmer over a very low heat for 20 minutes while you cook the polenta.

For the polenta, place the onion, garlic and rosemary into a saucepan and cover with the milk. Over a medium heat, bring to the boil gradually, being careful not to let it boil over. Set aside for 10 minutes to infuse.

ALTERNATIVE WINE MATCHES

'Flaccianello della Pieve', Fontodi, Tuscany
☞ *page 112*

Brunello di Montalcino, Argiano
☞ *page 112*

Brunello di Montalcino 'Tenuta Greppo Riserva', Biondi-Santi ☞ *page 112*

Strain the milk infusion through a sieve into a clean heavy-based saucepan. Over a medium heat, return it to the boil gradually. Slowly whisk in the instant polenta and reduce the heat to low. Be careful, as the polenta bubbles up like thick lava and can cause a nasty burn. Cook for a few minutes, stirring regularly to keep it from catching on the pan.

The polenta will quickly thicken to a creamy, smooth porridge consistency. You can adjust the consistency by adding a little milk to loosen, or a little polenta to thicken if required. After a few minutes the polenta will be cooked and will have lost its grainy texture. At this stage, stir in the butter and Parmesan. Stir the basil into the meatballs and sauce.

To serve, pour the polenta into bowls and serve with the meatballs and sauce, finishing with a few basil tips.

GRAND VIN
DE
LATOUR
GRAND CRU CLASSE
2006
PAUILLAC

Fillet of beef Wellington
Grand Vin de Château Latour, Pauillac

☞ page 100

SERVES 8

See previous page for picture

I assumed this dish was named after the Duke of Wellington. The late Clarissa Dickson Wright, however, claimed the dish was invented for a civic reception in Wellington, New Zealand's capital city. I'll take that.

The recipe for the crêpes makes 8 and you only need 4 for the recipe, but you'll need to make the full quantity of batter, as it's not good if made in smaller amounts. Store the rest in the fridge overnight, without the added parsley, and you've got breakfast sorted for the morning.

A rolling lattice cutter (optional) is good for presentation here. Give yourself plenty of time for preparing this; there are a lot of components, so it is a labour of love.

With such an iconic dish we needed an equally iconic wine. Château Latour is a blend of Cabernet and Merlot grapes that is wonderful with beef, while the mushroom duxelles and truffle oil-spiked chicken mousse also really complement the wine.

FOR THE MUSHROOM DUXELLES

200g shallots, finely chopped
leaves from 5 thyme sprigs, chopped
3 garlic cloves, finely chopped
100g unsalted butter
1kg button mushrooms, finely sliced
salt and pepper

FOR THE CHICKEN MOUSSE

250g chicken breast, finely chopped and chilled
½ tsp salt
1 egg, plus 1 egg yolk, chilled
200ml double cream, chilled
1 tbsp truffle oil

FOR THE CRÊPES

240ml whole milk
20g unsalted butter, plus a little more to fry
100g plain flour
2 eggs
1 tbsp chopped parsley leaves

FOR THE WELLINGTON

50ml vegetable oil
1.5kg centre-cut beef fillet, fully trimmed of sinew
500g spinach, coarse stalks removed
2 tbsp English mustard
plain flour, to dust
1.2kg all-butter puff pastry
8 egg yolks, lightly beaten
500ml hot Red wine jus (see page 209)
roast potatoes, to serve

Start with the duxelles. In a large saucepan, sweat the shallots, thyme and garlic in the butter over a gentle heat. Once the shallots are soft, add the mushrooms and season sparingly. Now cook slowly, to reduce the water content and intensify the flavour. Adjust the seasoning and leave to cool.

For the mousse, blitz the chicken and salt in a blender until very smooth. Add a few twists of pepper, then slowly blend in the egg, egg yolk, cream and truffle oil. To check the seasoning, roll a sausage of mousse in cling film, then poach for a few minutes in boiling water. Taste and adjust accordingly. Keep chilled.

Now for the crêpes. Heat the milk and butter gently in a small saucepan until the butter melts, then cool. Sift the flour into a bowl and make a well in the centre. Crack the eggs into the well and whisk. Add the milk mixture and whisk to a smooth batter. Pass through a sieve, then add the parsley.

Heat a large non-stick frying pan over a medium heat. Melt a small knob of butter in the pan, then add a small ladleful of batter (the crêpes should be very thin). Tilt the pan, spreading the batter to the edges. After a minute, the crêpe will have set on the surface; at this point, if you're not game enough to flip, turn it carefully with a spatula and cook on the other side for about 30 seconds. Refrigerate.

Preheat a large frying pan with the vegetable oil over a high heat. Season the beef liberally. Once the oil starts to smoke, carefully sear the fillet on all sides, then place straight in the fridge to cool down quickly.

ALTERNATIVE WINE MATCHES

Château Pédesclaux, Pauillac ☞ *page 100*

Château Chasse-Spleen, Moulis-en-Médoc, Bordeaux ☞ *page 100*

Château Angélus, St-Emilion ☞ *page 116*

Bring a large pan of salted water to the boil and blanch the spinach for a few seconds, then plunge into iced water. Drain, then lay out to dry on a towel.

To roll the Wellington, cover a work top with 2 sheets of cling film. Cut the rounded edges off each crêpe to make squares and lay them on the cling film like tiles, overlapping slightly. Lift the tea towel containing the spinach and carefully turn it out over the pancakes. In a mixing bowl, fold the duxelles into the chicken mousse, then spread in an even layer over the spinach.

Rub the mustard into the beef and place it in the very centre of the layers, crossways. Lift the edge of the cling film carefully over the meat. Without rolling the cling film inside, tuck the crêpes underneath the far side of the fillet and roll, encasing it. Wrap it in the cling film, then wrap in several layers more until the Wellington is tight. Chill overnight to set.

Dust a work top with flour and roll out two-thirds of the pastry into a rectangle big enough to wrap the Wellington.

Carefully cut the cling film from the rolled Wellington. Place it crossways in the middle of the rolled-out pastry. Using a pastry brush, brush the far edge of the pastry with the egg yolk. Lift the edge of the pastry closest to you over the Wellington, then pull the edge with the egg yolk tight across, sticking them together. With a pair of scissors, trim the pastry at each end to leave 2 rectangular flaps. Brush these with egg yolk and stretch over each end, sealing neatly. The side with all the seams of pastry is the underside. Carefully roll the Wellington on to a baking tray lined with baking parchment. Brush it all over with egg yolk.

Dust the work top with flour and roll out the remaining pastry into a sheet slightly longer than the Wellington and slightly wider than the width of the lattice roller. Dust the lattice roller with a little flour so it doesn't stick, then roll it firmly along the length of the pastry. (If you don't have a lattice roller, use a small knife to cut leaves, or whatever else takes your fancy.) Stretch the pastry lattice over the Wellington to cover completely, trimming the edges with scissors. Ensure the lattice is stuck fast to the Wellington and brush with a final layer of egg yolk. Place your beautiful creation in the fridge to relax for at least 30 minutes before you bake it.

Preheat the oven to 180°C. Bake for 45–50 minutes, until golden brown, covering loosely with foil if it browns too much. If you have a temperature probe, the core temperature should reach 35°C for medium-rare beef. If you don't have a probe, pierce the meat with a metal skewer and touch it on the inside of your forearm; it should feel warm, but not hot.

When the Wellington is ready, rest it in a warm place for 10 minutes. Carve with a large, sharp serrated knife, to saw through the crisp pastry.

Serve with the hot red wine jus and roast potatoes.

Roast fillet of beef, blue cheese-stuffed fig, candied prosciutto, Bourbon jus, collard greens Cabernet Sauvignon 'Martha's Vineyard', Heitz Cellar

☞ *page 103*

SERVES 6

Ronan and I got really excited when tasting Napa Cabernet Sauvignon and coming up with this dish. Such bold wines need bold flavours to pair well, and these Napa reds are definitely bold. With flavours of ripe red and black fruits, we thought of jammy figs stuffed with tangy *Gorgonzola dolce*. The ageing of the wine in toasted oak barrels imparts flavours of vanilla, smoke and toffee, which are represented in the dish by the addition of a splash of Bourbon as well as the prosciutto brushed with maple syrup.

Serving with smoked bacon collard greens reinforces the obvious American slant of this dish. Don't despair if you can't get collards, as kale and spring greens are in the same family and work just as well.

ALTERNATIVE WINE MATCHES

'Destinae', Destiny Bay, Waiheke Island ☞ *page 98*

'La Muse', Vérité, Sonoma ☞ *page 116*

Cabernet Sauvignon 'Howell Mountain', Dunn Vineyards, Napa ☞ *page 103*

FOR THE GREENS

12 rashers of smoked streaky bacon
2 tbsp sunflower oil
30g unsalted butter
1 large onion, sliced
2 garlic cloves, finely chopped
1kg collard greens, coarse stalks discarded, leaves shredded
salt and pepper

FOR THE BEEF

6 slices of prosciutto
50ml maple syrup
6 ripe, jammy black figs
120g *Gorgonzola dolce*
6 x 200g beef fillet steaks
50ml sunflower oil
300ml Red wine jus (see page 209)
50ml Bourbon

Place a large heavy-based saucepan over a medium-high heat. Slice the bacon across the rashers into 1cm pieces, then cook it in the sunflower oil until crispy and caramelised. Fat will render out, but don't be tempted to pour it off: bacon grease is the key to tasty greens. Reduce the heat to medium and add the butter, onion and garlic, then cook until soft and translucent. Don't worry if they caramelise a little, it adds to the flavour. Add the shredded greens and season. Place a lid on the pan so the greens cook down in their own steam. Cook for 20 minutes or so, stirring at regular intervals, until soft. Once done, check the seasoning and adjust as required.

Preheat the oven to 180°C. Place the slices of prosciutto on a baking tray lined with baking parchment and, using a pastry brush, brush them with the maple syrup. Bake for 7–8 minutes until crispy and caramelised.

To prepare the figs, using a sharp paring knife, cut off the stalks. Sit them upright on a chopping board and cut a criss-cross into the stalk end, going halfway down the fig. Squeeze the figs gently at their bases, opening them up like the petals of a flower. Place a 10g nugget of Gorgonzola into the middle of each fig. Place the figs on a baking tray lined with baking parchment and bake for 10 minutes. Don't worry if the cheese oozes out.

Place a large heavy-based frying pan over a medium-high heat. Season the fillet steaks liberally. Pour the sunflower oil into the hot pan and sear the steaks, caramelising them well on all sides. Transfer to an ovenproof dish and roast in the oven for 5–6 minutes. I use a temperature probe to ensure the right cooking degree. The core temperature should be 32°C for rare, 35°C for medium-rare, 42°C for medium, 55°C for medium-well and 65°C for well-done. Remember, the temperature will rise as the meat rests. Allow to rest for 5–6 minutes. Pour the jus into a small saucepan and add the Bourbon. Bring it to the boil, then reduce it to a rich sauce consistency.

Divide the remaining cheese between each fig and flash them through the oven for a couple of minutes along with the candied prosciutto. (If the steaks have cooled during the resting process, give them a flash also.) Serve on warmed plates with the greens on the side.

Braised short ribs with thyme-roast sweet potato
Château Rayas, Châteauneuf-du-Pape

☞ page 106

SERVES 8

Unusually for Châteauneuf-du-Pape, Rayas is 100 per cent Grenache, which is grown in cooler, sandier soils, so the levels of alcohol or spice never reach dizzy heights. Short ribs can have a very intense, quite smoky flavour, and the sweetness of the potato works well with the ripe fruit and the dried herbs in the wine, while the use of thyme accentuates the natural *garrigue* flavours of the Southern Rhône.

Short ribs, also known as Jacob's Ladder, are a good braising cut. They are the rib bones that extend out from the classic forerib joint, and have a generous portion of meat attached. Ask your butcher to cut them into 8cm lengths, so they're easier to manage.

The sweet potatoes help balance the tannins in this strong red wine.

ALTERNATIVE WINE MATCHES

'Menagerie of the Barossa', Dandelion Vineyards, Barossa Valley ☞ *page 108*

Clos Erasmus, Priorat ☞ *page 106*

'Da Capo', Domaine du Pégau, Châteauneuf-du-Pape ☞ *page 106*

4kg beef short ribs, cut to 8cm
120g plain flour
120ml sunflower oil
50g unsalted butter
3 onions, chopped
3 garlic cloves, finely chopped
1 bay leaf
2 tbsp chopped thyme leaves
2 tbsp tomato purée
750ml good-quality red wine
2 litres hot Demi-glace (see page 279)
4 sweet potatoes
1 tsp cornflour (optional)
salt and pepper

Preheat the oven to 150°C.

Season the short ribs and place in a large plastic bag. Add the flour and, holding the bag closed, give it a good shake to coat the beef pieces. Remove the beef from the bag; reserve the flour.

Place a large saucepan over a high heat. Add half the oil and fry the ribs in 3–4 batches, until evenly browned. Transfer to an ovenproof casserole.

Reduce the heat under the saucepan to medium and tip in the butter, onions, garlic, bay leaf and half the thyme. Cook for 4–5 minutes, or until the onions are soft and slightly caramelised, stirring regularly to release any tasty morsels left by the beef. Stir in the reserved flour and tomato purée and cook for another minute, stirring so they don't catch on the pan. Stir in the wine, a little at a time, so lumps don't form.

Once all the wine has been added, pour in the hot demi-glace and bring to the boil. Pour the gravy over the ribs and cover. Place in the oven and braise for 2½–3 hours, until the meat is tender. It's difficult to put an exact time on braising meats; sometimes an extra 30 minutes is needed. The best way to check is by tasting the meat.

Meanwhile, bake the sweet potatoes alongside the meat. They take about 1 hour, depending on size. Test they are ready by piercing them with a small knife: if cooked, they should offer no resistance. Allow to cool enough to handle, then peel away the skins. Cut into large pieces suitable for roasting.

Once the ribs are cooked, carefully remove them with a slotted spoon. If the gravy seems thin, pour it into a saucepan set over a medium heat and bring it to a simmer. Dissolve the cornflour in a little cold water, stir it in and simmer, skimming off any fat that may rise to the surface. Once the gravy is the correct consistency, check the seasoning, then pour it over the ribs.

Increase the oven temperature to 250°C, or as high as it will go. To finish the sweet potato, heat a large non-stick frying pan over a medium heat. Cook the sweet potato in the remaining oil until well caramelised on all sides. Season well and add the remaining thyme. Transfer to a roasting tray and finish them in the oven for a final 10 minutes. Serve the short ribs with the roast sweet potato.

Stir-fried Szechuan beef
Cabernet Sauvignon, Ao Yun, Yunnan

☞ *page 98*

SERVES 4

Szechuan cuisine is known for its fiery heat. If you're not a fan, reduce or omit the dried chilli flakes from the marinade.

China is now the country with the second biggest plantings of vines and, with three-quarters of this being Cabernet Sauvignon, we will soon be seeing a lot of it. It may seem clichéd to go for a Chinese dish, but they work really well together... just go easy on the chilli.

Make sure, when sealing the beef strips, that the wok or pan is very hot, so the beef caramelises without releasing its juices. Timing is everything when cooking a stir-fry, so make sure you have all the ingredients prepared and to hand.

ALTERNATIVE WINE MATCHES

Carmenere 'Legado' Gran Reserva, De Martino, Maipo ☞ *page 118*

'Chairman's Reserve', Grace Vineyard, Shanxi ☞ *page 98*

Cabernet Sauvignon 'Black Label', Wynns, Coonawarra ☞ *page 102*

FOR THE MARINADE

- 2 tbsp Shaoxing rice wine (dry Sherry makes a good substitute)
- 2 tbsp dark soy sauce
- 1 tbsp ground Szechuan pepper
- ½ tbsp Chinese five spice
- 1 tbsp finely grated or very finely chopped garlic
- 1 tbsp peeled and finely grated fresh root ginger
- 1 tsp chilli flakes
- 800g beef skirt, sliced against the grain into thin strips (5–8mm)
- 2 tbsp cornflour

FOR THE SAUCE

- 2 tbsp hoisin sauce
- 1 tbsp sesame oil
- 3 tbsp dark soy sauce
- 1 tbsp soft brown sugar
- 2 tbsp Shaoxing rice wine (dry Sherry makes a good substitute)

FOR THE STIR-FRY

- groundnut oil, to fry
- 1 small carrot, finely sliced
- ½ small red onion, finely sliced
- 2 red chillies, deseeded and finely sliced
- 4 baby sweetcorn, split lengthways
- ½ red pepper, finely sliced
- 100g mangetout, finely sliced
- 4 tbsp roughly chopped coriander leaves
- 60g beansprouts
- 3 spring onions, finely sliced
- 1 tbsp sesame seeds
- steamed jasmine rice, to serve

To marinate the beef, place all the marinade ingredients into a bowl except the cornflour and mix well until all ingredients are well incorporated, then stir in the beef. Cover and leave to marinate in the fridge for at least 2 hours.

In a separate bowl, whisk all the sauce ingredients together and set aside.

Remove the strips of beef from the marinade and place them in a bowl. Add the cornflour and mix it through the beef well.

Preheat a wok or a large non-stick frying pan over a high heat and add about 50ml of groundnut oil. When the oil begins to lightly smoke, add half the beef, evenly spread out in the pan. Don't be tempted to shake the pan or give it a toss, as that will cool the pan down and your strips of beef will boil rather than caramelise. Once browned on one side, turn them over to caramelise the other side. Remove the beef from the pan and repeat the process with the remaining beef.

Once the beef is cooked, place the empty pan back on the heat and add a little more oil. Cook the carrot, onion, chillies, baby corn and red pepper for a minute or so, stirring constantly, until starting to soften slightly. Add the sauce, along with the caramelised beef and mangetout. Cook for a couple of minutes until the sauce thickens. Toss in half the coriander and the beansprouts. Serve immediately in bowls sprinkled with the spring onions, sesame seeds and remaining coriander, with steamed jasmine rice.

AoYun

HARLAN ESTATE
BODEGA
NOEMIA

Penfolds
BIN 707
CABERNET
SAUVIGNON
HAUT-BRION

Steak

As many of our Club members are partial to big, full-bodied red wines, naturally we sell a lot of steaks. To keep it interesting, we regularly change the cuts, ageing periods, breeds, provenance and so on of the steaks on the menu.

When buying beef, if you want quality, you must be ready to pay for it. Supermarkets have driven demand for cheap meat from intensively farmed cattle. These are fattened quickly and slaughtered young, sometimes at just 12–15 months. Obviously, the longer a farmer has to feed and maintain an animal, the higher price that animal must be sold for to account for this.

In 2015, Galician beef made an appearance on menus in the UK. Much of this was from retired dairy cows as old as 17 years. I must admit that initially I was very sceptical, as it's not easy to turn hard-working dairy cows into premium beef. I was wrong.

When you're spending a lot of money on steak, you need to be aware of how it has lived and – vitally – how it has died. These are a few things you need to ask about before you get out your wallet.

'Slow-grown' beef has a fuller, deeper flavour, and has developed marbling and texture. This is true for all beef, but husbandry grows more complex for the ex-dairy Galician beef – and increasingly, its British equivalent – that is hurtling upwards in popularity. Dairy breeds, unless properly reared, once retired at anywhere from five to ten years old, will produce poor-quality beef. To make good eating, they need to be finished with a long grazing period, to slowly develop the intermuscular fat that gives this meat so much flavour.

Also critical to the meat's quality is the treatment of the animal at slaughter. A farmer's hard work can be for nothing if the animal is stressed. Cattle don't like travel, and are social animals with a pecking order, so become stressed if forced to socialise with unfamiliar beasts. It's vital that they are not having to travel too far and are rested at the abattoir, to alleviate the stress of their journey. Meat from a stressed animal will be spoiled: dark in colour and lacking tenderness and moisture, as the muscles are depleted of their stored energy, which hinders the natural decrease in aged meat's pH level.

What we have found at the Club through cooking Galician steaks is that, as they are from older animals, the meat can sometimes be less tender. So you sacrifice a little tenderness for flavour. But you can't judge a steak by how tender it is. Some cuts, such as fillet, are very tender but have less flavour. Older Galician steak you may need to chew, but the flavour from intermuscular marbling will knock you over.

Dry-Aged Steak

The length of time beef should be aged is a matter of personal preference, though I would advise you never to buy (or order) a steak aged for less than 28 days. At the Club, we sell steaks aged from as little as 28 days, for a fillet, to as much as 100 days, for a côte de boeuf.

There are varying methods of ageing. Dry-ageing is the best. (Some of the best beef I've tried has been aged in rooms lined with Himalayan salt.) After 28 days of dry-ageing, a joint has lost 12–15 per cent of its weight in water content, which intensifies the flavour. This makes the final cut more expensive. You can take this process so far, but eventually you have to make a choice. The longer a joint has been aged, the more flavour it has, but the more moisture it loses. Lesser-quality steak on the market is wet-aged in vacuum packs without any weight reduction, which makes it more cost effective.

If you cook two steaks of the same weight side by side, one dry-aged and the other wet-aged, you will find that in the pan the wet-aged steak shrinks significantly more than the dry-aged beef. Also, the flavour and texture of dry-aged beef will be far superior.

PREVIOUS PAGES From left: steak and blue cheese sauce, with Harlan Estate Cabernet Sauvignon; steak and chimichurri, with Bodega Noemia Malbec; steak and peppercorn sauce, with Penfolds 'Bin 707' Cabernet Sauvignon; steak and béarnaise sauce, with Château Haut-Brion

HOW TO CHOOSE YOUR CUT

RIB EYE My favourite cut, this has got great flavour, a good fat content and great marbling throughout.
FILLET This is extremely tender, with no sinew, and is especially enjoyed by people who don't want any fat.
SIRLOIN A bit leaner than ribeye, with a bit of fat coverage, but between the fat and the muscle there is a layer of sinew, which can be off-putting.
SKIRT A cheaper cut, great for griddling or the barbecue, as it is quite thin. Carve it finely across the grain after a very good rest and it will be very tender. (See page 280.)
CÔTE DE BOEUF This is a rib eye on the bone, cut thick, for two people to share. It's harder to judge the cooking of this, due both to its size and to the presence of the bone.
PORTERHOUSE This is made of up two muscles: one side of the T-shaped bone is a sirloin and on the other is a smaller fillet. The fillet does less work, so is more tender and cooks more quickly; when it's done, try to arrange the steak so the fillet is over a cool area of the barbecue (see below), or even hangs off the edge.

HOW TO COOK STEAK

Sorry, but we can't give you the time it will take to cook a steak. It's not that simple.

There are so many factors that change how to cook a steak: size; density; the temperature of the meat and of the grill, or pan. Experience is really the only thing that will teach you.

- ☞ A steak will cook more slowly if it's straight out of the fridge. Large, thick steaks are better cooked from room temperature.
- ☞ A thick steak takes longer to cook.
- ☞ Density and age. Older steaks, such as those from ex-dairy beef, are denser and may need longer both to cook and to rest.
- ☞ Cooking a steak to perfection is a case of trial and error. I wouldn't recommend that you go out and spend £100 on a Wagyu steak if you are an inexperienced steak cook.

Let's face it. Steaks are better cooked over charcoal, which at home means the barbecue. If you don't have a barbecue, use a griddle pan and a little oil (oiling the meat, not the barbecue or the pan).

Allow the flames on the barbecue to die down so you're left with hot glowing coals. Push the hot coals to one side, to create a hot side and a cooler side.

Season the steaks well. Place the steaks over the hot coals to sear the meat. As the fat melts, it will drip on to the coals and ignite, creating flame and smoke. The smoke is good, as it flavours the meat, but the flames tend to burn, so keep moving the steaks around. Sear both sides of the meat until you are happy with the level of caramelisation.

If you want to cook the steaks to medium-well or well-done, place them on a tray in the oven to finish, as they will char too much if left on the barbecue. If you want rare, medium-rare or medium steaks, pull them to the cooler side of the barbecue and finish cooking here, turning regularly so they cook evenly but don't burn.

Resting Steak

Steaks tighten up as they cook in intense heat. They need time at an ambient temperature for the muscles to relax and the temperature to spread evenly throughout.

For rare steak, rest the meat for four minutes, adding an extra two minutes for every cooking degree. Older Galician beef, larger steaks and tougher cuts such as skirt will need more resting.

ERIC CHAVOT AND THE JOSPER GRILL I had never worked with a Josper grill before I accepted the job at 67 Pall Mall. (The Josper is an enclosed charcoal barbecue that reaches temperatures in excess of 500°C, though at 67 Pall Mall, we run ours at 350–400°C.) So my friend, Eric Chavot, took me in hand in his kitchen at the Westbury Hotel, which had a Josper at its heart.

Eric par-cooked his steaks in a water bath and used the Josper to finish and flavour them as they were ordered. This is great for quality, consistency, and for speed of service. I do the same at the Club with our larger steaks, to be shared by two or more. So, if you come to the Club and order a 1kg porterhouse, côte de boeuf or châteaubriand, it has been prepared the following way. When the beef comes into the kitchen we vacuum pack it and par-cook it in a water bath set at 62°C, in which it is cooked slowly to a core temperature of 38°C. The steaks are then plunged into iced water to arrest the cooking and the vacuum bag replaced with a fresh one. During service we have a water bath running at 42°C. The steaks sit in the water bath until they reach that 42°C core temperature and, when they come on order, are removed from the bag, seasoned and cooked in the Josper grill to the degree requested.

continued overleaf ☞

BLUE CHEESE SAUCE
HARLAN ESTATE, NAPA

SERVES 6 (MAKES ABOUT 350ML)

150ml whole milk
1 small onion, peeled and quartered
1 thyme sprig
2 bay leaves
1 small garlic clove, crushed
20g unsalted butter
1 tsp plain flour
100ml double cream
100g blue cheese, crumbled
½ tsp English mustard
salt and pepper

Pour the milk into a heavy-based saucepan and add the onion, thyme, bay and garlic. Set over a medium heat and bring to the boil, then remove from the heat. Allow to infuse for around 20 minutes, then strain.

In a separate pan over a low heat, melt the butter, then stir in the flour to form a roux. Cook the roux for a minute or so, then add the warm milk infusion slowly, stirring constantly to ensure there are no lumps. Cook, again stirring constantly so it doesn't catch on the pan, for a further 3–4 minutes, then have a taste: the flavour of raw flour should no longer be apparent.

Add the cream, cheese and mustard, stirring over the heat until they have melted. Continue to cook gently until it reaches a rich sauce consistency. Remove from the heat, season and serve immediately.

CHIMICHURRI
BODEGA NOEMIA, PATAGONIA

SERVES 5 (MAKES ABOUT 250ML)

Chimichurri should be made fresh and served straight away. If it sits around for too long, the herbs lose all their flavour and the vinegar turns them brown.

4 tbsp chopped parsley leaves
2 tbsp chopped oregano leaves
40g jalapeño (tinned or jarred), drained and finely chopped
1 shallot, finely chopped, rinsed, then patted dry
2 Preserved lemons (for home-made, see page 181), pulp discarded, rind shredded
120ml extra virgin olive oil
1 tbsp red wine vinegar
2 garlic cloves, finely chopped
salt and pepper

Mix all the ingredients in a bowl and season to taste.

PEPPERCORN SAUCE
'BIN 707', PENFOLDS, SOUTH AUSTRALIA

SERVES 6 (MAKES ABOUT 300ML)

1 tbsp tinned green peppercorns in brine, dried
30g unsalted butter
2 shallots, finely chopped
4 tbsp brandy
2 tsp Worcestershire sauce
250ml Demi-glace (see right)
150ml double cream
salt

FOR THE DEMI-GLACE
3kg beef or veal bones
1 onion, quartered
1 leek, white part only
3 celery sticks, halved
3 carrots, halved
3 garlic cloves, crushed
1 tbsp tomato purée
a few sprigs of thyme
1 bay leaf
10 black peppercorns

Preheat the oven to 200°C. Place the bones in a roasting tin and roast for 30 minutes. Turn and roast for a further 15–20 minutes. Transfer to a stockpot and cover with water, leaving the fat behind. Bring to the boil, then reduce to a simmer. Scatter the vegetables into the tin and coat with the fat. Roast for 20–30 minutes, stirring halfway. Stir in the garlic and tomato purée. Roast for 10 minutes, then stir into the stock with the herbs and peppercorns. Simmer for 3–4 hours, topping up with water when needed. Turn off the heat and rest for 20 minutes. Strain, then bring to the boil and reduce to 1.5 litres, skimming from time to time. Cool, then chill and discard the fat. Chill for 1 week, or freeze for 3 months.

Crack the peppercorns in a mortar and pestle. Melt the butter in a large, heavy saucepan set over a medium heat, then cook the shallots until soft. Pour the brandy over and set it alight. When the flame dies, add the peppercorns, Worcestershire sauce and demi-glace. Bring to the boil, then reduce the heat to a simmer. Reduce the sauce by half, then add the cream. Again, reduce to a consistency that coats the back of a spoon. Season with salt and serve as soon as possible.

BÉARNAISE SAUCE
CHÂTEAU HAUT-BRION, PESSAC-LÉOGNAN

SERVES 6 (MAKES ABOUT 300ML)

This is my favourite of all steak condiments. At the Club we aerate our béarnaise in a cream whipping bottle, a little trick I learned from chef Eric Chavot (see previous page). It transforms it to a light sauce that just melts in your mouth.

80ml white wine vinegar
80ml white wine
1 small shallot, chopped
a few tarragon sprigs, plus 3 tbsp finely chopped tarragon leaves
6 black peppercorns
300g unsalted butter
3 egg yolks
1 tbsp double cream (optional)
salt and pepper

Place the vinegar, wine, shallot, tarragon and peppercorns in a saucepan over a medium heat and boil until reduced to about 3 tbsp. Strain and set aside.

Melt the butter in a saucepan and simmer it over a low heat for 5–10 minutes until it separates. Remove from the heat and allow to cool for a few minutes. The whey will settle on the bottom, leaving the clarified butter on top. Pour off the clarified butter and discard the whey.

Put the egg yolks into a heatproof bowl with half the vinegar reduction. Place over a pan of barely simmering water, making sure the base of the bowl does not touch the water, then whisk until the mixture becomes light and fluffy. Be careful not to heat the mixture too much at this stage, as that will cause the eggs to scramble; remove the pan from the heat if necessary.

Slowly drizzle the warm clarified butter into the eggs, whisking over the heat to form an emulsion. You may need to add a little warm water if the sauce becomes too thick, then continue with the butter. Season. Taste to see if you want more vinegar reduction. Stir in the tarragon, and the cream only if you're going to aerate it with a whipping bottle. Aerate, if you like, then serve.

Barbecued beef skirt, stuffed green pepper with creamed sweetcorn, smoked bacon & merkén chilli
'Coyam', Emiliana, Colchagua

☞ page 118

SERVES 4

Skirt is a great cut for a quick grill on the barbecue and it benefits from rubs and marinades. It is cut from under the breast of the cow and is no more than 2.5cm thick, so needs to be cooked quickly. When you buy skirt steak, ask your butcher for the outside cut, which is a little more tender.

Skirt is best served thinly sliced against the grain; this way the knife is doing the work, so your jaw doesn't have to, and it makes the difference between a good meal and a disaster.

Merkén chilli is a traditional condiment in Mapuche cuisine. The chillies are smoked and dried, so they work well with the smoky, spicy flavours in the Carmenere. This grape also has a pyrazine characteristic you find in capsicum, hence the green peppers in this recipe.

ALTERNATIVE WINE MATCHES

Antiyal, Alvaro Espinosa, Maipo ☞ *page 118*

'Millia Cala', VIK, Cachapoal ☞ *page 118*

Carmenere 'Purple Angel', Montes, Colchagua ☞ *page 118*

FOR THE CREAMED SWEETCORN

- 4 ears of sweetcorn, husks and silks removed
- 30g unsalted butter
- 3 smoked streaky bacon rashers, finely sliced
- 2 small banana shallots, finely chopped
- leaves from 2 rosemary sprigs, chopped
- 1 tsp merkén chilli powder
- 250ml double cream
- salt and pepper

FOR THE STEAK

- 50g Barbecue spice rub (see page 259)
- 80ml vegetable oil
- 1 tsp merkén chilli powder
- 1.5kg beef skirt, outside cut (see recipe introduction)
- 2 large green peppers
- 1 quantity Chimichurri (see page 278)

Light a barbecue and leave it until the flames have subsided. (Or you can use a griddle pan.)

For the creamed sweetcorn, run a sharp knife down the cobs, slicing off the kernels. Scrape out all the juices and pulp with the sharp edge of the knife.

Melt the butter in a large saucepan over a medium heat, then add the bacon. Allow it to caramelise slightly before adding the shallots and rosemary. Cook gently, stirring, until the shallots are soft and translucent (3–4 minutes). Add the corn, its scraped juices and the merkén chilli. Cook for 2–3 minutes, stirring. Pour in the cream and bring to a simmer. Cook for a final 4–5 minutes until the cream has reduced and the corn is cooked through. Season to taste, decant into a heatproof container and chill quickly.

Preheat the oven to 180°C.

Now for the steak. Put the spice rub in a mixing bowl with the oil and merkén chilli powder. Rub this marinade into the beef on both sides, cover and refrigerate for an hour or so to marinate.

Halve each pepper lengthways, splitting the stalk down the middle. Remove the pith, ribs and seeds. Fill each half with creamed sweetcorn, then place, skin side down, on the barbecue grill, or in a griddle pan. Allow to blister and blacken slightly, then finish them in the oven for 10 minutes, so the filling heats through.

Place the steak over the hottest part of the barbecue to seal, or into a blisteringly hot griddle pan, turning often, then move to a cooler part to finish. It's a thin cut, so this only takes a few more minutes. Once it is cooked medium-rare, rest for 8–10 minutes.

Slice the steak into slices 1cm thick across the grain. Serve with the peppers and chimichurri.

Oxtail & celery ravioli, root vegetables
Sassicaia, Tenuta San Guido, Bolgheri

☞ page 102

SERVES 4 AS A STARTER

This iconic Cabernet Sauvignon needs deep and bold flavours, and oxtail inside ravioli is a great choice, as it also brings Italian pasta to the match and to the table.

This is a fantastic, heart-warming dish, but not one for the faint hearted. You will need to spend a long time in the kitchen to put it together, but your guests will love you for it. Cooking and serving ravioli successfully to many more than four people is a tall order, even for an experienced cook.

It may seem like an excessive quantity of oxtail for four people but, trust me, once you have removed the meat from the bones you will have a very large pile of bones and a very small pile of meat. Take your time making the ravioli, as anything with a hole in it will just fill with water when cooked, so they must all be well sealed. Good luck!

FOR THE BRAISE

2.5kg oxtail, cut into 5cm pieces
150g plain flour, plus more to dust
sunflower oil
1 large onion, quartered
1 large carrot, cut into large pieces
3 celery sticks, roughly chopped, plus a few celery leaves to serve
4 garlic cloves, unpeeled
2 tbsp tomato purée
500ml red wine
1.5 litres hot Demi-glace (see page 279)
6 thyme sprigs
1 bay leaf
1 tsp cornflour (optional)
salt and pepper

FOR THE RAVIOLI

1 quantity home-made pasta dough (see page 234)
2 heads of leafy celery
2 eggs, lightly beaten
100g semolina

FOR THE SAUCE

40g unsalted butter
80g carrot, finely chopped
80g celeriac, finely chopped
80g swede, finely chopped
80g Parmesan cheese, finely grated

Preheat the oven to 200°C. Season the oxtail and place it into a large plastic bag. Add the flour and, holding the bag closed, give it a good shake to coat. Remove the oxtail from the bag and save the flour. Place the oxtail in a large, heavy roasting tray and rub with sunflower oil. Add the onion, carrot, celery sticks and garlic and roast on the middle shelf for 30–40 minutes, until golden. Turn the oxtail halfway through and give the vegetables a stir. Remove from the oven and lift the meat and vegetables into a casserole dish.

Place the roasting tray over a medium heat to make the gravy. Stir in the reserved flour and tomato purée and cook for 1 minute, stirring. Stir in the wine a little at a time, so lumps don't form. Pour in the hot demi-glace and bring to the boil, using your spoon to release any tasty morsels left in the tin by the oxtail. Pour over the oxtail and vegetables and add the thyme and bay. Cover with a lid or foil and put in the oven, reducing the oven temperature to 150°C. Braise for 3 hours, until the oxtail falls from the bone.

Remove the oxtail pieces from the gravy with a slotted spoon and set aside. Strain the sauce through a sieve. If it seems too thin, pour it into a saucepan over medium heat, bring to a simmer, then stir in the cornflour dissolved in a little cold water. Once the gravy has reached the correct consistency, adjust the seasoning. Once the oxtail is cool enough, flake the meat from the bones and chop larger pieces. Return it to the sauce, cool, then refrigerate.

To make the celery-flavoured pasta, use the recipe on page 234, substituting 20g of the flour for 2 tbsp celery dust. Making the celery dust is easy. Just pick the leaves from the 2 heads of celery and dry them in the oven on its lowest setting with the door ajar. This will take 2 hours, turning from time to time. Once they are crisp and dry, blitz them in a food processor to a fine

ALTERNATIVE WINE MATCHES

'Le Difese', Tenuta San Guido, Bolgheri
☞ *page 102*

'Le Serre Nuove dell'Ornellaia', Bolgheri
☞ *page 102*

'Guado al Tasso', Marchesi Antinori, Bolgheri
☞ *page 102*

powder and sift. Roll the pasta into sheets (see page 234), cut into 7cm discs with a cookie cutter, then place under damp kitchen paper.

Place a small spoon of oxtail filling on a disc of pasta. Brush the edge of the pasta with egg and place another disc on top. Holding the raviolo in your hand, pinch the edges together, sealing the raviolo and forcing out as much air as possible. Place on a work surface and cut a clean edge with a smaller fluted cutter. Place on a tray and scatter with semolina. Repeat to use up the pasta. You will serve only 16 pieces, but you'll need extras up your sleeve, as you will have a few casualties. Any filling you have left will be used as sauce.

To make the sauce, place a large, heavy-based saucepan over a medium heat, melt the butter and add the carrot, celeriac and swede. Season, cover and cook, stirring, until soft (about 6 minutes). Add the leftover oxtail sauce, bring to the boil, adjust the seasoning and cover to keep warm. Put a large saucepan of salted water over a high heat and bring to the boil. Carefully drop in the ravioli, adding extras in case of casualties. Cook for 4 minutes, then test one. When it is *al dente*, lift them all out with a slotted spoon.

Divide the ravioli between 4 warmed plates. Spoon over the sauce and sprinkle with a few fresh celery leaves. Serve the Parmesan at the table.

2013
ECKEN
ARKT
MORIC

Roasted haunch of roe deer, braised cabbage, bilberries, spätzle
Blaufränkisch 'Neckenmarkt', Weingut Moric

☞ page 120

SERVES 4

Roe deer are a small species with lighter, more delicate meat than the larger red or fallow deer, and Blaufränkisch pairs well with lighter meats. This dish is a tribute to those Austrian hunter-gatherers who would be likely to stumble across juniper and bilberries while stalking roe deer. Blaufränkisch likes a little acidity and spice, so this spiced and lightly vinegared cabbage is ideal.

Spätzle is a kind of egg noodle, traditional to Germany, Austria and Switzerland. It can be eaten boiled and soft, or fried and crispy. There is a bit of work involved, but it's rewarding to watch the 'little sparrows' instantly puff up in the frying pan.

ALTERNATIVE WINE MATCHES

Egri Bikavér 'Titi' Bull's Blood, Gál Tibor, North Hungary ☞ page 120

Rosso del Ticino, Castello Luigi, Switzerland ☞ page 114

Blaufränkisch 'Goldberg', Weingut Prieler, Burgenland ☞ page 120

1 tbsp chopped thyme leaves
1 tbsp finely ground juniper berries
150ml sunflower oil
4 x 200g portions haunch of roe deer
300ml chicken stock
2 tbsp white wine vinegar
80g unsalted butter
1 small Savoy cabbage heart
1 tsp sweet paprika
200ml Red wine jus (see page 209)
100g bilberries, or blueberries
salt and pepper

FOR THE SPÄTZLE

300g plain flour
½ tsp fine salt
¼ nutmeg, finely grated
4 eggs
100ml whole milk
a little olive oil
handful of chopped parsley leaves

Preheat the oven to 180°C. Place all the thyme, half the juniper and 50ml of the sunflower oil into a large bowl. Add the deer, coat well, then chill.

Bring the stock, vinegar and half the butter to the boil in a small saucepan. Cut the cabbage into 4 wedges, leaving the core intact so they hold together. Put them in a baking dish and season well with salt, pepper, the paprika and remaining juniper. Pour over the stock, cover, then braise for 30–40 minutes until tender. After 25 minutes, proceed with the rest of the dish.

For the spätzle, sift the flour into a large bowl. Add the salt and nutmeg and make a well in the centre. In a separate bowl, beat the eggs with the milk and pour them into the well. Whisk to a wet, sticky dough. Transfer to a food mixer fitted with the paddle attachment and beat for 10–15 minutes. Set up a steamer pan over a pan of salted water. Using a plastic scraper or spatula, push the mix through the holes in the pan into the boiling water in 2–3 batches. Cook for 30–40 seconds or until they float, then lift out and plunge into iced water. Drain and toss in a little oil to stop them sticking together. At this stage the spätzle can be chilled for up to 2 days.

Preheat a heavy-based frying pan over a high heat. Lift the venison from the marinade and season well. Add 50ml more sunflower oil to the pan and sear until caramelised on all sides. Reduce the heat and allow the meat to cook more gently for 3 minutes, turning regularly. Remove from the pan to rest.

Place the red wine jus into a small saucepan over a high heat and bring to the boil. Add the bilberries and turn off the heat.

In a small frying pan over a medium-high heat, melt the remaining butter and sunflower oil. As it starts to bubble, add the spätzle. Move them around constantly so they crisp evenly. They will swell quickly to 3 times their original size and turn golden. Season with salt and drain on kitchen paper. Remove the cabbage from the oven and drain it well in a colander.

Carve the venison against the grain and serve in warmed bowls. Add a wedge of cabbage and spoon over the jus. Scatter the spätzle over and serve.

Rigatoni of braised venison shank ragù, sour cherries & chocolate 'Cerequio', Roberto Voerzio, Barolo

☞ page 112

SERVES 4

Venison, cherries and a hint of chocolate are the flavours of Barolo, so this is a great match.

There are six different species of deer in the UK, red deer being the largest. Four shanks from a red deer is more than enough for this recipe, but if you are cooking shanks from a smaller animal such as a fallow deer, you will probably have to use 6.

If you find the Morello cherries difficult to get hold of, try online. They are a great, versatile product, so it's worth sourcing the correct variety.

140g dried Morello cherries
1 bottle red wine
4 red deer shanks
100g plain flour
vegetable oil
1 large onion, quartered
1 large carrot, cut into large pieces
3 celery sticks, roughly chopped
4 garlic cloves, unpeeled
2 tbsp tomato purée
1.5 litres hot Demi-glace (see page 279)
6 thyme sprigs
1 bay leaf
1 tsp cornflour (optional)
500g dried rigatoni
40g 70% cocoa cooking chocolate, finely grated
80g Parmesan cheese, finely grated
salt and pepper

Preheat the oven to 200°C.

Place the dried cherries in a large bowl. In a saucepan, bring the red wine to the boil and pour it over the cherries. Allow to cool, then place the venison in the liquid. Cover and let them marinate in the fridge in the cherry-infused wine for 24 hours, turning the shanks a couple of times as the wine will not totally cover them.

The next day, remove the shanks and pat them dry with kitchen paper. Strain the wine, reserving it and the cherries separately.

Season the shanks and place them into a large plastic bag. Add the flour and, holding the bag closed, give it a good shake to coat the shanks with the flour. Remove the venison from the bag and save the flour for later.

Place the shanks in a large roasting tin and rub them with a little vegetable oil. Add the onion, carrot, celery and garlic and place on the middle shelf of the oven to roast for 30–40 minutes, until the meat is golden brown and retracting from the bone, turning the shanks over halfway and giving the vegetables a good stir. Remove the tin from the oven and lift both the meat and vegetables into a casserole dish.

Place the roasting tin over a medium heat. Stir in the reserved flour and the tomato purée and cook for 1 minute, stirring constantly with a wooden spoon so they don't catch. Stir in the reserved wine a little at a time so lumps don't form, then pour in the hot demi-glace and bring it to the boil, using a spoon to release any tasty morsels left on the tin by the meat.

Pour the gravy over the meat and vegetables and add the thyme and bay leaf. Cover with a lid or foil and return to the oven, reducing the oven temperature to 150°C. Braise for 3 hours, until the shanks are tender and just falling from the bone. Remove the shanks carefully from the gravy with a slotted spoon and set aside to cool.

Strain the sauce through a sieve. If it seems too thin, pour it into a saucepan, and, over a medium heat, bring to a simmer. Stir in the cornflour dissolved in a little cold water. Once the gravy has reached the correct consistency,

ALTERNATIVE WINE MATCHES

Barbaresco, Produttori de Barbaresco, Piedmont
☞ *page 112*

Nebbiolo, Luke Lambert Wines, Yarra Valley
☞ *page 110*

Barolo, Bartolo Mascarello, Piedmont
☞ *page 112*

taste and adjust the seasoning. Once the shanks are cool enough to handle, flake the meat from the bone into small chunks and return them to the sauce.

Place a large saucepan of water over a high heat and bring to the boil, adding plenty of salt. Cook the rigatoni to al dente. You can follow the time specified on the packet, but sometimes I never trust it. Once cooked, strain the pasta through a colander.

Finish the sauce with the macerated cherries and stir in the chocolate. Fold the rigatoni through the sauce and serve, topped with the Parmesan.

Peppered venison striploin, sprout tops & black pudding, blackcurrant jus
Côte-Rôtie 'La Turque', Maison Guigal

☞ page 94

SERVES 6

Northern Rhône Syrah is full of dark berry fruit, earthy and gamey, a perfect match with venison, plus the rotundone chemical in the grape skins exudes black pepper spice.

The richness of black pudding balances the natural acidity from the blackcurrants in this recipe. It's best to tweak the sauce to work with the wine you are enjoying on the night. Some examples of Syrah can also have a smooth, chocolatey finish. For these, melt a few 70 per cent cocoa solids dark chocolate buttons into the jus just before serving. The chocolate also complements the venison.

ALTERNATIVE WINE MATCHES

Crozes-Hermitage, Domaine Alain Graillot, Northern Rhône ☞ *page 94*

'Little William', Pieter H Walser, Blank Bottle, South Africa ☞ *page 92*

Syrah 'IX Estate', Colgin Cellars, Napa ☞ *page 92*

1.2kg venison striploin, membrane removed by your butcher, cut into 6 even-sized portions
50ml sunflower oil, plus more to cook the black pudding
6 sprout hearts
200g black pudding
50g unsalted butter
250ml Red wine jus (see page 209)
200g blackcurrants
salt and pepper

Sprinkle a sheet of baking parchment evenly with a generous amount of salt and pepper. Don't be shy with the pepper; it will complement the Syrah. Roll each portion of venison in the salt and pepper, coating it well.

Heat a large heavy-based frying pan over a medium–high heat, add the sunflower oil and cook the venison, caramelising it evenly on all sides. The venison should be served rare to medium-rare, so should not need any time in the oven. Once caramelised, reduce the heat and continue to cook the venison for 3 minutes, turning it regularly so it cooks evenly. Remove from the heat and rest for another 3–4 minutes.

Meanwhile, to prepare the sprout hearts, bring a large saucepan of lightly salted water to the boil. Cut each sprout heart in half, splitting the stalk end down the middle, then rinse under cold water to remove any undesirables lurking between the leafy layers. Add the washed sprout hearts to the boiling water and cook for 2 minutes until tender.

Cut the black pudding into 6 even-sized portions. Heat a large heavy-based frying pan over a medium heat, add a little sunflower oil and fry the black pudding until it is crisp on the outside and warmed through.

Drain the sprout hearts in a large colander with their cut sides pointing down, to allow the water to drain off. Place the pan back on the heat and melt the butter. Return the sprout hearts to the pan, season with salt and pepper and coat with the butter.

In a small saucepan, bring the jus to the boil and add the blackcurrants.

To serve, place 2 sprout hearts on each of 6 warmed plates with their cut sides facing upwards. Carve each portion of venison into 4–5 slices and place on the plates. Serve a piece of black pudding with each and, finally, spoon the blackcurrant jus over the meat and sprout hearts.

LA TURQUE
CÔTE BRUNE
Côte-Rôtie
E. GUIGAL

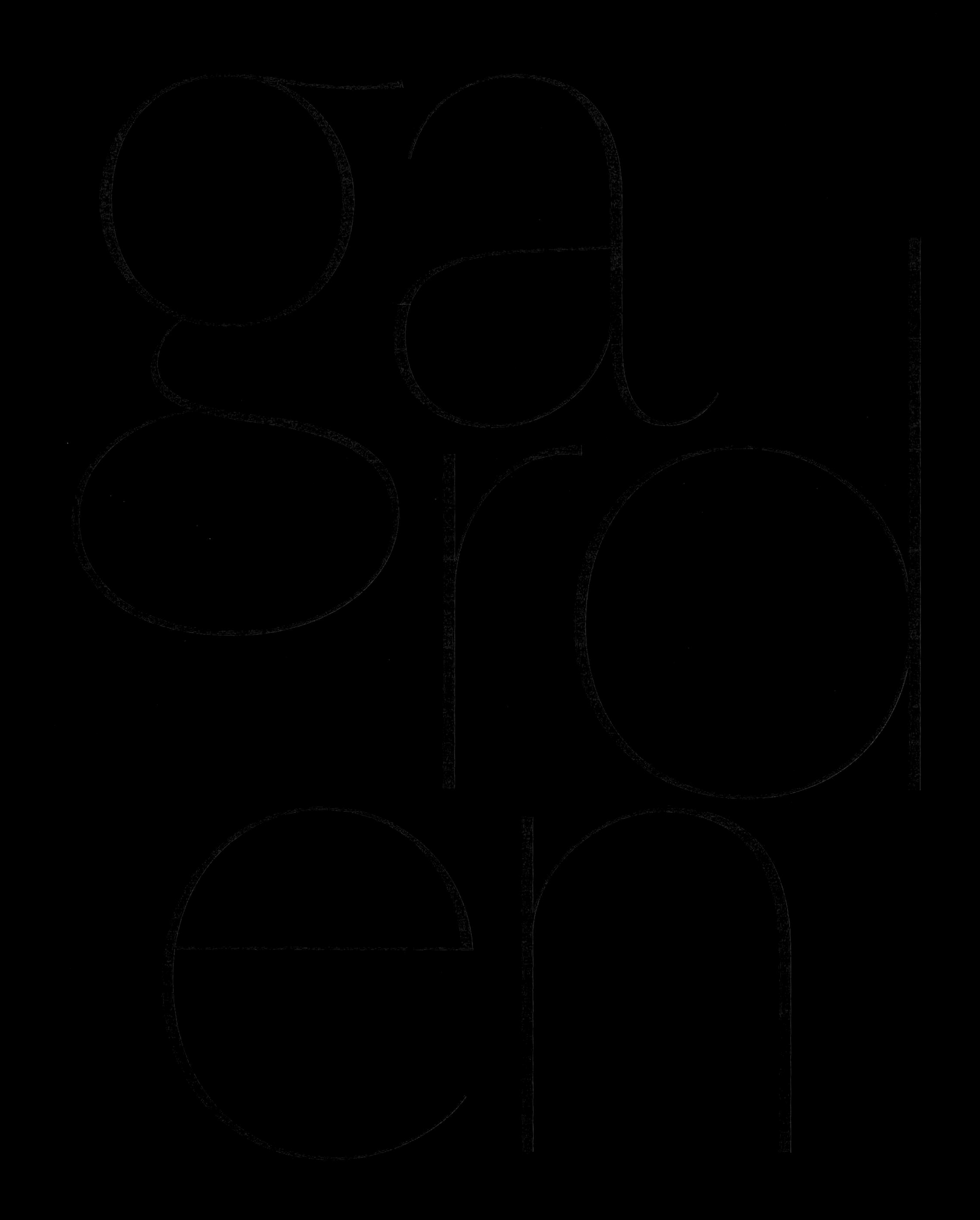
garden

Starting a meal: appetisers & aperitifs

CHEESE STRAW TRIO
NV CHAMPAGNE 'LES CHÉTILLONS', PIERRE PÉTERS

☞ *page 85*

MAKES ABOUT 24 OF EACH STRAW

The perfect pairing for non-vintage Champagne or sparkling wine. Rather than just one flavour, we are giving you three: both salted anchovies and olives are great with Champagne and sparkling wine, so we are using those. These are so easy to make. The lactic and nutty nature of cheese, and the toasty, yeasty character of pastry both work well with Champagne, which can have similar flavours. Its acidity will also cut through the richness of the pastry.

- 100g pitted Kalamata olives
- 100g salted anchovies
- 600g all-butter puff pastry
- plain flour, to dust
- 2 eggs, lightly beaten
- 300g finely grated Parmesan cheese
- 100g finely grated Emmental cheese

Preheat the oven to 180°C.

Finely chop the olives and then grind them to a paste in a mortar and pestle. Wash out the mortar and pestle and do the same with the anchovies. Reserve both the pastes, separately, for later.

Cut the pastry into 3 x 200g portions. Dust a worktop with flour and roll each into a large square. Prick heavily with a fork. Trim the edges to get 3 x 30cm squares.

Using a pastry brush, brush a coating of egg on the first pastry square right to the edges. Mix 100g of the Parmesan in a bowl with all the Emmental. Sprinkle half of this evenly over the egg-washed pastry right to the edges. Cover with a sheet of baking parchment and, using a rolling pin with no force, gently roll it across the pastry so the cheese sticks. Remove the parchment and lay it flat on the worktop. Carefully turn the pastry sheet over on to the parchment, then repeat the process on the other side, with more egg and the other half of the cheese mixture. Cut each pastry sheet into 12 x 2.5cm strips.

Line several baking trays with baking parchment. Twist the ends of each strip in opposite directions until you have a tight straw and lay them out on the baking trays, leaving space between them so they crisp up (you may have to bake these in batches).

Bake for 10–12 minutes until golden and crispy. While they are still warm, using a serrated knife, trim each end and cut each straw in half. Cool on a wire rack.

Meanwhile, spread the second pastry sheet with half the olive paste and scatter with another 50g of the Parmesan. Cover with a sheet of baking parchment and, using a rolling pin with no force, gently roll it across the pastry so the cheese sticks. Remove the parchment and lay it flat on the worktop. Carefully turn the pastry sheet over on to the parchment, then repeat the process on the other side, using the remaining olive paste and 50g more Parmesan. Form the straws and bake as above.

Make the anchovy straws in the same way as the olive straws, replacing the olive paste with anchovy paste.

Serve at room temperature, or flash back through the oven for a couple of minutes to serve warm.

ALTERNATIVE WINE MATCHES

Champagne 'Cuvée Vénus', Agrapart & Fils ☞ *page 85*

Champagne 'Les Pierrières', Ulysse Collin ☞ *page 85*

Champagne 'Les Ursules' Blanc de Noirs, Roses de Jeanne ☞ *page 85*

Starting a meal: appetisers & aperitifs

GOUGÈRES FILLED WITH GRUYÈRE MORNAY CHABLIS GRAND CRU 'GRENOUILLES', DOMAINE LOUIS MICHEL & FILS

☞ page 68

MAKES ABOUT 30

In Chablis, you can buy these freshly cooked from the *boulangerie* and sold in paper bags, to be eaten as a snack while still warm. We added extra cheesse, and it's their lactic quality that make them so perfect with a Chablis that has been aged on its lees. The mornay centre explodes, filling your mouth with the rich, cheesy sauce.

FOR THE GOUGÈRES

65ml whole milk
50ml water
50g unsalted butter
½ tsp sugar
½ tsp salt
65g plain flour, sifted
95g eggs (excluding shell)
45g grated Parmesan

FOR THE MORNAY SAUCE

125ml whole milk
1 small onion, quartered
1 thyme sprig
1 bay leaf
1 garlic clove, crushed
20g unsalted butter
20g plain flour
35g Gruyère, grated
15g Parmesan, grated
½ tsp English mustard
50ml double cream
1 egg yolk
salt and pepper

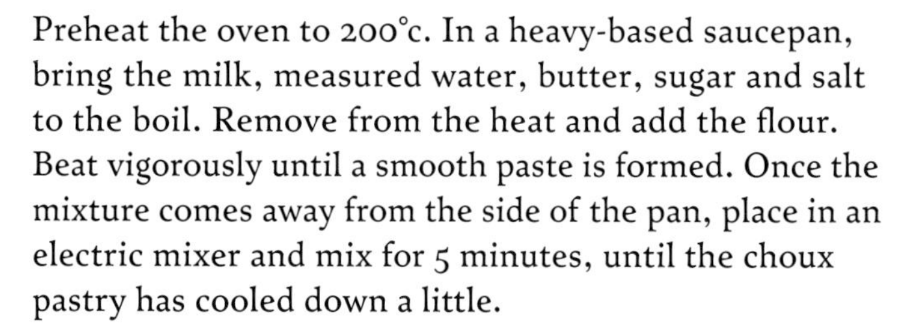

Preheat the oven to 200°c. In a heavy-based saucepan, bring the milk, measured water, butter, sugar and salt to the boil. Remove from the heat and add the flour. Beat vigorously until a smooth paste is formed. Once the mixture comes away from the side of the pan, place in an electric mixer and mix for 5 minutes, until the choux pastry has cooled down a little.

Increase the speed of the mixer and gradually beat in the eggs, until the mixture is smooth and glossy and has a soft dropping consistency. Fold in half the Parmesan, then spoon into a piping bag fitted with a 1cm plain nozzle. Pipe balls on to bakings tray lined with baking parchment, each about the size of a 10 pence piece. Leave space between them to allow for expansion in the oven. (You may have to bake these in batches.)

Place in the middle of the oven, then reduce the oven temperature to 160°C. Bake for 15 minutes until crisp on the outside and dry in the middle. (Check by breaking one in half.) Allow to cool.

Over a medium heat in a heavy-based saucepan, bring the milk to the boil with the onion, thyme, bay and garlic. Remove from the heat and infuse for 5 minutes, then pass through a sieve and set aside.

In a separate saucepan over a low heat, melt the butter, then add the flour to form a roux. Cook for a minute or so, then add the milk slowly, stirring to ensure there are no lumps. Cook, stirring, for 3–4 minutes, then add the cheeses and mustard. Remove from the heat and season. Cool for 10 minutes, stirring so a skin doesn't form. Meanwhile, whip the cream until semi-whipped. Stir the egg yolk into the mornay sauce, then fold in the cream. Spoon into a piping bag fitted with a small nozzle and pipe a small amount into each gougère from underneath.

When ready to serve, preheat the oven to 180°C. Sprinkle a little grated Parmesan on top of each gougère and bake for 4 minutes, until the cheese on top has melted and the mornay sauce has warmed through. Serve immediately.

ALTERNATIVE WINE MATCHES

Amontillado 'El Tresillo Viejo 1874', Bodegas Emilio Hidalgo ☞ *page 125*
Chardonnay 'Trout Gulch Vineyard', Arnot-Roberts, Sonoma ☞ *page 71*
Chablis Grand Cru 'Moutonne', Domaine Long-Depaquit ☞ *page 68*

MINI TOMATO BRUSCHETTA WITH BAKED BOCCONCINI IN PROSCIUTTO GRECO 'MASTRO', MASTROBERARDINO, CAMPANIA

☞ *page 78*

MAKES 12 BITE-SIZED BRUSCHETTA

Because of its high acidity, Greco is the perfect match for fresh tomatoes. It tends to oxidise in the bottle within a few years of vintage, producing nutty, caramelised flavours that echo those of the baked prosciutto encasing the cheese here.

These mini bruschetta make a great little snack before a barbecue in the hot summer months. The flavour achieved by charring the bread over hot coals and rubbing it lightly with raw garlic is the cornerstone of any good bruschetta. After that, the choice of toppings is endless...

3 ripe vine tomatoes, chopped
½ small red onion, finely chopped
10 basil leaves, shredded
100ml extra virgin olive oil
6 slices of prosciutto
12 bocconcini balls
1 baguette
1 garlic clove
salt and pepper

Place the tomatoes, onion and basil in a mixing bowl with 50ml of the olive oil. Season well and mix to combine.

Preheat the oven to 220°C. Cut each slice of prosciutto in half and use them to encase the bocconcini, folding the edges underneath and neatly trimming off any excess.

Place the bocconcini balls on an oven tray lined with baking parchment. Bake for about 4 minutes, until the cheese in the centre is gooey.

Meanwhile, slice 12 x 1cm-thick discs of baguette. Brush them with the remaining olive oil and char both sides on a griddle pan, or a barbecue. If they are still a little soft, having already achieved the right level of charring, finish them off in the oven for a couple of minutes. When they are ready, cut the garlic clove in half and gently rub it into the charred baguette slices. Don't overdo it, as the garlic can be a bit overpowering.

Spoon a little tomato mixture on to each bruschetta with plenty of the juices. Top each with a ball of prosciutto-wrapped bocconcini and serve while the cheese is hot.

ALTERNATIVE WINE MATCHES

Carricante 'Eruzione 1614', Planeta, Sicily ☞ *page 78*

Grechetto 'Montefalco', Antonelli San Marco, Umbria ☞ *page 78*

Aubergine chickpea fritters, barrel-aged feta & pesto St Laurent 'Jungle', Weingut Jurtschitsch

☞ page 121

SERVES 6 AS A STARTER

This is inspired by the Arabic meze dip, baba ganoush. The key is to make sure the skins of the aubergine are charred to ash; only then will you achieve the smoky flavour integral to the dish. These are also great served smaller, as a canapé.

St Laurent is a deep and dark wine with a smoky character, and this is mirrored in the charred aubergines that go into these fritters.

ALTERNATIVE WINE MATCHES

Petit Verdot, Casa de la Ermita, Jumilla ☞ page 118

Grand Eschola, Quinta do Côtto, Douro ☞ page 127

Spätburgunder, Jean Stodden, Ahr ☞ page 86

FOR THE FRITTERS

4 large aubergines
2 garlic cloves
200g canned chickpeas, drained and rinsed
50g gram flour, plus more if needed
pinch of cayenne pepper
1 tbsp tahini paste
juice of 2 lemons, or to taste
1 tsp ground cumin
200g feta cheese, chopped into 1cm cubes
vegetable oil, to deep-fry
basil cress, to serve (optional)

FOR THE PESTO

40g pine nuts
80g basil leaves
80g Parmesan cheese, finely grated
1 garlic clove, finely chopped
1 chilli, deseeded and finely chopped
300ml extra virgin olive oil
salt and pepper

To produce 400g aubergine pulp, burn the aubergine skins over a charcoal barbecue, or the flame of a gas hob. Turn to char all sides evenly, until the aubergines start to collapse. When cool enough to handle, remove the skins and tops. Spoon the pulp into a muslin cloth, tie it to form a bag and, using string, hang it over a bowl in the fridge overnight.

The following day, put the garlic cloves in a small saucepan, cover with water and set over a high heat. Boil for 8 minutes, then drain and cool.

To make the pesto, preheat the oven to 170°C. Place the pine nuts on a tray and toast in the oven for 5–7 minutes, or until golden. Remove from the oven and spread out to cool. After about 10 minutes, add all the ingredients to a blender and pulse-blend until amalgamated but still a little coarse; be careful not to over-blend the pesto. Taste and adjust the seasoning.

Pulse the chickpeas coarsely in a food processor, then remove. Peel and finely chop the garlic. Put the aubergine in the food processor with the gram flour, cayenne, garlic, tahini, lemon juice and cumin. Blend to a purée, put in a bowl and fold in the chickpeas. Season, adding lemon juice if needed.

Set up a deep-fat fryer to 190°C, or use a saucepan, taking the same precautions and care as usual (see page 138).

Test a spoon of fritter mix in the fryer. If it disintegrates, you will need to add a little more gram flour. Once adjusted (if needed), fold in the feta.

At the Club we use 2 dessert spoons to shape the mixture into quenelles, but this is a difficult skill for a novice, so don't feel defeated if you choose to drop the mixture from a spoon instead. They will still taste great!

Deep-fry the fritters for a couple of minutes until golden and crispy. You'll need to do this in batches. Once ready, drain on kitchen paper to soak up any oil. Serve with the pesto and sprinkle basil cress over, if you like.

Baked crottin de Chavignol en croûte, beetroot, orange & watercress salad
Clos Rougeard, Saumur-Champigny

☞ page 118

SERVES 4

Beetroot's sweet, earthy flavour makes it ideal with cheese, and goat's cheese in particular. Crottin de Chavignol, from a village in the Loire, is a tiny ripened cheese of just 40g, created as a snack during the grape harvest. Its nutty – sometimes mushroomy – flavours complement the beetroot.

Saumur-Champigny from the Loire Valley is made with Cabernet Franc and, in the relatively cool climate, can produce grassy, earthy styles of red wine, sometimes described as like damp straw. High-acid Cabernet Franc stands up well to goat's cheese, which is itself naturally acidic, while the earthy flavours of beetroot are a good match to both cheese and wine.

This dressing recipe makes about 800ml, but it keeps for months in the fridge and is very versatile.

ALTERNATIVE WINE MATCHES

Sancerre 'La Moussière', Alphonse Mellot
☞ page 58

Pinot Noir 'Les Chailloux', Claude Riffault, Sancerre ☞ page 86

Savennières 'Coulée de Serrant', Nicolas Joly
☞ page 64

FOR THE DRESSING (MAKES 800ML)

500ml freshly squeezed orange juice
100ml red wine vinegar
3 tbsp clear honey
3 tbsp wholegrain mustard
600ml extra virgin rapeseed oil
salt and pepper

FOR THE CROTTINS

300g baby beetroot (ideally red, golden and candy)
80ml extra virgin rapeseed oil
5 thyme sprigs
100g clarified unsalted butter
4 baguette slices
4 crottins de Chavignol
a few watercress sprigs, any coarse stalks removed
2 oranges, segmented

First make the dressing. In a saucepan, bring the orange juice and vinegar to the boil and reduce to about 150ml. Cool, then chill. Once the mixture is cold, pour it into a large bowl with the honey and mustard. Slowly drizzle in the oil, whisking to emulsify, then season well. Store in a bottle or jar in the fridge. If the dressing separates, just give it a good shake before you use it.

Preheat the oven to 180°C. Remove the stems and leaves from the beetroot, saving any delicate new leaves for the salad. Save a couple of raw candy beetroot; they make a striking garnish sliced into thin discs on a mandolin. Wash the beetroot and place it on a large sheet of foil. Drizzle over the oil, add the thyme and season liberally. Lift the sides of the foil and pour in 80ml of water, then seal the parcel at the top, place in the middle of the oven and bake for 40 minutes, until cooked through. (Test a beetroot with the tip of a knife, to check.)

Once cool enough to handle, rub off the skins. (Peel the red beetroot last, or its dye will mark the others.) Cut into bite-sized wedges and set aside.

Melt the clarified butter in a small frying pan over a medium heat. Once it is hot, add the baguette slices. If the butter is hot enough, they should gently bubble on entry. Cook until golden and crisp, then turn to toast the other side. They should be soft in the middle. Lay them on kitchen paper.

Place the crottins on a baking tray and bake for 8–10 minutes until softened and starting to bubble around the bases. Remove from the oven and rest for a couple of minutes.

Place a crouton on each of 4 plates.

In a small bowl, dress the beetroot lightly with some of the dressing and season. Place around the croutons and scatter over the watercress, any reserved beetroot leaves and the orange segments. Garnish the salad with a few candy beetroot discs. Drizzle a little more dressing over, sit a crottin on each crouton and serve.

Parmesan-battered courgette flower, courgette vinaigrette, anchovies & soft-boiled quail's eggs Trebbiano d'Abruzzo, Valentini

☞ page 78

SERVES 6

Courgette flowers are one of those prized summer vegetables that chefs eagerly await. They are great torn into salads, or stuffed with ricotta or goat's cheese, cooked into risotto, or eaten like this: deep-fried in a light Parmesan batter. Anchovies and capers are delicious with courgettes and great with a chilled glass of crisp Trebbiano on a hot summer day.

Trebbiano is good with this dish because of its acidity, which stands up to the light vinaigrette used here while also helping to cut through the cheese and oil in the crispy batter.

FOR THE VINAIGRETTE

1 tbsp white wine vinegar, ideally Chardonnay vinegar
juice of ½ lemon
1 tbsp Dijon mustard
80ml extra virgin olive oil, plus more if needed
40ml sunflower oil
salt and pepper

FOR THE DISH

12 quail's eggs
300ml chilled sparkling water
1 ice cube
150g tempura flour, plus more to dust
60g Parmesan cheese, finely grated
1 courgette
2 Preserved lemons (see page 181)
30g small capers in brine, drained
1 small shallot, finely chopped
80ml Vinaigrette (see left)
sunflower oil, to deep-fry
6 courgette flowers
12 salted anchovies, split lengthways

All the ingredients for the vinaigrette must be cold, to help it to emulsify.

Place the vinegar, lemon juice and mustard into a mixing bowl. Place a tea towel under the bowl to help stop it from moving around while you whisk. Drizzle the oils very slowly into the bowl, whisking vigorously to create an emulsion. If the emulsion becomes too thick, add a little cold water. Once completely emulsified, season to taste. If the vinaigrette is too acidic for your liking, whisk in a little more olive oil.

Bring a small saucepan of water to the boil. Carefully add the quail's eggs and boil for 2 minutes 45 seconds. Lift out with a slotted spoon and plunge them into iced water to arrest the cooking. Carefully peel, then set aside.

When making the tempura batter, it's important the sparkling water is chilled. To keep it cold, slide an ice cube inside the whisk. Place the tempura flour into a bowl. Slowly whisk in the sparkling water a little at a time until all has been incorporated. The consistency of the batter should be light enough to just coat the courgette flowers. Fold in the Parmesan and chill.

Halve the courgette lengthways and scoop out the seeds with a teaspoon. Cut the courgette into 5mm dice and place in a bowl. Cut the preserved lemons into quarters, scoop out and discard the flesh, then shred the rind and add to the courgette. Add the capers, shallot and vinaigrette and season.

Once the batter has rested, set a deep-fryer to 170°C, or use a saucepan, taking the same precautions and care as usual (see page 138).

Place a little tempura flour into a bowl. Carefully remove the stigma from inside each courgette flower and, one by one, coat the courgette flowers with tempura flour, shaking off any excess. Gently drop the floured flowers into the batter.

continued overleaf ☞

continued from previous page

ALTERNATIVE WINE MATCHES

Verdicchio di Matelica Riserva 'Mirum', La Monacesca, Marches page 78

Trebbiano d'Abruzzo, Emidio Pepe, Abruzzo page 78

When you're ready to cook the flowers, lift them out one by one, holding the tip of the baby courgette. Allow the excess batter to run off back into the batter bowl and carefully lower it, flower first, into the hot oil. Don't drop it yet: wait for the flower end to rise to the surface and then carefully let go of the courgette. Now that it's floating it won't stick to the bottom of the fryer basket. Repeat with the other flowers, being careful to keep them separated so they don't stick together. Depending on the size of your fryer it may be best to cook in 2 batches. Deep-fry them for about 2 minutes, until golden and crispy. You may need to turn them over halfway, so they cook evenly.

Once they are cooked, lift them out of the fryer with a slotted spoon. Rest them on kitchen paper to drain the oil. (Be careful that the oil hasn't collected inside the flower; this can happen occasionally.)

Spread a little courgette vinaigrette out on each plate, with 4 strips of anchovy, followed by 2 quail's eggs, cut in half. Arrange a battered courgette flower on top and serve.

Crisp spring vegetable salad with capers & preserved lemon Picpoul de Pinet, Domaine Gaujal

☞ page 82

SERVES 4

See overleaf (right) for picture

This salad is on the menu at the Club throughout spring and summer. When we've taken it off before, we've been bombarded with complaints.

Picpoul literally translates as 'lip stinger'. It is the Muscadet of the Languedoc: the crisp, dry white wine of choice to pair with the seafood and shellfish found in abundance along the coast. A fresh lemony nature and high acidity means it works with preserved lemon and sharp capers.

ALTERNATIVE WINE MATCHES

Bosco, Cantina Cinque Terre, Costa da' Posa ☞ *page 78*

Château de Caseneuve Blanc, Pic St-Loup, Languedoc ☞ *page 82*

Pinot Grigio, Marjam Simčič, Goriška Brda, Slovenia ☞ *page 77*

- 400g broad beans in pods (to yield 100g beans)
- 1 fennel bulb, halved lengthways and cored
- 1 small Preserved lemon (see page 181)
- 6 radishes, finely sliced into discs
- 300g peas in pods (to yield 100g peas)
- 100g mangetout, very finely sliced lengthways
- 8 asparagus spears, trimmed, very finely sliced on the diagonal
- 60g capers in brine, drained
- 10 mint leaves, shredded
- a few dill sprigs or fennel tops, roughly picked
- handful of pea shoots
- 100ml Lemon dressing (see page 134)
- salt and pepper

Remove the broad beans from their pods. Blanch the beans for 30 seconds in boiling water, then refresh in iced water. Once cold, pop them out of their bitter skins.

Shave the fennel finely with a sharp knife, or a mandolin. Plunge it into a bowl of iced water for 30 seconds; it will emerge very crisp. Drain in a colander. Cut the preserved lemon into quarters, discard the flesh and shred the rind.

Toss all the ingredients into a large bowl, dress liberally with the lemon dressing and season to taste.

Superfood salad
Cinsault 'Pofadder', Sadie Family Wines, Swartland

☞ page 121

SERVES 6

See previous page (left) for picture

Cinsault in South Africa is making its renaissance. It's a variety that's been there for a long time, but has been underused up until now. A younger generation of winemakers are making excellent wines from very old vines found in places such as Swartland. It can have Gamay-like flavours of fresh red berries, cherry, strawberry and especially pomegranate, with a hint of citrusy orange. Cinsault is perfect to serve slightly chilled and matches many elements found in this dish.

This is a riot of colours, flavours and textures that work harmoniously. Quinoa is one of the few plant foods that has all nine essential amino acids, while kale and orange are high in vitamin C, so with each mouthful you're doing yourself a huge favour.

This makes 800ml dressing, but it keeps for months and is very versatile.

ALTERNATIVE WINE MATCHES

Côte-de-Brouilly, Château Thivin, Beaujolais ☞ page 91

Pinot Noir 'True Point Vineyard', Adelsheim, Oregon ☞ page 90

FOR THE ORANGE, MAPLE SYRUP AND GRAIN MUSTARD DRESSING (MAKES 800ML)

500ml freshly squeezed orange juice
100ml red wine vinegar
3 tbsp maple syrup
3 tbsp wholegrain mustard
600ml extra virgin rapeseed oil
salt and pepper

FOR THE SALAD

45g pumpkin seeds
45g sunflower seeds
2 tbsp extra virgin olive oil
300g curly kale, ribs stripped out, chopped
225g quinoa
1 pomegranate
90g dried cherries
1 orange, segmented
120g blueberries
100g fresh edamame beans, podded (frozen and defrosted are fine)

First, make the dressing. In a saucepan, bring the orange juice and vinegar to the boil and reduce to 150ml. Chill. Place in a large bowl with the maple syrup and mustard. Slowly drizzle in the rapeseed oil, whisking quickly to emulsify the dressing, then season. Store in the fridge. If it separates, just give it a good shake before you use it.

Preheat the oven to 180°C.

Spread the pumpkin and sunflower seeds on a baking tray, drizzle with oil, season with salt and mix to coat. Bake for 5–7 minutes, or until golden. You'll need to stir them a couple of times, so they cook evenly. Once toasted, leave them to cool. Try to resist the temptation to eat them all...

Bring a saucepan of lightly salted water to the boil over a high heat, then blanch the kale in it for 30 seconds. Strain, plunge into iced water to refresh it, then drain on kitchen paper.

Bring another saucepan of lightly salted water to the boil over a high heat. Place the quinoa in a sieve and give it a good rinse. Add the quinoa to the boiling water and return to the boil, then reduce the heat to a simmer. Cook until soft; this takes 10–12 minutes. Strain through a sieve and run it under cold water to cool it down. Place the sieve over the saucepan and leave the quinoa to drain.

Remove the seeds from the pomegranate by cutting it in half. Holding each half at a time, cut-side down, over a bowl, give it a good bash with the back of a ladle. The seeds will fall through your fingers into the bowl. Pick out any bits of bitter white pith that have also made it through your fingers.

Place all the ingredients into a large bowl, season lightly and toss with 80ml of the dressing to serve.

Waldorf salad
Bacchus, Chapel Down, Kent

☞ page 80

SERVES 6

See previous page (centre) for picture

Bacchus is a wine grape variety of German origin and was one of the first to be planted in England. Although English producers are now moving mainly to Chardonnay and Pinot Noir, some Bacchus has remained. It's intensely aromatic, with the green aromas of fresh-cut celery, plus a tart green apple acidity, so Waldorf salad is a pretty obvious great match.

This famous salad, first served at the Waldorf Astoria in 1896, is also good with crumbled blue cheese. I have lightened my version by cutting the rich mayonnaise with yogurt.

ALTERNATIVE WINE MATCHES

Vermentino 'Is Argiolas', Argiolas, Sardinia *☞ page 78*

Bacchus, Weingut Hans Wirsching, Franken *☞ page 80*

Viognier 'The Wingwalker' Alpha Domus, Hawke's Bay *☞ page 83*

FOR THE MAYONNAISE

6 egg yolks
20g English mustard
40g Dijon mustard
35ml white wine vinegar
500ml vegetable oil
250ml olive oil
juice of ½ lemon, or to taste
salt and pepper

FOR THE SALAD

20 walnut halves
2 tbsp Mayonnaise (see left)
2 tbsp Greek-style yogurt
1 tsp walnut oil
2 celery sticks
200g celeriac
2 Granny Smith apples
1 tsp apple cider vinegar
20 seedless red grapes, halved
a few leaves from the heart of the celery

First make the mayonnaise. This is easiest in an electric mixer with a whisk attachment, but if you don't have one it's still very simple by hand.

In a large bowl, whisk the egg yolks, mustards and vinegar until well combined. Slowly drizzle in the oils, still whisking continuously, until the mixture thickens and emulsifies. Don't rush this stage, or the oils won't incorporate with the egg yolks and the mayonnaise will split. If you don't have a spare set of hands around to hold the bowl steady, try resting it on a folded tea towel. Add the lemon juice and season to taste. If the mayonnaise is too thick, add a touch of warm water. It keeps for 2 weeks in the fridge.

Now for the salad. Preheat the oven to 170°C. Scatter the walnuts over a small baking tray and toast in the oven with a little salt for 7–8 minutes until golden, then leave to cool.

To make the dressing, whisk the mayonnaise, yogurt and walnut oil in a small bowl.

Peel the outside of the celery sticks with a vegetable peeler to remove the stringy fibres. Slice into thin crescents and place in a large mixing bowl.

Peel the celeriac and slice it into long thin julienne – about 2–3mm wide – and add to the bowl. Julienne the apples, too, leaving the skin on. (If you have a mandolin, use it to slice the celeriac and apple for a more uniform finish.) Toss the apples in the vinegar, to stop them turning brown, then mix with the celery and celeriac. Add the grapes, walnuts and celery leaves.

Fold the dressing into the salad, season and serve.

Orecchiette of summer vegetables, capers, preserved lemon & feta
Vernaccia di San Gimignano, Cesani

☞ *page 79*

SERVES 4

I cook this lovely simple Italian pasta at home often; it's great during the summer, so quick and easy and there is very little washing up. Tossing the hot pasta and vegetables over the cheese, olive oil and herbs ensures the herbs retain their delicate freshness and the olive oil's flavour remains true. Find a good-quality oil for this dish; it makes all the difference.

The feta and the olive oil emulsify into a beautiful creamy sauce and the classic Tuscan white wine, made from the Vernaccia grape, is a wonderful accompaniment to the pasta. The wine is full-bodied, but has an underlying backbone of crisp acidity that matches well with the fresh green herbs, lemon and capers in this recipe.

ALTERNATIVE WINE MATCHES

Assyrtiko, Jim Barry, Clare Valley ☞ *page 80*

100% Rolle Domaine de la Source, Bellet ☞ *page 82*

200g feta cheese
2 tbsp Parmesan cheese, finely grated
2 tbsp chopped mint leaves
2 tbsp chopped dill, any coarse stalks removed
2 tbsp capers in brine, drained
70ml extra virgin olive oil
2 Preserved lemons (see page 181)
600g broad beans, in their pods (to yield 150g beans)
4 asparagus spears, trimmed
12 fine green beans
100g sugar snap peas
500g orecchiette pasta
450g peas, in their pods (to yield 150g peas)
salt and pepper

Crumble the feta into a very large bowl. Add the Parmesan, mint, dill, capers and olive oil. Cut the preserved lemons into quarters and discard the flesh. Shred the rind and add it to the bowl.

Bring a small saucepan of water to the boil and season it with salt. Fill a bowl with cold water and add a handful of ice cubes. Drop the podded broad beans into the boiling water and blanch for 30 seconds. Strain, then plunge into the iced water. Pop the beans out of their bitter skins and set aside.

Remove the woody ends of the asparagus and cut them into 2.5cm lengths. Top and tail the beans and cut those in the same way. Halve the sugar snaps.

Fill a large saucepan with water, set it over a high heat and bring to the boil. Season generously with salt and add the orecchiette. You can follow the time specified on the packet, but I never trust it. Once the pasta is very nearly *al dente*, add the asparagus, beans and podded peas. Allow the vegetables to cook with the pasta for 30 seconds before adding the sugar snaps and broad beans. Cook for a further 30 seconds, then strain through a colander.

Shake off the excess water and toss the hot pasta and vegetables into the bowl with all the other ingredients. Season and fold everything together. The heat from the pasta will melt the Parmesan and (partially) the feta, creating a creamy emulsion with the oil. Serve immediately.

Chargrilled asparagus, romesco sauce, toasted almonds & fennel
Verdejo, Bodegas Naia, Rueda

☞ page 80

SERVES 4 AS A STARTER

In Catalonia in the spring, romesco sauce is served as a dip for calçots, a large spring onion celebrated in the region. Asparagus is the most celebrated UK spring vegetable, so we are showcasing these fat juicy spears instead. They are sublime cooked on the grill, but take care, as they cook deceptively quickly and you want them to char but still retain a little crunch.

We chose a Verdejo with a few years of bottle age with this dish; it's similar to Sauvignon Blanc, so makes a great match to asparagus. As time passes in the bottle, unlike some whites, Verdejo improves, gaining a rich texture and flavours of toasted almonds, making it a good match with romesco sauce. Flavours of grass and fennel come in on the finish, hence the garnish of fennel fronds.

ALTERNATIVE WINE MATCHES

Sauvignon Blanc, Casa Marín, San Antonio ☞ page 56

Riesling 'Les Jardins', Domaine André Ostertag, Alsace ☞ page 52

Château Pape-Clément Blanc, Pessac-Léognan ☞ page 60

FOR THE ROMESCO SAUCE

5 red peppers
120ml olive oil
60g flaked almonds
4 garlic cloves, finely chopped
2 red chillies, deseeded and finely chopped
½ tbsp tomato purée
1 tbsp Sherry vinegar
2 pinches of smoked paprika
pinch of cayenne pepper
salt and pepper

FOR THE ASPARAGUS

50g flaked almonds
600g thick asparagus spears
extra virgin olive oil
200g Romesco sauce (see left)
fennel fronds, to serve

Preheat the oven to 200°C.

Start with the sauce. Place the peppers in a roasting tray and drizzle a little of the olive oil over them. Season with salt and cover with foil. Bake for 30 minutes, then allow to cool for 15 minutes, still covered. Remove the ribs and seeds, then peel off the skins and chop the flesh roughly.

Reduce the oven temperature to 170°C.

Scatter the flaked almonds, both for the asparagus and for the sauce, separately on 2 baking trays, making sure you know which is which. Drizzle a little olive oil over, season with salt and place in the oven for 5–7 minutes until lightly toasted.

Preheat a heavy-based saucepan over a medium heat. Cook the roasted peppers, garlic and chillies in the remaining olive oil, stirring regularly, for 5 minutes, or until the garlic and chillies are softened. Season, then add the tomato purée, vinegar, paprika and cayenne and cook gently for a further 2 minutes. Remove from the heat and place in a food processor with the 60g of toasted almonds for the sauce, then pulse until you have a coarse sauce. Adjust the seasoning if required.

Prepare a barbecue until the coals are white and the flames have died down, or set a griddle pan over a high heat.

To prepare the asparagus, remove the woody ends and place the raw spears on a tray. Drizzle with a generous amount of olive oil and season with salt and pepper. Chargrill the asparagus on an area of your barbecue that is not too intensely hot, or in the griddle pan, adjusting the heat as needed. Keep turning the asparagus until its sufficiently charred. Once charred, the thick, juicy spears should still have a little bite. Serve straight from the grill with the warm romesco sauce, sprinkled with the 50g of toasted flaked almonds and the fennel fronds.

Domaine
BERTHET-BONDET
2011
2011
CHATEAU - CHALON
Appellation d'origine contrôlée

Champagne & white Alba truffle risotto Cuvée Dom Pérignon

☞ page 85

SERVES 6 AS A STARTER

The pungent aroma given off by white truffle shavings landing on hot creamy risotto cannot be equalled. Aged Champagne takes on a mushroom character, so the creamy risotto and rich truffle are perfect with it.

We use carnaroli rice, which is higher in starch, giving a creamier texture. It's also more forgiving. (Arborio is prone to overcooking.)

Evenly cooked *al dente* grains are what you're striving for, so it is important that your stock is hot and is added gradually. Stir constantly so the grains cook at the same rate.

At the Club we store our truffles in uncooked carnaroli rice. This protects the truffles by keeping them in a dry atmosphere, while the truffles impart flavour to the rice. We then use the rice for risotto. If you store truffles with eggs, the same happens. Try scrambling the eggs and shaving a little truffle over the top… delicious!

ALTERNATIVE WINE MATCHES

Old Champagne, 25+ years
☞ page 85

FOR THE STOCK

1 onion, chopped
1 leek, white part only, chopped
3 celery sticks, chopped
3 garlic cloves, chopped
10 thyme sprigs
1 bay leaf
50ml extra virgin olive oil
2kg button mushrooms, finely sliced
2.5 litres water
salt
palmful of white peppercorns

FOR THE RISOTTO

80g unsalted butter
2 tbsp extra virgin olive oil
2 large shallots, finely chopped
300g carnaroli rice
180ml Champagne
50ml double cream
100g Parmesan cheese, finely grated, plus more to serve
white truffle oil
freshly ground white pepper
40g white Alba truffle, to serve

Make the stock in a large, heavy-based saucepan over a medium heat. Cook the onion, leek, celery, garlic, thyme and bay leaf gently in the olive oil until they soften. Add the sliced mushrooms and season with salt. Cook gently for 5 minutes, or until the mushrooms have released their water and the liquid is starting to reduce. Add the measured water and peppercorns, increase the heat and bring to the boil, then reduce the heat to a gentle simmer. Simmer for 30–40 minutes or so, skimming the surface. Strain through a sieve. (The stock will keep in the fridge for 5 days, or can be frozen.) Bring the stock to the boil, then set it over a medium-low heat at the back of the stove.

In a large, heavy-based saucepan over a medium heat, melt half the butter with the olive oil and add the shallots. Cook for a few minutes until soft and translucent. Add the rice and season with a few pinches of salt. Seasoning at this stage means that, when the wine and stock are added, they will absorb into the rice, taking the salt with them. Stir for 2 minutes, until the rice starts to give off a subtle toasted aroma.

Add half the Champagne and continue to stir until it has been absorbed into the rice. This will happen quickly. Gradually add the hot stock a ladle at a time, stirring constantly and ensuring each addition is fully absorbed by the rice before adding the next. Taste the risotto regularly, so you don't go past the *al dente* stage.

Just before you are there, add the remaining butter, the cream and the Parmesan, stirring until it all emulsifies with the stock. Add the rest of the Champagne and a few drops of white truffle oil; be cautious with the oil, as a little goes a long way. Finally, adjust the seasoning with salt and white pepper and check the risotto has the correct consistency: it should feel like a loose creamy porridge and, when spooning it on to the plate, it should roll off the spoon and fall gently, spreading slightly under its own weight. If it's too dry, add a little more stock.

Shave the truffle over the plates at the table, and offer Parmesan to serve.

Risotto primavera with robiola cheese
Sauvignon Blanc 'Saurint', Miani, Friuli

☞ *page 58*

SERVES 6 AS A STARTER

I would never usually put green peppers into a risotto, but one of the unique flavour notes in Sauvignon Blanc comes from aromatic compounds called pyrazines, which are also found in green peppers. Sauvignon Blanc has citrus and herbaceous flavours, too, so a fistful of chervil and mint and a squeeze of lemon juice added at the end make this a great marriage.

Goat's cheese is also a great match for Sauvignon Blanc and I have chosen robiola. Although it is made with a mixture of cow's, sheep's and goat's milks, it captures that definitive tangy and mildly sour flavour you find in a typical goat's cheese. It also comes from Friuli in the north, where some of the best examples of Italian Sauvignon Blanc are produced.

ALTERNATIVE WINE MATCHES

Riesling 'Hochäcker', Weingut Nigl, Kremstal
☞ *page 50*
Riesling Trocken, Weingut Wittmann, Rheinhessen
☞ *page 52*
Toscana Bianco, Ornellaia, Tuscany
☞ *page 58*

6 asparagus spears
120g fine green beans
4 tbsp extra virgin olive oil
½ green pepper, deseeded and cut into 1cm cubes
½ courgette, deseeded and cut into 1cm cubes
about 1 litre vegetable stock (home-made is best here)
80g unsalted butter
2 large shallots, finely chopped
400g carnaroli rice
150ml white wine
40ml double cream
100g Parmesan cheese, finely grated, plus more to serve
150g frozen peas, defrosted
150g frozen broad beans, defrosted, bitter skins peeled off
juice of ½ lemon
3 tbsp chopped chervil or dill leaves
1 tbsp chopped mint leaves
250g robiola cheese
salt and pepper

Bring a large saucepan of salted water to the boil over a high heat.

Remove the woody ends from the asparagus spears and slice them into 2.5cm batons. Top and tail the green beans and cut these also into 2.5cm batons. Blanch the asparagus and beans in the boiling water for 1 minute, then drain and plunge them into iced water to retain their colour. Once cold, remove from the water and set aside.

Heat half the olive oil in a frying pan over a medium heat. Add the green pepper and courgette and season. Cook gently for 2–3 minutes, then remove them from the pan on to kitchen paper and allow to cool.

Bring the vegetable stock to the boil, then keep it hot on the stove.

In a large heavy-based saucepan over a medium heat, melt 30g of the butter with the remaining olive oil and add the shallots. Cook for a few minutes until soft and translucent. Add the rice and season with a few pinches of salt. Stir constantly for 2 minutes or so until the rice starts to give off a subtle toasted aroma. Add the wine and stir until it has been absorbed.

Gradually add the hot stock, a ladle at a time; it is very important that your stock is hot and that it's added gradually. Stir the risotto constantly so the grains cook at the same rate. If some grains get stuck on the side of the pan, push them back in. Ensure each addition of stock is fully absorbed before adding the next and taste the risotto regularly so you don't go past *al dente*.

Just before you are there, add the rest of the butter, the cream and the Parmesan, stirring until it all emulsifies with the stock. Add all the vegetables, adjust the seasoning and squeeze in the lemon juice. Check your risotto has the correct consistency: it should feel like a loose creamy porridge and roll off the spoon and fall gently, spreading slightly under its own weight. If it's too dry, add a little more stock.

Add the chervil and mint at the last minute, so they hold their fresh flavour. Serve immediately, with a few nuggets of robiola cheese.

Black rice & squash salad, quinoa, cumin, orange & pomegranate
Semillon 'La Colline', Raised by Wolves, Franschhoek

☞ pages 76 & 83

SERVES 4

Made in the Franschhoek ('French corner') region of South Africa, this is an orange wine that has been left on its skins for a long time; essentially it is a white wine made like a red wine. (Usually, the skins in white wine are removed early on.) This wine therefore has a pale orange-rosé colour, and a richness that works really well with the squash and dark rice here.

This delicious vegan salad presents beautifully. The black rice serves as a dramatic backdrop studded with orange segments, squash and ruby red pomegranate seeds. I love using sunflower and pumpkin seeds in salads. They are very healthy and add such a delightful crunch and an additional nutty flavour.

ALTERNATIVE WINE MATCHES

Rkatsiteli, Pheasant's Tears, Kakheti, Georgia
☞ page 83

'Libiamo Field Blend', Libiamo, Millton, Gisborne
☞ page 83

100g black rice
100g red quinoa
1 butternut squash
80g pumpkin seeds
80g sunflower seeds
80ml olive oil
2 tsp cumin seeds
1 large shallot, finely chopped
2 red chillies, deseeded and finely chopped
400ml freshly squeezed orange juice
2 tsp wholegrain mustard
3 tbsp maple syrup
3 spring onions, finely sliced
handful of coriander leaves, plus coriander sprigs to serve
seeds from 1 pomegranate
2 oranges, segmented
salt and pepper

Bring a saucepan of lightly salted water to the boil over a high heat. Place the black rice into a sieve and give it a good rinse. Put the rice in the boiling water, return to the boil, then reduce the heat to a simmer and cook until tender (15–20 minutes). Strain the rice and run it under cold water to cool it down. Place the sieve over the saucepan and leave it to drain. Prepare and cook the quinoa in the same way, it will take 10–12 minutes.

Peel and deseed the squash, then chop it into 1cm cubes.

Preheat the oven to 180°C.

Spread the pumpkin and sunflower seeds out on a baking tray and drizzle with a little olive oil. Season with salt and mix together so they have a shiny coating of oil. Spread the cumin seeds out on a second, smaller baking tray.

Put both trays into the oven and toast for 5–7 minutes or until they turn golden. You'll need to give the pumpkin and sunflower seeds a stir halfway through, so they cook evenly. Once toasted, pull them all out of the oven to cool.

Place a heavy-based saucepan over a medium heat and cook the shallot, chillies and toasted cumin seeds in the remaining olive oil until the shallots are translucent but without colour.

Add the chopped squash, orange juice, mustard and maple syrup, season with salt and pepper and cook, stirring regularly, until the squash is *al dente*. As the squash is cooking, the orange juice will reduce and create an emulsion. Once the squash is cooked, remove the pan from the heat and allow to cool to room temperature.

In a large bowl, fold the rice and quinoa together. Add the toasted sunflower and pumpkin seeds, spring onions, coriander leaves and squash. Fold it all together and season with salt and pepper.

Finally, fold in most of the pomegranate seeds and orange segments, then scatter the remainder over the top of the salad with the coriander sprigs.

RAISED
BY
WOLVES

Griddled giant puffball, sautéed wild mushrooms, spelt & cavolo nero
Etna Rosso 'Feudo di Mezzo', Girolamo Russo

☞ *page 121*

SERVES 4

Giant puffball mushrooms are fairly prolific during late summer and early autumn. They resemble a football and are hard to miss. Keep your eyes peeled for them during your weekend stroll in the countryside, as they are a real treat. They are best when still young. (As they mature, the bright white flesh on the inside starts to turn yellow and they aren't nearly as good.) They have a very delicate flavour and a lovely soft, creamy texture.

We have paired this dish with the Sicilian Nerello Mascalese grape variety from Mount Etna, which has flavour notes of resinous herbs, hence the echo in the dish of oregano or marjoram. (A little thyme would work well, too.) Don't hold back with the black pepper, the mushrooms love it and so does the wine.

ALTERNATIVE WINE MATCHES

Sciaccarellu 'Rouge Frais Impérial', Domaine Comte Abatucci, Corsica ☞ *page 121*

Merlot, Leonetti Cellar, Walla Walla, Washington ☞ *page 116*

150g pearled spelt, or pearled barley
200g cavolo nero, ribs stripped out, leaves chopped
400g wild mushrooms (we used porcini, *pied du mouton*, chanterelles and girolles)
1 giant puffball mushroom
100ml extra virgin olive oil
2 garlic cloves, finely chopped
1 tbsp chopped oregano or marjoram leaves
salt and pepper

Cook the spelt in well-salted boiling water for 15–20 minutes, until it's cooked but still has a little bite to it. Strain through a sieve and set aside.

Bring a saucepan of water to the boil and season with a good handful of salt. Fill a bowl with water and add a few ice cubes. Blanch the cavolo nero in the boiling water for 30 seconds, then strain and plunge into the iced water, so it keeps its vibrant green colour. Once cold, drain well and set aside.

If the wild mushrooms are dirty, give the stalks a good scrape with a paring knife and then rub off any dirt or grit with a clean damp cloth. Cut the larger mushrooms into bite-sized pieces and leave the smaller ones whole.

Preheat the oven to 100°C.

Slice 4 discs of puffball about 2cm thick and season with salt and pepper. Preheat a large griddle pan over a medium-high heat and drizzle on about half the oil. Mark the puffball with a criss-cross pattern in the griddle pan. (You may need to do this in batches, depending on the size of your pan.) Place the slices of puffball into the low oven to keep warm.

Set a large frying pan over a medium-high heat and add the remaining olive oil. Add the larger wild mushrooms to the pan with the garlic and season them. If you are using a very delicate mushroom, such as a chanterelle, these should be added right at the end, so they cook through but still hold their shape. Toss the mushrooms in the pan until they are cooked. (Be careful not to burn the garlic, or it will ruin the dish.) Add the oregano or marjoram, spelt and cavolo nero. Give the pan a toss and cook until all is warmed though. Taste and adjust the seasoning, if required.

Place a disc of puffball on each of 4 warmed plates and spoon over the wild mushrooms, spelt and cavolo nero.

Feudo 2012

Malva pudding, Amarula sauce, vanilla ice cream
Vin de Constance, Klein Constantia

☞ page 124

MAKES 12

In 2016, our South African assistant head sommelier and I ran a dinner celebrating South African wines. Not having a vast knowledge of the country's food, I called upon a good South African friend of mine, Sarah Houghting, a great all-rounder accomplished at desserts. Sarah gave me this recipe, passed on to her by her Aunt Colleen, a talented baker. We had great feedback, so over the cooler months I put it on our regular menu. Cheers Sarah (and Colleen)!

Amarula is a creamy South African liqueur made from the yellow fruit of the Marula tree, a favourite snack for elephants that are drawn by the exotic fragrance, travelling miles for a taste.

Vin de Constance is a wine with more than 300 years of history. Its rich honeyed and tropical flavours are great with this rich, buttery dessert.

ALTERNATIVE WINE MATCHES

'T' Noble Late Harvest, Ken Forrester, Stellenbosch ☞ *page 64*

Chenin Blanc 'Straw Wine', Mullineux & Leeu, Swartland ☞ *page 64*

FOR THE PUDDING

- 60g unsalted butter, softened, plus more for the tin
- 500g plain flour, plus more to dust
- 2 eggs
- 500g caster sugar
- 30g apricot jam
- 2 tsp bicarbonate of soda
- 500ml whole milk
- ½ tsp salt
- 2 tsp malt vinegar
- Vanilla ice cream, to serve (see page 342)

FOR THE SAUCE

- 400ml double cream
- 250g caster sugar
- 250g unsalted butter
- 160ml Amarula liqueur

Preheat the oven to 180°C. Butter a deep 30 x 25cm square cake tin, or the equivalent, then dust it with flour.

It's best to use an electric mixer to make this, but it is also achievable by hand, if a lot harder work. In a large mixing bowl, whisk the eggs and sugar together until light and fluffy. Add the apricot jam and softened butter and continue whisking to combine thoroughly. Sift the flour and bicarbonate of soda and mix it into the egg mixture. Pour in the milk slowly, until it is all incorporated and the mixture is smooth. Finally, mix in the salt and vinegar.

Give the tin a couple of taps over the sink to release any excess flour. Pour the mixture into the prepared tin and cover it with foil, then place on the middle shelf of the oven and bake for 50 minutes.

Meanwhile, prepare the sauce. In a heavy-based saucepan over a medium heat, bring the cream, sugar and butter to the boil. Reduce the heat to a simmer until the sauce emulsifies and thickens slightly; this should take 4–5 minutes. Remove from the heat and whisk in the Amarula.

Once the 50 minutes has elapsed, remove the foil and continue to bake the pudding for another 10 minutes, until golden brown. To test if it's cooked in the middle, push the blade of a small knife or a skewer into the centre. If it comes out clean, the pudding is ready. When the pudding comes out of the oven, while it's still hot, trickle 300ml of the sauce over the top of it. The sauce will seep into the pudding, making it deliciously moist.

Allow to cool in the tin for 30 minutes before turning out carefully on to a wire cooling rack. Once cool, trim the edges from the pudding and slice off the number of portions you intend to serve. Whatever is left can be stored in a sealed container in the fridge for up to 4 days.

Just before serving, place the pudding portions into a microwaveable container and microwave until hot. Serve in a bowl, pouring the hot Amarula sauce over generously. Finish with a ball of vanilla ice cream.

Pavlova, passion fruit cream & mango
Riesling TBA 'Forster Ungeheuer', Weingut Reichsrat von Buhl, Pfalz

☞ *page 123*

SERVES 6

There's a friendly rivalry between New Zealand and Australia regarding the origins of the pavlova, but having looked into it I've found that Keith Money, biographer of the ballerina Anna Pavlova, wrote that a chef in Wellington, New Zealand, created this dessert when she visited in 1926 on her world tour. (I'm not biased at all!)

This recipe makes 10 pavlovas, but it's tricky to make a smaller quantity of meringue, and any extras will keep for a few days in an airtight container in a cool, dark, dry cupboard.

Trockenbeerenauslese – thankfully usually known as TBA – is a heavily botrytised wine that takes on an incredible deep and rich tropical fruit flavour while retaining its high acidity. The tartness of passion fruit is a great match to a sweet Riesling such as this.

ALTERNATIVE WINE MATCHES

Sauvignon Blanc 'Noble', Amisfield, Central Otago ☞ *page 61*

TBA 'Zwischen den Seen No. 4', Kracher, Burgenland ☞ *page 123*

TBA 'Brauneberger Juffer Sonnenuhr', Fritz Haag, Mosel ☞ *page 123*

6 medium egg whites
340g caster sugar
1 tsp white wine vinegar
1 tbsp cornflour
500ml passion fruit purée
500ml whipping cream
80g icing sugar
10 passion fruits
3 ripe mangos

There are certain rules you must follow when making meringue. Make sure your equipment, the mixing bowl and whisk are spotlessly clean, dry and free from any grease. It's also important your egg whites have not been contaminated with any yolk. It's best to use an electric mixer for this; mixing meringue by hand is far too much of a work out.

Place the egg whites into a mixing bowl and whisk on high speed until they reach soft peak stage, but no further. Slowly add the caster sugar in 4 stages over about 5 minutes. As the sugar slowly dissolves into the egg whites, they will become glossy and very stiff. Taste the raw meringue to ensure there are no undissolved sugar granules before whisking in the vinegar and cornflour.

Preheat the oven to 160°C.

Using 2 large serving spoons, quenelle the raw meringue on to a baking tray covered with greaseproof baking parchment. Put on the middle shelf of the oven and immediately reduce the oven temperature to 100°C. Bake for 1 hour. Without opening the door, turn off the oven and allow the meringues to cool inside for another hour. Remove from the oven and carefully transfer to a wire rack to cool completely. Be careful, they are very fragile. Once totally cooled, transfer to an airtight plastic container until ready to use. It is important the container is sealed, as any humidity will soften the crust of the pavlovas and they will be ruined.

To make the passion fruit cream, place a saucepan over a high heat. Pour in the passion fruit purée and reduce it until you're left with about 80ml of thick syrup. Remove from the heat and allow to cool completely. Once the passion fruit syrup has cooled, place it in a mixing bowl with the whipping cream, icing sugar and the seeds and pulp of 3 of the passion fruits. Whip the cream until you reach the soft peak stage, but do not over-whip.

Carve the mango from its large stone and then into 1cm slices lengthways. With a small knife, remove the skin from each slice.

To serve, 'glue' each pavlova to its plate with a little passion fruit cream. Using the handle of a spoon, break a hole in the top of each, exposing the soft marshmallowy centre. Place a few slices of mango inside so they're protruding from the hole. Top with a generous dollop of passion fruit cream and a few more slices of mango. Finally cut the remaining passion fruits in half and squeeze the seeds and pulp over each pavlova.

Poached white peaches with zabaglione & amaretti Zibibbo 'Ben Ryé', Donnafugata, Passito di Pantelleria, Sicily

☞ page 124

SERVES 6

I like to make my zabaglione using a little soft brown sugar, as I find it complements the Marsala. It is traditionally made with only Marsala, but I have substituted some of it for the Zibibbo di Pantellaria with which we have paired the dish. Wow, what a wine, like the nectar of exquisitely ripe stone fruit; truly a wondrous experience. What a combination. Just try it, and thank us later.

In the pudding, the peaches are the stars of the show alongside the neutral richness of the zabaglione, while the amaretti add texture and are a great flavour with the peaches. Semi-ripe peaches are fine for poaching, as anything too soft will not give up its stone. If you're at the market and find the apricots look better than the peaches, go with those instead; they work just as well with the Zibibbo.

ALTERNATIVE WINE MATCHES

Viognier 'La Linda', Bodega Luigi Bosca, Mendoza ☞ page 83

Zibibbo 'Integer', Marco De Bartoli, Sicily ☞ page 124

FOR THE POACHED PEACHES

- 500ml water
- 500g granulated sugar
- juice of ½ lemon
- 1 vanilla pod, split in half, seeds scraped out
- 6 semi-ripe peaches, ideally white peaches, halved and pitted

FOR THE ZABAGLIONE

- 5 medium egg yolks
- 3 tbsp caster sugar
- 2 tbsp soft brown sugar
- 3 tbsp Marsala
- 2 tbsp Zibibbo di Pantellaria
- 6 crunchy amaretti biscuits

To prepare the peaches, bring the measured water to the boil in a saucepan with the sugar, lemon juice and vanilla seeds, then reduce the temperature to a simmer. Add the peach halves and simmer gently until they are soft. The cooking time depends on how ripe they are, but they shouldn't take longer than 3–5 minutes.

Using a slotted spoon, carefully remove the peaches from the syrup and lay them on a tray to cool. Once cool, remove and discard the skins from the peaches and store the fruits in their poaching syrup in the fridge until required. The peaches are best poached on the day of serving, as they discolour if left overnight.

Start preparing the zabaglione just before you want to serve it. It's not one of those desserts you can make in advance and store in the fridge. You will need a stainless-steel bowl that fits over a saucepan of simmering water, without touching the water, to avoid direct heat. Bring a large saucepan about one-quarter filled with water to the boil, then reduce the heat to a very gentle simmer.

Place the egg yolks, caster sugar, brown sugar, Marsala and Zibibbo di Pantellaria into the bowl and whisk together. Place the bowl over the saucepan and whisk vigorously, incorporating air and cooking the eggs gently at the same time. If you feel the mixture is getting too hot and may scramble, remove it from the heat and keep whisking. Persevere with the whisking until the zabaglione has thickened and quadrupled in volume.

To serve, place 2 peach halves into 6 stemmed pudding glasses. Spoon over the zabaglione and crumble an amaretti biscuit over each.

Pannacotta with macerated strawberries, lime & basil
Pink Moscato, Stella Bella, Margaret River

☞ page 123

SERVES 6

A fun pairing, in which pink moscato and strawberries work in perfect harmony. Chefs welcome strawberries with open arms when they come in season and this dessert goes on the menu in late spring when the first of them come in. At the beginning of the season they are a bit sharp, so need a bit of help, and macerating them transforms them into something special. The sugar and lime juice create a balanced sauce with a slight acidity, which works well with the wine.

A pannacotta should be light, and contain just enough gelatine to hold its own weight without collapsing, so it almost melts in the mouth.

You will need either 6 small plastic pudding basins, or tea cups will do the trick. Any leftover pannacottas will keep in the fridge for up to 4 days.

ALTERNATIVE WINE MATCHES

Moscato d'Asti 'Bricco Quaglia', La Spinetta, Piedmont *☞ page 123*

Pink Moscato, Innocent Bystander, Yarra Valley *☞ page 123*

Lambrusco Rosso 'Vecchia Modena', Cleto Chiarli, Emilia Romagna, Italy *☞ page 120*

FOR THE PANNACOTTA

6g gelatine leaves (gold strength)
1 vanilla pod
375ml double cream
375ml milk
100g caster sugar
a little vegetable oil

FOR THE STRAWBERRIES

400g strawberries
60g caster sugar
finely grated zest of 1 lime and the juice of 2 limes
6 basil leaves, plus basil cress or small leaves to serve

Soak the gelatine leaves in a small bowl of cold water to soften them.

Split the vanilla pod lengthways with a small sharp knife and scrape out the tiny black seeds with the tip.

Set a large, heavy-based saucepan over a medium heat and pour in the cream, milk, sugar and vanilla seeds. To extract the maximum flavour from the vanilla, add the scraped-out pod halves to the pan, too. Heat gently, stirring until the sugar has dissolved.

Squeeze the water out of the gelatine. Remove the saucepan from the heat and stir in the softened gelatine until it, too, has dissolved. Strain through a fine-meshed sieve into a bowl and discard the spent vanilla pod halves.

Fill a larger bowl with iced water and place the smaller bowl containing the pannacotta mixture into it to cool. As it cools, stir regularly until it starts to thicken. This is important as, when the mixture is hot and thin, all the vanilla seeds drop to the bottom, but as it cools and thickens, the tiny seeds stay suspended throughout the pannacotta.

Meanwhile, rub a little vegetable oil on the inside of 6 pudding basins or tea cups and place them in the freezer to cool. Pour the pannacotta mixture into the moulds and place them into the fridge to set for 3–4 hours.

About 45 minutes before serving, prepare the strawberries. Hull them with a small sharp knife and cut each in half or quarters, depending on size. Place in a bowl and dust them with the sugar, lime zest and juice. Slice the basil into fine strips and sprinkle it in. Gently fold all the ingredients together, cover and place it in a warm place, such as a sunny windowsill. The sugar will draw juice from the strawberries. Allow to macerate for 20 minutes, then uncover and put them in a cool part of the kitchen.

Removing the pannacottas from their moulds can be a little tricky. Hold the mould in one hand, tipping it to one side and – with the index finger of the other hand – pull the pannacotta away from the side of the mould at the top edge. Once one side has been released, slowly roll the mould and let gravity do the rest.

Tip the pannacottas out into serving bowls and spoon the berries and their juices around. Sprinkle with basil cress or small basil leaves and serve.

Chocolate & honeycomb semifreddo
Banyuls 'Quintessence', Coume del Mas, Roussillon

☞ page 127

SERVES UP TO 12

This is the perfect dessert if you love ice cream but don't own an ice-cream maker. It's so easy to prepare and serve, and incredibly moreish. Semifreddo, in this case, basically means 'semi-frozen', so it's vital you let it soften slightly on the plate before serving. This recipe makes 1.5 litres of semifreddo, so you will have plenty left in the freezer to enjoy on another occasion; it will happily keep in there for up to three months.

Banyuls, in the Roussillon area of southern France, is the French equivalent to Port: rich and deep with plenty of sweetness and dark berry fruit. Chocolate is a tricky thing to match (see page 41), as it's full of flavour and coats the mouth, but this style of fortified wine can work well.

ALTERNATIVE WINE MATCHES

Black Muscat 'Elysium', Quady Winery, California ☞ page 123

Recioto della Valpolicella Classico, Giuseppe Quintarelli, Veneto ☞ page 121 & 123

FOR THE HONEYCOMB

- 200g caster sugar
- 50ml water
- 1 tsp liquid glucose
- 1 tsp bicarbonate of soda

FOR THE SEMIFREDDO

- 950ml double cream
- 300g 70% cocoa solids chocolate buttons
- 100g honey
- 6 egg yolks
- 50g caster sugar

Line a baking tray with silicon paper.

For the honeycomb, place the sugar, measured water and glucose in a heavy-based saucepan. Set over a high heat, melt the sugar and boil until it reaches a light caramel. Remove from the heat and stir in the bicarbonate of soda: be careful, when it hits the caramel it will froth violently.

Quickly pour the molten honeycomb on to the prepared tray and spread it out to 1cm thick with a palette knife. Allow to cool completely and harden. Once cool and set, break off a few shards of honeycomb to garnish the semifreddo and chop the rest into rough 1cm nuggets. Store in an airtight container in a cool dry cupboard until ready to use.

To make the semifreddo, bring 200g of the double cream to the boil in a heavy-based saucepan over a medium heat. Remove from the heat and immediately stir in the chocolate, until completely melted. (Set over a very low heat, stirring constantly, if the chocolate doesn't melt entirely.) Pour the smooth mixture into a large bowl, cover with cling film and set aside.

In a heavy-based saucepan over a medium heat, gently heat the remaining cream and the honey until it almost reaches boiling point. Stir occasionally to ensure it doesn't catch on the pan.

In a clean, dry mixing bowl, whisk the egg yolks and sugar until they start to lighten in colour. Slowly pour the hot honey mixture over, whisking quickly so it doesn't scramble, then return the whole mixture to the saucepan. Set over a very low heat and cook, stirring constantly, until it starts to thicken slightly and coats the back of the spoon. Be patient; don't be tempted to increase the temperature, or you run the risk of scrambling the custard.

Pass the custard through a sieve into the chocolate mixture and stir gently. Fold in the chopped honeycomb and pour into a loaf tin. Place in the freezer to set. This will take a few hours, so it's best to prepare it the day before you would like to serve it, to ensure it is properly frozen.

When ready to serve, remove the semifreddo from the freezer and suspend in a sink of hot water for a couple of seconds, to release it from the tin. Tip it on to a cutting board and, using a hot knife, cut into slices. Place the slices on serving plates and allow to soften for a few minutes. Stab a shard of honeycomb into the middle of each slice and serve immediately.

Black Forest trifle
Tannat 'Alcyone', Viñedo de los Vientos, Uruguay

☞ page 126

SERVES 8

Uruguay makes fantastic red wines from the Tannat grape (see page 121), which are normally deep, full-bodied and tannic, but this is a dessert wine. The winemaker aromatises it to a secret recipe and then fortifies it in a similar way to Marsala (a nod to his Italian ancestry). The wine has deep, black kirsch cherry flavours, chocolate, coffee and vanilla bean. We've twisted the flavours in this pudding to match those in the delicious Tannat.

Give yourself plenty of time to prepare this dessert, as there are a few stages involved, but you can assemble the trifles a day in advance and store, covered, in the fridge. All that is left to do before serving is whip the cream and sprinkle the chocolate. Which gives you more time with your guests and a glass of wine in your hand!

ALTERNATIVE WINE MATCHES

Mavrodaphne 'Chortais', Mercouri Estate, Peloponnese ☞ *page 121*

Zinfandel Late Harvest 'Aida Estate', Vineyard 29, Napa ☞ *page 121*

FOR THE CHERRIES AND JELLY
- 200ml Port
- 350ml red wine
- 200g granulated sugar
- 2 star anise
- ½ vanilla pod, seeds scraped out
- 500g pitted cherries
- 10g gelatine leaves (gold strength)

FOR THE COFFEE SPONGE
- 4 eggs
- 125g caster sugar
- 125g plain flour, sifted
- 2 tbsp instant coffee
- 2 tbsp boiling water

FOR THE CHOCOLATE CUSTARD
- 300ml double cream
- 300ml milk
- ½ vanilla pod, seeds scraped out
- 7 egg yolks
- 120g caster sugar
- 1 tbsp cocoa powder
- 1½ tbsp cornflour

TO SERVE
- 300ml whipping cream
- ½ vanilla pod, seeds scraped out
- 2 tbsp icing sugar
- 100g 70% cocoa solids chocolate

For the cherries, pour the Port and wine into a saucepan. Add the sugar, star anise, vanilla seeds and scraped-out pod and bring to the boil. Drop in the cherries, return to the boil, then reduce the heat to a simmer. Simmer for 2 minutes, then allow the cherries to cool in the liquor.

Now make the sponge. Preheat the oven to 170°C. In a bowl or electric mixer, whisk the eggs and sugar until tripled in volume, light and fluffy. Sift the flour and gently fold it in. Dissolve the coffee in a cup with the boiling water, then fold it in. Line a baking tray with baking parchment and spread the batter out evenly 2cm thick. Bake for 6–8 minutes, then cool on a wire rack. Once cooled, using a sharp serrated knife, cut into 2cm cubes. Place a few cubes into the bottom of 8 dessert coupes, or other glasses.

For the jelly, soak the gelatine leaves in cold water for 5 minutes, until soft. Bring 700ml of the strained cherry liquor to the boil, then remove from the heat. Drain the gelatine well, then add it to the liquor and stir to dissolve (it takes a few seconds). Pass through a sieve, then pour enough into each glass to just cover the sponge. Leave to set in the fridge for at least 3 hours.

For the custard, put the cream, milk, vanilla pod and seeds into a saucepan and bring to the boil. Remove from the heat. In a bowl, whisk the egg yolks, sugar, cocoa powder and cornflour. Remove the vanilla pod from the cream and gradually whisk it into the egg mixture. Return to the pan and cook over a low heat, stirring until it thickens. Strain through a sieve into a bowl and cover with a sheet of baking parchment so a skin doesn't form. Cool.

Using a piping bag, pipe a layer of custard over the set jelly. Place 5 poached cherries into each glass on top of the custard. Just before serving, whip the cream in a large bowl with the vanilla seeds and icing sugar. Using a star nozzle, pipe the whipped cream on to the trifles. Top with a generous sprinkling of grated chocolate and serve straight away.

Port-poached pear, whipped Stilton, honeyed walnuts Quinta do Noval, 40-year Tawny Port

☞ *page 127*

SERVES 8

Tawny Port is aged for a long time in barrels, losing its colour and oxidising to a brownish tone while taking on its nutty, orange rind, caramelised flavour. It is traditionally matched with Stilton, because of the opposing flavours of saltiness and sweetness (see page 39). Honey-roast walnuts accentuate the Madeirised nature of the wine and the poached pears in orange and spices make a great – but not too rich or sweet – dessert.

The cooking time for the pears can vary greatly depending how ripe they are. It's a good idea to cook them a day or so in advance, making sure they're soft before you take them off the heat. A good poached pear should be soft enough to cut using a spoon. The longer they spend in the cooking liquor, the deeper red they become.

ALTERNATIVE WINE MATCHES

Commandaría 'St John', Keo, Cyprus
☞ *page 123*

Occhio di Pernice Vin Santo di Montepulciano, Avignonesi, Tuscany ☞ *page 124*

600ml red wine
600ml Port
300g granulated sugar
pared zest of ¼ orange
3 cloves
¼ cinnamon stick
½ vanilla pod

8 Williams pears
125g Stilton cheese
450ml whipping cream
200g walnut halves
100g clear honey

Place the red wine, Port, sugar, orange zest, cloves, cinnamon and vanilla into a heavy-based saucepan. Peel the pears and cut a thin slice from the base of each so they can stand upright. Using a melon baller, core the pears. (In order to get the whole core, you will need to remove at least 2 balls.) Place the peeled, cored pears in the wine and set over a high heat. Bring to the boil, then reduce the heat to a gentle simmer. Once the pears are softly poached (10–15 minutes, but check they're soft first), remove them from the heat and allow to cool in the liquor, then chill.

To make the Stilton cream, crumble the Stilton into a blender and add 150ml of the whipping cream. Very quickly blend into a paste, then stop the blender. Add the remaining cream and blend for 10 seconds, so it is slightly whipped but not firm. Remove from the blender and pass it through a sieve into a large bowl. Finish whipping it to semi-firm by hand, as you have more control. Spoon it into a shallow container or tray to a depth of 5cm.

Preheat the oven to 170°C.

Place the walnuts on a baking tray and toast in the oven for 7–8 minutes until golden. Remove them from the oven, drizzle half the honey over, then cook for a further 2–3 minutes until the honey starts to caramelise. Place into a bowl to cool. Mix them around so they have a good coating of honey.

To serve, place the poached pears in a saucepan with their cooking liquor. Set over a medium-low heat and bring the pears to a warm temperature. Stand the pears upright on the plates.

To serve the Stilton cream, heat a dessertspoon under a hot tap. Drag the hot spoon across the cream to form an attractive scoop. (This is more difficult than it sounds, but you can use a piping bag and nozzle instead.) Spoon on the walnuts and drizzle the remaining honey over the cream to sweeten it.

Sticky date pudding, salted toffee sauce, walnut praline & clotted cream
Rutherglen Muscat, Stanton & Killeen, Victoria

☞ *page 123*

SERVES UP TO 12

I've been making this delicious, rich, comforting pudding for more than 20 years. When Ronan and I tasted the Australian Muscat we have paired with it, we were overwhelmed by its rich flavour of dates, so it was an obvious choice for a match.

But this combination is not for the faint hearted. It is a sugar attack, of the most delicious kind. Dates and walnuts are the main flavours of this wine, and match perfectly. It might seem curious to us these days, but this is in fact what most Australian wine was like before the 1950s.

You will need a deep 30 x 25cm cake tin, or the equivalent.

ALTERNATIVE WINE MATCHES

Pedro Ximénez 'de Añada', Bodegas Alvear, Montilla-Moriles ☞ *page 123*

Boal Reserva Vintage, D'Oliveiras, Madeira ☞ *page 126*

FOR THE WALNUT PRALINE
50g walnuts
150g caster sugar
50ml cold water

FOR THE PUDDING
120g softened unsalted butter, plus more for the tin
340g plain flour, plus more for the tin
600ml water
340g pitted dates
2 tsp bicarbonate of soda
340g caster sugar
4 eggs
2 tsp baking powder
1 tsp vanilla extract
clotted cream, to serve

FOR THE TOFFEE SAUCE
150g caster sugar
50ml water
150ml double cream
20g unsalted butter
couple of pinches of salt

Start with the praline. Preheat the oven to 180°C. Place the nuts on an oven tray and toast in the oven for 7–8 minutes until golden. Remove from the oven and lay on a heatproof tray lined with baking parchment. Place the sugar and measured water in a small clean saucepan and, over a high heat, bring to the boil. Boil rapidly until the sugar turns into a dark caramel. Pour over the nuts and leave for 2 hours, until it sets to a hard toffee. Break up into pieces and pulse it in a food processor into coarse crumbs. Set aside.

For the pudding, preheat the oven to 160°C. Butter the cake tin, then dust with flour. Give the tin a couple of taps over the sink to remove any excess. Bring the measured water to the boil in a saucepan. Add the dates and simmer for a couple of minutes until they soften. Mix in the bicarb, leave for 10 minutes, then blend with a stick blender to break up large pieces.

Beat the butter and sugar until light and fluffy. Add the eggs, one at a time, mixing well after each addition. Sift the flour and baking powder together then stir them in with the date mixture and vanilla extract. It will seem a little wet, but rest assured, all will be fine. Pour into the tin, place in the middle of the oven and bake for 35 minutes, or until a knife emerges clean. Allow to cool in the tin for 30 minutes, then turn out carefully on to a wire cooling rack. Slice off the number of portions you intend to serve.

Meanwhile, make the toffee sauce. Place the sugar in a heavy-based saucepan and mix in the measured water so all the sugar is wet. Set over a medium-high heat to melt the sugar, then bring to the boil. Have a pastry brush and a glass of water to hand to brush down the sides of the pan should any sugar crystals form. Once the sugar has reached a dark caramel, switch off the heat and gently stir in the cream, followed by the butter. Be careful as it will boil violently. Stir until you have a smooth sauce. Season with salt.

Just before serving, place the pudding portions into a microwaveable container and microwave until hot. Place in warmed bowls and pour over the sauce. Finish with a spoon of clotted cream and a sprinkling of praline.

MUSCAT

Fig galette with a blue cheese-stuffed crust
Graham's Vintage Port

☞ page 127

SERVES 8

This rustic galette is relatively quick and easy to make. You could assemble it in advance and keep it in the fridge, unbaked, until you're ready to serve it. Put it in the oven as you sit down for your main course and it will be ready in time for dessert with a glass of vintage Port! I like the yin-yang of sweet jammy figs and savoury blue cheese here, while ripe red fruit and blue cheese are classic pairings with Port. Feel free to change it up: the galette is great made with pears, Roquefort and walnuts, all flavours that work with a glass of Sauternes.

The heavier the oven tray the better for this tart, as it will help the pastry cook from the bottom. This pastry recipe makes twice the quantity needed, but freezes well wrapped in cling film. Don't try halving the recipe; it's easier to make in this quantity.

ALTERNATIVE WINE MATCHES

Taylor's Late Bottled Vintage Port ☞ page 127

Recioto della Valpolicella 'Vigneto di Monte Lodoletta', Dal Forno Romano, Veneto ☞ pages 121 & 123

FOR THE FLAKY CREAM CHEESE PASTRY (MAKES ENOUGH FOR 2 GALETTES)

- 230g unsalted butter, chilled and chopped into 1cm cubes
- 370g plain flour
- ¼ tsp sea salt
- ¼ tsp baking powder
- 170g cream cheese, chilled
- 40ml iced water
- 1 tbsp cider vinegar

FOR THE GALETTE

- 150g good-quality fig conserve
- plain flour, to dust
- 400g Flaky cream cheese pastry (see left)
- 12 ripe jammy black figs, quartered
- 300g blue cheese, ideally Stilton
- 1 egg white, lightly beaten
- 70g caster sugar
- Vanilla ice cream, to serve (see page 342)

Place the butter in the freezer for at least 30 minutes. Sift the flour, salt and baking powder into an airtight plastic container and freeze this, too. After 30 minutes in the freezer, place the dry ingredients into a food processor fitted with a blade. Cut the cream cheese into 4–5 pieces and add to the processor. Process for 20 seconds, until the mixture resembles coarse meal. Add the frozen butter and pulse until it breaks into pea-sized pieces.

Add the iced water and vinegar and pulse for 10–15 seconds, or until the butter has broken down into smaller pieces. The mixture should be in particles, it is crucial that a flaky pastry such as this is not overworked at this stage. Place into a food-safe plastic bag and press it together from the outside, gently kneading into a mass. Split into 2 pieces and shape carefully into flat discs. Wrap them with cling film and refrigerate for 1 hour. (Freeze one of the pieces at this stage, unless you are making 2 galettes at once.)

Preheat the oven to 190°C. Microwave the fig conserve for 30 seconds or so, to soften. Dust a work top with flour and roll out one of the portions of pastry into a 40cm circle. Cover a large oven tray – or shallow pizza tray – with baking parchment. Roll the pastry on to the rolling pin and carefully lay it out on the parchment. If your pastry is soft and difficult to work with, give it a few minutes in the fridge to harden before continuing.

Using a pastry brush, coat the pastry with a generous layer of conserve, leaving an 8cm rim. Place the fig quarters on the conserve, flesh-sides up and packed together. Crumble 200g of the blue cheese in a ring around the outside of the circle of figs, still leaving the 8cm border. Fold the edges of the pastry towards the centre, pleating them at regular intervals, encasing the cheese and overlapping the outer ring of figs. Brush the crust with egg white and sprinkle the caster sugar over the crust and figs.

Bake on the middle shelf of the oven for 20 minutes, until golden and crisp. During the last 2 minutes, sprinkle the remaining cheese over the figs.

Cut into wedges and serve hot, with vanilla ice cream.

BOTTLED AND SHIPPED BY
PORTUGAL

Tarte Tatin with vanilla ice cream
'5 Puttonyos Aszú', Royal Tokaji Wine Company

☞ page 124

SERVES 6

Tokaji is one of the world's most classic dessert wines. It was thought some of the world's first botrytis wines were made in Hungary by accident, when a Turkish incursion caused grapes to be left on the vine until they were fully rotten and shrivelled. The grape variety used here is Furmint, which has a beautiful crisp acidity that balances with the rich, caramelised orange flavours of the wine. An underlying acidity can also be found in the apples, which balance beautifully with the caramelised sugar in the tarte. This is a glorious food match for those with a sweet tooth.

You will need a good heavy-based frying pan with an ovenproof handle.

ALTERNATIVE WINE MATCHES

Vin Santo, Argyros Estate, Santorini
☞ page 124

Tokaji Aszú Esszencia, Chateau Pajzos, Hungary
☞ page 124

FOR THE VANILLA ICE CREAM (MAKES ABOUT 1.5 LITRES)

500ml whole milk
500ml double cream
1 vanilla pod, split in half, seeds scraped out
250g caster sugar
12 egg yolks

FOR THE TARTE

plain flour, to dust
125g all-butter puff pastry
6 large Braeburn apples
180g granulated sugar
70g unsalted butter, cut into small cubes and chilled

Start with the ice cream. In a heavy-based saucepan, gently heat the milk, cream, vanilla pod and seeds and half the sugar until almost boiling. Stir occasionally, to ensure it doesn't catch on the pan.

In a clean, dry bowl, whisk the egg yolks and remaining sugar until the yolks start to lighten in colour. Slowly pour the hot milk mixture over, whisking quickly so it doesn't scramble, then return it to the saucepan. Fill a large bowl with iced water and have a slightly smaller bowl and a sieve to hand.

Cook the custard slowly over a low heat, stirring constantly, until it thickens and will coat the back of the spoon. Pour it through the sieve into the empty bowl and place into the ice bath. Lay baking parchment on the surface so a skin doesn't form. Cool completely, then churn in an ice-cream machine.

Preheat the oven to 180°C. Dust a work top with flour. Roll out the pastry into a disc a bit larger than a 24cm ovenproof frying pan. Cover and refrigerate to rest, while you get on with the apples and caramel.

Peel the apples, quarter them and remove the cores with a small knife. Sprinkle a little of the sugar into the frying pan. Pack the pan with the apple quarters as best you can. Don't be worried about trying to make them look pretty, if you're struggling to get them all in a single layer, just start a second, they will cook down in the oven. Sprinkle the remaining sugar over the top and dot the cubed butter throughout. Place over a medium-high heat. As it heats up, the sugar and butter will melt and the apples will start to release their juice. Eventually all will boil together, caramelising into the most heavenly toffee apple emulsion. The process will take 8–10 minutes, depending on how fierce the heat is. Once you're happy with the colour of the caramel (bearing in mind it will darken a couple of shades in the oven), remove from the heat. Lay the pastry over, tucking it in at the sides.

Place in the middle of the oven for 20 minutes or so, until the pastry is golden and cooked through. Allow a few minutes to rest and settle.

Before attempting to turn the tart out, place the pan over a medium heat to soften the caramel. Now the moment of truth! Place a serving plate over the pan and flip them over together (wearing oven gloves to protect your hands and arms). Slice at the table and serve with the vanilla ice cream.

ROYAL TOKAJI

Saffron-poached apricot & almond tart, Roquefort ice cream Château d'Yquem, Sauternes

☞ *page 124*

SERVES 6
Chateau d'Yquem has stand-out flavours of ripe apricots and saffron. It's also often enjoyed with Roquefort. Initially, I found it a little odd putting blue cheese with apricots, but it's sublime with this iconic Sauternes.

The recipe for the almond cream makes more than you need for this dessert. However, it will keep in the fridge for about a week and can be used to enhance any fruit tarts. To complement the Château d'Yquem, we've folded a few chopped golden raisins through the almond cream.

A rolling lattice cutter (optional) is good for presentation here.

FOR THE ROQUEFORT ICE CREAM (MAKES ABOUT 1.5 LITRES)
500ml whole milk
500ml double cream
250g caster sugar
12 egg yolks
300g Roquefort cheese

FOR THE ALMOND CREAM (MAKES ABOUT 500G)
125g unsalted butter
125g caster sugar, plus more to dust
2 eggs
½ tsp lemon juice
2 tsp Amaretto liqueur (optional)
125g ground almonds
1 tbsp plain flour

FOR THE TART
500ml water
500g granulated sugar
generous pinch of saffron threads
1 vanilla pod, split in half, seeds scraped out
6 ripe apricots, halved and pitted
600g all-butter puff pastry, chilled
plain flour, to dust
30g golden raisins
120g Almond cream (see left), at room temperature
3 egg whites, lightly beaten
50g flaked almonds

First make the ice cream. In a heavy-based saucepan, gently heat the milk, cream and half the sugar until it is almost boiling, stirring occasionally to ensure it doesn't catch. In a clean, dry bowl, whisk the egg yolks and remaining sugar until it starts to lighten in colour. Slowly pour the hot cream mixture over the yolks, whisking all the time, then return all the mixture to the saucepan. Remove any rind from the Roquefort, cut it into small pieces and add it to the pan. Fill a large bowl with iced water and have another slightly smaller bowl and a sieve to hand.

Place the ice cream mixture over a very low heat and cook the custard, stirring constantly with a wooden spoon, until it starts to thicken slightly and coats the back of the spoon. As it cooks, the cheese will melt and incorporate into the custard. Be patient: don't be tempted to raise the temperature, as you will run the risk of scrambling the custard.

When ready, pour the custard through the sieve into the smaller bowl. Place into the ice bath. Cover the custard directly with baking parchment, so a skin doesn't form. Cool completely, then churn in an ice-cream machine.

Now make the almond cream. In a mixing bowl, whisk the butter and sugar until light and fluffy. Add the eggs one at a time, mixing gently after each addition; don't be too vigorous, or the cream may curdle. Carefully fold in the lemon juice, Amaretto, if using, almonds and flour. Mix well, then chill. Return to room temperature before using, so it's easier to work with.

To poach the apricots, bring the measured water to the boil in a saucepan with the sugar, saffron and vanilla seeds, then reduce the heat to a simmer.

continued overleaf ☞

☜ *continued from perious page*

ALTERNATIVE WINE MATCHES

Jurançon Doux 'Les Jardins de Babylone', Didier Dagueneau ☞ *page 123*

Sauternes, Château Rieussec ☞ *page 124*

Sauternes, Château de Fargues ☞ *page 124*

Add the apricots and simmer gently until soft. The cooking time depends on how ripe they are, but they shouldn't take longer than 5–7 minutes. Allow to cool. Store them in their poaching syrup in the fridge until required. (They are best poached on the day of serving, as they discolour if left overnight.)

Preheat the oven to 200°C.

Cut the chilled pastry into 2 even pieces and, on a lightly floured surface, roll each out to a thickness of 3–4mm. Out of one, cut 6 x 12cm discs for the tart bases and, out of the other, use a rolling lattice cutter to cut a sheet of lattice about 35cm long, large enough to stretch across all the bases at once. (If you don't have a lattice cutter, create your own lattice by criss-crossing thin strips of pastry.) Transfer the bases to a sheet of baking parchment, and place the lattice on a separate sheet, then chill for 20 minutes. (Puff pastry is much easier to work with when chilled.)

Place the bases, still on their baking parchment, on a large baking tray. Using a fork, prick holes into the centre of each disc, leaving a 1.5cm border around the edge free of holes. 'Docking' in this way stops the pastry from rising so freely, enabling the undocked edges to rise up and encase the tart.

Chop the golden raisins and fold them through the almond cream. Spread evenly on to each pastry base, still leaving the edges clear. Lay the poached apricots, skin-side down, on the thin layer of almond cream.

Using a pastry brush, brush the exposed edge of each tart base lightly with the egg whites, so the lattice tops have something to stick to. Stretch the piece of lattice pastry across the tarts and press down gently around the edges, so it sticks into place. Using the same cutter used for the bases, cut around the tarts again and remove the excess lattice. Brush the lattice tops with egg white and sprinkle with the flaked almonds and a little caster sugar.

Bake for 25–30 minutes, until the pastry is golden and crispy. Serve hot, with a ball of Roquefort ice cream.

Index

WINE INDEX

RECIPE INDEX

Acknowledgements

GRANT ASHTON, FOUNDER & CEO My original plan to open a 'wine bar in Marylebone', a place where my friends and I could enjoy our wine, ended up being a bit larger than intended... This is what my children describe as an 'epic fail'. The scale of what 67 Pall Mall required meant leaving my comfortable job and throwing myself into the hospitality industry. My wife Grainne's willingness to join me in that risk is a cause of constant amazement; my love for her is unbounded. Our children, Cameron, Georgia and Alexandra, deserve a mention for enduring the inability to explain to friends what their father did, as we struggled to turn Hambros Bank's ex-West-End branch into the world's first private members' club for wine lovers.

The path to opening the Club was only made possible by the support and advice of my board of directors, so I would like to thank my board, past and present – Geoff Fink, Olivier Herregods, Alec Innes, Marzena Niziol, Charlotte Morton, Ian Smith, Olivier Staub and Chris Tuffey – for their wise counsel.

The undertaking required many people to back my vision with hard-earned cash. It must be admitted that the proposition of a ground-breaking business model for a wine club is more obvious with the benefit of nearly five years of hindsight! Thanks to you all for taking the risk...

Thanks to the 5000+ members who have joined, both in London and now in Singapore. You make this book and everything we have achieved possible.

Finally, I thank my team, who deliver my vision day in, day out. I reserve a special mention for Niels Sherry, who helped me construct and run the original Club, and with whose help I hope to open many more outposts in the coming years.

NIELS SHERRY, COO A friend introduced me to Grant Ashton in 2014. Sitting in the empty shell of the old Hambros Bank, Grant shared his vision for 67 Pall Mall. What a vision it was. After that, we were joined at the hip, building and opening an outstanding club. Of course, it wouldn't happened without the amazing team that came together.

We have an incredible membership, passionate about wine; wine is the thread that ties us together. The diversity of our members is magical and their support unquestionable. When a member says: 'this club has changed my life,' you know you have helped to create something unique and special.

This book celebrates the very best of 67 Pall Mall. Bringing wine and food together under the expertise of Ronan and Marcus is at the heart of our success, and now, with this book, we can reach many more.

RONAN SAYBURN Many thanks to all the great sommeliers, chefs and restaurant staff that I have had the privilege to work with over the years; your passion has been an inspiration. Thanks to the wine merchants, wine makers and winery owners who have endured my endless questioning over the years in pursuit of my Master Sommelier qualification.

Thanks to all those at 67, especially our great team of sommeliers led by Terry Kandylis, our front-of-house team, cellar and kitchen brigade, plus the ladies in the office (the original three being Steph, Bash and Shallot) and our management from Niels Sherry and Mark Watts. And to Grant Ashton, whose vision and determination has made 67PM a remarkable place for sommeliers to work and wine lovers to visit.

Big thanks to co-conspirator Marcus, who does a fantastic job with the food at 67; working with him is a total pleasure. He is a very talented chef who is open to suggestions, curious about wine flavours and composition and flexible about our wine-led events and what food we serve.

Many thanks to our production team led by the lovely Jacqui Small, with Lawrence Morton, Joakim Blockström and Cynthia Inions providing the beautiful photography and design.

Finally, many thanks to my family Maria, James and Eddie, my sister Julia and brother Rob, who along with my parents Mary and Robert didn't quite make it to see me in print, but I hope it would have made them proud.

MARCUS VERBERNE To the love of my life, and my best friend, Masha for her constant love, support and belief in me. No one knows me like Masha. She is my everything and brings out the best in me.

For the support and encouragement from my rather large family: my dad Han and his wife Maggie, my mum Anna and her husband David, my stepmother Sharron and her husband Salvatore and my brothers and sisters, Scott, Jo, Nicky, Suny, Shahan and Jan. It's the most difficult sacrifice to be so far away from you all. Not a day passes when I don't wish at some point that I was home in New Zealand with you all. I love you all so much.

Huge homage to my friend and colleague Ronan Sayburn. What I have learned from you is priceless and I am indebted to you for sharing with me your vast knowledge of wine and food harmony. You've made me a better chef.

Massive gratitude to Jacqui Small (our superb conductor) and the orchestra of talented individuals she assembled to bring our book to life. Jacqui, thank you for wise guidance and endless support in this enjoyable and fulfilling project.

Joakim Blockstrom, Lucy Bannell, Lawrence Morton, Cynthia Inions. I was nervous before the first shoot. It was so important we all clicked, and we did. It has been a privilege working with you.

To Grant, Niels and Mark Watts. Thanks for your support over the years. It's been a pride and pleasure to play my part in the evolution of 67PM. I look forward to what the future has in store.

To the 67 kitchen team, past and present. This project has taken me out of the kitchen, but I have always felt confident that my team was more than capable of sustaining the high standards we set for ourselves. Thank you for holding the fort in my absence and of course for help in testing the recipes.

Finally, thanks to all our suppliers at the Club, in particular: Chloe Cleverley (First Choice), Phil Reed (The Upper Scale Ltd), Darren North (Billfields of London), George Blackwell (The Rare Breed Meat Company), Guy & Juliet Grieve (The Ethical Shellfish Company) Shaun Henderson (Henderson Seafood), Ruth Holbrook (Paxton & Whitfield) and Simon Smith (Aubrey Allen). We couldn't do what we do without you.

IMAGE CREDITS: Alamy: p54 (Robert Harding), 79 (Brian Jannsen), 91 (Hervé Lenain), 105 (Park Dale), 110 (Old Images), 115 (Tim Graham), 119 (Anton Petrus). Bridgeman Art Gallery / Dagli Orti: p50, 62, 66, 72, 86, 92, 98, 104, 114. Chateau Latour p13 (top). Getty Images / Dagli Orti: p56. Jackson Family Wines p17, 71, 90, 99, 103. Keith Barnes p7 (image of Oz Clarke). Ronan Sayburn MS p13 (bottom), 14, 15, 16, 60, 73, 76, 81, 96, 109. Shutterstock: p19, 63. Tim Atkin MW p67, 87, 111. Wine Australia p18, 93 (Andre Castelluci). Wines of Austria p82. Wines of New Zealand p8, 51, 57, 70